From Louis XIV to Napoleon

From Louis XIV to Napoleon: The Fate of a Great Power

Jeremy Black

University of Exeter

First published 1999 in the UK and the USA
by UCL Press
11 New Fetter Lane, London EC4P 4EE

The name of University College London (UCL) is a registered trade mark used by
UCL Press with the consent of the owner.

UCL Press is an imprint of the Taylor & Francis Group

British Library Cataloguing in Publication Data
A catalogue record for this book is available from the British Library

Library of Congress Cataloging in Publication Data
A catalogue record for this book has been requested

ISBN   1-85728-933-1 HB
       1-85728-934-X PB

Typeset in Bembo by Best-set Typesetter Ltd., Hong Kong
Printed and bound in Great Britain by T.J. International Ltd, Padstow, UK

For Gill Carey and Nick Lewis

Contents

Preface

The absence of a major modern study of this subject is worrying, because France's political and military impact in Europe and the world in this period was of great importance. The purpose of this work is not to provide a blow-by-blow narrative, for such a task would require a multi-volume approach and would be unlikely to attract the interest of publishers and readers. Instead, while providing a chronological framework, this study seeks to concentrate on major themes. These include the objectives of French policy, the degree of continuity it possessed, and the reasons for its successes and failures. Particular effort is devoted to considering continuity or otherwise across the period of the French Revolution.

France's global position is also addressed. This is a question of the conflation of foreign policy, mercantile interests, colonial roles and military preferences. The trajectory of colonial policy and strength is considered, as is the question of why France 'lost out' to Britain in the maritime and colonial sphere. It is necessary to integrate this aspect of foreign policy with that of policy within Europe in order to demonstrate the range of French options. For example, in 1778 there was a choice between intervening in North America or fulfilling treaty commitments to Austria in the War of the Bavarian Succession. Had the latter choice been taken, France might well not have benefited from the weakening of British power caused by the loss of the Thirteen Colonies.

There were also choices within Europe. Thus, in 1805 Napoleon did not have to turn against Austria. An emphasis on the choices facing French policy-makers ensures that there is no suggestion of geopolitical determinism. Indeed modern France was shaped by the substantial acquisitions of territory made by Louis XIV and Louis XV. No pre-ordained French foreign policy existed, French foreign relations were unpredictable and fluid, and French interests were varied and episodic. The role of choice focuses on the importance of France's alliances and her failure to produce lasting effective relationships with the Dutch, Britain,

Austria, Spain and Russia. The impact of these foreign policy failures greatly affected France's maritime and colonial position.

This study is based on extensive work in the French archives, especially that of the Foreign Ministry, since 1979. During this period, I have accumulated a number of institutional and personal debts. A number of bodies supported research in Paris, particularly the British Academy, the Leverhulme Foundation, and the University of Exeter. I am most grateful to the hospitality offered there by Rory Browne, Mat Burrows, Jacques Carré, Michel Fleury, Hugues Mantoux, Bruno Neveu, Peter Sheldrick and Peter Tibber. I have benefited greatly from the advice of Matthew Anderson, Nigel Aston, Ken Banks, John Bosher, Eveline Cruickshank, Kate Desbarats, Charles Esdaile, Jan Glete, Allan Greer, Harald Kleinschmidt, Jean-Marie Lafont, Peter Marshall, John Rule, Bailey Stone, and David Sturdy on sections of an earlier draft, and from the comments of Bill Doyle on the entire draft. I am grateful for the opportunities provided to discuss the subject by invitations to speak at the conference of the Society for Seventeenth-Century French Studies in 1989, the 1994 Strasbourg conference on Schoepflin and eighteenth-century Europe, the 1997 Mainz conference on the Peace of Rijswijk, the Consortium on Revolutionary Europe in 1999, and at the University of Tsukuba and George Mason University. Wendy Duery provided crucial secretarial assistance, and I am most grateful to Gerard Hill, Chris Hughes and Luciana O'Flaherty for speeding the typescript through the press in a competent and friendly manner. Sarah has been a great support.

Jeremy Black
University of Exeter
January 1999

Abbreviations

Add.	BL, Additional Manuscripts
AE	Paris, Archives du Ministère des Affaires Etrangères (now Ministère des Relations Extérieures)
AG	Paris, Archives de la Guerre (sometimes cited as Vincennes)
AM	Paris, Archives de la Marine
AN	Paris, Archives Nationales
Ang.	Angleterre
AP	*Archives parlementaires de 1787 à 1860: Recueil complet des débats législatifs et politiques des chambres françaises* (127 vols., Paris, 1879–1913)
Arsenal	Paris, Bibliothèque de L'Arsenal, Archives de la Bastille, Gazetins secrets de la Police
AST	Turin, Archivio di Stato
Aut.	Autriche
BL	London, British Library
BN	Paris, Bibliothèque Nationale
Bod.	Oxford, Bodleian Library
BVC	Paris, Bibliothèque Victor Cousin, Fonds Richelieu
Chewton	Chewton Mendip, Somerset, Chewton Hall, papers of James, 1st Earl Waldegrave
Consortium	*Consortium on Revolutionary Europe: Proceedings* (year is that of conference rather than year of publication)
CP	Paris, Archives du Ministère des Affaires Etrangères, Correspondance Politique
Dresden	Dresden, Hauptstaatsarchiv, Geheimes Kabinett, Gesandtschaften
Esp.	Espagne
HHStA	Vienna, Haus-, Hof- und Staatsarchiv, Staatenabteilung
LM	Lettere Ministri

Marburg	Marburg, Staatsarchiv, Bestand 4 Politisiche Akten nach Philipp d. Gr.
MD	Paris, Ministère des Affaires Etrangères, Mémoires et Documents
MF	Manuscrits Français
Munich	Bayerische Hauptstaatsarchiv
NAF	Nouvelles Acquisitions Françaises
Nancy	Nancy, Archives départementales de Meurthe-et-Moselle, Fonds de Vienne
Polit. Corr.	R. Koser (ed.), *Politische Correspondenz Friedrichs des Grossen* (46 vols, Berlin, 1879–1939)
PRO	London, Public Record Office
PWSF	*Proceedings of the Western Society for French History*
Recueil	*Recueil des Instructions données aux Ambassadeurs et Ministres de France depuis les Traités de Westphalie jusqu'à la Révolution Française* (Paris, 1884–)
RHD	*Revue d'Histoire Diplomatique*
Sbornik	*Sbornik imperatorskago russkago ostoricheskago obshchestva* (148 vols, St Petersburg, 1867–1916)
SP	State Papers, Public Record Office, London
sup.	supplement

The eastward expansion of France 1659–1766

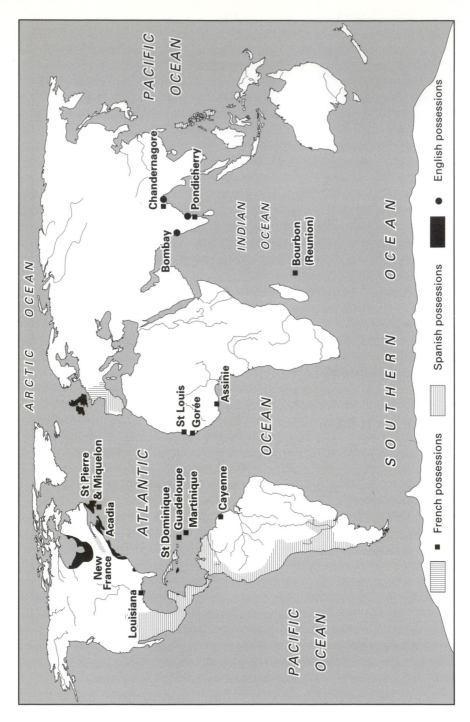

The world in 1700

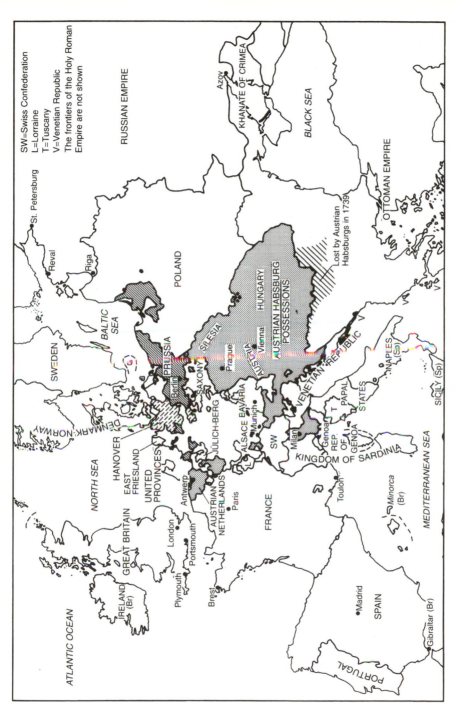

Europe in 1739

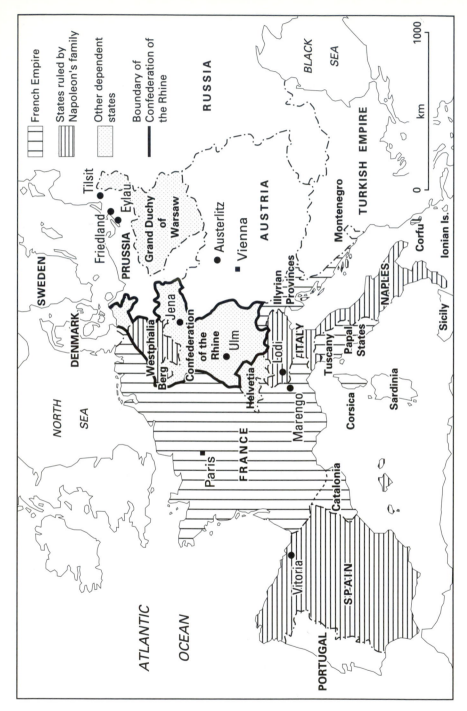

Europe in 1812

CHAPTER ONE

Introduction: A European and world power

Why didn't she make it? Much of the period 1661–1815 appeared to be the age of France. France was the greatest power in Western Europe in the late seventeenth and eighteenth centuries. Two of France's leaders, Louis XIV and Napoleon, seemed – and still seem – to dominate their periods of power. If France was dominant in any age of world history, it was in this age.

And yet when Louis XIV died in 1715, and, again, after Napoleon's attempt to resume power was defeated at Waterloo a century later, France appeared as a failed power. This failure in Europe, which led to a brief occupation by the victorious powers after Waterloo, was matched by failure on the world scale, seriously so in an age of European expansion. France was beaten by Britain in the struggle for maritime predominance, and ended the period with her empire in ruins. The British had lost much of their empire in 1775–83 during the War of American Independence, but they returned, to become, within three decades, the leading European colonial empire. France made no such revival after her losses in the Seven Years' War of 1756–63, and, as a result of the overthrow of her imperial system in 1793–1815, she entered the subsequent age of European expansion at a serious disadvantage *vis-à-vis* Britain, one from which she was not to recover. Thus France's new empire, that began with the occupation of Algiers in 1830, was very much the second-best, and this conditioned her self-awareness as a world power.

Why was France not more successful? Such a counterfactual may appear methodologically questionable. It is in fact of considerable value. First, it gives particular point to the chronological approach. Secondly, it serves as an important reminder that what did not happen is as important an aspect and outcome of past events as what did. This underlines the approach of this book.

A system in flux

A second, and related, conceptual thesis is the notion that international relations, both in Europe and in the world, were fluid. The notion that the European

1

warfare of the period was indecisive is inaccurate.[1] So also is any understanding of international relations as rigid and limited. This is the case not only for the age of the French Revolution, but also for the preceding period of the *ancien régime* (1661–1789). That was an age that saw major changes in European power politics and territorial control, as well as a massive expansion of European power elsewhere in the world, particularly in North America and India.

The resulting sense of fluidity, that also owed much to cyclical notions of decadence and long-term historical flux,[2] was accompanied by one of unpredictability. The latter owed much to the central role of monarchs, both French and foreign, and their personalities. Huxelles, the foreign minister, observed in 1717 that 'events often lead to situations that it is difficult to predict'.[3] The French envoy in Berlin complained in 1732 of Frederick William I of Prussia 'ni luy, ni ses ministres n'ont jamais de plan fixe'.[4]

Hereditary monarchy also entailed the vagaries of dynastic chance. Born in 1638, Louis XIV came to the throne in 1643. In 1661, when the powerful first minister Cardinal Mazarin died, the personal rule of the young and dynamic Louis began. He ruled until 1715, personally directing his kingdom throughout this period and holding the reins of power until his death. In 1665, in contrast, the sickly Charles II came to the throne of Spain. He failed to provide strong direction and died in 1700, without providing the prime obligation of a monarch, a son.

Had each of these two men succeeded, instead, to the other's kingdom then it is interesting to speculate how this would have affected international relations. Under more powerful monarchs, Philip V (r. 1700–46), Louis XIV's younger grandson, and, in particular, Charles III (r. 1759–88), eighteenth-century Spain was to show itself more dynamic. On the other hand, the divisions and political disorder of France in the 1610s and 1640s had indicated the problems posed by French monarchs who were unable, in their case for reasons of youth, to cope with the difficulties of maintaining the political momentum of personal monarchy. Louis XIV's reign also exemplified another aspect of dynastic anxiety, the succession. While unmarried, he had a near-fatal illness on campaign in 1658. Later, he had only one son who survived, and even this son, the Grand Dauphin, predeceased him. These problems encouraged Louis to legitimate illegitimate children and to attempt (unsuccessfully) to have two of his legitimated sons recognized as possible successors to the throne.

As another illustration of dynastic chance, in 1730 the young Peter II of Russia died of smallpox, leading to a major change of direction in Russian policy. Two years earlier, Louis XIV's great-grandson the young Louis XV (1710–72, r. 1715–72) had also been attacked by smallpox. Although married, he then lacked a son, and his uncle, Philip V of Spain – formerly Philip, Duke of Anjou – made preparations to take the throne. Such a step would have led to a major change in French foreign policy, not least by dissolving the Anglo-French alliance, and even more so if Philip had maintained his control over Spanish policy and his alliance with Austria, but Louis recovered and lived until 1774.

Nevertheless, Louis XV only had two sons, the second of whom died young, while the Dauphin nearly died of smallpox in 1752. The Dauphin had no son by his first marriage in 1745 and his eldest son by his second marriage died in 1761. Fortunately, the second marriage produced five boys between 1751 and 1757, thus ending any possible succession dispute, specifically one between the house of Orléans (the descendants of Louis XIV's brother) and the line of Philip V. Lastly, as an example not of hereditary but of meritocratic monarchy, Napoleon was struck on the chest by a bullet at the siege of Regensburg in 1809. As this was at a great range, the bullet only gave him a bruise, but it served as a reminder of the dangers of military command.

This sense of fluidity, of dynastic change and international uncertainty, may not seem readily apparent, because of the contemporary conceptualization of international relations in terms of an apparently rigid set of notions that left scant role for chance. The idea of a balance of power, combined with that of the natural interests of states, appeared to establish an equilibrium model of international relations, in which the balance worked to reconcile the pursuit of these interests. If any one state was unwilling to accept the constraints of this essentially static system, then others would combine to prevent it overthrowing the equipoise of Europe.

Such a system can be approached in two ways: firstly, in terms of contemporary understandings of European power politics and, secondly, with reference to modern assessments of their means of operation. In the first case, it can be suggested that contemporary conceptualization was normative – an account of what they believed ought to happen, rather than descriptive – an account of what did happen and why. For example, Chauvelin, the French foreign minister, claimed that as the Austro–Spanish alliance of 1725 was a caprice, contrary to natural interests, it ought not persist.[5] Indeed, the very notion of the balance can be seen as a compensatory response to the chaos of international relations, a desperate attempt to reduce to form and order the inchoate nature of volatile reality.

The sense of unpredictability was captured in January 1789 by the French envoy in Berlin. He drew attention to past transformations in Russian policy when rulers changed, and warned about the danger of constructing diplomatic systems on the basis of Catherine the Great's longevity. In 1728 Chauvelin had anticipated major changes if Osterman, his Russian counterpart, died, which he did not do; while Argenson, the foreign minister in 1745, was concerned about the health of Frederick II – 'the Great' – of Prussia, fearing that his successor might follow a different policy or be less capable.[6] Frederick did not die until 1786. The French were especially prone to argue that Russian politics were affected by favouritism and Russian policies pursued without due consideration. Vergennes, the foreign minister at the time, took this view in 1785.[7] This was an important aspect of the way in which the French sought to 'primitivize' Russia and to treat it as a non-European power.

The balance of power was also employed both as a diplomatic tool, in order

3

to try to persuade allies to act as desired, and as a polemical device, in order to condemn opposing states. Far from offering an obviously accurate description of international relations, as far as contemporaries were concerned, the notion of the balance is also a questionable modern analytical device. This is directly relevant to the case of France.

Coalitions of other European states stopped both Louis XIV and Napoleon. If it is argued that a balance of power operated to prevent the growth of hegemony by any one power, then expansionist foreign policies on the part of both rulers can be regarded as foredoomed to failure; indeed the course of their reigns becomes an account of how their policies aroused opposition, and were eventually thwarted by it, so that the balance was maintained and hegemony thwarted. In contrast, with the important exception of Marshal Belle Isle's creation of an anti-Austrian alliance in 1741, French policy in 1715–91 was different. It was generally less aggressive and expansionist, and did not arouse opposition comparable to that created by Louis XIV and Napoleon. As a result, French policy in 1715–91 did not structure western European international relations around a polarity based on an alleged struggle to overthrow or maintain the balance of power, as support and opposition for French plans.

Such a thesis is implicit, certainly as far as Louis XIV and Napoleon are concerned, in much of the literature on their foreign policy; although Paul Schroeder has recently queried this assessment of Napoleon and suggested that many powers were willing to accommodate themselves to his power and to French hegemony, only, however, to be thwarted by his unwillingness to accept limits.[8] As a consequence of the general assumption of the normative character of the balance of power, discussion usually focuses on the details of policy, the 'did Louis go too far here?' approach, rather than addressing the theoretical underpinnings of the approach. Yet the use of this thesis is not only suspect as a method, but also questionable as an analysis.

Firstly, it is by no means clear that Europe was inevitably multipolar (composed of several independent powers), or, rather, that the diversity of polities precluded at least regional hegemony. Successive failures to sustain such an hegemony in Western Europe, not least by Louis XIV and Napoleon, have diverted attention both from the Russian success in creating one in Eastern Europe in this period, and from the process of historical cannibalization, by which a large number of European polities lost their capacity for independent political action from the fifteenth century. If this was true of Aragon, Scotland, Bohemia and Hungary, it was not clear why other states should not follow. There was no inevitability about the number of states nor, therefore, about relationships within a European states system.

Many of these political entities had lost their independence as a consequence of dynastic unions. This was the case with those already mentioned. That, however, served to underline the unpredictability of international relations, and raised the question whether the process might not recur, possibly to the benefit of France. Many of the *ancien régime* wars were directly related to succession disputes. This was true of the War of Devolution (1667–8), the War of the Spanish Succession (1701–14), the War of the Polish Succession (1733–5), the War of the Austrian Succession (1740–48), and the War of the Bavarian Succession (1778–9). Other wars can be related to these succession issues. The Dutch War of 1672–8 can, in part, be seen as an attempt to disable an opponent to French ambitions on the Spanish Succession. The Seven Years' War (1756–63) can, in part, be seen as the second round of the War of the Austrian Succession.

Conquest, as well as dynastic union, was responsible for a decline in the number of European sovereign polities. In Eastern Europe, independent states had been swept aside since the fourteenth century by the rise of empires, especially Turkey and Moscow. Hitherto independent territories, including those of the Teutonic Order along the eastern Baltic, independent Russian principalities, such as Novgorod and Pskov, Islamic ones, such as the khanates of Kazan and Astrakhan, and Balkan states, such as Bulgaria, Moldavia, Wallachia, Serbia and Bosnia, were all conquered. The absorption of independent or autonomous polities by larger neighbours continued in Eastern Europe in the eighteenth century and the Napoleonic period. Poland was partitioned (1772–95), and the khanate of the Crimea annexed by Russia in 1783, the kingdom of Georgia following in 1801.

In Western Europe, the French Revolutionary and Napoleonic period saw a dramatic decline in the number of independent polities. This culminated, in 1810–12, at the height of Napoleonic power, with much of Western Europe being part of France, including the Netherlands, Hamburg, Lübeck, Genoa, Tuscany, Savoy–Piedmont, the Papal States, Trieste, Dalmatia and Catalonia. Client states, such as the new kingdoms of Bavaria, Italy and Westphalia, were similarly engorged. Although the treaty settlements of 1814–15 reversed this trend, and even created new units, such as the republic of Krakow, there were fewer states in Western and Central Europe in 1815 than there had been in 1789.

If the distribution of territorial power was far from fixed, that created opportunities for expansionist rulers. Far from seeing Louis XIV, Napoleon and other French governments as being bound to fail, because of some self-righting mechanism within a multipolar European balance of power, it is appropriate to note the fluid state of European international relations and to ask why the various French governments were not more successful, or rather why they were unable to sustain the highpoints of their achievements.

The World Outside Europe

The same point can be made at the global level. There was no inherent reason why France should not have been as successful as Britain, or, indeed, more so. Oceanic power did not depend on being an island. Portugal, Spain and the Dutch, the other leading European oceanic and colonial powers, were not

5

islands. Furthermore, even more clearly than within Europe, there were no obvious bounds to the ambition of powers. It was possible with a modest outlay of effort to make major territorial acquisitions, as the French discovered in Canada and Louisiana, areas where the native population was relatively small. If the demographic (population) balance between European and non-European was very different in South Asia, and far less favourable there than in North America, it was also possible for European powers to make gains and exert influence there through fitting into local power struggles. The British were ultimately more successful at that than the French; but, similarly, with a modest investment of manpower and other resources, the French had played a major role in southern Indian power politics in the 1740s and 1750s, and sought to do so again in the 1780s.

By 1661 France had some important bases around the world, including Acadia (1604), Québec (1608), Trois-Rivières (1634) and Montreal (1642) in New France (Canada), St Christopher (1625), Martinique (1635), Guadeloupe (1635), Dominica (1635), Grenada (1650), and St Domingue (now Haiti, 1660) in the West Indies, Cayenne (1635) on the Guiana coast of South America, St Louis (1638) in West Africa, and Réunion (1642) in the Indian Ocean. By 1715 this list had expanded to include Pondicherry (1674) and Chandernagore (1693) in India, Mauritius (1715) in the Indian Ocean, Gorée (1677) and Assine (1687) in West Africa, and Biloxi (1699) and Mobile (1710) on the Gulf of Mexico, as well as major expansion in New France, through trade and native alliances,[9] from the base at Québec, both to the Mississippi and to the head of Lake Superior.

There was no inherent reason why this process should not continue. As in Europe, there was a fluidity in international affairs. This was a matter not solely of the activities of European states across the oceans, but also of those other powers, many of which were also dynamic. In North America and, more clearly, India and South East Asia, the activities of the latter provided opportunities for the Europeans.

The prospect of gain in this wider world is the subtext of any assesssment of foreign policy within Europe, for this was an age of major European expansion. This was particularly so in North America, the Indian subcontinent, Australasia and the Pacific; although far less the case in Africa, let alone South-East and East Asia. Thus any assessment of success in foreign policy has to consider success outside Europe, although this is generally underrated in studies of early-modern international relations.

In part, this is a matter of institutional practice. France's global position was a matter of relations with non-European powers, with competing European powers that also had a global presence, and with European powers whose competition within Europe absorbed French energies. Relations with non-European powers were generally handled either by royal agents, generally colonial officials and military personnel, or by the agents of chartered companies who represented French interests in many regions; the same was true of other European powers. As a result, in the Foreign Ministry archives, there is not a massive Correspondance Politique Haiderabad or Mysore or Oroquois or Siam, to complement those marked Autriche, Angleterre, Espagne and Prusse. Colonial matters also played a major role in French relations with other European states, sometimes very much so, as in the case of Anglo-French relations in 1763–90. It is important to consider whether they could, and should, have played a greater role in French foreign policy.

France and the need for allies

This sense of international volatility and opportunity has to be complemented by an understanding of France's resources, of her allies and rivals, and of the context within which French decision-making was made. If the emphasis in this study is on choices, then the pressures and processes of choice have to be considered. In terms of resources, between 1660 and 1815 France was better placed with regard to her rivals than she was thereafter. Her population rose, only partly as a result of the annexation of Lorraine and Corsica, from about 21.9 million in 1675 to about 22.4 million in 1705, about 24.6 million in 1740 and possibly close to 30 million in 1800. This was less than the growth of Russia's population, where territorial gains, especially from Poland, helped to push her population from 15 million in 1719 to 35 million in 1800.

Furthermore, the growth of the French population was less in percentage terms than that of a number of other European states, including Britain. France's relative demographic decline, relative to most other European countries, dates from the early eighteenth century. Despite this, the French population was still far greater than those of Britain, Spain, the United Provinces or any of the German states. This demographic lead was important, because human labour was the crucial source of power for the economy and because manpower was the vital ingredient of military strength. Without the manpower at their disposal, neither Louis XIV nor Napoleon could have sustained their rate of military activity. They certainly could not have combined operations in so many regions at once, and thus have fought off coalitions of several states. The vast French human resources were augmented, especially under Napoleon, by employing large numbers of foreign troops.

This demographic resource also enabled France to limit one of the major problems of diplomacy, reliance on allies. Allies could be very beneficial, and were, indeed, necessary for France at sea, where military strength was far more than just a function of manpower. However, reliance on allies created severe problems, both in peacetime and at war. This was true for France, but even more for her opponents, for resistance to France was generally a matter of alliances. The problems of organizing and sustaining alliances greatly lessened the effectiveness of opposition to France, both during Louis XIV's reign and in that of Napoleon.

The apparent relative absence of need for allies was a characteristic of French policy within Europe for part of the period, and also of British policy at sea, and had an impact on French effectiveness, on the character of French policy, and on the decision-making procedure. All powers encountered difficulties in making alliances work, and in India, the French met serious difficulties when attempting to get Hyderabad, Mysore and the Marathas to co-operate against Britain in the early 1780s. As with attempts to create an alliance system in Eastern Europe, the French suffered from the contradictory interests of their allies, but the solution to the problem was the task of their diplomacy. Under both Louis XIV and Napoleon, the problem of European alliances was in a fashion evaded because neither ruler really sought allies. Instead, they were interested in clients, powers that could be manipulated, indeed controlled, their resources directed, as France required. This process reached its height under Napoleon.

When Louis XIV and Napoleon were given the challenge of sustaining an alliance in which compromise played a role, they failed; although it is not clear that either alliance could have lasted for long. Louis XIV negotiated treaties for the partition of the Spanish Empire with William III in 1698 and 1700, but war broke out with Britain and the United Provinces in 1702. Napoleon negotiated peace with Alexander I of Russia in 1807, but their relationship broke down in 1810, and they went to war in 1812.

This situation of perfunctory alliances and limited co-operation did not, however, define French policy throughout the period, for there were also serious efforts at alliance diplomacy based on mutuality, an understanding of different ethos as well as interests. These alliances helped to frame ideas of what French foreign policy was for. Furthermore, successive French governments were willing to seek and maintain alliances with powers and groups that did not share their ideological suppositions. In the United Provinces the French rarely sought alliance with the House of Orange, which was associated with pro-British and anti-French views. Instead, much effort was devoted to relations with the Protestant mercantile groups that dominated the province of Holland, those referred to by the French foreign minister in 1756 as 'republicans who have at heart the liberty and peace of their country'.[10] More generally, from the 1710s until the Revolution there were attempts to obtain French goals in a more consensual fashion.

Such a remark might appear ridiculous, as France went to war with Spain in 1719, Austria in 1733 and 1741, Britain in 1743 and 1754 (war was not formally declared until 1744 and 1756), and Prussia in 1756. However, these were wars in which France was very much part of an alliance system, with the exception of that of 1754, which was colonial in origin. France was not responsible for the wars that began in 1719 and 1756, nor for the breakdown of peace in Central Europe that led to war with Austria in 1741. Furthermore, far from being an account solely of war, French foreign policy in the eighteenth century is frequently thought about in terms of alliances, such as the Anglo-French one of 1716–31, or those between France and Spain after the Family Compacts of 1733, 1743 and 1761, or that with Austria in 1756–92. These alliances were not free of tension, indeed sometimes debilitating differences, but French policy depended on those alliances and the process of policy formation was, therefore, not the same as when France was acting essentially on her own.

Crucially, diplomacy played a major role in the process. Representations from allies, sent either via French envoys or via allied diplomats in Paris, were important, as were French perceptions of the views, strength and reliability of allies. These representations and perceptions were mediated through French ministerial and court politics, but they proved significant, sometimes crucial, in the timing and content of any debate about policy. Thus in 1729 the development of policy towards Spain, in part, reflected the views of France's leading ally, Britain, and the French perception of British determination.

Royal power

With the exception of the Revolutionary period, policy was the view of the ruler, either formally so, or – when the ruler was a minor, in Louis XV's early years – through the structure of a regency government presided over by a regent, then Philip, Duke of Orléans. His was the dominant voice in French foreign policy from 1715 until his death in 1723, although he met with opposition from some ministers and courtiers, especially when resisting the plans of Philip V of Spain, Louis XV's uncle.[11] Until Louis XV had a son in 1729, Philip was his heir, and the reversionary interest (the views associated with the heir) was of great importance both then and earlier. For example, the then Dauphin's support (the Dauphin being the king's eldest son) for the acceptance of Charles II of Spain's will in 1700 was accompanied by angry threats of the consequences for ministerial opponents when he succeeded to the throne, a scenario pre-empted by smallpox. Louis XV's son was a bitter opponent to Choiseul.

Different monarchs had particular methods of control and styles of command. Louis XIV was concerned to take the decisions, a course he pressed on his grandson Philip when he became king of Spain in 1700. He made it clear in 1661 that he would be his own principal minister by saying that no dispatches or orders were to be sent by the Secretaries of State without his permission and/or signature. Ministers were not allowed to meet unless Louis was present. Policy was discussed in the *Conseil d'en haut*, but it was Louis who decided whom to call there and what decision to take.[12] The foreign minister received his orders from the king. Important diplomatic instructions were read to Louis before he approved them. Louis XV was less directly and publicly assertive than Louis XIV, but gained and maintained control through a manipulative style of kingship. Initially, the young monarch was very much under the tutelage of his leading ministers – successively Orléans (1715–23), Bourbon (1723–6) and Fleury (1726–43) – so that the British envoy reported in 1740 that it was only for 'form's sake' that diplomats waited on the king.[13]

The decline of the elderly Fleury's grasp in his last years matched and helped a growing independence on the part of Louis XV. In 1744 Argenson, newly appointed as foreign minister, wrote to French envoys about the importance of 'fixed and precise rules' for their conduct, and informed them that it was by the express orders of Louis XV that all his envoys report only to the foreign minister and take instructions from him alone,[14] rather than from other ministers or directly from the king. In practice, Louis encouraged envoys to do the exact opposite, but only if allowed to do so by him. Secretive and frequently inscrutable, Louis sought to keep court factions from controlling his options.[15] The Bavarian envoy noted in February 1738 that Louis XV's intentions over what would happen should Fleury die, as then appeared likely, were impenetrable.[16] There was a lack of certainty about Louis's intentions, for both his ministers and for foreign envoys.

Although not without views – and indeed willing to oppose his wife, Marie Antoinette, in her attempt to encourage support for her brother, the Emperor Joseph II, ruler of Austria[17] – Louis XVI had less of a direct impact on policy than Louis XV, his grandfather, had done. Personality, here as elsewhere, counted for so much. He tended to follow the advice of his foreign minister, who, for most of the reign, until his death in early 1787, was the experienced diplomat Vergennes. In 1784 the Emperor Joseph was convinced that Louis would follow the lead of Vergennes on the Bavarian Exchange scheme.[18] Louis allowed Brienne to become Principal Minister in August 1787, the first such appointment since Richelieu.

The personal interactions of rulers were important. Tsar Alexander I of Russia's respect for Napoleon encouraged him to try to build on their agreement at Tilsit in 1807, while Napoleon's failure to reciprocate helped to wreck such hopes. Monarchs could write directly to foreign sovereigns. From 1757, Louis XV had a correspondence with Tsarina Elizabeth, unknown to his ministers, and in 1759 he persisted with it against the advice of the Duke of Broglie. At the end of 1756 Louis XV ordered Broglie, one of his leading diplomats, to accept the new Austro-French alignment, an order repeated in January 1757 with the words 'it is my work'. He made the same point in 1773.[19]

Reality was sometimes different. The volume of diplomatic business was such that, even when the monarch was able and active, many affairs were handled without his direct oversight. Furthermore, there were periods when the monarch was not able to handle important business. This was especially so when he was very ill or away on campaign. Yet, permanent mechanisms to cope with such eventualities did not have to be developed because the French crown in this period was not for long incapacitated by ill-health or compromised by a distant absence on campaign. In the first case, Louis XIV and Louis XV were seriously ill on occasion, but there was nothing to match George III's bouts of ill-health. As far as absence on campaign was concerned, neither Louis XIV nor Louis XV operated at any great distance from Paris/Versailles, while Louis XVI never did. None of these monarchs can be compared with such peripatetic rulers as Peter I, the Great, of Russia, Charles XII of Sweden or Joseph II.

Napoleon, in contrast, went considerable distances, for example to Central and Eastern Europe in 1805–7, 1809 and 1812–13, and to Spain in 1808. As his government was intensely personal, a government of personal empire rather than of France, the policymaking process was an adjunct of his travels, rather than being greatly hindered by them, although his commanders in Spain suffered from the time it took to send instructions from Eastern Europe. The situation under Napoleon was more stable than during the government of the Directory (a five-strong executive) in 1795–9. Then, in the absence of a single leader, there was division over policy, with particular Directors arguing for concentration on Continental or oceanic goals, and with a debate over where France's German frontiers should be. In 1797 there was division within the Directory over whether to accept the peace terms with Britain negotiated by the foreign minister, Talleyrand.

Despite the limitations on their role, the views and personalities of the monarchs, whether Bourbon or Napoleon, were still of great significance. However, it is important not to abstract royal views from the court ideologies and cultures that influenced them. Thus, Louis XIV was more affected by counter-Reformation mentality[20] than an emphasis on *raison d'état* politics might suggest.

Royal prestige was a major objective of French policy. When, on 1 June 1727, the distinguished veteran Marshal Villars, a glorious survivor from the reign of Louis XIV, complimented the young Louis XV in the council, 'on the glory of being the arbiter of Europe',[21] he was referring specifically to the fact that the preliminaries for a European peace settlement had been signed at Paris on 31 May, owed much to French diplomacy, and stipulated a peace congress in France that was to meet at Soissons, but also, more generally, to the close identification of diplomacy with the position of the crown. In 1727 Parisian opinion also registered that Louis XV was to be the arbiter of the differences of other monarchs.[22]

Prestige was also very much involved in royal marital diplomacy. This was designed to enhance the dynasty. Dynastic advantage could be a matter of gaining territories or territorial claims for the main line by marriage, or of placing junior members of the royal family in territories, or of benefiting cadet branches of the royal house, or of a more general sense of *gloire*. The Sardinian envoy was convinced in 1734 that France would prefer her alliance with Spain to that with Sardinia, because Philip V of Spain was a Bourbon and the 'prestige of [Louis XV's] family' was involved.[23]

Dynastic prestige also played a major role in Napoleon's creation of kingdoms and principalities for his family. Napoleon's stepson, Eugène de Beauharnais, became Viceroy for the new King of Italy, who was none other than Napoleon. The Dutch made one of Napoleon's brothers, Louis, king in 1806, in order to avoid annexation to France. Another brother, Joseph, became King of the Two Sicilies the same year. In 1808 Joseph was given the Spanish crown after Louis had turned it down. Joseph was replaced by Joachim Murat, Napoleon's brother-in-law, while another brother, Jerome, became King of Westphalia, a new state created by Napoleon that reflected French dominance of Germany. Murat was moved from being Grand Duke of Berg. The monarchs proved less pliable and reliable than Napoleon had hoped. Louis was obliged to abdicate as king in 1810, because he came to identify with the Dutch. Murat deserted Napoleon in 1814.

Ministers

Aside from rulers and their surrogates, the principal figures involved in the formation of foreign policy were foreign ministers and other leading ministers. Foreign ministers were major figures, playing a crucial role in the mechanics of policy – the drafting and dispatch of instructions, the receipt of reports, and interviews with foreign diplomats. They were also important in the formulation of policy, although they had to respond to the monarch and other ministers.

Relations within this ministerial group reflected not institutional position, but the interplay of personalities. The Council was often circumvented. Among the foreign ministers, Pomponne (1671–9) was less central to decision-making than Lionne (1663–71), Huxelles (1715–18) less so than Torcy (1696–1715), and Amelot (1737–44) less so than Dubois (1718–23). In 1727 the role of the foreign minister, first Morville and then Chauvelin, was lessened by the direct intervention in foreign policy of Fleury, the leading minister: he corresponded, that year, with Charles VI of Austria, the Duke of Richelieu, French envoy in Vienna, Count Rottembourg, envoy in Spain,[24] and Fonseca, one of the Austrian plenipotentiaries in Paris,[25] and discussed developments with other foreign diplomats in Paris. Fleury succeeded in his objectives of securing an agreement with Austria and then persuading Spain to accept it without losing the British alliance. In 1730 he corresponded with the Spanish minister La Paz. The previous year, Villars claimed that Fleury did not tell the Council anything, and in December 1728 he complained that Fleury consulted neither him nor Huxelles.[26] In 1744, in contrast, Argenson emphasized to Chavigny, when he reprimanded him, that the latter's dispatch, advocating major new French commitments in Germany, had been read to the Council and been the subject of very serious reflections on the part of Louis XV and his ministers.[27]

Foreign ministers who pressed unwelcome advice could be replaced: Huxelles, seen as overly anti-British and pro-Philip V, in 1718; Chauvelin, seen as anti-Austrian and too close to Philip V, in 1737. Champagny, an opponent of any invasion of Russia, was removed in April 1811. His replacement, Hugues Maret, Duke of Bassano, was a pliant nonentity who did not offer Napoleon unwelcome advice.

The interplay between monarch and ministers has been ably studied for certain periods and crises.[28] Thus, Paul Sonnino's detailed account of French policy before the Dutch War of 1672 was based on a comprehensive study of interconciliar correspondence.[29] In addition, careful dating of texts, verifications of authorship, and comparisons with other references, permitted an evaluation of *mémoires*, an oft-scorned source that Sonnino probed both for information and for psychological evidence about the formulation of foreign policy.[30] Sonnino placed great weight on Louis XIV's personal support for the war, but also investigated the role of the leading ministers. Lionne, the foreign minister, was unenthusiastic about war. Le Tellier, the army minister, was brought round by royal favour for his son, Louvois. Colbert, the Finance Minister, was opposed to war, but outmanoeuvred by Louvois and humiliated by Louis. Turenne, a leading general, but without any formal competence in the field of foreign policy, emerged as the adviser with the greatest responsibility for the conflict, and thus of the limitation of any analysis of policy based solely on official ministerial spheres of responsibility.

The role of Turenne also serves as a reminder that important decisions about foreign policy were in fact more wide-ranging, and, thus, necessarily involved other advisers. Financial, military, religious and domestic political considerations could all be important. Ministers of war and generals played a major role in alliance diplomacy in wartime and could also be important in peacetime. Furthermore, those decisions that could be described as narrowly diplomatic were not protected from intervention by other ministers and advisers. The French Foreign Office grew greatly in size during the reign of Louis XIV, and was the biggest in Western Europe,[31] but, despite its efficiency, crucial memoranda were mislaid.[32] More generally, the ministry was not strong enough to provide an institutional insulation for the conduct of foreign policy, let alone for its formulation.

Nevertheless, the views of individual officials within the ministry, such as Nicholas Louis Le Dran and Jean-Gabriel de La Porte du Theil, were of considerable importance. Their longevity of service provided continuity. La Porte du Theil, a nephew of one of Torcy's secretaries, served in the ministry in 1706–12, was then at Utrecht, The Hague and Baden, crucial postings during the peace negotiations, and from 1715 until 1745 was one of the *premiers commis*, or heads, of the bureaus into which the ministry was divided. He was particularly influential under Amelot. La Porte du Theil was a supporter of alliance with Austria, the policy with which Amelot was associated in his early years, and in 1745 was accordingly demoted by Argenson. Such officials could also serve as diplomats: La Porte du Theil at Madrid in 1733–4 and Vienna in 1736–7, Bussy in Hanover in 1741 and London in 1761. The younger Pecquet, an official who was influential under Chauvelin, was very hostile to Austria. He was dismissed and imprisoned in 1740 for supporting war with Austria, a policy then unacceptable to Fleury.[33]

Foreign envoys frequently complained of divisions within the French government, and an inability to provide consistency in policy and the necessary resources to effect plans. The Austrian envoy, Starhemberg, expressed his frustration in July 1758, when the two powers were wartime allies. He complained about overly frequent changes in government, ministerial intrigues, poor administration and exhausted finances. The previous month, Kaunitz, the Austrian Chancellor and a former envoy to Paris, contrasted the failure of the French to tap their resources adequately with what he saw as the greater success of the Habsburgs in galvanizing their resources.[34]

Ministerial divisions were related to clashes between French diplomats. In 1728 Chavigny – the firmly anti-Austrian envoy at the Imperial Diet, who was trying to persuade Belle Isle, an influential general, of the need to plan for the death of the Emperor Charles VI – was encouraged by what he saw as a more favourable attitude by Chauvelin than that of Fleury.[35] Personality also played a major role. Thus, in Russia in 1742–5, the ambassador, La Chétardie, clashed with the minister plenipotentiary, D'Alion.[36] Such clashes were exacerbated by the extent to which envoys were accompanied by representatives of a more junior rank who often reported on them and/or disagreed with them, rather than co-operating. This was a particular problem at the time of the Revolution, but not only then. In the winter of 1746–7 the Duke of Richelieu, then ambassador extraordinary at Dresden, sought to win Saxon help for an Austro-French reconciliation without keeping the Marquis of Issarts, the envoy extraordinary, informed.[37]

Aside from clashes between diplomats, there were also serious differences between the *premiers commis*. Nicholas Louis Le Dran, the *premier commis* of the second bureau, disagreed with Pecquet and in 1727 was ordered to deal only with the records of the ministry. When Pecquet fell in 1740, Le Dran was appointed *premier commis* of the first bureau.

Personal diplomacies

An extreme example of uncertainty over policy was provided by personal diplomacies, in which envoys received instructions and correspondence from ministers and advisers other than the foreign minister. Thus, the Count of Gergy, minister at the Imperial Diet at Regensburg 1716–21, had a secret correspondence with Orléans, unknown to Huxelles. He was employed to probe the possibility of better relations with Austria.[38]

Such diplomacies were important not only at the time of the famous *Secret du Roi* of the mid–eighteenth century, an unofficial diplomacy that began in 1745, initially directed to furthering the possibility of the Prince of Conti becoming next king of Poland and, more generally, seeking to limit Russian power in Eastern Europe. Louis XV supported Conti, but insisted that the scheme be kept separate from the foreign ministry and the Council. Diplomats were appointed who were expected to report not only to the Ministry, but also, separately and secretly, to Conti and Louis. Envoys were also given secret instructions.

The *Secret* led to difficulties for both diplomats and ministers. In 1754 the foreign minister, Saint-Contest, congratulated Aubeterre, the envoy in Vienna, for rejecting pressure from members of the *Secret du Roi*, led by the Duke of Broglie, that he should correspond with the *Voivode* of Wallachia, a Turkish client ruler. He warned that any such correspondence would have been soon discovered by Austria.[39] It would have harmed attempts to improve relations with her. In 1755, Vergennes at Constantinople received cautious official instructions that differed from his secret orders from Louis XV to secure a treaty of friendship with the Turks, a treaty moreover that included a secret article committing the Turks to support Polish 'liberties' against Russian aggression. In 1757, the French confidential agent Douglas was disavowed for agreeing certain terms with Russia – a secret clause obliging France to help Russia if she was attacked by the Turks – that did not conform to the *Secret*.[40] The *Secret* itself eventually became both cause and means of criticism and opposition to the official government foreign policy within the court, ministry and diplomatic service.

The French were by no means unique in having such personal diplomacies. The Austrian diplomatic service under Charles VI (1711–40), the Saxon under Augustus II (1696–1733), and the Prussian under Frederick William I (1713–40), were all characterized by the same situation, as was the British diplomatic service for periods during the eighteenth century. This practice indicates that any presentation of foreign policy in terms of bureaucratic regularity is questionable. This is also true, more generally, of the overt intervention of other ministers in policy formulation. The absence of any system of collective ministerial responsibility in France contributed to a situation in which foreign ministers did not always enjoy the support of their colleagues and of other influential figures. Thus, in 1727 Villars criticized the replacement of Morville by Chauvelin.[41] The extent to which the latter was a protégé of Huxelles became a matter for diplomatic speculation.

Foreign envoys, at times, reported as if ministerial divisions drove the pace of French diplomacy. Thus, in November 1753 the Prussian envoy, the Lord Marshal, noted Saint-Contest's request for a letter from Frederick II pressing for a French approach to the Elector of Cologne. The envoy suggested that the foreign minister wanted this, 'in order to justify himself in the Council where he will need to cite your views in order to prevail over his opponents'.[42] In 1773 there was a conspiracy to replace D'Aiguillon, the foreign minister, and the alliance with Austria, by another with Prussia.[43]

The folly of presenting foreign policy in terms of bureaucratic regularity was even more the case with the participation of favourites and other courtiers in policy-making.[44] Thus, in 1752, Kaunitz, the Austrian envoy, was confident that what he saw as an anti-Austrian war party would be held at bay while Madame de Pompadour remained Louis XV's mistress. The following year, Frederick II saw her as pro-British, while in 1757 he speculated that the unsuccessful attempt by Damiens to assassinate Louis XV might make the king more devout, and, thus, weaken the position of his mistress and lessen the influence of the 'pro-Austrian clique'. Frederick was ready to accept Belle Isle's idea of ceding the

Prussian possession of Neuchâtel to Madame de Pompadour for life in return for obtaining peace.[45] Foreign rulers thought it worth appealing for her help.[46] Her enmity to Conti affected Louis XV's support for his cousin's pursuit of the Polish crown. Madame de Pompadour backed the alliance with Austria in 1756, in part to thwart the *Secret du Roi*, although her hostility to Frederick was also important. Her favourite, the Abbé de Bernis, became foreign minister in 1757. His earlier influence had infuriated his predecessor as foreign minister, Rouillé. Pompadour's counterpart at the close of Louis XV's reign, Madame Du Barry, was opposed to Choiseul and supported his replacement in 1771 by the Duke of Aiguillon.

The future Louis XVI's 1770 marriage to Maria Theresa's daughter, Marie Antoinette, a move seen as anchoring Austro-French relations, was actively discussed from the 1750s. In 1777 Frederick speculated about the possibility of interesting Louis XVI in mistresses, in order to lessen the influence of his Austrian wife.[47] Foreign diplomats in Paris were certain that she influenced policy,[48] and this belief itself was important.

Speculation about such issues reflected the widespread sense that rational policies could be abandoned in favour of what a French diplomatic instruction of 1737 termed 'the particular and internal circumstances of courts'.[49] Seven years later, the Swedish envoy complained from the court that

> the government is divided, and cabals and intrigues delay all the decisions
> of war and government, making public matters depend on private views.
> To send a mistress away, to prevent a general from having command or a
> minister from wielding influence, or a courtesan from approaching the
> king; these are the matters to which courtiers devote themselves.[50]

Government could not be separated from court party, indeed became an aspect of the pursuit of power by such parties.[51] The situation was similar in many other states, notably Russia.

In certain spheres, there was a formal competence for French ministers other than the foreign minister. This was true, most importantly, of the secretary of state for the marine in colonial issues and disputes, and in consular matters. Thus it was Jérome Phélypeaux, Count of Pontchartrain, who in 1698 organized the expedition to establish the colony of Louisiana. This role created the possibility of disputes. In 1724 the French envoy in Vienna was uncertain whether, in the absence of orders from the foreign minister, to respond to instructions from the minister of the marine to complain about hostile actions towards French merchant shipping off Austrian Italy.[52] Smuggling led controllers-general, the finance ministers, to take an interest in relations with neighbouring states.[53]

At a less senior level, the *intendant* (central government representative) for Bresse was often the agent for relations with neighbouring Geneva and Savoy.[54] Relations with enclaves in French territory also involved the agents of the king's domestic power, as well as his envoys. This was true of the papal enclaves in southern France – Avignon and the Comtat Venaissin – as in the case of the commercial struggle in 1730–34.[55]

Ecclesiastical diplomacy

In relations with Rome, diplomacy was widely defined, and the crucial issues generally related to the situation of the Church within France, rather than to matters of wider diplomatic import, let alone the affairs of the Papal State. The Gallican privileges of the Church in France, the controversies arising from Jansenism, a Catholic movement eventually judged heretical, and the response to papal bulls affecting France, especially *Unigenitus* of 1713, all kept France's envoys in Rome very busy.[56] Ministers and diplomats such as Choiseul who are generally associated with international power politics also had to spend much time on negotiations with Rome. The fate of the Jesuits was a major issue in the 1760s and 1770s, and a sign of the decline of Catholic internationalism and counter-Reformation politics. The order was expelled from France in 1764. In 1768–74 Avignon and the Comtat Venaissin were confiscated, in order to pressurise the papacy to abolish the Jesuit order. The choice of pope was also important as an aspect of international prestige, dynastic legitimacy, and Italian politics, each of which was important to France. Austria and France clashed in the 1724 conclave,[57] France and Spain in that of 1740. Such clashes were central to prestige and primacy in the Catholic world, one of the major issues at stake in relations between Austria, France and Spain. In 1730 the French tried to win papal support for the Alliance of Seville.[58]

French envoys supported the foreign interests of monastic orders and houses under royal protection, such as the Carthusians, both in Spain and in Naples;[59] and, also, the Catholic Church in areas such as the Ottoman Empire and Ragusa, where it was not the official religion. The Very Christian King of France was the Protector of the Catholics in the Ottoman (Turkish) Empire. In 1757 Vergennes, then envoy in Constantinople, had to respond to an attack by Greek Orthodox on the Catholics in the Church of the Holy Sepulchre in Jerusalem.[60] Interventions were also made on behalf of Catholics in Protestant-ruled states, for example in Ireland in 1738.[61] Louis XIV took seriously his role as 'Protector' of the Order of Malta, a Catholic crusading order that ruled Malta.[62] Three-fifths of the order's income came from its French property. It was typical of the changing attitude to power, privilege and sovereignty, that constituted the French Revolution, that in 1791–2 these properties were confiscated, while in 1798 Napoleon seized Malta. The position of Protector was then held by Tsar Paul I. Ecclesiastical jurisdiction could be an issue on France's borders affecting France's diplomacy with her neighbours: the jurisdiction of the Bishop of Grenoble was at issue in relations with Savoy–Piedmont in 1728.[63]

A number of senior French politicians, such as Fleury, Bernis and Brienne, were clerics, and their ecclesiastical role had an impact on policy, albeit to very varying degrees. Fleury's commitment to peace owed much to his personality, but his religiosity was also important. Church politics and attitudes were less important to Bernis. Cardinals Richelieu and Mazarin, the leading ministers in 1624–61, had been largely responsible for the strongly anti-Habsburg policies of that period. Yet, within the French Church there was also a sense that Catholic France should not fight other Catholics and this played a role in encouraging eighteenth-century moves towards a realignment with Austria.

In the sixteenth and seventeenth centuries, French rulers frequently – although not invariably – allied with Protestant powers against the Habsburgs: with the Schmalkaldic League of German Protestants in the mid-sixteenth century, the Dutch during the Thirty Years' War, and the Swedes both then and subsequently. Co-operation with Frederick the Great of Prussia in the 1740s and early 1750s was a continuance of this pattern. Generally – certainly up to 1756 – allied to at least one major Protestant state, French governments sought to lessen confessional differences that might affect their ability to persuade allies to co-operate. This was particularly important in Germany where the French needed the alliance of both Protestant and Catholic powers, for example Hanover and Prussia, and the Wittelsbach rulers of Bavaria and the Palatinate respectively.[64]

Prestige

The importance of the Rome embassy, and indeed of the papal nuncio in Paris, is a valuable reminder that the issues at stake in foreign policy were not simply, or even at times largely, those of power politics. This was also true of the mass of effort devoted to dynastic diplomacy that cannot be seen only, or even primarily, in terms of politics. Thus, concern about the state of other ruling houses, matters of precedence, rank, inheritance and matrimony, all took up a great amount of diplomatic time and effort. A prudential, *raison d'état* interpretation of this effort can be offered in terms of the role of the prestige gained and maintained in the international and domestic position of the regime, and this was, in part, the case. Nevertheless, it was not the entire explanation.

The extent to which the foreign service was just that for the sovereign ruler was, indeed, central to the ruler's view of their duties. Diplomats were the personal representatives of the monarch and, as such, could be expected to discharge family or, indeed, commercial and cultural commissions, as well as what might be regarded as political tasks. Marital diplomacy took up much time, and ministers devoted much consideration to the subject. In 1762, Choiseul was concerned to ensure the best marriages for Louis XV's grandchildren.[65] Relations with the Spanish Bourbons were very much a matter of family politics during the reign of Philip V (r. 1700–46), although far less so under his successors, and Louis XV's first cousins, Ferdinand VI (r. 1746–59) and Charles III (r. 1759–88). Interest in better relations with other powers was frequently accompanied by consideration of dynastic links, as in 1734 for a double marriage of the Dauphin and a Bavarian princess, and the Bavarian heir with a daughter of Louis XV.

Royal *gloire* was maintained by diplomats, and this encouraged the Bourbons to prefer nobles of the sword for important postings, rather than their less prestigious robe counterparts. Envoys were supposed to act with a style, even magnificence, that supported royal dignity, and to report fully on such magnificence. In 1729 the birth of the Dauphin led to costly celebrations by French envoys, including both a concert and a fête in Rome. At Vienna in 1752, Hautefort was very concerned to ensure that the ceremonial observed on his public entry and audiences accorded with the respect paid to his predecessors. Louis XV approved. Such ceremonial was very expensive.[66] Newly appointed to London in 1762, the Duke of Nivernais was anxious to secure a house appropriate to his rank.

Much time was taken up with struggles with governments and other envoys over protocol and precedence. This was a particular problem at Lisbon. In 1746 Chavigny's arrival at Lisbon was delayed while France refused pressure for their envoy to address the Portuguese foreign minister as 'Your Excellency'. Disputes were also frequent at other courts. In 1699 the Count of Ferriol was thrown out of his audience with the Sultan for wearing his sword. He spent a decade in Constantinople without presenting his credentials. In 1732 Villeneuve quarrelled with the Austrian envoy over his entry into Constantinople.[67] Difficulties over precedence prevented Louis XIV from sending an ambassador to Vienna. The stress on prestige and its outward symbols slackened slowly in the second half of the eighteenth century. As part of the Third Family Pact, France and Spain sought in 1761 to prevent disputes over precedence, such as that between their envoys in Vienna in 1725. Nevertheless disputes persisted and French diplomats continued anxious to preserve their ceremonial position. In 1769 the French envoy in London tried to insist that he, and not his Russian counterpart, should sit next to the Austrian ambassador. The Russian allegedly insulted Châtelet and a duel was fought. In 1785 the French clashed with the British over etiquette at the court in Naples.[68]

Diplomats

As the representative of the sovereign, envoys were also expected to provide whatever services were required. Louis XV enquired about British condoms through a British diplomat, but used his own diplomats to try unsuccessfully to prevent the publication in London in 1771–2 of fictitious letters by Madame de Pompadour; while his grandson used his representative in Algiers to obtain animals for his menagerie in the 1780s, including four ostriches.[69]

The French government also had to confront the problems of ensuring that diplomats obeyed orders and did not take unwelcome initiatives. In 1757 Louis

XV and his foreign minister, Bernis, were furious when Ogier arranged Danish intervention to secure an armistice for the Hanoverian army that failed to contain sufficient provisions to prevent the danger of it being subsequently ignored when the Hanoverians might be relatively stronger. Marshal Richelieu, then in command of the army in Hanover, was told to restrict himself to hearing proposals and forwarding them to Paris for consideration, since

> diplomats are not able to see the totality of combinations, an understanding of which is necessary in order to relate operations to the general plan. Only the royal Council can therefore settle policy . . . envoys should restrict themselves to overtures approved and ordered by the king.

Four years earlier, Bonnac had stressed his care not to take discussions with the Dutch too far in the absence of instructions.[70]

In 1727 Fleury was told that Cardinal Polignac, the envoy in Rome, was not pressing the pope sufficiently hard to have 'James III', the Stuart Pretender to the British throne, expelled from Avignon, as instructed, because he owed his cardinalcy to the Pretender's support. In fact, Pope Benedict XIII was resisting pressure.[71] Fleury, himself, criticized Rottembourg that year for reaching an agreement with Spain without permission,[72] a step that angered France's ally, Britain. In 1742 La Chétardie was reprimanded for urging Russia to stop operations against France's ally Sweden, and told that he had underestimated the quality of the Swedish army.[73] In the event, the Russians were to defeat the Swedes easily. There were comparable problems with the colonial diplomacy of officials of the Ministry of the Marine. Agents on the spot were frequently bolder than was intended, as in the case with expansion west from Louisiana in 1716– 17 and its unintended impact of worrying Spain.[74] The Revolutionary governments faced problems with independent-minded envoys and generals who pursued their own policies. Thus the Directory had only limited control over Bernadotte, the envoy in Vienna in 1798, and over generals such as Hoche and Napoleon.

Aside from issues of policy, diplomats could also appear to commit, or at least embarrass, the crown and government by their language and behaviour. Thus, the response of French envoys in Italy to 'James III' and his family angered British ministers and diplomats at a time when the two powers were not hostile. This was especially true of representatives in Rome, such as Cardinal Rohan in 1722 and the Duke of Saint-Aignan in 1731–40, and also of Count Froulay when James's eldest son, Bonnie Prince Charles, visited Venice in 1737.[75]

Most of the time, the government defended its envoys against criticism. This was a particular issue during alliances. Allies often argued that French envoys at third courts were pursuing hostile views, and this was especially an issue when France was allied to a traditional enemy: Britain in 1716–31 and Austria in 1756– 91. In 1785 Kaunitz claimed that Choiseul-Gouffier, the envoy in Constantinople, was stirring up the Turks against Austria. Vergennes argued that this was unjust and defended the envoy at length.[76]

Intelligence gathering was an important aspect of diplomatic activity,[77] but it was — and often is — difficult to judge the accuracy of the reports. The problem of control over diplomats was exacerbated by the nature of communications. Naturally slow, these were further affected by the weather, for example the heavy rains that stopped nearly all posts in mid-January 1728, or the ice in the Baltic five years earlier.[78] The unpredictability of communications was as big a problem as the delays. In 1731 Villars commented on dispatches that took only 39 days to arrive from Constantinople by sea. Choiseul-Gouffier wrote from Constantinople to the foreign minister, Montmorin, on 25 April 1787, and again the following day. The first dispatch was received on 26 May, the second, sent by sea, on 3 July. Those of 11, 15, 16, 25 January, 10, 23 February, 10, 17, 24 March, 10, 25 May and 9 June arrived on 11 February, 6 April, 29 March, 26 February, 11 March, 25 March, 8 April, 31 May, 24 April, 9 June, 23 June and 7 July respectively. Dispatches of 18 and 25 June and 24 July 1787 from St Petersburg were received on 12 and 19 July and 17 August.[79]

Journey times were greatly affected by wind direction. Such delays and uncertainties were worse in wartime. The uncertainty of sea routes led Villeneuve, when war with Austria broke out in 1733, to prefer to send his mail across the Adriatic to Ancona in the Papal States rather than along the Adriatic to Venice, a route that increased the risk of interception. Eleven years later, the hazards of voyages by sea, combined with dangers from hostile British warships, left the French envoy in Genoa without messages for up to three weeks at a time, and led to the hope that Nice, then a possession of the rulers of Savoy–Piedmont, would be captured by French forces so as to improve communications. On an overland route, two successive couriers from Naples were taken by Austrian hussars.[80]

The situation put further pressure on diplomats, obliging them to respond to developments without being able to obtain fresh instructions. This was a particular problem at the most distant embassies. Constantinople was the furthest permanent one. Delays and the unpredictability of communications also affected the journeys of envoys. Leaving St Petersburg in June 1726, Campredon's boat ran aground.[81] Vergennes's voyage to Constantinople in 1755 was affected by contrary winds. It took 49 days from Marseille.

The degree to which diplomats had to cope with urgent business varied greatly, both between postings and during the course of individual embassies. Thus, the envoy at Venice was expected to do and report more when French troops campaigned in northern Italy, as in the 1690s, 1700s, 1730s and 1740s, but not during the remainder of the *ancien régime*.[82] Furthermore, the degree of initiative left to envoys varied greatly. The freedom granted Villeneuve at Constantinople in the 1730s was not offered Jonville and Guymont in Genoa in the 1740s: they found everything decided at Paris, and were not even kept informed.[83]

Like all governments, the French was aware that it was liable to have its views judged by the conduct of its envoys and that these could be contradictory.[84] This became a more acute issue at the time of the Revolution, when the chilly injunction 'the French nation counts on the zeal and fidelity of its foreign agents',[85] in part, reflected the difficulty of matching the views of diplomats to the volatile politics of Paris. The Foreign Ministry itself was placed under the scrutiny of the Diplomatic Committee that the National Assembly created on 29 July 1790. Furthermore, difficulties between French diplomats were exacerbated by accusations of obstruction, disobedience and treason.[86]

Individual careers reflected the disruption of the Revolution. This was especially true at the senior level. Thus, many envoys, for example Choiseul-Gouffier from Constantinople, were recalled after the declaration of the republic in August 1792. Disruption was not only the case at the senior level. Charles Flüry, secretary of legation at Munich, joined the *émigrés* after his father was killed in the storming of the Tuileries by the Revolutionaries on 10 August 1792. He then returned to Paris, where in 1793 he was appointed secretary of legation at Dresden. Unable, owing to the war, to take up the post, he became secretary of legation to the Republic of the Valais, a French client state, in 1793–6. Denounced as disloyal in 1796 he was, nevertheless, appointed consul general to Wallachia, Moldavia and Bessarabia.[87]

If the service of the monarch, and, briefly, the republic, was the task of diplomats, that does not explain their instructions, nor indeed the choices that policymakers had to implement. How monarchs developed their ideas is not very clear, not least because a revelatory, still more autobiographical, stance was not expected from the ruler. Louis XIV's *Mémoires* offer a partial, propagandist view of his views, and then only for a part of the reign. Monarchs tended to think in terms of generalities, rather than specifics, and then it was up to both the rulers and their advisers to try to respond to particular issues. This was as much a matter of re-action as of being pro-active. The policies and actions of the rulers and ministers of other states provided much of the agenda of French policy. Thus, Sonnino shows that the Dutch war of 1672 developed in the midst of a complex and volatile international system which greatly affected its aims and timing.

Yet, operating within a system and being re-active, did not preclude ideas and policies. These will emerge within the chronological chapters, but, in essence, the bold hopes of Louis XIV's reign were not sustained under his two successors, although there were moments, such as 1741, when French ministers convinced themselves that they could reconfigure European power politics. Furthermore, thanks in large part to its role in Constantinople and Stockholm, the peacetime ambit of seventeenth- and eighteenth-century French diplomacy was greater than the wartime range of French power. That altered during the Revolutionary and Napoleonic period, as 'diplomacy' with states outside this range declined, while, instead, a pseudo-diplomacy developed with client republics and rulers within the French world.[88]

The impact of domestic politics

The extent to which public opinion, and aspects of domestic politics without any formal part in foreign policy, played a part in affecting its formulation and conduct, as was the case with other states, is difficult to establish. At one extreme, there was the belief that policy was affected by domestic agitation that had been deliberately stirred up by foreign powers to that end, a practice indeed followed by both France and Spain during their frequent conflicts in the sixteenth and early seventeenth centuries. In 1674 William III of Orange and the Queen Regent of Spain sought to encourage conspiracies in France, including one for an insurrection in Normandy. In 1719 Philip V of Spain supported opposition to Orléans and tried to overthrow him in favour of the Duke of Maine.[89] Thereafter, such intervention diminished until it was greatly revived after the French Revolutionary War broke out in 1792. In 1732 the British ambassador to Austria reported the Chancellor as interested in 'intriguing' in French internal disputes: 'he thinks they may be forwarded to advantage'.[90] The government and the *Parlement* of Paris were then embroiled. The same month, a police spy in Paris noted the belief that dissidence in Dauphiné was encouraged by foreign powers.[91] There was no evidence for this claim and the Austrians did not intervene in the disputes involving the *Parlement*. The British were believed to be behind Huguenot schemes in 1757[92] and Parisian radicals in 1789–90,[93] although their interest and role were greatly exaggerated in both cases and many Huguenot leaders refused anyway to take part in the plotting of 1756–7.

Nevertheless, even if there was no active intervention in French domestic politics and problems, these were still believed to affect the foreign perception of French strength and policy. In December 1725 the French envoy in St Petersburg reported that Russian views of France were based on diplomatic accounts of discontent and poverty there. He was told that France was in no state to fight Austria,[94] a view that was reasonably well founded then, in so far as sustained conflict was concerned. In November 1753 the Swedish envoy in The Hague told his French counterpart that disputes involving the *Parlement* of Paris were encouraging Britain to take steps against France,[95] an opinion without much basis. In September 1782 Rayneval reported from London that the previous British government had encouraged George III to persist in the War of American Independence by telling him that France had internal and financial problems.[96]

The French complained about hostile envoys.[97] Sensitivity to foreign views was increased by the degree to which the French themselves gauged the likely actions of foreign states as arising from their degree of domestic stability. Thus, disorder in Hungary led Vergennes to argue in 1784 that Joseph II would not act in the Scheldt crisis.[98] Such assessments were linked to the belief that domestic opponents looked to foreign powers. In November 1730 the consul general in Spain wrote, 'I'm assured there is a direct correspondence between the Spanish court and French opponents of the government'.[99] Such activity was far less common than was rumoured. In February 1728 the Saxon envoy in Paris reported that domestic critics would approach the plenipotentiaries at the forthcoming international peace congress and request their intervention; and Chauvelin was also concerned. There was in fact no approach.[100]

Foreign powers were affected by their perception of French stability, particularly so at the time of the Revolution.[101] Then, as at other times, French governments resisted any idea that domestic affairs should be influenced by foreign negotiations and powers. Just as Louis XIV did not want the position of the Huguenots made an issue of international negotiations,[102] so, in October 1792, Lebrun emphasized that the government could not guarantee the life of Louis XVI in any treaty with Prussia. He argued that this would compromise French independence and that only the nation could judge Louis.[103]

Prior to the Revolution, foreign views on the domestic situation within France also affected the judgement of her actual and likely foreign policy. Thus, the replacement of Louis XIV by a minor in 1715 led to the assumption that France would take a generally quiescent role, a response, in part, to Louis's international image. There was also interest in the state of the economy and its likely impact on policy. In January 1740 Earl Waldegrave, the British envoy, reported on the possibility that France might support Spain against Britain: 'though the Cardinal [Fleury] affects in his discourses a great deal more courage than usual, I fancy he will consider of it more than once before he venture out of his road. The misery of the country is excessive, and the weather seems tending to increase rather than to lessen it'.[104] That did not prevent Fleury from sending a fleet to the Caribbean later in the year, although it did not act against the British. At times of domestic political crisis or uncertainty, for example 1732, when there was a serious clash between the government and the *Parlement* of Paris, less attention was devoted, by both the French government and French public opinion, to foreign policy. Stainville, the Lorraine envoy, reported on 3 July 1732, 'internal matters so dominate government attention that there is no time for those of Europe'.[105] Police reports on Parisian opinion that year were dominated by domestic politics.

Royal glory

The existence and expression of public opinion on the content and conduct of foreign policy was far from new. Indeed, the extent to which policy aligned or clashed with the confessional divides that were so important within France had helped to politicize foreign policy both during the (civil) Wars of Religion of the late sixteenth century and in the first half of the seventeenth century. Far from ignoring public opinion, Louis XIV sought to win domestic support for, as well as by, his foreign policy. He developed his *gloire* through war. Louis accompanied the army under Turenne that invaded the Spanish Netherlands in 1667 and enjoyed both commanding and reviewing troops.[106] Royal princes were given titular command of armies, Louis's eldest grandson, the Duke of Burgundy, on the Rhine in 1703 and in Italy in 1706. Louis's triumphs, such as the crossing of the Rhine in 1672, and the successful sieges of Maastricht (1673), Ghent (1678), Mons (1691) and Namur (1692), were celebrated with religious services and commemorative display.

Louis had begun such commemoration at the outset of his personal reign, commissioning Gobelins tapestries to record the public apologies made by Spain (1662) and the Papacy (1664) after clashes over precedence and recognition. The *Galerie des Glaces* at Versailles, the largest long gallery yet built, had ceiling paintings commemorating in particular triumphs during the Dutch War of 1672–8.[107] The *Salon de la Guerre* in the palace was finished and opened to the public in 1686. In it, Antoine Coysevox presented Louis as a stuccoed Mars, the God of War. Engravings and medals spread images of glory. Masques, plays and operas focused on French victories. Philippe Quinault's libretto for Lully's 1677 opera *Issus* presented Louis XIV as Neptune and referred to recent Mediterranean successes. It was considered important that the court opera at Versailles was more magnificent than that at Vienna.[108]

Royal military spectacle had a secular and sacral symbolism.[109] Symbolism linked royal power and French strength, and made both normative. This was particularly so at Versailles, the new palace that proclaimed the power of Louis XIV.[110] In addition, building in Paris under Louis – with its repertoire of royal column, triumphal arch and monumental avenue – was designed to enhance the splendour of the capital and of the monarchy. The monarchy symbolized France, a symbolization and ideological centrality that was pushed hard during this reign. It has been argued that 'the ideology of hierarchy and lineage' pressed more heavily within France in the seventeenth century than hitherto.[111] This ideology was deployed in the context of an internationally assertive dynasty. Much of the nobility, conditioned to respond to royal martial leadership, responded with an often exuberant patriotism.[112] By the 1690s over 20,000 nobles were serving in the army and navy, a bond that testified to aristocratic confidence in Louis and his policies.

Although it is difficult to measure, there was considerable elite bellicosity in 1667, 1672, 1688, 1733 and 1741, although less so in 1701, possibly as a consequence of difficulties and setbacks during the Nine Years' War of 1688–97.[113] In addition, there was a shift in style from the 1680s as Louis and his advisers adopted a new attitude towards his public image. Although the use of the device of the sun in glorification of the 'Sun King' was never abandoned, it lost its earlier importance. Attempts to draw connections with Alexander and Augustus also declined. There was a new emphasis on the statistics of conquered territory and population. A less 'glorious' note was struck, and this can be related to the attempts to avoid war in the negotiations of 1698–1700 over the future of the Spanish Empire.

In 1734 Louis's surviving grandson, Philip V, told the French envoy that war was necessary for the political stability of the French monarchy.[114] Louis XV presented himself as a warrior in the 1740s, although not during the War of the Polish Succession (1733–5), while the Parisian rumour in December 1728 that he would lead an army into Germany[115] was baseless. Nevertheless, Louis was at the siege of Freiburg in 1744, received the keys of surrendered Ghent in 1745, and was at the siege of Antwerp in 1746. He was also present at the battles of Fontenoy (1745) and Lawfeldt (1747); the Dauphin was also at the first. Louis XV benefited from his association with Marshal Saxe's victories. Having followed Louis on his 1745 campaign, the Parisian painter Charles Parrocel exhibited ten paintings of Louis's victories the following year.

Public opinion

Increasingly, the government also sought both to influence public opinion through printed propaganda, and to gain an insight into the public mood through systematic police reporting.[116] Printed propaganda, directed both at domestic and foreign opinion, was produced in greater quantities from the 1700s.[117] The public mood within France was seen as important, although it was not until the second half of the eighteenth century that it was regarded as a source of political legitimacy.[118] The notion of honour and *gloire*, generally presented in the seventeenth century in personal (the monarch) and dynastic terms, was, increasingly, seen in terms of the nation and country. Considering in 1782 how best to persuade the government of his ally France to support his aggressive Balkan views, Joseph II included the need for 'a means to cover itself *vis-à-vis* the French public',[119] an indication of the potential importance of public opinion and of the appeal to it as a lever on and within government.

Popular opinion could, however, be regarded as factious, and it is difficult to show that well-entrenched ministers were overly concerned by it.[120] In November 1735 Fleury wrote to the Emperor Charles VI concerning popular views about the, as yet, undisclosed peace terms with Austria: 'there are, as usual, critics who in fostering impracticable expectations prepare the way for criticism. It is necessary to be prepared for their clamours'.[121] Having seen off disaffection over ecclesiastical and constitutional issues,[122] Fleury knew that he would not be overthrown over peace with Austria at the close of a successful war. More generally, success in war, rather than responses to specific policy initiatives, was crucial to public judgements of rulers and their governments.[123]

Public opinion was, and is, open to multiple definitions. It is most helpful to think of a number of widely held opinions that lacked specific force, such as the wish to be seen to do well and the need to protect national territorial and commercial interests, as well as more particular notions that were not so widely held, but which were presented as public opinion by their protagonists. Hostility to the Austrian alliance of 1756–91 is the best example of the latter. While widely expressed,[124] it was still a minority view. Nevertheless, efforts were made to elicit support for this view through writings. Broglie hired Jean-Louis Favier, formerly a minor diplomat, to produce tracts directed against the alliance with Austria. In 1756 he wrote *Doutes et questions sur le traité de Versailles* and in 1773 *Conjectures raisonnées sur la situation actuelle de la France dans le système politique de l'Europe*. Marie Antoinette's alleged influence focused this issue in often scurrilous printed attacks during the reign of Louis XVI (r. 1774–92).[125] Claims on behalf of public opinion climaxed during the Revolution. In January 1792, after the previous foreign minister, Montmorin, was blamed for French isolation, his successor was told to recall 'that the nation has its eyes on you'.[126]

Domestic pressures and problems were frequently (but not only) most serious in periods of financial difficulty. This was especially so in wartime. Thus, in early July 1761 Choiseul sought a rapid peace, largely due to financial problems and troubles arising from *parlementaire* opposition.[127] However, in a *lit de justice* on 21 July, Louis XV overcame the opposition and the war continued.

The nature of public opinion was, in part, a matter of knowledge. Travellers could comment on French ignorance about the outside world – the notion in Orléans in 1728 that Britain was a town of the same size – or the French officer who allegedly asked if Scotland was adjacent to Pondicherry in India[128] – and some plays presupposed 'general ignorance': Lesage's *Sophie et Sigismond* (1732) about Hungary.[129] Nevertheless, there was a growing amount of information about the outside world available in the culture of print, whether books or journals, newspapers or maps. The *Gazette* reprinted items of foreign news from the Dutch and English press, and foreign newspapers circulated in France.

Trade and foreign policy

The correspondence of those not responsible for diplomacy, for example Mathieu Marais, a member of the *Parlement* of Paris in the 1720s, indicated familiarity with foreign policy.[130] In 1735 another Parisian lawyer conversant with foreign policy, D'Aube, was convinced that alliance with Spain was crucial to French wealth.[131] Trade, and thus knowledge of the wider world, was important to urban opinion. In November 1728 a Parisian police spy noted comments that the government had not re-established trade: 'there are complaints, as usual, against the government'.[132] Mercantile views were not those of the army officers. The latter, naturally bellicose, were reported in January 1728 as publicly attacking Fleury in the Versailles cafés, and claiming that he would be overthrown by the aristocracy.[133]

The spatial composition of French power was that of inland France.[134] The landed nobility was crucial, and the role of land in elite identity was underlined under Napoleon by his reliance on a new service aristocracy who were provided with estates. The nobility were far more interested in the army than the navy, in the land rather than trade or empire. These values affected French society as a whole. The loss of Canada in 1760 and Louisiana in 1763 was criticized in mercantile circles in the Atlantic ports, but had only limited impact elsewhere, not least because they were seen in fashionable circles as barren and profitless. Aristocratic families had scant presence in French North America.

The values of aristocratic power were important to French policy-making and diplomacy. The ready transfer between war and diplomacy was noticeable in many careers. One of Louis's leading generals, Villars, sought as a diplomat to win the alliance of Max Emmanuel of Bavaria in 1687–8. He advised the advance of French troops to Ulm in order to persuade the Elector of French power to threaten or protect.[135] The Count of Vaulgrenant became a colonel before being appointed to Turin in 1732. He transferred as a lieutenant general to Madrid in 1734 and was a supporter of Chauvelin's bellicose anti-Austrian policies. The Marquis of Fénelon, ambassador to the United Provinces in 1724–44, was a veteran of the Wars of the Spanish Succession and the Quadruple Alliance, in both of which he had been wounded, served as a lieutenant general in the War of the Austrian Succession from 1744, and was shot dead in 1746.[136] The Count of Plélo, envoy in Copenhagen, was killed in 1734 during the War of the Polish Succession while trying to relieve Danzig (Gdańsk).[137]

A strong belief in the importance of the economy to the strength of the state, of the international competitiveness of economies, and of the need for state intervention and support, led to policies and attitudes later described as mercantilism. They predated Louis XIV, being particularly associated with Henry IV's principal minister, Sully, in the 1600s, and with Louis XIII's Cardinal Richelieu, but from the 1660s were pushed with great energy by Colbert. He was in effect chief economic minister from 1661 until his death in 1683, sufficiently so for French mercantilism to be sometimes described as Colbertism.[138]

Mercantilism, however, did not provide France with a state bank, or with a financial infrastructure sufficient to fund and sustain large-scale imperial and trans-oceanic activity, whether government or private. Marked oscillations of national credit in the early eighteenth century, particularly the 1720 crash of John Law's government-backed Mississippi Company, ended an experiment with paper credit. The crash sapped confidence in the idea of national financial institutions and ensured that public banking, thereafter, played little part in pre-Revolutionary France. The discount bank established in 1776 was a relative failure partly because it was compelled to make excessive loans to the government.

Credit was provided by private individuals or consortia, neither of which were particularly interested in long-term investment, especially in infrastructure. Significant commercial activity tended to look for its credit, as for its political support, to Paris, thus helping to increase its dependence on the vicissitudes of national credit, particularly state borrowing. While Mediterranean commerce at the beginning of the eighteenth century remained largely a monopoly of Marseille, Parisian financiers were significantly involved in, or actually dominated, almost all the other commercial companies. In the 1780s merchants in the French ports relied on Parisian financiers for credit and basic banking facilities.

The nature of the financial system had harmful economic consequences.

Much investment was short-term, hitting, for example, marine insurance,[139] while interest rates varied greatly, a major disincentive to long-term investment, and government borrowing drove up the cost of credit. In 1786 interest rates of 10 per cent for commercial loans to French merchants were normal. Much of the French economy was undercapitalized. In the 1780s many of the Bordeaux merchant firms trading with the West Indian colonies were financially weak, with a limited margin of security and little liquid money; and this was the most profitable large-scale trans-oceanic trade of the period. Britain and the Dutch, in contrast, had more sophisticated credit systems. Although French overseas trade increased greatly during periods of peace in the eighteenth century, especially from the ports on the Atlantic coast,[140] investment and profitability at the level of individual traders and companies were frequently low,[141] while the impact of the trade on the rest of the economy was limited, not least owing to internal tariffs. Thus, La Rochelle, with its restricted network of communications into the interior, had an enclave economy,[142] while in the 1780s the major industrial centre of Lyon did not benefit greatly from the activity in the Atlantic ports.

Commercial interests played only a small role in French foreign policy, and this was even more true of colonial groups. Commercial interests were represented in national Councils of Commerce,[143] but these councils had a patchy history, and there was no equivalent to the British Board of Trade. The Council created in 1664 was dominated by administrators and financiers, not merchants, and ceased to meet in 1676. The Council, established in 1700, sought specific privileges for individual ports, rather than free trade. Furthermore, internal tariffs made it difficult to think in national terms. For example, French cider-based liqueurs could be sold only in Normandy and Brittany, lest they compete with the wine brandies which alone could be sold to Paris and the French colonies. Norman requests in the mid-eighteenth century for permission to sell to the colonies were rejected. In the late seventeenth century, economic links between the Dutch and Brittany were closer than those between Brittany and Paris.

Representations could be made directly to the government, rather than through national Councils of Commerce. Thus, in 1727, the Chamber of Commerce of Marseille[144] complained that British merchantmen were driving their counterparts from the carrying trade. The same year, French diplomats in London were instructed to find out if linen imports from Cambrai were to be banned, as the town feared. The British government had already been pressed on the issue in 1726. In 1728 a memorandum from Agde emphasized the importance of the Spanish trade and the value of a trade treaty with Russia, while memoranda on trade with Spain were produced for the minister of the marine by the Chambers of Commerce of Bayonne, La Rochelle and Nantes. In 1726 the Bayonne Chamber was worried about the impact of British blockade on trade with Spanish America via Spain.[145] In 1764 the foreign minister, Praslin, consulted the St Malo deputies about the Newfoundland fisheries.[146] French merchants abroad could also influence policy through the consular system, which was particularly well developed in Spain. The French mercantile community at Cadiz was especially influential.[147]

The scope of such groups reached to little more than the details of commercial regulation, and did not contribute to a powerful impact on foreign policy. In late 1727, despite great pressure from mercantile circles (pressure referred to by Fleury),[148] to reach an agreement with Spain, so that the latter would release goods and funds owed to French merchants in the *flota* from the New World, the government refused to satisfy Spain at the expense of the views of her leading ally, Britain. Police reports had noted concern in Paris about the issue.[149] Chauvelin had told the British envoys that the government 'could not stand the clamour which would be occasioned by the breaking [bankruptcy] of many considerable merchants, for want of the effects they had on board'.[150] However, it had to withstand the outcry, a valuable comment on the nature of contemporary and modern arguments of policy changing as a result of public pressure based on such evidence.

Indeed, both the Councils of Commerce and the consular system were tangential to the processes of foreign policy formulation and execution, although they were capable of ensuring a degree of support for French commercial interests. Such interests were prominent in disputes over customs regulations on France's borders, for example between Strasbourg and Baden-Baden in 1738.[151] Further afield, commercial interests were most important where serious political issues were absent, as for example in relations with Ragusa (Dubrovnik).[152]

Consuls regularly reported on trade, as they were, indeed, instructed to do.[153] They did not always support French merchants, not least because they sometimes thought them shortsighted, motivated solely by gain, rash, and prone to complain unreasonably. Jean-Baptiste Daubenton de Vauraoux, who was made consul general to Spain in 1728, reported contemptuously about the French merchants there the following year, and in 1730 was unsympathetic to their complaints about Spanish customs. Benoît de Maillet was similarly angry, first at Cairo (1692–1708) and then at Livorno (1712–17). In 1728 the minister of the marine, Maurepas, noted the number of disputes between consuls and merchants, especially in Salonica, Sidon and Tripoli (in Lebanon).[154] The agreement by which the French merchants were invited back into Palestine in 1790 by Jezzar Ahmed Pasha, the Governor, was denounced by the consul in Syria and Palestine, Jean-Pierre Renaudot, as demeaning, and he complained that the merchants had come to terms against his wishes. Villeneuve was typical of many diplomats in preferring a regulated trade, rather than liberty of commerce, which he referred to as disorderly, repeating the views of the Marquis of Bonnac, envoy at Constantinople in 1716–24.[155] The Marseilles Chamber of Commerce corresponded directly with the envoys in Constantinople, but it clashed with Villeneuve and its influence declined during the century.[156]

Relations between consuls and diplomats could be poor. In 1740 Pierre

Bigodet des Varennes, consul general in Spain, complained that the ambassador, Count La Marck, refused to co-operate or, indeed, to say much to him. Seven years later, La Marck's replacement, the Bishop of Rennes, complained that Bigodet des Varennes did nothing, and, in 1748, he was replaced.[157] In 1776 the Marquis de Clermont d'Amboise reported that the Neapolitan government would only pay attention to him, and not to the consul.[158]

Clermont d'Amboise repeatedly pressed the Neapolitan government on the treatment of French shipping. In July 1776 he complained that, whereas the British were allowed to sell prohibited goods, the French were not and that their ships were searched despite their privilege to the contrary. He added that French vice-consuls were alone threatened with the loss of the privilege of putting up their ruler's arms. The following month, he complained about the more favourable treatment of the Genoese in the Calabrian oil trade, while in September the Neapolitans protested that a French ship had given a murderer refuge, episodes which reflected the fact that commerce and national rights and sensibilities were never truly separate. In 1776 disputes over the conduct of customs officers multiplied, although Clermont d'Amboise admitted in November that French traders were guilty of smuggling. Nevertheless, he complained of preferential treatment for the British. 1777 brought renewed disputes over the customs, the respect not paid to the French flag, and the debts owed to Marseille grain merchants. The French were concerned about the willingness of Neapolitan consuls to allow Genoese and Tuscan smugglers to use their flag. In 1778 Clermont d'Amboise pressed the Neapolitan government to allow grain exports to France and to stop the imprisonment of French sailors for smuggling.[159]

Compared to many British and Dutch envoys, their French counterparts mostly devoted relatively little attention to trade. The weakness of trade in French political culture, and as a symbol of national interest, was, in part, responsible for the degree to which Austrophobia increasingly overshadowed Anglophobia in court and public debate about foreign policy in the 1780s and early 1790s: Austria to many appeared more of a threat than the commercial rival, Britain.

In Britain, trade was not the prime concern of the monarchs. Nor did the trans-oceanic global dimension play much of a role in the views of Georges I and II. George III's firm response to the demands of the American colonists was the first major royal intervention in imperial matters. The lack of a consistent royal interest can be seen in terms of salutary neglect, or it can be regarded as less benign. None of the Hanoverians took a positive role akin to that of Charles III of Spain (r. 1759–88). Imperial, like industrial, growth is a central feature of the period in Britain that does not bear a royal imprint. Yet, that did not matter. So many other aspects of the British political system were conducive to commercial interests, that modest royal support was not a bar.

The situation in France was different. There the crown had little real interest in matters maritime. Louis XIV only once went to sea, and then briefly. His visit to Dunkirk in 1680, when he embarked on the *Entreprenant*, one of his ships of the line, was the sole occasion when he boarded one of his ships, and the only time after 1660 that he saw a ship. This contrasted greatly with William III's experience and with Peter the Great's determination to learn about ships. Louis XIV's interest in the navy was episodic, and his failure to maintain financial support has been seen as crucial to its institutional weaknesses in the mid- and late 1680s and to its consequent operational limitations in 1690.[160] Louis gave little thought to the overseas world, and his failure to support Colbert in developing France's position in Asia, specifically to reinforce the expedition sent to the Indian Ocean in 1670, has been criticized.[161] Louis failed to appreciate the potential importance of British and Russian developments. Louis XVI only once visited a port: Cherbourg in June 1786, to see the major harbour works being constructed. Louis XIV and Louis XV sought military glory by accompanying their armies and not their fleets. Louis XVI's visit to Cherbourg, commemorated in a painting by Gapin, brought him no glory and was no substitute for Louis XIV's heroic poses.

Conclusions

Royal preferences were serious because the emphasis within French government and politics was not on matters maritime, commercial or colonial. Louis XIV was no Peter the Great, keen to develop and sustain a navy and to move the capital to the coast, while Louis XV lacked the Emperor Charles VI's ostentatious commitment to trading companies ('the Emperor is so bent upon making a figure at sea' according to the British envoy in 1728)[162] and Louis XVI failed to match Charles III of Spain's interest in the colonies and trade. Nor were their leading ministers as committed to trade as, for example, the Portuguese first minister, Pombal. French failure in the struggle for oceanic power, and thus dominance of the maritime trade of the world, has been traced in part to the impact of aristocratic political culture and priorities over those of bourgeois origin.

Yet, before this is seen as the failure of an entire governing order, it is worth stressing that, at various times, powerful ministers were committed to naval power and colonial expansion. This was particularly true of Colbert, who went to La Rochelle in 1669, and of Maurepas, minister of the marine 1723–49, and also of the years after the Seven Years' War. In July 1761 Choiseul consulted mercantile opinion over which colonial losses France should seek to regain in her peace negotiations with Britain.[163] Commerce has been seen as playing a larger role in French policy from the 1760s.[164] There was nothing pre-ordained about French priorities and policies, in Europe or outside.

CHAPTER TWO

Louis XIV and Europe: French foreign policy, 1661–1715

As generations of history undergraduates knew only too well, Louis XIV's foreign policy was a subject that fascinated their teachers, at least to the extent of providing steady essay and lecture fodder. It is also the aspect of international relations in the period that has attracted most scholarly study and debate. The traditional nationalist historiography of other western-European states, often highly unsympathetic to Louis, was challenged from the 1960s, especially by Ragnhild Hatton, who showed that harsh criticism of Louis was inappropriate.[1] Since then much excellent work has appeared, but it has, on the whole, addressed particular periods of Ludovician foreign policy, rather than dealing with the reign as a whole. Lucien Bély's publications are especially welcome as they indicate a return of French historians to the study of international relations.[2] Recent work helps to clarify the extent to which Louis's policy neither conformed to any master plan nor consistently centred on one issue. Rather, the picture that emerges is a fractured one.

This empirical development is underlined by two conceptual points. Firstly, the reification of early-modern foreign policy has not been without unfortunate consequences, not least in providing an analytical imperative for historians to clothe actions and events with signs of coherence and consistency, and especially to show that there was long-term planning. Secondly, consideration of how decisions were taken calls into question any presentation of a defined policy springing from bureaucratic agencies. The unpredictability of royal interventions was combined with a significant inchoate element in the processes by which advice was given. Furthermore, the degree to which the formal mechanisms for the conduct of diplomacy can be referred to as mature, in a bureaucratic, institutional sense, is open to question. The patron/client relationship which flourished among the officials in the ministry of foreign affairs was also found in the diplomatic service, if that is not a misleading term for what was for many simply another way to serve the king.[3]

Any attempt to fit French policy throughout the reign of Louis XIV into a procrustean mould thus appears inappropriate. Nevertheless, historians of other aspects of Louis's reign, aware of the political importance of foreign policy and the tremendous burden of war, are entitled to expect an answer to questions concerning Louis's purposes and success; and these are also important because accounts of his purposes and success thereafter played an important role in judging French foreign policy. The need to consider such issues is made more apparent by the realization that Louis's domestic power rested on uncertain foundations, that what was subsequently termed absolutism required – and was, indeed, the product of – consent, and that success was a vital lubricant of obedience. Equally, it is apparent that Louis's attitudes varied during his reign. His readiness to turn to force was not constant, and from the late 1690s he was more flexible than in the 1680s.[4] The varying independent scope of his foreign ministers was also important.

The strength of Spain

In light of the habitual tendency to present Louis's policy in an aggressive light, it is worth noting that anxiety about France's strategic position was a persistent theme during the reign. The Peace of the Pyrenees of 7 November 1659, that closed 24 years of continuous war with the Spanish Habsburgs, was less decisive than is generally appreciated.[5] The resilience of mid-century Spain tends to be forgotten beneath the blanket depiction of the 'Decline of Spain'.

In fact, Spain had not only preserved her Italian possessions (Sicily, Sardinia, the kingdom of Naples – southern Italy – and the Duchy of Milan – Lombardy). She had also, thanks in part to the effects of the *Frondes*, regained Catalonia, which had rebelled in 1640, and she proved capable of attempting, albeit without success, to regain Portugal, which had also rebelled in 1640. The French had sent support to the Portuguese and, particularly, the Catalans. Despite its Iberian and Italian commitments, the Spanish government was also able in the 1650s to make a major effort to retain the Spanish Netherlands (modern Belgium and Luxembourg), one that the young Louis XIV's government led by Cardinal Mazarin required the assistance of English forces sent by Oliver Cromwell to challenge. Aside from her European possessions, Spain ruled the largest empire in the world. Most of South and Central America and the West Indies was under her control, as was much of Florida and the Philippines.

Spanish security appeared to depend on French weakness, a situation that in turn encouraged French desires to harm Spain. In the 1520s, and from the 1560s onwards, the Spaniards had been able and willing to encourage disaffection within France, and thus to challenge the power of the crown, its ability to wage war and the appearance of stability that was so important to a successful foreign policy. This policy reached a high point in 1585, when the Spaniards formally allied with the Guise family, the leaders of the Catholic League, in the Treaty of

Joinville, and, again, from 1648 when Philip IV provided support for those aristocrats led by Condé who sought to overthrow Mazarin's government in the *Fronde*. A settlement of Condé's position was an aspect of the Peace of the Pyrenees. Such sponsorship of aristocratic opposition was both dangerous and humiliating for French monarchs, and only Spain was well placed to do so.

Under the Peace, the French made gains from Spain. The acquisition of Artois pushed the frontier with the Spanish Netherlands back and that of Roussillon strengthened France's position in Languedoc. Louis married Philip IV's daughter, Marie-Thérèse, in June 1660 and thus gained another diplomatic prize: pretensions to the Spanish succession. The infanta's renunciation of her rights to the Spanish succession was made conditional on the payment of the substantial dowry. The marriage also served as an opportunity to develop an iconography of royal virility and Bourbon hegemony.[6] Louis reached for his new opportunities in 1661 when unsuccessfully he asked Philip IV for an annulment of Marie-Thérèse's renunciation and the immediate gain of Aire, Saint-Omer, Cambrai, Hainault, Luxembourg and Franche-Comté, in return for abandoning his links with England and Portugal.[7] The position on the north-east frontier was enhanced in 1662 when Louis purchased Dunkirk, England's European gain from the war, from the recently restored Charles II. The English kept Jamaica. Artois and Roussillon were useful acquisitions for France, but far less than had been hoped for, and less than is suggested by much of the discussion of the 'Decline of Spain'.

An awareness of Spanish resilience makes French policy in the 1660s easier to comprehend. It was felt necessary to take measures to guard France against a revival of the Spanish threat, an attitude encapsulated by Louis's frequent references to his grandfather, Henry IV (r. 1589–1610), who had been an active opponent of Spain and had also faced Spanish support for aristocratic opponents.

This can be seen clearly in French policy towards Portugal. The Peace of the Pyrenees had been a great blow to Portugal, as it had prohibited French assistance and left her to fight Spain alone. This repeated the serious situation in which France had found herself in 1648 when the United Provinces and Sweden, to whom France had been allied in the latter stages of the Thirty Years' War (1618–48), had negotiated peace with the Habsburgs. In 1661, when Mazarin died (on 9 March), and Louis announced that he would dispense with a prime minister (10 March), the king sought the opinion of his ministers on aid to Portugal, and all agreed that France could assist Portugal because of Spanish violations of the Pyrenees treaty. Turenne, Louis's leading general, who had wanted to fight on against Spain in 1659, argued that it was indispensable to preserve Portuguese independence and that France must not be weak. In 1664 Philip IV still had 77,000 men under arms, the largest force in this army being located along the Portuguese border. As a result, Louis sent military assistance to Portugal. Furthermore, in 1665 he dispatched an ambassador to Lisbon with instructions to thwart any peace settlement between Portugal and Spain.[8]

This policy was scarcely new. Henry II of France had supported the German Protestants against the Emperor Charles V in the 1550s, while, from the fourteenth century, Scottish opposition to England had been backed by successive monarchs. Louis was to be a major proponent of such diversionary tactics; indeed they were crucial to his diplomatic and military strategies. Such tactics entailed benefits and commitments for France. It was necessary to support allies. Thus in December 1659 the French threatened to invade the nearby Duchy of Cleves in order to persuade its ruler, Frederick William, Elector of Brandenburg–Prussia, the 'Great Elector', to restore gains from France's ally Charles X of Sweden.

Aggression in the 1660s

Honour and prestige were central values for Louis[9] and from the outset of his personal reign (from 1661) his concern with his *gloire* influenced policy. On 10 October 1661 a dispute over precedence between the Count of Estrades and the Baron of Vatteville, the French and Spanish envoys in London, erupted into a serious clash, with the Spaniards forcing their way ahead at the celebration of the arrival of a new Swedish envoy. Louis at once convened an extraordinary council, and when it unanimously advised moderation, the king, instead, decided to push the issue, expelling the Spanish envoy, and obliging Philip IV to recall Vatteville and to have his new envoy in France declare publicly before Louis on 24 March 1662 that all Spanish diplomats had been instructed not to contest precedence with their French counterparts. The dispute reflected Louis's concern about prestige, his aggressive tactics and his particular sensitivity about Franco-Spanish relations.

In August 1662 a dispute between papal guards and the armed following of the French envoy in Rome, the Duke of Créqui, led to violence. Louis broke diplomatic relations and began preparations for military action, leading again to concessions – for both Louis and his Italian allies – in 1664. Yet this quarrel was not solely about prestige: it also related to wider considerations, especially French hopes of weakening the Spanish position in Italy.[10] Expenditure on the galley fleet – half of naval costs in 1663[11] – reflected the importance of Mediterranean concerns. France was the strongest naval power there, but not in the Atlantic or the Channel.

The foreign minister in this period, Hugues de Lionne, had been a trusted agent of Mazarin. He helped to maintain a measure of continuity, but policy was very much set by Louis. A series of treaties reflected France's diplomatic presence and pressure, and the new opportunities opened up by the end of the war with Spain: treaties with Sweden (1661), Lorraine (1662), the Dutch (Treaty of Paris, 22 April 1662), Denmark (1662 and 1663), and the Swiss cantons (1663). Charles II of England was pressed to help Portugal.[12] French troops joined the forces of the French-sponsored League of the Rhine in 1664 in subjugating Erfurt to the authority of the Archbishop of Mainz and the following year Frederick William of Brandenburg joined the League.

Louis also took a more assertive line in New France: the French colony centred on the St Lawrence valley of modern Canada. Louis XIV took over its administration in 1663, having dissolved the Company of New France, and in 1664–5 sent 1,200 troops who helped encourage the Iroquois, the dynamic Native Americans to the south of New France, to terms. The Mohawk were forced to terms, although not defeated, by the burning of villages and crops. In 1665–6 five forts were built along the Richelieu River, giving control over the route from the St Lawrence to Lake Champlain. Jean-Baptiste Colbert, who became controller general of finances in 1665, wished to develop the St Lawrence valley as a source of food and industry that would complement the fishing off Newfoundland and the colonial goods from the West Indies, producing mutually supportive and profitable interactions in the French colonial world. New France itself had a population of only 3,200 French colonists in 1666, but in the 1660s and early 1670s the government sent both money and settlers, including *filles du roi*, mostly orphans, whose immigration was subsidized in 1663–73 in order to offset the overwhelming preponderance of men. A governor, some settlers and a small force of about 50 troops had been sent to Newfoundland in 1662–3 to develop a base at Plaisance.

To the west of New France the journeys of Jesuit missionaries and of *coureurs du bois* (fur traders) extended French influence and knowledge. Trading bases were established at Sault-Ste-Marie and St-Ignace in 1668, giving the French an important presence in the strategic region where Lake Huron joined Lakes Michigan and Superior (to use the subsequent English names). There were hopes that waterways, and thus trade routes, would lead from Lake Superior to Hudson Bay and the Gulfs of Mexico and California. Travelling into Wisconsin in 1669, Father Allouez heard of the Mississippi. Two years later, at a ceremonial meeting of Native Americans at Sault-Ste-Marie, French officials laid claim to North America as far as the 'South Sea'. In 1673 a seven-strong mission led by Louis Jolliet, a fur trader, and Father Jacques Marquette, set off to find the Mississippi and to travel to its outlet. They travelled as far as the confluence with the Arkansas River and, on their return, used a shorter route via the Illinois River and the Chicago Portage. Marquette reported that a route from the Great Lakes to the Gulf of Mexico had been discovered. Further north, an expedition from the St Lawrence reached Hudson Bay in 1672 but the English Hudson's Bay Company was already established there.

A growing consciousness of the importance of maritime and colonial interests led in 1669 to the creation of the secretaryship of state for the navy, a post occupied by Colbert. He was motivated by a desire to challenge and emulate, if not replace, the profitable and powerful maritime position of the Dutch. French West India and East India Companies were founded in 1664,[13] and the Dutch were driven from Cayenne (later French Guiana on the northern coast of South America) the same year. The earlier French company that had sought to develop a colony there had gone bankrupt in 1654. Troops were also sent to strengthen the crown's position on Martinique in the West Indies. The first French trading base in India was founded at Surat in 1668, and in February 1669 the first East India Company ship returned from India to France, bringing pepper, saltpetre and indigo from Surat. Northern (Baltic) and Levant Companies followed in 1669 and 1670 respectively, and in 1670 Colbert sent an expedition on a fruitless attempt to occupy Hudson Bay. A large squadron was sent to the Indian Ocean in 1670, instructed to found fortified establishments near the Cape of Good Hope, on Ceylon (Sri Lanka) and in the East Indies.[14] French trade in the Mediterranean was helped by the imposition in 1669 of a prohibitive 20 per cent tariff on all goods brought to Marseille from the Ottoman Empire in foreign ships. Colbert sought to organize an effective system of raising sailors for the navy, announced in 1663 that the crown would purchase no more ships abroad, and in 1664 created a system of subsidies to support shipbuilding in France. He encouraged the development of Rochefort, La Rochelle, Québec, Brest, Lorient and Sète as a system of naval ports.

The death of Philip IV of Spain on 17 September 1665 both provided Louis with an opportunity to act and served as a reminder of the challenges and volatility provided by dynastic chance. Had Philip's successor, Charles II, been a strong ruler, then traditional French fears of Spain might well have been renewed. However, the four-year-old Charles was mentally and physically weak and apparently unlikely to have children: he never did so, despite two marriages. His speedy death appeared sufficiently possible that Louis and Leopold I, the (Holy Roman) Emperor and the ruler of the Austrian Habsburg inheritance, were to reach a secret agreement in 1668 for the partition of the Spanish inheritance. This agreement was not to be carried out and the two powers were to be at war by 1673, but, like other examples of interest in better relations with Austria, it serves as a reminder of the volatility of the international system.[15]

The opportunity presented by Charles's succession appears clear in hindsight, naturally so in light of Louis's exploitation of his position as Philip IV's son-in-law in order to seize part of the Spanish Netherlands in the War of Devolution (1667–8). The French claims were themselves tenuous: an application of private laws of inheritance in the Spanish Netherlands under which children of a first marriage, such as Louis's wife, took precedence over those of a second marriage, such as Charles.[16]

There was also a danger. Aside from the possibility of Spanish regeneration if Louis did not act, there was the prospect that part of the inheritance would be acquired by another ruler. The likely candidate was one of the prospective children of Leopold, who was shortly to marry Philip's other daughter. Philip's will left the inheritance to this line in the event of Charles's death without children. Such a development would have led to a major establishment of Austrian power on France's borders, prefiguring and greatly exceeding that of Prussia under the Congress of Vienna in 1815.

Aside from the possibility of such gains, there was also the danger of a closer union between the Austrian and Spanish Habsburgs. It was not necessary to go back to the 1550s, to the reign of the Emperor Charles V (Charles I of Spain), when the dominions had been united in the hands of one man, in order to appreciate the danger to France of such a union. In 1617, when the question of a successor to the Emperor Mathias was urgent, Philip III of Spain proposed a reunion of all Habsburg territories under a Spanish prince. The Austrian Habsburgs instead chose Ferdinand of Styria. Although the Austrian Habsburgs were in favour of collaboration with the Spanish branch, they resisted any notion of going back to Charles V.

Nevertheless, in the Thirty Years' War (1618–48), Austro-Spanish co-operation, celebrated in Rubens's triumphalist painting of their joint victory over France's ally Sweden at Nördlingen in southern Germany in 1634, had posed major problems for France. Such co-operation limited her influence in the Empire (the term used for the Holy Roman Empire, which covered modern Germany and some neighbouring regions) and threatened her from the east. Austro-Spanish co-operation also restricted French influence in Italy. This was true both militarily, as in the War of the Mantuan Succession in 1628–31, and also in diplomatic terms. Furthermore, Austro-Spanish co-operation limited French influence with the papacy.

Far from simply being a Franco-Spanish duel, the French struggle with the Habsburgs involved an important Austrian dimension, not least in terms of the French reaction: sponsorship of Austria's leading German rival, Maximilian of Bavaria, and also of the Swedes, who had invaded the Empire in the 1630s. If French rivalry with Austria receded after 1648, when the two powers made peace, it was still present in Mazarin's successful arrangement in 1658 of a French-sponsored league of German allies, the League of the Rhine. The powers were officially under the protection of Louis, and the League was an aspect of a forward policy in Germany,[17] that included in 1664 the negotiation of a defensive alliance with Frederick William of Brandenburg, and the dispatch of French troops, to help resist a Turkish invasion of Austria.

Thus the Spanish succession focused a long-standing French problem, that of Austro-Spanish co-operation. It also served as a reminder that France's European opportunities and challenges were linked, and that the number of her options were limited. Louis has traditionally been criticized for pushing his schemes for territorial expansion too hard. This analysis is open to a number of qualifications. It is difficult to assess how much expansion is 'enough' and, therefore, question-able to suggest that, up to such a date or such a frontier, policy was justified and that, thereafter, folly had been embraced. To many Germans, any French expansion was not immutable, but rather the product of French strength that could be reversed. Ultimately, French hegemony over the lands between the Saône/Marne and Rhine depended on military strength, for the Dukes of Lorraine were traditional Habsburg allies, and the Emperor and Empire keenly concerned to prevent the consolidation of the position the French had acquired in Alsace under the Peace of Westphalia of 1648.[18]

From the inheritance of Philip IV, Louis claimed Brabant, Antwerp, Namur, Limbourg, and parts of Franche-Comté and Luxembourg. He sent troops in to enforce his claims in May 1667, leading Spain to declare war on 14 July. Militarily, the War of Devolution was a major success for France, demonstrating the vulnerability of the Spanish Netherlands and of Franche-Comté, part of the Burgundian inheritance, with its capital at Besançon, that belonged to Spain. French forces made major inroads in both. Lille fell in 1667, Besançon the following year. Lionne sought as France's gain from the war an equivalent for the queen's claims: Franche-Comté, Luxembourg, Aire, Cambrai, Charleroi, Douai, Saint-Omer and Tournai.

The war also had an unfortunate diplomatic consequence. French successes led, in January 1668, to the negotiation of a Triple Alliance of England, Sweden and the Dutch Republic, each of which had been important allies of France during the previous quarter-century: indeed, by the Treaty of Paris of 1662, France had renewed her alliance with the Dutch, and in January 1666 Louis had declared war on England in support of his Dutch ally in the Second Anglo-Dutch War. The ostensible purpose of the Triple Alliance was to mediate between the combatants, in order to produce a compromise peace that would include some French concessions,[19] but the Alliance secretly agreed to back Spain if Louis refused to compromise. To help Spain, the English, in spite of French opposition, negotiated a settlement of the conflict between Spain and Portugal.

Although his leading generals wished to fight on, the creation of the Triple Alliance led Louis to accept terms in the Treaty of Aix-la-Chapelle, signed on 2 March 1668. This extended France's frontiers in the Low Countries, in particular with the retention of conquered Lille and Tournai, but far less so than those of Russia, at the expense of Poland, in the Truce of Andrusovo of 1667. The last left Russia with Smolensk, Kiev and the eastern Ukraine, a major extension of her territorial area.

The contrast between the two treaties is instructive. That with Poland came at the end of a war that had started in 1654, and revived in 1658 after a settlement in 1656, whereas the War of Devolution had been but brief. In part this was a matter of the differing nature of the international situation in the two halves of Europe. In Western Europe, where the number of independent states and density of interests were greater, any advance of a certain distance potentially brought more powers into play.

In Eastern Europe, however, there were fewer players. Russian pressure on Poland directly involved, in addition, only Sweden and the Turkish Empire. Indeed Charles X of Sweden both attacked Poland (1655–60) and fought Russia (1656–8) in what was a tripartite struggle. However, once differences with Sweden had been accommodated, in an armistice (1658) and then the Treaty of Kardis (1661), Alexis of Russia was able to press forward against the Poles with no further bar. The Turks had many other commitments: aside from a long-standing conflict with Venice over Crete (1645–69), they intervened in

Transylvania (1660–61) and fought Austria (1663–4). Louis sought to play a role in Eastern Europe. The elective character of the crown of Poland attracted his attention. In 1666–7 he wanted to send troops to Poland in order to provoke the abdication of the king, Jean-Casimir, and ensure the election of the Prince of Condé. However, events further west demanded his attention, and Polish candidates were elected to the throne in 1669 and 1674. In order to assert his role, Louis also sent troops in 1668 and 1669 to help in the defence of Venetian-ruled Candia in Crete against Turkish attack. Many were killed and the remainder were withdrawn in 1669.

Whereas in Eastern Europe there were major opportunities for territorial gain, in the west this process appeared far less likely because of the number of second-rank powers willing to combine against any potential hegemon. Yet, Louis XIV did have a prospect of major gains in 1668, a prospect provided by the means of dynastic claim. The prize was the Spanish succession. The secret partition agreement with Leopold I, signed on 19 January 1668, the Treaty of Grémonville, promised that on the death of Charles II without children, Louis and his heirs would receive the Spanish Netherlands, Franche-Comté, Navarre in northern Spain, Naples, Sicily and the Philippines. This was a rich prize, and an acceptance that Louis did have a claim to the Spanish succession, although the Austrian Habsburgs were left the New World, as well as Spain, Milan and Sardinia. A parallel can be found in the French failure to obtain colonial acquisitions from Spain in the War of Devolution or the subsequent peace. Nevertheless, as a permanent gain to the French royal house, the agreement promised much, especially as the Spanish Council of State felt obliged to concur. This seemed a more appropriate way to make gains than that of conquest. Austrian consent would prevent a lengthy war, akin to that with Spain in 1635–59.

The Dutch War

The existence of the Triple Alliance suggested that other powers might have a view on the Spanish succession, and this represented an irritation for a monarch unused to compromise. Louis had found that his control of military developments was not matched by international deference. As a result, he devoted the postwar years to preparing fresh action in the Low Countries. This time, however, his target was the Dutch, who in May 1669, with the other powers of the Triple Alliance, guaranteed the Spanish Netherlands. Louis correctly anticipated Dutch hostility to an extension of French power in the Spanish Netherlands, but also was swayed by scorn and spite. The United Provinces was a republican, Protestant, commercial state with a political culture to match, and there was a powerful element of instinctive hostility in Louis's aggressive approach. As a result, he misjudged the potential of Dutch politics. Divisions within the United Provinces between the princely House of Orange, the traditional source of the *stadtholders* (provincial governors) who provided the monarchical element in Dutch politics, and the more republican town oligarchies of the wealthiest province, Holland, provided Louis with a chance to intervene. He indeed did so, but lacked the necessary acuteness to succeed in the long term.

Louis also sought to benefit from divisions within English politics, encouraging Charles II to abandon the Dutch and, by the Treaty of Dover, to ally with France against them in an alliance that included secret clauses loosely committing Charles to support the Catholic cause in England, and Louis to secret subsidies that would improve Charles's position *vis-à-vis* Parliament.[20] Pedro of Portugal was offered an agreement directed at the power of the Dutch in the Indian Ocean, but he refused, fearing that Anglo-French naval assistance would be inadequate and that Spain would support the Dutch.[21] The French fleet greatly increased in size in the late 1660s and early 1670s, so that by 1675 it was the largest in the world.[22]

Louis's system extended to Germany where, with some difficulties, the major rulers near the United Provinces were persuaded to provide a route for French attack. He had allowed the League of the Rhine to decline in importance, instead preferring alliances with individual rulers. Frederick William of Brandenburg–Prussia signed a treaty with Louis at the close of 1669, accepting the promise of (the region of) Guelders, which was to be seized from Spain.[23] Charles of Lorraine was intimidated in early 1669 when the French assembled troops at Metz. The following year, Lorraine was occupied, a step that encouraged anti-French feeling in the Austrian court. On 16 February 1670 a treaty with Bavaria committed the Elector to close his territory to Austrian troops in return for a French subsidy. Treaties of neutrality with Cologne and Hanover were concluded in July 1671. By a treaty of neutrality of 1 November 1671, Leopold I promised not to intervene, so long as Spain was not attacked. Louis, indeed, would have preferred such an attack, another triumphal march into the Spanish Netherlands, this time without the prospect of English intervention. However, his English ally was against such a step.

Instead, the French invaded the Dutch Republic in 1672, declaring war on 4 April.[24] Thanks, in part, to the support of the local ruler, the Elector of Cologne, French forces crossed the Rhine and invaded the United Provinces from the east, only being stopped when the dykes were breached on 20 June. The province of Holland had been saved, but the French had made a far greater impact in one campaign than the Spaniards had done in over a quarter-century of war (1621–48).

The Dutch offered terms, but an over-confident Louis, hopeful that the war would widen to include Spain, issued excessive demands, including major territorial gains and the acceptance of Catholic worship. This was unwise, not least because an Orangeist *coup* in Holland in July 1672 brought the anti-French William III of Orange to power as *stadtholder*. He was to prove Louis's staunchest opponent. William was unwilling to accept a settlement under which he became hereditary ruler of the United Provinces in return for yielding to English and French demands.

In 1673–4 the conflict changed shape, but not as Louis had wanted, in part because of his over-confidence and his maladroit handling of others, but also because the coalition that Louis had created was unstable. He lost his ability to manipulate German politics in order to create an important alliance system, while the Austrians became increasingly successful at doing so. A peace congress at Cologne failed, in part because Louis was insufficiently conciliatory, and Spain, the Emperor and the Empire joined the struggle against him, while in February 1674, angry at the lack of sufficient French naval support, Charles II abandoned the war, ending Anglo-French naval pressure on the Dutch.[25] The Dutch were no longer interested in negotiations. Louis failed to draw Portugal into the war against Spain and the Dutch, and his difficulties led Denmark and the Palatinate to join Austria. Louis was not helped by an Eastern European diversion of Austrian strength. The Turks were more concerned about war with Poland than Austria.

In August 1673 Leopold, the Dutch, Spain and Charles IV of Lorraine had agreed to try to force Louis back to the frontiers laid down at the Peace of the Pyrenees. To try to undo both his gains in the War of Devolution and his conquests in 1672–3 was a bold objective, but France had not hitherto that century had to face a comparable coalition. In 1673 and 1675 French forces were pushed back by the skilful Austrian general Montecucculi. However, the threat to eastern France was held, lightly-defended Franche-Comté was conquered in 1674, and major advances were made in the Spanish Netherlands and Catalonia. From 1674 the French sent troops, by 1677 over 11,000 men, to assist the Sicilian rebels against Spanish rule. There was a series of successful naval engagements with Dutch–Spanish squadrons off Sicily in 1675–6, but in 1678 the French recalled their forces, leaving Spain in control.[26]

Outside Europe, the French position was weakened by the failure of attempts to win Portuguese support. French attacks on the Dutch in Sri Lanka and southern India failed. A base was established at Trincomalee on Sri Lanka in the spring of 1672 and approaches made to Sinha II, ruler of the interior kingdom of Kandy, then at war with the Dutch. He was willing to negotiate an alliance, but French inaction led to a failure to co-operate and in July 1672 the base capitulated to a Dutch fleet. That month the French captured São Tomé on the Coromandel coast of India from the ruler of Golconda, but the pressure of France's European commitments led to failure to send necessary reinforcements and in 1674 an alliance of Golconda and the Dutch forced the French at Masulipatam to surrender. No French fleet of comparable size was sent to the Indian Ocean during the rest of the century. François Martin established a position on the Coromandel coast of India at Pondicherry in 1674, but the French had failed in their best chance that century to establish a powerful position in the Indian Ocean.[27]

There was extensive conflict in the Caribbean. The French re-captured St

Martin (1676) and Tobago (1677) after Jean, Count of Estrées, defeated a Dutch squadron off the latter island, but an expedition sent against Curaçao in 1678 ran aground in May on the Isle of Aves off the South American coast with the loss of seven ships of the line. The Dutch were unable to capture Martinique (1674), although in May 1676 they recaptured Cayenne from the French. It was taken back by Estrées in December 1676.[28] In West Africa, the French took Gorée (1677) and Arquin (1678) from the Dutch, ruining their trade on the coast. The loss of much of Estrées's fleet was a serious blow, but the opportunities for further conquests were soon to be ended by the coming of peace.

French trade and commercial networks were hit by the war. The French depended heavily on Dutch intermediaries in order to trade with the Baltic and to re-export their colonial products. This system had thrived in the 1660s, but was hit in the 1670s.[29] In 1669 Colbert had founded the *Compagnie du Nord* to limit the Dutch role as intermediaries, but it was unsuccessful and, after its ships were seized by the Dutch, folded in 1677.[30] The number of ships sent annually to the Indian Ocean by the East India Company fell after 1676, and by 1680 the company had ceased paying dividends. The tonnage of French shipping itself continued to rise,[31] while the first slaving voyage from Bordeaux sailed in 1672.

The war did not stop French expansion in North America. Louis de Buade de Frontenac, the Governor, strengthened the French position on Lake Ontario by building Fort Frontenac (1673). His protégé René-Robert, Cavalier de La Salle founded a series of trading posts on the Illinois River.

The Peace of Nijmegen

The war was brought to a close by a series of treaties signed in 1678–9, known collectively as the Peace of Nijmegen. Their terms reflected French military success in the recent war, and this success had led the Dutch to negotiate. Gains and exchanges gave France a far stronger frontier with the Spanish Netherlands. Acquisitions included Bouchain, Bouillon, Charlemont, Condé, Longwy and Valenciennes. None was as dramatic a gain as Namur or Luxembourg would have been, but, individually and collectively, they altered the balance of vulnerability between France and the Spanish Netherlands. Further south, the Spanish loss of Franche-Comté consolidated French links with Alsace and weakened the position of the Emperor's ally, the Duke of Lorraine. The gain of Freiburg in the Black Forest took French power east of the Rhine, further strengthening Alsace and giving France greater influence in the Upper Rhineland. Within Alsace the French had replaced the ambiguous relationship established by the terms of their acquisitions there under the Peace of Westphalia of 1648 by more clear-cut control. In the New World, French possession of Cayenne and Tobago was confirmed, although Spain refused to acknowledge French claims to Hispaniola.[32]

Aside from these valuable gains, there was also a diplomatic victory. The Dutch War was very different to that with Spain in 1635–59, because it was fought against a coalition. The destruction of this was instrumental in France's success, both in obtaining satisfactory peace terms and in launching a postwar diplomatic offensive. French diplomacy played on divisions between her opponents, ensuring that there was no single treaty ending the war, but, instead, a number of agreements. The Dutch, who lost no territory, settled before the Spaniards, while Leopold I, who had hoped to see France out of Alsace, was isolated and forced to abandon his schemes. Frederick William was obliged by French military moves to return his gains from France's ally, Sweden, and felt it necessary to ally with France from October 1679.

The politics of intimidation

Louis's opponents were left divided and without strong leadership. This provided a background for reversion to the intimidatory tactics of the 1660s. In the winter of 1678–9 French forces occupied much of the Spanish Netherlands, in order to collect contributions owed to the army, and also fortresses in the lower Rhineland, in order to exert pressure on the local rulers. Using force, Louis advanced a series of claims in a unilateral fashion. Claims to the dependencies of territories ceded to the French crown, including the prince-bishoprics of Metz, Toul and Verdun and the Landgravate of Upper Alsace, led to demands for much of the Spanish Netherlands and of the Empire west of the Rhine and south of the Moselle. Many of these territories were reunited by force in the early 1680s, the *réunions*, named after the *Chambre de Réunion* at Metz. For example, the French took the Marquisate of Franchimont from the Prince-Bishopric of Liège, claiming it as an indirect dependency of the Duchy of Bar, which had been ceded to the French crown. Further claims were then advanced, leading to the seizure of Theux and Verviers, and threats to Huy. In 1682 Maximilian-Henry, the Prince-Bishop of Liège, agreed with Louis that the French would return their gains and abandon their claims in return for a thirty-year occupation of Bouillon and Dinant. As the chapter of Liège refused, however, to agree, the French continued in occupation, and in 1684 French troops helped the bishop regain control.[33]

Other gains were also made in this period. Strasbourg, the major crossing place between Alsace and Germany, was occupied in 1681, a step that alienated opinion in Berlin, and that was part of Louis's replacement of Richelieu's more cautious approach to German politics by one of wholesale territorial advance. The French attitude to the German constitution had become more contemptuous.[34] The north-Italian fortress of Casale was also purchased in 1681. The gain of Freiburg and Casale extended Louis's power far beyond what were subsequently seen as the natural frontiers of Rhine and the Alps. They provided bases for the projection of force into southern Germany and northern Italy. In addition, many of the gains made strategic sense in terms of avoiding a repetition of the difficulties that had affected France during the Dutch War.

Louis's successes in these years were a product not simply of military strength, but also of the strengths of France's diplomatic position. The wartime attempt to arouse and direct anti-hegemonic fears against France was not successfully sustained. This was despite the efforts of William III who argued that Louis's strength and attitudes were a threat to what he presented as a European system in which sovereign powers, however weak, were guaranteed by the restraint of the powerful. Louis, a monarch who – to William – represented an absence of restraint, appeared the principal threat to such a situation. William negotiated a series of treaties against Louis and in 1682 the threat of Dutch attack led Louis to raise the siege of Luxembourg, the crucial military base in the Spanish Netherlands and one from which France could be threatened and links with Germany maintained.

William's position was weakened by French diplomacy. This included intervention in the factional politics of potential opponents. In the United Provinces itself the French envoy, D'Avaux, was able to exploit the anti-Orangeist feeling of the Louvestein party and the sense that Spain and England were broken reeds, while favourable French tariff changes and the consequent revival of trade influenced Dutch opinion.[35] In England, Louis was willing in 1678 to help opposition politicians attack the government and bring down Charles II's leading minister, the Earl of Danby, when it appeared that English foreign policy would be maintained in an anti-French direction. In 1681 Louis switched to supporting Charles, providing him with funds to keep Parliament dissolved.[36]

The weakness of potential opponents encouraged Louis to press on with his aggressive schemes. Intimidation seemed an end as much as a means, the creation of a situation in which diplomacy was not necessary other than to cement military gains. This was clearly seen in the Spanish Netherlands. In 1683 troops were sent into Spanish Flanders, ordered to live off the land, and Spanish responses led to an escalation of French intimidation.[37] Spain declared war in December 1683, only to lose Luxembourg the following June and then to negotiate the Truce of Regensburg (Ratisbon).

No other power was in a position to help Spain. In part, this was a matter of French action. Many of the German princes were in receipt of subsidies; Charles II of England responded to his French subsidies, not to his treaty with Spain; and pressure from Amsterdam, encouraged by France, blocked William III's attempt to increase his army and paralysed his attempts to aid Spain. Although Brandenburg and Denmark did not act against William's allies in Brunswick, as Louis had hoped, they also did not support Louis's opponents. The dispatch of a fleet to the Baltic in 1683 reflected France's ability to challenge the Dutch in an area of traditional interest, although Louis rejected Danish pressure for joint action against Sweden.[38]

Other aspects of the situation were only fortuitously favourable. In 1683 the Turks attacked Austria, leading Leopold I and many of the German princes to concentrate on the defence of Vienna. Unlike in 1664, when he had sent Leopold help against the Turks, Louis had encouraged this crisis. In 1681–2 he provided support to Turkish-backed Hungarian opponents of Leopold (opponents with whom Louis had allied in 1677).[39] Nevertheless, Turkish intervention did not represent an alliance that Louis could dominate or even much influence. As such, it was different to alliances with Sweden in the Thirty Years' War or with Charles II of England. In particular, the likely longevity of the crisis in the east was unclear.

This wider international context affected Louis in the 1680s, the pivotal decade of his reign.[40] Louis's success in negotiating with his rivals separately in 1684 brought him the twenty-year Truce of Regensburg, leaving him in possession of his *réunion* gains, Strasbourg, Luxembourg, and Charolais, a Spanish enclave in France; but not a definitive peace ceding them to France. The importance of this can be exaggerated. Although their gains from Poland under Andrusovo (1667) were only those of a truce, the Russians made them permanent by the Treaty of Eternal Peace (1686). Louis could have tried to match this achievement, but, unless he wanted a full scale war in 1684, it was sensible for him to accept what could be obtained.

The opinion was expressed in France that such a war was indeed what he should have sought, and that the opportunity to grasp the entire Spanish Netherlands had been lost.[41] Nevertheless, 1673–4 served as a warning about how a situation could suddenly deteriorate. Louis had to consider the danger of provoking Leopold to settle with the Turks, as he had done in 1664, and also had to assess the effects of his policies on the Spanish government and Charles II of Spain's likely will. The Franco-Spanish armistice of 1684 had included a Spanish agreement to Louis's demand that his elder grandson, the Duke of Burgundy, become Governor of the Spanish Netherlands.

In Canada, the French found themselves vulnerable to Iroquois pressure. An attempt to crush the Western Iroquois in 1682 led to a humiliating climbdown after influenza and logistical problems weakened the French force.[42] Further west, positions were established at Fort St Joseph (1679), Fort Crèvecoeur (1680) and Fort St Louis (1682), consolidating France's presence between Lake Michigan and the Mississippi, and in 1682 La Salle canoed down the Mississippi to its mouth. On 9 April he planted the cross, raised the arms of France, and claimed the river, its tributaries and the lands they watered for Louis.

Angered by the failure to defeat the Iroquois, Louis disgraced Frontenac in 1683 and criticized La Salle's discoveries as worthless; but his opinion was changed by clerics eager to extend the Catholic Church. An energetic new governor, Jacques-René de Brisay de Denonville, arrived in 1685 with 500 troops, part of the force of 1,750 sent in 1683–8. He successfully attacked the villages of the Seneca in 1687, and negotiated an acceptable peace with the Iroquois in 1688. In 1686 a force captured the English bases on James Bay. Further west, the network of French posts extended with the foundation of Fort Ste-Croix (1683), St-Antoine (1686) and Fort La Pointe (1693) south of

Lake Superior. North of Lake Superior, bases were founded at Fort Kaministiquia (1678), Fort Népigon (1679) and Fort La Tourette (1684).

La Salle found little support in Québec for his plan for a series of forts down the Mississippi, but he met with a better reception in France in 1684, in large part because Louis was then at war with Spain. La Salle was sent to the Gulf of Mexico with four ships and 300 settlers but, missing the Mississippi delta, landed 400 miles west at Matagorda Bay where he founded Fort St Louis. This fell foul to the barrenness of the coast, divisions in the expedition (which cost La Salle his life in March 1687), and the hostility of the Karankawa who wiped out the surviving colonists at the close of 1688. All France had to show was the post on the Arkansas River near the confluence with the Mississippi founded by an unsuccessful relief expedition in 1686. Fort St Louis had provoked a series of Spanish expeditions into Texas and along the Gulf of Mexico.

In India, peace with other European powers helped the French as they expanded their network of trading bases. They fortified Pondicherry in 1682 and received permission to settle in Balasore in 1684, Masulipatam in 1687 and Tellicherry in 1690.

1685–8: Louis's position deteriorates

Louis hoped to turn the terms of the Truce of Regensburg into a peace so that his *réunion* gains were confirmed, and the acceptance in the truce of his right to fortify the *réunion* territories was an important bonus. A series of developments in the mid-1680s undermined the French position. The order in which these are presented is important as it reflects a prioritization that is, in fact, difficult to make. The Revocation of the Edict of Nantes in 1685, the change in international relations produced by Austrian success against the Turks, and the breakdown of France's position in the Rhineland, were all of consequence, but possibly most important was the sense of power ebbing that affected Louis in the mid-1680s and the consequences both of this and of the king's continued insensitivity, for the handling of developments in an increasingly volatile situation. Having long had a low view of Leopold and Austria, Louis was disconcerted by the Austrian advance into Hungary.

Louis's attempt to use Hungarian pressure on the Austrians in order to secure his eastern frontier was greeted with suspicion. An instinctive bellicosity can be seen in the willingness of French envoys to suggest a resort to force, as Rebenac, the envoy in Spain, did in 1688 in response to Spanish measures against French trade.[43] The French readily employed violence and the threat of violence to force the Barbary States to respect French trade. Algiers was heavily bombarded in 1682, 1683 and 1688, each attack producing a treaty. Tripoli (North Africa) accepted terms after bombardment in 1685, returning all French captives and paying a ransom of 500,000 *livres*, and Tunis agreed terms under the threat of bombardment. The navy was also used to bombard Genoa in 1684, to blockade

Cadiz in 1682 and 1684, and in a major show of force off Cadiz in 1686.[44] The devastating attack on Genoa was a punishment for its support of Spain.[45] French warships forced their Spanish counterparts to lower their flags as a mark of French maritime predominance.[46]

Force also played a role in Louis's attempts to develop a relationship with Siam (Thailand). This owed much to his desire to present himself as a champion of the Church, a desire strengthened by his disputes with Pope Innocent XI and by Leopold I's successes against the Turks. This theme was probably far more important than trade, despite the role of the latter in contemporary equations of power and prestige and the wish to surpass the wealth derived by the Dutch from Asia. In 1685 Louis sent Abbé François-Timoléon de Choisy to Siam in an unsuccessful attempt to convert its ruler, Phra Narai. Choisy also failed to gain the privileges he sought for missionaries and converts, while commercial hopes proved abortive. Nevertheless, a Siamese embassy was sent to France, and suggestions from Constantin Phaulkon, a Greek favourite of Phra Narai, that the French establish garrisons in Bangkok and Mergu to protect local Christians were taken up. In January 1687 Louis ordered the dispatch of troops and a new embassy.[47]

Suspicion of French policy in Europe was accentuated by a belief that the Truce of Regensburg did not necessarily represent the conclusion of Louis's aggression and the end of French expansion. Louis, anyway, appeared to be unwilling to respect the provisions of the Truce. His construction of new fortifications in the Empire at strategic points, including Landau and Trarbach, led to protests and confirmed the feeling that Louis was unwilling to confine himself, notwithstanding specific assurances.

This feeling encouraged the pursuit of agreements aimed against France, despite the failure of earlier efforts. In 1686 many of the princes of the Empire, including Leopold, created the League of Augsburg to which Spain and Sweden adhered, a union designed to guarantee the public security of the Empire and the agreements of Westphalia, Nijmegen and Regensburg. Military quotas were stipulated. Although not in theory aimed at any particular ruler, the intention of the League was to prevent France from disrupting the struggle against the Turks. That the League was formed under Imperial sponsorship and was a vehicle for the revival of Austrian Habsburg influence within the Empire constituted an obvious contrast to Mazarin's sponsorship of the League of the Rhine less than thirty years earlier. Combined with the repulse of the Turks, the League was an occasion for the revival of the ideology as well as the mechanisms of empire.

The League reflected and strengthened a growing hostility towards France within the Empire and an increased tendency to rally to the emperor, a marked reversal of the situation for most of the previous 150 years. This was linked to, but more immediate for France than, the success of the emperor against the Turks. It was also important to the eventual role of England and the Dutch, for their military capability against France in 1689–1713 was, in large part, to depend on their ability to hire and subsidize the forces of German allies. Aside from the League, Leopold and Frederick William I of Brandenburg signed an anti-French defensive alliance in March 1686. The previous year, Max Emmanuel of Bavaria married Leopold's daughter, Maria Antonia, while the Habsburg succession was strengthened by the birth of Leopold's second son, Charles, later the Austrian candidate for the Spanish succession and eventually the Emperor Charles VI. But for this birth, there might have been a War of the Austrian Succession in 1711 – when Leopold's elder son, Joseph I (r. 1705–11) died without any sons of his own – rather than in 1740 when Charles died.

Closer relations between Bavaria and the emperor and the failure to secure a pro-French second wife for Pedro II of Portugal[48] indicated that the decline in France's position was not restricted to Louis's relations with Protestant powers. However, the latter was important and owed much to the Edict of Fontainebleau of 15 October 1685, by which Louis XIV revoked what little remained of the privileges of the French Protestants, the Huguenots, as originally conferred by the Edict of Nantes (1598). This step, bitterly denounced in Protestant Europe, produced a mass of hostile propaganda that owed much to the rigours, extent and prominence of the Huguenot diaspora. French envoys noted that Protestant groups that might hitherto have been sympathetic to France became hostile.[49]

The Revocation did not produce commensurate gains for Louis in Catholic Europe where, thanks to his successes against the Turks, Leopold appeared a more convincing champion. Leopold supported the Revocation in theory, but was also able to benefit from Louis's unpopularity.[50] In November 1687 Max Emmanuel rejected a French approach designed to whet his appetite for gains from the Habsburgs, by arguing that Louis would be unable to provide effective support. A fresh approach the following month, offering support over the Imperial succession and the acquisition of Augsburg, Nuremberg, Regensburg, and, if Bavaria backed French claims to the Spanish succession, Naples and Sicily, was rejected in January 1688.[51]

Dutch anger about the treatment of the Huguenots was exacerbated by a more hostile treatment of Dutch trade from the summer of 1687. Tariffs on cloth imports rose, and imports of herring were banned unless French salt was used in the curing. Having tried to solve the situation by diplomatic means, the Dutch retaliated.[52] The Dutch were also concerned by the build-up of the French navy. The French envoy complained of a collapse of Dutch support.[53] Swedish anger was exacerbated by the impact of the *réunions* on the Duchy of Zweibrücken, a German possession of the house of Vasa adjudged to Louis in 1680. More generally, there was widespread resentment about the *réunions* and especially at the combination of force and legal chicanery.

As yet there was no specific issue to test the impact of these shifts. This was to be provided as tension mounted over uncertainty as to Louis's intentions towards two contentious issues. In 1685 the succession of a new ruler to the Electorate of the Palatinate, the leading territory on the Middle Rhine, led Louis to advance claims on behalf of his Palatine sister-in-law. In addition, the apparently imminent death of another Rhenish elector, the Archbishop of Cologne, led Louis to seek the succession of a sympathetic cleric. These were crises in near-Germany. Louis did not want war, but if he could not determine developments there then he had little hope of having an impact further afield in the Empire.

The outbreak of the Nine Years' War

Neither issue, however, was really important to French power, and, in both cases, it appears that irritation at an inability to determine events, combined with a sense of being overshadowed by the emperor and overtaken by change, led Louis to resort to force. There was a sense of brittleness about France's eastern frontier. In April 1688 the envoy in Vienna reported an alleged plan for a peasant uprising in Franche-Comté based on Austrian arms and supported by Austrian troops commanded by Charles V of Lorraine. Six months later, the envoy in the United Provinces reported talk of forcing Louis back to the frontiers of the Peace of the Pyrenees. In 1689 the Marquis de Chamlay was concerned that Charles would invade Lower Alsace.[54] Conversely, Louis was widely distrusted, sufficiently so for him to have to deny in May 1688 that he planned to invade Switzerland.[55]

The disputes over Cologne and the Palatinate became important tests of determination in Europe where the respective strengths of the major powers appeared to be altering considerably. The pope, Innocent XI, was unwilling to support William Egon von Fürstenberg, Bishop of Strasbourg, the French candidate for Cologne, when the elector died in June 1688. Unpersuaded by poorly handled French approaches, Innocent backed the rival claimant, Joseph Clement, the brother of the Elector of Bavaria. This led Louis, possibly affected by a failure of nerve, to decide that a military demonstration was necessary in order to display his power and the vulnerability of the Rhineland. French diplomats claimed that Louis's *gloire* and honour were bound up with the Cologne election,[56] and that Innocent and German opponents needed to be overawed, a course urged from Rome by Chamlay.[57] The French military were not prepared for a major war, but in October 1688 a large army under the ostensible command of the Dauphin (the title given to the eldest son of a king of France) besieged Philippsburg, the major fortress of the Empire in the Middle Rhine. Another force occupied the papal enclave of Avignon in southern France.

Louis claimed that the League of Augsburg was an aggressive coalition aimed against France, and he gave an ultimatum of three months within which Leopold and the Empire were to convert the Truce of Regensburg into a treaty and to accept Fürstenberg in Cologne. In return, his manifesto offered the restitution of Freiburg and the abandonment of territorial claims to the Palatinate, in exchange for a cash settlement to be reached by arbitration.

Louis was to be proved wrong in his expectation that the electors who understood their 'true interests' would not support Leopold and that his attack would lead to a limited, short and successful conflict, in which French triumphs would drive Leopold to terms. There were no preparations for a lengthy conflict.[58] Instead, Louis found himself involved in an intractable conflict in Germany, while changes in the British Isles produced an even more serious headache. Philippsburg fell on 30 October and Mannheim on 12 November, but German resistance gathered pace. On 15 October 1688, reflecting a rise in German patriotism, the rulers of Brandenburg, Hanover, Hesse–Cassel and Saxony concluded a treaty of alliance for the defence of the Middle Rhine, stiffening resistance there. Louis XIV, Louvois and the generals resorted to crude intimidation. In order to intimidate their opponents and to strengthen their defences, the French devastated much of south-western Germany in 1689, touching off a guerrilla struggle in the Palatinate and accentuating the anti-French nature of German patriotism.

The conflict was not restricted to Germany. In 1688 James II of England, a Catholic with autocratic tendencies, was overthrown by his nephew and son-in-law, William III, as the result of an invasion that Louis XIV had failed to predict or prevent. The same year, a *coup* in Siam (Thailand) ended Louis's hope of alliance. Phra Narai fell, his adopted son and Phaulkon were killed, the French garrisons lost many men and were expelled, and the new monarch, Phra Petratcha (*r.* 1688–1703) put a stop to hopes of good, or indeed any, relations.

In England, James II had been unwilling to associate himself too closely with Louis, for both domestic and international reasons, and sought to win the support of the Catholic powers, the pope, Leopold and Spain. His departure itself was not a crisis for Louis, but his replacement by William was. It was to lead to a major war between England and France, a conflict that was subsequently presented by Whigs as the natural and necessary product of British history and of Britain's place in Europe.

What is interesting about the crisis in 1688 is not that it led to war, but that the conflict proved to be a major one, and this despite the fact that the Austrians remained at war with the Turks. This was not what Louis wanted, and to a considerable extent it can be attributed to chance factors, in particular William III's seizure of Britain. His subsequent commitment to the defence of the Spanish Netherlands, a defence that Spain was no longer able to provide, played a crucial role in the continuation of the anti-French coalition.

Louis's attitude to Jacobitism, the cause of the exiled James, highlights the role of contingency. Pride, personal commitment, and a sense of royal dignity were reflected in Louis's recognition of the Jacobite claim, and, in turn, helped to make it difficult to negotiate. On the English part, the recognition was a direct challenge to the domestic political situation. It was very different from the French co-operation with the Cromwellian regime in the 1650s. Instead, this policy helped to give Anglo-French rivalry an added degree of tension and made it recognizably different in kind from that between France and the United Provinces. Although concern about French intentions and policies had risen from the 1660s onwards, especially from 1673–4, with French aggression on the Continent, bold commercial schemes, and the Revocation of the Edict of Nantes, this concern was given focus and intensity by the events of 1688–90. The Williamite moment in English foreign policy was one in which a major disjuncture was followed by a rapid process of state formation, constitutional and governmental change, and ideological formulation, all in close association with a perception and policy not only that France was a major threat, but also that it was England's task and necessity to thwart her.

Indeed, it could be argued that Louis established himself as the enemy of Britain that so alarmed the Whigs more by his real and apparent backing for the Stuarts and their British supporters than by his activities on the continent. Louis's military support for the Jacobite cause in Ireland in 1689–91 was significant, as Ireland was the focus and source of a number of English and Scottish phobias. There was an immediacy about such action that contrasted with the English perception of the situation in northern Italy, the Rhineland and the Low Countries, although the apparently inexorable nature of Louis's ambitions ensured that developments there were seen in a context that automatically made them a matter for concern.

Louis had to decide how far he was to support James II. His policies ensured that France clearly emerged as the leading challenge to the Protestant succession. Far from such a development being inevitable, it was at variance with one of the central themes of French foreign policy since the 1530s. Louis restricted his freedom of manoeuvre by sheltering James, while, in contrast, the more distant and manipulative French policy towards the Jacobites that followed the death of Louis in 1715 was more successful in respecting British sensitivities on the subject of the succession, and, thus, easing tensions.

Nevertheless, it is all too easy to be wise after the event. Legitimism was not only an automatic attitude and ideology for Louis; it also seemed prudent, both with reference to Britain and because of Bourbon interest in the Spanish succession. William was an enemy whom Louis was convinced was uninterested in compromise. It also did not seem impossible that William could be defeated, and a Britain under a suitably grateful and subservient James II would have been the best possible scenario for Louis, albeit a risky and long-term one that restricted his freedom of manoeuvre in the short term. In 1689 William faced serious opposition in both Scotland and Ireland, and in 1690 the French defeated the English fleet at the battle of Beachy Head creating the possibility for amphibious attacks. Had Tourville and the Brest fleet been permitted by Louis to wait for the Toulon fleet in 1692, the battle of Barfleur with the Anglo-Dutch fleet might have been a French success, and an invasion of Britain could have been mounted. William, an active soldier-monarch who was wounded at the Battle of the Boyne in 1690, could have been killed during the war, as Turenne had been in 1675, or as Charles XII of Sweden was to be in 1718 and the Duke of Berwick,

James II's illegitimate son, in 1734, or he could have been murdered in the Jacobite Assassination Plot of 1696. If so, it is probable that British policy would have become less anti-French, and/or possible that the policies of reinsurance on the part of the politicians who continued links with the exiled James might have weakened the response to a French invasion or a Jacobite rising.

The issue of Louis's folly or otherwise in supporting James raises more generally the problem of assessing his policies and conduct in the light of the contemporary culture of royal power. There has been considerable criticism of Louis's skill in foreign policy in the middle period of his reign,[59] but some of it assumes an unrealistic level of superhuman or disembodied competence on the part of Louis.

The Nine Years' War

In the immediate term, however, William III's role ensured that the war would not be restricted to the Rhineland. In November 1688 Louis declared war against the United Provinces. The following May, William, as king of England, declared war on Louis, while Leopold and the Dutch made an alliance with the declared aims of returning France to the frontiers stipulated by the treaties of Westphalia and the Pyrenees and of returning Charles of Lorraine to his duchy. Habsburg claims to the entire Spanish succession were backed. As king of England, William acceded to this Grand Alliance later in the year. The treaty also provided for joint peace negotiations and for the continuation of the alliance after the war.

The conflict itself widened. On 15 April 1689 Louis declared war on Spain, which had refused to promise to be neutral and presented a vulnerable target in the Spanish Netherlands. Three months earlier, he had sought to woo Charles II of Spain with Casale, territorial cessions in Roussillon and four million *livres* support for the Spanish attack on Portugal he proposed.[60] The Spanish government was more impressed by William III's success in England. In May an Austro-Bavarian treaty brought Bavaria into the war, and in 1690 Victor Amadeus II of Savoy–Piedmont, fed up with French tutelage and eager to dislodge the French from Pinerolo and Casale, joined the alliance.[61] Unlike in the Thirty Years' and Dutch Wars, France did not benefit from Swedish attacks on her German opponents. The opposition of most of Western Europe was a comment not only on Louis's policies but also on the sense that he was now vulnerable and that he would not determine any re-ordering of Europe. Princes keenly aware of shifts in the wind, such as Victor Amadeus and Max Emmanuel of Bavaria, now looked for opportunity at the expense of Louis. As later with Napoleon when his position began to deteriorate, it no longer appeared prudent, or indeed wise, to accommodate Louis's pretensions and goals. There was also a degree of unease on the part of informed French commentators. In October 1689 Louis's commissioner general of fortifications, Sébastien le Prestre de Vauban, suggested the recall of the Huguenots.

Louis sought to overcome this crisis by a string of victories that would divide his opponents, but he was no more able to provide them than he had been in the Dutch War. Although successful in the Spanish Netherlands at Fleurus (1 July 1690), Leuze (19 September 1691), Steenkerk (3 August 1692) and Neerwinden (29 July 1693), and able to defeat Victor Amadeus at Marsaglia (1693), Louis was unable to make significant inroads into the Empire or northern Italy, to maintain James II in Ireland or to sustain early naval success in the Channel. The outnumbered fleet was defeated by the English and Dutch at Barfleur–La Hogue. Furthermore, French military prestige was hit when Namur was recaptured in 1695 by William III. 1693 was the last year when Louis XIV campaigned in person. In contrast, despite being pushed back in 1690, the Austrians continued their conquest of Hungary from the Turks. The Treaty of Karlowitz of 1699 left them with most of Hungary, and with their Hungarian opponents also beaten. Louis had been unable to prevent this major shift in the European system.

From 1693, the French increasingly concentrated their naval efforts in the Mediterranean. Their trade was harmed by commercial embargoes by England, the Dutch and the Empire. English and Dutch warships enforced the Imperial embargo on Hamburg. These moves hit French shipping and trade hard. As in the 1670s, wine exports collapsed, hitting rents and wages.

The mixed fortunes of war encouraged negotiations. William's refusal to make his succession a subject of discussion ended talks with him begun in 1693, while longer-lasting discussions with Leopold begun in 1692 were also stalled by the English succession. However, in a difficult situation in 1696 and with his war effort under great pressure, Louis bought off Victor Amadeus in the Treaty of Turin, at the price of Pinerolo and Casale, enabling the French to transfer forces to Catalonia where Barcelona fell in 1697. This led Spain to press for peace, thus contributing to an impetus that owed much to growing war-weariness among the combatants and their interest in the Spanish succession. In 1697 terms were negotiated at Rijswijk. All the powers signed on 20 September, apart from Leopold, who still hoped to weaken France and drive her from Alsace, but – now isolated – he had to abandon such hopes and to sign on 30 October.

The peace was no confirmation of the Truce of Regensburg. Louis returned many *réunion* gains, as well as Freiburg and Luxembourg, although his position in Alsace, including Strasbourg, was recognized. The return of Luxembourg was a gesture intended to please Charles II at a time when the issue of the Spanish succession was becoming more acute. Lorraine was restored to the duke, although on terms which left it vulnerable to French occupation. Louis got his way over neither Cologne nor the Palatinate. Max Emmanuel continued as Governor of the Spanish Netherlands to which he, rather than the Duke of Burgundy, had been appointed in 1691. William III was recognized as king and Louis promised not to support Jacobite schemes. Vauban condemned the peace as dishonourable. He was particularly opposed to the return of Luxembourg. In 1748 the then foreign minister, Puysieulx, complained that the cessions made in the Treaty of Turin shut the doors of Italy to France. Indeed, in 1689 Louis had indicated that he wanted to retain possession of Casale as it provided a base for operations in Lombardy.[62]

Thus, peace was made at the expense of legitimist principles, Catholic fellow-feeling, Jacobite hopes, and the long-standing French practice of meddling in the internal affairs of rivals. As recently as 1696, Louis had shown both his commitment to the Jacobites and the political strength of the Jacobite card, by massing troops – joined by James II – at Calais, in order to invade England. This plan, however, had to be abandoned, because there was no Jacobite rising in England and in the face of a major Anglo-Dutch naval presence:[63] the rising depended on a French invasion, the invasion on a rising, a problem that frequently affected Jacobite conspiracies. The silence of the Treaty of Rijswijk about the interests and privileges of Scotland and Ireland reflected the inability of the expeditionary force sent to Ireland in 1689 to prevent Williamite conquest. Louis did not devote sufficient attention or military resources to Ireland, and, unlike his successors, he could not employ the excuse of conspicuous naval inferiority.[64] The failure to support the Stuarts also entailed an inability to prevent the British statebuilding that followed William III's accession. As a consequence, Louis and his successors were unable to benefit from differences between the parts of Britain to the extent that his predecessors had done.

France as an imperial power

The treaty also specified the return to France of Rupert House, Moose Factory and Fort Albany, fur-trading posts on James Bay in north Canada, captured by the French under Pierre de Troyes in 1686, the last-named being recaptured by the British in 1693; and the return to England of York Fort. The French also regained Pondicherry, which had been captured by the Dutch in 1693, bringing the French East India Company to the verge of bankruptcy. The following year, the Dutch blocked river traffic to the French Bengal base of Chandernagore. Colonial issues played a far smaller role at Rijswijk than they were to do in the Anglo-French negotiations that led to the treaties of Utrecht (1713), Aix-la-Chapelle (1748) and, even more, Paris (1763). This reflected the nature of the Nine Years' War. Anglo-French hostilities had been concentrated, on land, in Ireland and the Low Countries, and, at sea, in European waters, particularly the Channel. In contrast, conflict in the West Indies and North America had been small-scale and largely inconsequential. The English had failed to capture Québec in 1690, Guadeloupe in 1691, Martinique in 1693, and St Domingue in 1695. There was nothing to compare with the colonial campaigning in 1745–8, let alone that in the Seven Years' War (1756–63), although mention of the James Bay forts anticipated more extensive future discussions of colonial issues.

Nevertheless, the French sent six expeditions to the Caribbean in 1689–97 and ten in 1701–13. Threats to Jamaica from St Domingue led the English to send fleets to the Caribbean in 1694 and 1696.[65] A French imperial drive can be seen at the close of the 1690s. Having devastated the Mohawk villages in 1693 and those of the Onondaga and Oneida in 1696, the French consolidated their position on the St Lawrence in 1701 when the Iroquois promised neutrality in the event of a future Anglo-French conflict.[66] The same year, against the advice of the Governor of Canada, Jérome Phélypeaux, Count of Pontchartrain, the secretary of state for the marine, backed Cadillac's plan to develop a base at Detroit in order to secure France's position in the Great Lakes and also communications with Louisiana. In the winter of 1696–7 a French force seized most of the British positions on the Newfoundland coast.[67] In 1697 the French claim to St Domingue, the western half of the Caribbean island of Hispaniola, was recognized. Two years later an expedition was sent to Louisiana, which had been claimed by La Salle in 1682 and was named after Louis XIV. La Salle's subsequent attempt to found a colony on the lower Mississippi gained the support of Louis XIV, but was wrecked by La Salle's failure to co-operate with his naval counterpart. Having landed by mistake on the Texan coast, the colony fell victim to disease and native hostility.[68]

In contrast, in 1699 Pierre Le Moyne, Sieur d'Iberville, founded Fort Maurepas in Biloxi Bay on the Gulf of Mexico coast of the modern state of Mississippi.[69] Mobile followed in 1702, New Orleans in 1718. Missions were established at Cahokia (1699) and Kaskaskia (1703) on the upper Mississippi.[70] In India the French extended their presence to Bengal, founding their first trading base in 1686 and their major Bengal base of Chandernagore in 1690. Pondicherry was regained in 1699 and, three years later, work started on its citadel, Fort Louis. Trans-oceanic trade from Saint Malo expanded greatly.[71]

French interest in the Spanish succession ensured that no major initiatives could be taken at the expense of the Spanish Empire at the close of the century, but Portuguese colonies could be treated differently. The two powers were in dispute over Maranhão, the area of Brazil north of the Amazon, or – from the French perspective – part of their colony of Cayenne. In 1688 Louis claimed the region, claiming that the French had been continually trading there since 1596, and had had permanent establishments there since 1626. Louis XIV instructed his envoy in Lisbon to devote as much attention to the issue as to the Spanish succession. However, this priority was not shared by all. Rouillé, the envoy, and Pontchartrain supported a hard line, while Torcy, the foreign minister, did not wish to lose Portugal's support in the Spanish succession. The Portuguese envoy in Paris, José da Cunha Brocado, was convinced that Torcy lacked the authority to thwart Pontchartrain, not least because the latter's views matched those of Louis. Louis had certainly argued that the best way to deal with Portugal was by fear, not good treatment.[72]

Rijswijk was also a prelude, not a conclusion, in that it left unsettled the leading issue in the European colonial world, the future of the Spanish succession. By ending the war before the succession was thrown open, Rijswijk brought Louis back into a central role in negotiations, creating an opportunity for him to reach an agreement that both served his interests and divided the Grand

Alliance. Such an option was to be presented by an unlikely combination, that of Louis and William III. The two rulers sought in 1698–1700 to create a diplomatic order based in co-operation, one able to surmount and settle the issue of the Spanish succession.

The partition treaties, 1698–1700

The role that dynastic considerations played in the diplomacy of the Spanish succession can be presented as another aspect of the conservatism of *ancien régime* international relations, a conservatism at odds with the more pragmatic 'rationalism' represented by interest in partition, as a means to avoid or resolve disputes and as a measure of strength. The subsequent War of the Spanish Succession (1701–14) can then be seen as the product of dynasticism, but one that led to an enforced partition. Such an interpretation is overly pat, but it raises the question whether excessive weight is commonly placed on the details of the dynastic claims. They are, however, worth discussing because they are important to the culture as well as content of the diplomacy of the period, and in many respects the claims represented the culmination of several important seventeenth-century dynastic strategies.

There were three principal claimants. The marriage of the daughters of Philip III of Spain (1598–1621) to Louis XIII and the Emperor Ferdinand III, and of their sons, Louis XIV and Leopold I, to Philip IV's daughters produced important interests on the part of the Bourbons and the Austrian Habsburgs. Both the princesses who married into the Bourbon dynasty specifically renounced their rights of succession for themselves and their heirs, but it was by no means clear how acceptable this was to Spanish custom and law. When Louis XIV married Marie-Thérèse in 1660 – part of the booty from the war with Spain, as Napoleon's second wife was to be from his with Austria – her renunciation was regarded, even then, as a matter of form only, entered into in order to allay international mistrust. Leopold's claim was better because his mother, Philip III's younger daughter, had not made any such renunciation. However, Leopold's sons, Joseph and Charles, were the sons not of his first, Spanish, wife, but of his third wife, Eleanor of Neuburg. By his first marriage, Leopold had only had a daughter, Maria Antonia, and her Bavarian marriage had produced a son, Joseph Ferdinand.

The inheritance 'rules' of the period were a combination of positive law, traditions, and the testaments (wills) of rulers. National conventions were frequently ambiguous, and they could clash with those of other countries. The relationship between dynastic and other inheritance practices was unclear. Legal claims played a major role in the diplomacy of 1698–1700, but such considerations did not greatly influence those rulers who had no dynastic claim to the succession and either wished to make gains for themselves or feared the consequences of acquisitions by others. Furthermore, the recent war suggested that compromise was a likely consequence of any conflict.

Against this background, Louis approached William in early 1698 to discuss the situation. He had correctly identified Leopold as likely to be his most obdurate opponent and had appreciated that the crucial point of tension in the Grand Alliance had been the relationship between Leopold and the maritime powers (England and the Dutch). Although Leopold had been willing to negotiate a partition treaty of the Spanish inheritance in 1668, success against the Turks had brought him an increased measure of determination. The French envoy, Tallard, told William that a failure to settle the succession would result in each ruler taking steps as soon as Charles II died and that it would then be too late to negotiate.[73]

In April 1698 Tallard proposed that the bulk of the Spanish Empire, including Spain, should go to a French prince. He claimed that such a monarch would quickly adopt the views of his new kingdom at the expense of France, and that France would have no authority or cabal in Madrid able to influence his conduct. To lessen Anglo-Dutch fears, the Spanish Netherlands was destined for Max Emmanuel of Bavaria, not a French prince. William was willing to consider a partition, although he pointed out that it was audacious to seek to determine matters which he and Louis could not control.[74]

French territorial aggrandizement remained a sensitive issue, a legacy of Louis's policies. In 1698, by agreement with Spain, Dutch troops had been moved into the leading fortresses of the Spanish Netherlands bordering France, in order to create a stronger 'barrier' against any future French advance. Stressing to Tallard the vulnerability of the region, William rejected suggestions that France needed Luxembourg for her security, instead claiming that it menaced the lower Rhine and could serve as the base for a French advance on Nijmegen and thus into the heart of the United Provinces. Aggrandisement was linked to fears about security. The French rejected William's suggestion that the Barrier be enlarged by French cessions, a reversal of Louis's gains, while William criticized the idea that France gain the Navarre region of northern Spain, arguing that it would allow France to dominate Spain.

On 11 October 1698 William signed what was to become the First Partition Treaty with France. Spain, her trans-oceanic possessions, the Spanish Netherlands and Sardinia were allocated to Joseph Ferdinand of Bavaria, while Naples, Sicily, the *presidii* (Tuscan coastal forts) and the Basque province of Guipuzcoa would go to Louis's heir, the Dauphin Louis. The treaty provided that the signatories should impose it by force if any power refused to comply. However, after a short illness that gave rise to rumours of Austrian poisoning, Joseph Ferdinand died on 6 February 1699. This contingency had not been provided for.

As there was no other suitable third party, Louis and William had, in their negotiations for the Second Partition Treaty, only to consider the distribution of territory among the Habsburgs and Bourbons. The treaty, concluded on 25

March 1700, gave the Dauphin the same portion as in the first treaty, with the addition of Lorraine. Tallard minimized the benefit, comparing Lorraine to a suburb or a small chateau in the midst of a landlord's estates,[75] but it was, in fact, a considerable strategic gain, and its acquisition had been sought by Vauban. Meanwhile, French attempts to reduce tension as part of a peaceful settlement of the Spanish succession led to the Treaty of Lille of 3 December 1699. This divided the territories in dispute between France and the Spanish Netherlands, although the claims of Liège were ignored.

French interest in a balance of power, or, at least, the prevention of any ruler gaining hegemonic power, was reflected in pressure on William to agree that if the Austrian beneficiary, Leopold I's second son, Archduke Charles, died without children his share was not to go to whoever held the Austrian possessions, but, rather, to a second son. Tallard was fearful that inheritance, in that case, by an archduchess would lead to a dynastic union with Portugal which he saw as very prejudicial to France.[76] This sense of a volatile international system and potential threats to France emerges clearly from the diplomatic correspondence of the period.

Neither Leopold nor the Spaniards accepted the new treaty. In order to prevent partition, Charles II signed a will leaving everything to the Dauphin's second son, Philip, Duke of Anjou, on condition that the crowns of France and Spain never be united in one person. If this was not accepted by the Bourbons, the whole empire was to be offered to Archduke Charles.

On 1 November 1700 Charles died, and on 16 November Louis presented Philip to his court as king of Spain. Explaining this decision, the French argued that it should please Europe more than the partition treaty, because, unlike under either Partition Treaty, by accepting the will, Louis won no territory for France. The French memorial to the Dutch States General claimed that this should assuage Anglo–Dutch fears about the impact on trade of a French acquisition of Naples and Sicily.

The will was a massive gain for the Bourbon dynasty and also broke any notion of equivalence of acquisitions and the satisfaction of different parties.[77] Philip was recognized by the Dutch and England, but Leopold was determined to gain Spanish Italy and sent a force to seize the Milanese, which he claimed as an escheated fief of the Empire. The first shots were exchanged on 19 June 1701, as the French sought to block the Austrian advance.

France was in a far stronger diplomatic position than she had been during the Nine Years' War. The Rijswijk negotiations and the partition treaties had clearly ended the Grand Alliance, and this encouraged second-rank powers, such as Portugal, to regard France as a possible ally. Better relations with the papacy enhanced Louis's position in Catholic Europe. In March 1701 Max Emmanuel negotiated a treaty by which the French agreed to maintain 10,000 Bavarian troops. His brother, the archbishop–elector, whose election to Cologne Louis had sought to prevent in 1688, signed a similar treaty that spring.

French actions elsewhere were considered provocative in both Britain and the

United Provinces. The replacement of the Dutch garrisons in the Barrier fortresses by French forces in February 1701 seemed to demonstrate the continued subservience of Philip to Louis, and led to Dutch protests. Concessions to France elsewhere in the Spanish Empire caused anger. French merchants were granted better conditions in Spain, and the French Guinea Company was granted the *Asiento* contract to transport slaves from West Africa to Spanish America for ten years, a lucrative opening into the protected trade of the Spanish Empire. Dutch ships carrying slaves under the former treaty were seized in the Caribbean by the French. In January 1701 French warships were granted permission to enter Spanish American ports and that March they were granted permission to sell goods there. This was to be the basis of extensive and unregulated sales of French goods. These developments encouraged alarmist, and misleading, rumours about French intentions.

Anglo-Dutch moves towards Austria led Louis to respond not by conciliatory offers, but by military and diplomatic preparations for war, which, in turn, made conflict more likely. On 7 September 1701 the Grand Alliance of The Hague brought Austria and the maritime powers together to support a partition. The treaty stipulated an attempt to achieve its ends by negotiation, but tensions rose, not least thanks to Louis's recognition of the son of the newly dead James II of England as James III, a step Torcy had unsuccessfully pressed might be kept quiet. The French and Spanish prohibition of English manufactures further embittered relations. After William died in March 1702, Louis sought to exploit the situation by opening negotiations with the Dutch, but he was unsuccessful, and in May Austria and the maritime powers simultaneously declared war on France.[78] Max Emmanuel and Louis agreed an offensive alliance the following month.

The War of the Spanish Succession

Louis started the war with a number of allies, but they changed sides or were overrun, his diplomatic strategy falling victim to the superior strength and greater success of his opponents. Attempts to expand the French alliance system largely failed. In 1701 Prussia and Saxony rejected French approaches. The Turks also rejected approaches to support the Hungarian opponents of Leopold.[79] Pedro II of Portugal, however, allied with Louis and Philip V in June 1701, and promised to support Philip in the Spanish succession.

In 1703 Louis was deserted by both Pedro II and Victor Amadeus II of Savoy–Piedmont, each being offered support and territorial gains by the Grand Alliance. Louis had been unable to offer Pedro naval protection against the threat of Anglo-Dutch naval attack. In 1702–3 the territories of two of Louis's German allies, the Elector of Cologne and the Duke of Brunswick–Wolfenbüttel, were overrun. To retain the support of the third, Max Emmanuel, Louis promised to support his acquisition of the Lower Palatinate and of full sovereignty over the Spanish Netherlands, with the exception of frontier fortresses reserved for France.

This threatened a total change in the political system within the Empire, which Louis deemed necessary if the Empire was not — as he preferred, and had sought in 1701–2 — neutral. By 1703 the objectives of both alliances had increased greatly, and Louis found himself committed to a major struggle. His opponents were now fighting to keep the Bourbons out of the entire Spanish inheritance. Such goals helped to make compromise difficult in the tentative and active negotiations that continued during much of the war.

Wartime diplomacy was both greatly affected by strategic considerations and intertwined with the fortunes of war. A cautious strategy in 1702–3 allowed France's opponents to gain the initiative in the Low Countries and the lower Rhineland. Further south, co-operation with Bavaria provided France with the opportunity for an advance on Vienna, possibly in concert with the Hungarians whose rebellion against Habsburg rule was encouraged from 1703. The opportunity was lost in 1704. The victory of an Anglo-Dutch-Austrian army over its Franco-Bavarian rival at Blenheim on 13 August 1704 was followed by the overrunning of Bavaria. French strategy became mostly a matter of frontier defence, a course of action that made it difficult to gain allies, that posed a serious logistical strain and which made victory impossible. The war indicated the strategic importance of the Empire to France, helping explain why Louis sought Friedlingen, Breisach, Freiburg, Kehl, Philippsburg and Landau, as well as fortresses that would aid advances, such as Villingen which controlled the route to Bavaria down the Upper Danube.[80] In addition, Louis believed his honour was involved in supporting Max Emmanuel. In November 1704, a Franco-Bavarian treaty committed Louis to continue the war until Bavaria was retaken, made a kingdom and embellished with much of Swabia, conditions that Louis indeed pressed in negotiations with the Dutch in 1706.

The French navy made scant impact. It suffered from limited investment, certainly in comparison with the British. The 1708 invasion attempt on Scotland failed.[81] The successful raid on Rio de Janiero mounted in 1712 by Duguay-Trouin was not part of any systematic attempt to overturn the colonial position of France's opponents. Instead, there was an emphasis on privateering.[82] The French were also driven from Italy and the Spanish Netherlands, although the Grand Alliance had far less success in conquering Spain and invading France.[83] After the battle of Turin on 7 September 1706, French influence in Italy was lost, although a subsequent invasion of Provence by Austrian and Savoyard forces, supported by the British fleet, was unsuccessful.

Furthermore, the Camisard (Huguenot) rising in the Cévennes was suppressed. Huguenot activists hoped for British and Dutch support, but there was a limit to what could be done even when the British had a fleet in the western Mediterranean. The Camisard rising did not prefigure the Peninsular War of 1808–13, and the fruitless wait for British support in 1704–5 cost the Camisards their vital momentum and their early strategic advantage. The British and the Dutch were more concerned to support Catholic opponents of the Bourbons in Iberia, and their alliance with Austria made them ambivalent about intervening in France. In addition, as in the case of action against the Revolutionary and Napoleonic regimes, it was easier to attack French power outside the borders of France.[84] Nevertheless, despite the problems facing his opponents, Louis was under tremendous pressure, a situation exacerbated by grave financial problems and by the serious consequences of the savage winter of 1708-9.

Peace negotiations, 1705-1714

Initially, Louis's overtures had been largely designed to divide the Grand Alliance by winning over the Dutch, a course defeated by Dutch determination to maintain their English alliance. In 1705 he proposed a partition of the Spanish inheritance, in which Naples, Sicily and the Spanish Netherlands were not to go to his grandson, Philip; but British insistence on the allocation of Spain to Archduke Charles led to the failure of the negotiations. Defeat at Ramillies on 23 May 1706 and the expulsion of the French from the Spanish Netherlands, led Louis to try again. He proposed that Spain and the Indies go to Charles, Spanish Italy to Philip and the Spanish Netherlands to the Dutch.

The proposals came to nothing, because Charles's elder brother, the Emperor Joseph I (r. 1705-11), wanted the Milanese for Austria, while the British were worried about the implications for Mediterranean trade of a Bourbon in Naples and Sicily. Nevertheless, the basis of the eventual settlement of 1713-14 was already present: a new partition treaty accompanied by a Dutch barrier and French recognition of the Protestant succession in Britain.

Defeat helped to alter the content and drive the pace of French diplomacy. From 1708 attempts to create an independent Hungarian state were abandoned. Marlborough's victory over the French at Oudenaarde on 11 August 1708 and his capture of Lille later that year, made Louis more eager to settle, but defeat also affected the room available for manoeuvre. In negotiations in 1709 Louis abandoned his demands for an establishment for Philip, agreed to restore Lille and all he had taken in Alsace since 1648, including Strasbourg, met British wishes about their succession, and agreed that 'James III' should leave France. The sticking point was that Louis could not guarantee that Philip would accept any settlement, and was unwilling to promise to help depose him, a step that might involve the use of French troops against the king's grandson.

Distrust of Louis played a major role in the formulation of this humiliating demand which was cited by Louis, in his inspiring appeals to the French public and his correspondence with Philip, as the reason why he rejected the preliminaries. Not everybody shared this opinion. The Austrian general Prince Eugene attributed Louis's decision to the provisions concerning Alsace, and it might be suggested that the refusal to leave Philip any compensation for what Louis saw as his right to the Spanish inheritance was decisive. The foreign minister, Torcy, had pressed for Philip to be given Naples and Sicily.

Louis's difficult position led to hopes on the part of his opponents that France could be forced to make major territorial cessions, including gains made in the sixteenth century. The Austrians sought a strong German barrier against France, demanding, for example, in September 1709, the three bishoprics of Metz, Toul and Verdun, which the French had acquired in 1552, and the restoration of Lorraine's 1624 frontier with France. A meeting of the representatives of the Imperial circles pressed, as a condition of any peace settlement, for a barrier that would include Landau, Metz, Strasbourg, Toul and Verdun. In 1709 the Allies invaded Franche-Comté.[85]

The eventual peace terms were not as bad as Louis had been prepared to accept in 1709, still less as bad as these demands. In part, this reflected the fate of war. Charles was unsuccessful in Spain, and Marlborough's pyrrhic victory at Malplaquet (11 September 1709) was followed by only slow progress in capturing French fortresses. Fresh negotiations at Geertruidenberg in early 1710 collapsed on the Dutch insistence that Louis expel Philip before peace could be considered. Louis was willing to accept Joseph I's demand for the exchange of Alsace for the restoration of the electors of Bavaria and Cologne, but, again, aid against Philip V was a sticking point.

Political changes in Britain in 1710 led to a Tory ministry prepared to compromise on its allies' demands in unilateral negotiations with France. In December 1710, following defeat at Brihuega in Spain, British willingness to leave Philip in possession of Spain and the Indies was signalled. The death, without sons, of Joseph I in April 1711 drove on the dissolution of the Grand Alliance, for Charles both succeeded his brother and maintained his own pretensions to the Spanish Empire, a strengthening of Austrian power that none of her allies sought.

Most of the terms of the eventual peace were settled in Anglo-French discussions in 1711. These served as the basis for the negotiations held at Utrecht in 1712–13. Matters were complicated in February–March 1712 when Philip's elder brother, the Duke of Burgundy, and the latter's eldest son, the Duke of Brittany, both died, while Burgundy's other son, the infant Duke of Anjou, nearly died. This brought Philip very close to Louis's succession, and revived fears of French influence in Spain.

The French insisted that diplomatic agreements could not contradict their fundamental laws and that any renunciation by Philip of his claim to the French succession would be of no value, because France was a patrimony that the monarch received not from his predecessor or the people, but in accordance with the law, which only God could change. It was stressed that as soon as one monarch died another succeeded, without his own personal choice or the consent of anyone being an issue. Torcy rejected the idea that any renunciation could be ratified by the Estates General or by the provincial Estates, and no such clause featured in the eventual peace treaty. A sense of monarchical responsibility was thus clearly enunciated, but without any suggestion of an institutional restriction comparable to that of the British Parliament.

Although both the British and French governments sought peace, it proved difficult to settle many issues. The Barrier and the settlements for Max Emmanuel and Victor Amadeus were especially contentious. Notions of honour and compensation were more important than any attempt to create a balance of power on a 'logical' basis.

The discussion of frontiers witnessed a mixture of strategic considerations and traditional bases for territorial claims. Resisting Dutch demands that the Barrier include part of French Flanders, the French pressed for the return to them of Lille, Tournai, Aire and a number of other captured fortresses. They argued that these positions would close the French frontier, without threatening their neighbours, and claimed that Tournai was part of the ancient domain of the kingdom. However, although they regained Lille, Valenciennes, Maubeuge and other forts promised to the Dutch by the Barrier Treaty, the French did not regain Tournai, which they had insisted on in June 1712.[86]

Victor Amadeus's demands for an extended alpine barrier were rejected by the French, as leaving the Dauphiné vulnerable, and, in a modern touch, Torcy urged his British counterpart, Bolingbroke, to consult a map. He also refused to accept Victor Amadeus's claim to Monaco, both because it was essential for the security of Provence and because it was important to protect the interests of the ruler of Monaco. Torcy also protested against the loss of any 'ancient domain of the Crown' to Victor Amadeus, leading to Bolingbroke's sceptical observation: 'yet this point of honour is to be got over, and this domain is to be parted with, provided the valley of Barcelonnette be given in exchange'.[87]

On 11 April 1713 the Treaty of Utrecht was signed. Britain and France had led the negotiations, and they pushed the Dutch, Victor Amadeus and Portugal into accepting their agreement. The Archduke Charles, now the Emperor Charles VI, was to receive the Spanish Netherlands and Spanish Italy – bar Sicily, which was to go to Victor Amadeus, along with a settlement of the latter's alpine frontier that was less generous than he had sought, but was more geographically consistent than the old frontier. Philip V gained Spain and the Indies, a triumph for the dynasty, but he renounced his claims to the French succession. Philip's renunciation was made by proxy in a full session of the *Parlement* of Paris with the peers of the realm present. Torcy informed Bolingbroke that even such a solemn occasion could not invalidate the fundamental laws of royal succession. Thanks to dynastic chance, the Bourbons, but not France, had gained territory, while the Habsburgs *and* Austria did the same. This was to prove an issue in the diplomacy of the following three decades.

The Dutch got a Barrier, while the nearby French privateering base of Dunkirk was to lose its fortifications. With the loss of Tournai, this greatly weakened the French defensive system on the vulnerable north-eastern frontier. From France, Britain gained Nova Scotia, Newfoundland, St Kitts, the return of the Hudson Bay forts and the recognition of the Protestant succession, and, from Spain, Gibraltar, Minorca and the *Asiento*, the right to send a boat once a year to trade directly with the Spanish New World. The last was at the expense of the French Company awarded the *Asiento* after the accession of Philip. French ambitions in Maranhão had been abandoned after the Spanish succession had come to the fore. The Huguenot cause was abandoned as, despite British pressure, was that of the Catalan opponents of Philip V, and the Hungarians were not mentioned in the treaty.[88]

The Imperial Diet at Regensburg declared in July 1713 that the French proposals would 'tarnish the glory of the German nation', but, outnumbered and pushed back by the French who captured Freiburg, Kehl and Landau in 1713, Charles was forced to negotiate. Desiring peace and fearful that a Hanoverian succession in Britain might lead to the revitalization of the Grand Alliance, Louis accepted terms reasonably favourable to Charles in the peace settlement agreed at Rastatt and Baden in 1714. Max Emmanuel was reinstated, although without the gain of the island of Sardinia that Louis had sought for him. The German border was based on the Peace of Rijswijk, with France retaining Alsace and Strasbourg, but not any possessions on the right bank of the Rhine. This essential repetition of the earlier terms helped to give them a degree of authority and normality that acted as an implicit restraint on further French expansion.

The retention of Alsace served to underline the futility of Duke Leopold's hopes that Lorraine could escape the influence of French power. In 1709 he had unsuccessfully offered the Allies subsidies if they would agree to the restoration of the duchy's 1624 borders, a reversal of successive French gains. Louis saw Lorraine as part of the ancestral patrimony of France which it was the duty of the crown to regain.[89] Leopold, nevertheless, continued to negotiate as an independent ruler, actively so in order to lessen the impact of French strength. He had been ignored at Utrecht[90] and his plan for an internationally-recognized barrier of forts directed against France, comparable to those in the Austrian Netherlands, was unsuccessful, as was his attempt to exchange Lorraine for other territories. Leopold's continued negotiations at Vienna, however, angered Louis. Leopold sought the governorship of the Austrian Netherlands and a dynastic link with the Habsburgs. In 1717 he attempted to gain ecclesiastical independence from France.[91]

Lorraine was a territory of the Holy Roman Empire that was to become part of the French royal inheritance. Some French aristocrats had their own territorial pretensions, but were scarcely able to follow an effective independent policy. The Duke of Luynes had a claim to the principality of Neuchâtel and in 1740 officially protested that it was ruled by the Hohenzollerns.[92] Such protests had little weight. However, the dynastic strategies and ambitions of the greater aristocracy[93] could indeed affect governmental policy. This was particularly the case with families such as the Orléans and the Contis that were cadet branches of the royal house. Presiding over what were in effect princely courts, they had a social role and important clientage systems that ensured that the crown took a concern in their interests. In 1777–8 the envoy in Naples repeatedly pressed for payments due to princes of the House of Bourbon.[94] Furthermore, the government took an interest in the dynastic and territorial interests of German princely houses that overlapped with those of France,[95] and in the concerns of French aristocrats with German interests, such as in the 1710s Cardinal Rohan, the bishop of Strasbourg.[96]

The reign assessed

Louis XIV died in 1715. It is worth considering his diplomacy from the 1680s not, as is so often suggested, largely in terms of failure, but rather by asking whether positive re-assessments of the quality and success of domestic governance, not least partnership with the nobility,[97] can be extended to foreign policy. The theme of a greater understanding of limits and thus enhanced effectiveness – at home, and in relations with the papacy – can be sketched,[98] although it is unclear how far Louis learned to place sufficient weight on supporting and reconciling the interests of allies. The insecurity that characterized French policy earlier in the century was lessened, in part because of the extensive fortification programme planned and implemented by Vauban, appointed commissioner general of fortifications in 1678. A decade later, Louis's confidence led him to write that 'whatever happens in this war, it is certain that the good state of my frontiers and of my troops, will prevent my enemies from troubling the peace of my kingdom and will give me the means to extend my possessions'.[99] He was wrong on the second but less so on the first.

Growing discrepancies in the 1690s and 1700s between the official rhetoric of triumph and the reality of defeats helped to tarnish the royal image. Louis's wars brought heavy costs – to government and people – but Louis's reign did not see the precarious evasion of crisis that had characterized those of his predecessors. Partly thanks to his achievements, the minority of his successor was less disturbed than his own or that of Louis XIII had been. The close of Louis's reign after Utrecht and Rastatt entailed clearing up diplomatic and territorial disputes left over from the war.[100] It also suggested new diplomatic possibilities, including Anglo-French co-operation in 1713–14, especially to keep the peace in Italy; and, after the Rastatt–Baden negotiations and the accession of George I in Britain in 1714, better relations between France and Austria. This sense of fluidity reflected, in part, the volatility that peace brought to diplomacy, but also the degree to which an agenda supposedly dominated by French aggression and aggrandizement was changing. Louis responded by revealing a willingness to seek better relations with Austria and Britain and a desire not to be trapped in the past. He refused to support Jacobite hopes for French intervention after the death of Queen Anne[101] and emphasized the need to avoid letting Protestant princes feel that he was out to form a Catholic League.[102] Louis also, however, reiterated his hostility to Peter the Great. Having helped persuade the Turks to attack Russia in 1711, Louis in April 1715 renewed his subsidy treaty with Charles XII of Sweden who was at war with Peter.

Turning points are always problematic, often only seen with the benefit of a hindsight that simplifies to a misleading degree. The wars fought in Western

Europe between 1717 and 1748 suggest that it is inaccurate to regard the peace settlements of 1713–14 as having created a new international order. Indeed, some of the major themes of the period, particularly Franco-Spanish differences in 1717–29, and French sponsorship of anti-Austrian German princes, especially the Wittelsbachs in the late 1720s, early 1730s and early 1740s, indicate that it is erroneous to exaggerate the changes created by the War of the Spanish Succession and the subsequent peace.

The continuation of diplomatic themes – alignments and rivalries – is compatible with a slackening of intensity and anxiety. It has been suggested that the war, and the subsequent peace, marked the end of French hegemony in Western Europe (and its replacement by an age of British power), but the existence of this hegemony can be questioned, especially in light of the willingness of many rulers to defy Louis in 1688. It was not so much that Louis's power had extended to hegemony, but, rather, that French hegemony had been widely feared. Even so, during the heyday of French power, many Austrian ministers had been more concerned by Turkey and Hungary, while the Scandinavian and north German rulers were more interested in Baltic affairs. At the same time, the prestige that Louis brought his family and country encouraged emulation, as with the impact of the model of Versailles – architecture, layout and protocol – on other courts including those, like Munich, that had hitherto looked to Habsburg models.[103]

The Spanish succession had suggested a new prospect, one very different to the piecemeal extensions of French power in the second half of the seventeenth century. The Bourbons would have gained the greatest inheritance in the world and became the dominant power in both Italy and the Low Countries. This would have been very different to the *réunions* or the gain of Casale. The predominance of one dynasty had been justifiably feared in 1700. This was a more realistic anxiety than earlier fears of French hegemony.

French claims that Philip V would not follow the French lead were to be fully vindicated after the war ended. Many German and Italian rulers were more concerned about Austrian than Bourbon power and intentions in the first three decades of the century. Their perspective was a valid one, was to be shared by the maritime powers in the 1720s, and should be placed alongside their earlier concern about the Bourbons. In 1715 Victor Amadeus II, a recent opponent of France, pressed on the French the threat from Austria and called for a countervailing league. Louis XIV had neither prevented the rise of Austria nor maintained and developed a system of alliances in Eastern Europe capable of balancing it. These related tasks were arguably outside French capability, not least because it was impossible to direct the policies of Eastern European powers, to overcome their own rivalries, especially that between Poland and the Turks, and to predict developments such as the course of the Great Northern War of 1700–21. Nevertheless, there was to a degree a lack of adroitness and lack of attention in Louis's handling of some aspects of Eastern European politics. In particular, attempts to co-operate with Hungarian rebellions and the Turks jeopardized relations with Poland.

In the global context, Louis left France with a valuable legacy. Although much of French industry showed signs of stagnation or depression in the last three decades of the reign, a number of key industries improved.[104] These included sugar refining in western France and cloth manufacture in Languedoc, both of which were dependent on foreign trade and France's international position. However, the Newfoundland cod fishery that was so important to western France and to France's trade in the Mediterranean, was hit by the wars of 1688–1713, as was trade to the Baltic, while the East India Company was crippled by a heavy debt.[105]

Louis's legacy was not so much one of colonial gain, although the foundation of Louisiana was important, as was the British failure to capture Québec in 1711 (although it was due to British mismanagement, not French strength). Rather, it was the case that in the eighteenth century France and Spain were to be aligned, and often allied, against Britain in a struggle for oceanic power. Possibly France and Spain would have co-operated anyway, whatever the state of their dynastic links. At any event, the value of this support was to be minimized because France lost the struggle with Britain. Links between Louis's policies and subsequent developments are tenuous: but consequences, whether intended or not, provide a basis for judgement. Louis left France with more secure land frontiers and with the possibility of allying with and benefiting from the leading European colonial power. Yet, Britain had clearly become the leading naval power during the War of the Spanish Succession, and this position could no longer be challenged by France alone. As a maritime state, France's effectiveness hereafter depended in large part on her ability to co-operate with other naval powers.

CHAPTER THREE

Foreign policy under the regency, Bourbon and Fleury, 1715–1743

France at present has only one aim: to obtain, one way or another,
a general peace for Europe and a long peace for herself.
Count Maffei, Sardinian envoy, 18 June 1728.[1]

The Orléans regency and the Anglo-French alliance

Louis XIV was succeeded in 1715 by his great-grandson, another Louis, born in
1710. Accession by such a young ruler constituted a serious dynastic problem.
Louis XV did not marry until 1725 or have a son until 1729, and it was not until
the mid-1750s that the succession to the throne was firmly assured in his line.
The strong claims of his uncle, Philip V of Spain, to the succession,[2] placed the
regent – Philip, Duke of Orléans (1674–1723), who controlled France from 1715
until his death[3] – in a precarious position, and encouraged him to look abroad for
allies who could counteract the Spanish threat to intervene if Louis died. Philip
of Spain doubted the validity of the Utrecht renunciation of his claims to the
French throne, which placed Orléans, Louis XIV's nephew, next in line.

When, in October 1728, Louis XV contracted smallpox, Philip of Spain
prepared to seize power in France and rumours spread of a possible civil war
between his supporters and those of Louis, Duke of Orléans (1703–52), the son
of the former regent.[4] Louis XV recovered swiftly, but the vulnerability of the
situation is suggested by the political crisis that affected Russia in early 1730
when the young, childless Peter II died of smallpox.

The peace settlements of 1713–14 had left a number of issues unsettled and
several rulers unsatisfied, and, although the principal sphere of tension was Italy,
this affected other powers, because of their interests there and their concern
about how changes in Italy might affect the rest of Europe. A bigger cause of
uncertainty was the coming of peace and the consequent dissolution of wartime

alliances. There were several policy options for France. One was a family compact with Spain. This was a popular option that would have consolidated and benefited from the placing of a branch of the Bourbon dynasty on the Spanish throne. The failure of this option cannot be explained in terms of any schematic theory of international relations. Instead, it reflected the contingent nature of French domestic politics and Anglo–French relations.

The accession of the Elector of Hanover in Britain as George I in August 1714 was followed by the replacement of the Tory government by the Whigs. The latter had bitterly opposed the Utrecht settlement and played a major role in 1713 in ensuring the parliamentary rejection of Bolingbroke's plan for improving Anglo–French commercial relations by a trade treaty. The French feared that the new Whig government would provoke war, while, in Britain, French action in support of the Jacobites was believed imminent. Relations were very poor in late 1714 and early 1715. The French failure to wreck the harbour of their North Sea privateering base at Dunkirk, as stipulated at Utrecht, had already caused tension between the Tory ministry and France. The issue was pressed with vigour by the new Whig government, and seen as an indication of French willingness to obey – and British ability to enforce – the provisions of Utrecht, and as a proof of French intentions.

Anglo–French relations also reflected relations and negotiations with other powers. The French were affected by the advance of Russia under Peter the Great and the weakness of their Eastern European allies, Poland, Sweden and the Hungarians. After his victory over Charles XII of Sweden at Poltava in 1709, Peter had overrun Sweden's possessions in the eastern Baltic and Charles's protégé, Stanislaus Leszczynski, had been driven from Poland. The Hungarians had been brought to accept Habsburg authority by the Peace of Szatmár of 1711.

Initially, the Whigs sought to recreate the Grand Alliance that had fought France in the War of the Spanish Succession. This provoked concern from the French. Their envoy in Vienna was certain, wrongly so, that the Whigs wished to fight France in order to win Alsace, Burgundy and Flanders for Charles VI. The Austrians, in turn, were anxious. Prince Eugene told the French envoy that fears aroused by Louis XIV's policies could not be swiftly assuaged and that there was a danger that Louis XV would follow the same policies.[5] Fear of Austrian plans, including the possibility that Charles VI would make most Italian rulers feudatories of the empire, led to French interest in sponsoring a league of Victor Amadeus II of Savoy–Piedmont and anti-Austrian German rulers. Orléans told the Piedmontese envoy that he did not want Charles VI to become more powerful in Italy. Pressed by the Papacy to promise not to attack Charles VI while the latter was at war with the Turks, Orléans replied that he would only give such an assurance if Charles promised that then, and thereafter, he would not attack in Italy or against Spain.[6]

However, it was clear to foreign envoys, such as that of Victor Amadeus, that the French government was more cautious than that of Louis XIV, and felt

France to be weaker.[7] Unexpectedly, Austro-Dutch differences over the Austrian Netherlands helped to clear the path towards better Anglo–French relations. This, in turn, left Orléans less threatened and less willing to listen to Spanish and Jacobite suggestions.

It might appear inevitable that the two weak leaders, George I and Orléans, should unite. The Jacobite and Spanish threats made a resolution of Anglo–French diplomatic difficulties urgent. Yet, distrust was strong in ministerial and diplomatic circles in both countries, and closer relations by either with Austria appeared at least as likely. The state of Anglo–French relations was linked closely to political struggles in London and Paris. Support for a Jacobite restoration was pushed in French court and ministerial circles. The policy apparently represented a continuation of that of Louis XIV and more particularly a fulfilment of aspirations for a pro–Catholic stance. Jacobitism offered France the prospect of a client Britain that would not ally with the Dutch and would not thwart French schemes on the Continent. The British ministry watched anxiously the fate of French factional struggles, fearing that Huxelles or Torcy would defeat Dubois in the battle to influence Orléans, or that Orléans himself would fall.

The negotiation of the Anglo–French alliance was conducted in a strained atmosphere. There was strong support within France for Philip V, and Orléans was very unpopular. The need for mutual support helped to drive the two regimes together, while better relations with Britain and the Dutch were a counterpart to the relative liberalism of the government of the pacific Orléans. It was not a politics of enthusiasm. The alliance was subsequently regarded by French diplomats such as the Marquis de Fénelon, ambassador at The Hague 1725–44, as very much motivated by Orléans' personal views and as being bad for France.[8]

On 28 November 1716, the Anglo–French treaty was signed. France guaranteed Hanover and the Protestant succession in Britain, and undertook to ensure that 'James III' left Avignon for Italy, while George promised military support if Philip V should seek to retract his renunciation of his rights to the French throne. Thanks to the Dutch accession on 4 January 1717, the alliance became a Triple Alliance. It was strengthened in 1718 when Huxelles was replaced as foreign minister by Guillaume Dubois, a protégé of Orléans'. The Anglo–French alliance was to persist until March 1731 when, with the Second Treaty of Vienna, Britain reached a unilateral agreement with Austria, that France both resented and refused to support.

Although there were periods of tension, particularly in 1721–2 and 1728–30, the alliance remained central to their respective foreign policies. Furthermore, there was no serious strategic or geopolitical clash between the two powers. Orléans and Dubois sought the maintenance of peace, and were prepared to accept that this essentially committed them to the Utrecht settlement. In addition, naval power did not play any real role in French foreign policy in this period, certainly in the 1710s. Expenditure was far less than that on the army.[9]

There was nothing to parallel the urgent Spanish attempts to rebuild a navy in the late 1710s. French naval policy suited British interests.

While the treaty was fairly clear on its aims – the maintenance of the essentials of the Utrecht settlement – it was less clear about what should be done to enforce these provisions. Both states unilaterally developed good relations with third parties, and, frequently, sought to persuade their ally to yield in disputes with other powers, France, for example, supporting Peter the Great's claims against Britain in 1724.

Nevertheless, France and Britain avoided supporting the interests of other powers when they threatened the vital concerns of their partner. In 1717, when, close to war with Hanover, Peter the Great visited Paris, the French rejected his offer of an alliance in return for subsidies. This policy was especially clear in the case of relations with Spain in the 1720s. France felt little support for the commercial privileges Britain had gained in the Spanish Empire at Utrecht, which led to persistent complaints from French mercantile circles, or for her retention of Gibraltar. French support for Spanish pretensions in Italy also reflected views different to those of Britain. Nonetheless, in the end the French stuck to their British alliance.

There was a measure of interest within France in better relations with Austria, again a continuation of policy at the close of Louis XIV's reign, and one helped by talk of common religious interests. The two powers were allied in the anti-Spanish Quadruple Alliance of 1718, and an attempt was made to have an Austro-French understanding as the basis of the Congress of Soissons in 1728. However, a major theme of French policy was opposition to Austria, the power that threatened to dominate post-Utrecht Germany and Italy, that intimidated France's allies in both regions, and that was now established in the Austrian Netherlands on France's north-eastern border. France's attitude encouraged the Austrians to accept Anglo-Dutch mediation in their peace negotiations with the Turks in 1718, and to reject that of France.

French hostility towards Austria encouraged French support for Spain, but the British were most suspicious of France in the case of Franco-Spanish relations, and the French were willing at moments of crisis between Britain and Spain to follow the British lead, as in 1718–19 and 1727. In the first, both countries declared war on Philip V when he challenged the peace settlement for Italy by invading Sicily. Dubois emphasized that war was being waged not against Philip or the Spanish nation, but to remove the leading minister, Alberoni, whom he blamed for Spanish aggression. He also called for Austrian pressure on the pope whom he saw as close to Spain and hostile to Orléans.[10] The war offered France little. It was unpopular and many generals refused to serve. A French army successfully invaded northern Spain in 1719, although the advance was not pushed far. There was also an attempt to expand from Louisiana in order to increase the French presence in the Gulf of Mexico.

Spanish defeats led Philip to accept terms in February 1720. This was followed by the development of a Franco-Spanish alignment that led to a convention signed at Madrid on 27 March 1721. The alliance was cemented by the betrothal of Louis XV to Philip's daughter Maria Anna, born in 1718, and by the marriage in January 1722 of Philip's heir, Louis, to one of Orléans' daughters. Dubois pushed hard the cause of the Orléans' dynasty, but dynastic links were also intended to secure the peace. The British were brought into the new alignment by the Triple Alliance of Madrid of 13 June 1721.

As in any alliance between major powers, there was tension within the Anglo-French alliance, and this was exacerbated by relations with third parties. It had been possible to reach agreement over creating an alliance in 1716, when it was a matter of mutual guarantees and a defensive mentality. Attempts to expand the alliance, both in intention and by means of negotiating additional agreements with other powers, proved to be very difficult, and productive of strain and quarrels. The two periods when the alliance worked best were those when it was clearly defensive, in 1716–17 and 1725–7.

In 1726 Charles-Jean-Baptiste Fleuriau, Count of Morville, the foreign minister who replaced the dead Dubois in 1723, presented the alliance as designed to establish 'a just balance in Europe'.[11] Five years earlier, Dubois had written to an envoy that France's principal objective was the consolidation of European tranquillity.[12] Indeed in 1721 Dubois pressed the Russian envoy on the value of a defensive alliance of France, Russia, Sweden, Britain and Prussia.[13] In 1719 he had wanted to ally with Prussia, in order to thwart Russian approaches,[14] and in 1723 Dubois told the Prussian envoy that France sought to protect the German Protestants, especially Prussia, and that the Emperor threatened to become the absolute master of the Empire, a reflection that led Frederick William I of Prussia to express support for a league of Britain, France and Prussia.[15] This re-active character to the alliance, designed to thwart disruption to a European system, especially from the rise of Austrian power, prefigured French intentions in their alliance with Austria in the second half of the century. Dubois sought to divide the expanding powers of Central and Eastern Europe – Austria, Prussia and Russia – and to gain the support of the last two against the first, but this policy was subordinate to his perception of French interests in Western Europe, not least in his acceptance that French approaches had to be compatible with British views. Proposals made by the Turks in 1721 of an alliance with Turkey directed against Austria were not followed up. They would have been unacceptable both to Britain and to international Catholic opinion.

In 1725–7 France and Britain were threatened by a new alignment, the Austro-Spanish alliance, formed in the negotiations leading to the First Treaty of Vienna in 1725. After the former regent Orléans' death on 2 December 1723, another prince of the blood, Louis-Henri, the Duke of Bourbon, had become the chief French minister, and, in order to weaken the position of his rival and Louis XV's heir, the new Duke of Orléans, he sought a speedy marriage for Louis, a policy lent weight by the king's ill-health.[16] Louis's return of Maria Anna, his intended bride, to her father and his uncle, Philip V in March 1725, so that he could marry a woman closer to childbearing age, led to an outraged reaction. The Russians were also angered because both Peter the Great and Catherine I had suggested that Louis marry Grand Duchess Elisabeth. The French preference for a Polish wife[17] helped encourage Russia to turn to Austria in 1726. In Paris, Russian strength was not appreciated.

The Austro-Spanish pact led to the reassertion of the Anglo-French alliance, first in the Treaty of Hanover between Britain, France and Prussia in September 1725, and secondly, in joint efforts to gain allies and to plan for war. Both the British government and Bourbon were worried by the consequences of the alliance between Philip and Charles VI.[18]

France and Britain appreciated their shared interests, and the unilateral policy-making that had characterized the early 1720s was replaced by a greater measure of co-operation. This was not free of dispute, and strains were if anything even greater as the attempt to co-operate led to quarrels that had been mostly avoided whilst each power had largely gone its separate way in the early 1720s. Nevertheless, the alliance was strengthened by outside threat, while Cardinal André-Hercule de Fleury, Louis XV's elderly ex-tutor, born in 1653, who, thanks to his former pupil's support, succeeded the displaced Bourbon in 1726, handled the British with some finesse, although he had to face criticism from senior figures that Britain controlled French policy.[19]

France now found herself part of a system that was dependent on her army. In 1727 and 1730 the alliance's plans for war with Austria and her allies included the movement of a French army into the Empire to protect Hanover from attack. In 1729 and 1730, when Prussia threatened to invade Hanover, the French position was again crucial. George II ascribed the Prussian decision not to attack in 1729 to the assistance of his allies. Within Germany, the French actively sought to build up opposition to Austria and, in particular, to stir up the Wittelsbachs: treaties were signed with Bavaria and the Palatinate respectively on 12 November 1727 and 15 February 1729, and the French helped overcome the division between the two main branches of the Wittelsbachs, a division that had greatly assisted the Austrians during the War of the Spanish Succession. Chavigny, the envoy at the Imperial Diet, was especially active. He argued that it was good for France if there were problems in the Empire,[20] and that France needed to separate Austria from the German princes, to raise the power of the latter at the expense of the former, and to combine the Wittelsbachs with the Protestant princes including George II, as Elector of Hanover.[21] Different territorial interests made this very difficult.[22] A protégé of Dubois, Chavigny's views looked back to seventeenth-century French efforts to develop a German league aimed against Austria, a power that, as Richelieu warned, was stronger than had been the case fifty years earlier.[23]

Fleury sought to avoid war, taking particular care to prevent hostilities with Spain in 1727. Affected by the War of the Spanish Succession, in which his Provencal bishopric of Fréjus had been briefly occupied in 1707, Fleury instead aimed to secure a general peace through the international congress that opened in Soissons in 1728. He wrote to the Emperor Charles VI the previous June: 'The object of the Congress should be a solid and general peace and that can only be obtained by settling everything that could lead to war. Palliative remedies will not suffice'. An Austrian envoy described Fleury's call for peace at the opening session at Soissons as like a short sermon.[24] Rather than see him as an idealist opposed to all war, or a statesman who hoped to solve France's historical rivalry with the Habsburgs and replace it with a bold détente, it is more accurate to view Fleury as a pragmatist aware of the costs of war and seeking to advance French interests without excessive risk.

Fleury used his direct correspondence with Charles and leading Austrian ministers to further peace,[25] and the Austrians had considerable trust in him.[26] Fleury was especially pleased with the views of the Austrian Chancellor, Sinzendorf,[27] but Austrian ministers who did not support his strategy prevailed. Austria was not willing to abandon Spain, and Spain would not yield to French pressure. Philip V argued that France was led by Britain.[28] The Congress failed to secure the peace and in 1729 war appeared imminent.

The Anglo-French alliance had survived changes in the British and French ministries and the accession of a new king in Britain in 1727. The French government had then reaffirmed their commitment to the alliance and the Hanoverian dynasty. They were pleased that George II had decided to maintain his father's policies and ministers. In 1729 the British pressed for action against Spain, but – after some frenetic diplomacy – Spain was, instead, detached from her Austrian alliance and allied to Britain and France by the Treaty of Seville of 9 November 1729. Fleury had already argued that only an alliance of the three powers could maintain the balance of power and free the German princes from Austrian control,[29] while Chauvelin, who replaced Morville in 1727, claimed that it was in France's interest to end the Austro-Spanish alliance.[30]

In 1730 the three powers sought to cajole Austria into accepting an Italian settlement agreeable to Spain, including the admission of Spanish troops into Parma and Tuscany. The Austrians responded negatively. In a conference at Compiègne in August 1730, the French government then pressed its allies for plans for a general war against Austria the following year that would entail military operations in Italy and the Empire, and subsidies to Sardinia and the Wittelsbachs. Chauvelin spoke of driving the Austrians from Italy and Fleury opposed any guarantee of the Pragmatic Sanction by which the undivided (Austrian) Habsburg inheritance was to pass on Charles VI's death to his elder daughter Maria Theresa, a measure that ignored the claims of the daughters of his elder brother, Joseph I, who had married into the houses of Saxony and Bavaria.[31] Charles's anxieties about the Pragmatic Sanction, and British governmental efforts to thwart Jacobite schemes, indicated that France was not alone in having an uncertain succession. The role of contested successions indicates the danger of assuming that eighteenth-century international relations can be understood in modern terms.

Anxious about Hanoverian security, fearful of the prospect of unilateral

French and Spanish approaches to Austria, and pressed by domestic criticism of its foreign policy, the British ministry began secret negotiations with Austria in the early autumn of 1730. Disquiet over long- and short-term French policies played a role, but there was no wish to end good relations with France, and the British hoped – wrongly – that France would accept the new agreement. In fact, the guarantee of the Pragmatic Sanction, a scheme to maintain the indivisibility of the Austrian succession, as part of the Anglo-Austrian Second Treaty of Vienna of March 1731, was unwelcome to France and destroyed her alliance with Britain. Rejecting French approaches, the Spaniards accepted the settlement in July.

France alone: 1731–3

The Austrians blocked a subsequent British proposal to reassure France about Anglo-Austrian intentions. Possibly it would have failed anyway, defeated by French unwillingness to accept a dictated settlement. The heir to Lorraine, who in 1729 became Duke Francis I, had gone to live in Vienna in 1723. He had been selected by Charles VI as a likely spouse for his daughter and heir, Maria Theresa, a marriage that was to occur in 1736, and to be followed by that of Francis's brother Charles to Maria Theresa's sister. This marriage project threatened to undo Louis XIV's settlement of his eastern frontier, which was based in part on a defenceless and easily-occupied Lorraine. In 1728 Fleury had told Sinzendorf that France was opposed to the Duchy of Lorraine ever being held by a Holy Roman Emperor. The failure to solve the diplomatic and strategic dilemma posed by the prospect of the Lorraine marriage made the international situation threatening for France once she lost the diplomatic initiative in 1731.

Without French consent, no western European peace settlement could be secure or lasting. Whilst France was isolated, in 1731–2, her diplomatic efforts – such as the attempt to gain the alliance of Sweden, Denmark, Saxony and Bavaria, to prevent the Imperial Diet accepting the Pragmatic Sanction,[32] and to block the Treaty of Copenhagen of 1732, by which Denmark and Russia settled their differences – were threats to European tranquillity. As soon as she could gain powerful allies willing to act, as in late 1733 with Sardinia and Spain, France was to prove a major threat.

However, the French presented their policy as being designed to resist the potential tyranny of an Austrian Habsburg dominance of the Empire and Italy. Villebois, envoy in Cassel, emphasized the dangers of Austrian desire for absolute authority in the Empire, and argued that the Pragmatic Sanction, and the likely retention of the Imperial succession in the Habsburg family, were dangerous.[33] These arguments reveal a sense of threat. Such language looked back to criticism of Habsburg universalism in the sixteenth and seventeenth centuries, and to arguments about the threat of Austrian power in the first three decades of the eighteenth century. In each case, French diplomats presented the rulers of France as determined to protect the liberties of other states. This combination looked forward to arguments that were to be made at the time of the French Revolution.

Both then and earlier envoys, however, had to face anxieties about the scope of French intentions, what La Chétardie in 1733 told Frederick William I of Prussia was 'the traditional view that France sought universal monarchy'.[34] Thus, the notion of the balance of power, either Continental or in part of Europe, could be used both against France and by her envoys opposing, in particular, Austria and/or Russia. In 1725 Cambis, the envoy in Turin, suggested to the French foreign minister, that France support schemes to gain Italian territory for Philip V's son Don Carlos, 'in order to establish there the balance so necessary for peace'.[35] Chavigny argued in 1727 that it was necessary to present Louis XV as motivated by 'the public good',[36] and to stop Austria from oppressing the weak rulers of Europe.[37]

In 1731 the French did not invade Britain on behalf of the Jacobites as was widely thought likely,[38] while talk of driving France from Alsace was pure bombast,[39] but in 1732 France sought to develop a German alliance system, directed against Austria. The opposition of Saxony and Bavaria to the Pragmatic Sanction was encouraged, and a subsidy treaty with Augustus II of Saxony concluded on 25 May 1732.[40] These moves, although peaceful, were essentially preparatory for a future conflict over the Austrian succession. In April 1732 Chauvelin discussed with Count Albert, the Bavarian envoy, the possibility of Saxon–Bavarian action against any election of a King of the Romans (successor to the Emperor) and offered the assistance of 50,000 French troops.[41] The diplomatic strategy that Belle Isle was to use so successfully in 1741 to create a coalition of German powers against Austria was already clearly developed in 1732 by Chauvelin.

The War of the Polish Succession: 1733–5

War, however, broke out over Poland, an elective monarchy. Augustus II died on 1 February 1733, supposedly as a result of gangrene suffered when he injured a toe getting out of his carriage. The two principal candidates for the Polish throne were Augustus III of Saxony, the son of Augustus II, and Stanislaus Leszczynski, who had been king in 1704–9. Stanislaus was Louis XV's father-in-law and the French government had encouraged the idea that he might return to the throne,[42] although without overcommitting itself. Stanislaus represented much more than French influence. The Russian General Münnich, who supported better Franco-Russian relations, explained to the French envoy, Magnan, that Stanislaus was an unacceptable candidate to Russia because of his French and Swedish connections. In their discussions with Magnan, Russian ministers stressed Stanislaus' support for the reconquest of former Polish territories in the

1700s. Chauvelin's hopes of Russian neutrality and Magnan's hopes of changes in the Russian government[43] proved abortive. As Chauvelin had noted in 1729, France's chances of better relations were hindered by Russian commitment to the Austrian alliance.[44] Both then and earlier, French ministers and diplomats hoped to use the Turks to restrain Russia.[45] Villeneuve, the French envoy, urged reform on the Turks.[46]

Stanislaus was elected in 1733, but displaced by an invading Russian force. Augustus III had allied himself to Austria and Russia, and the French-backed Bavarian–Saxon alliance had thus collapsed, as the Bavarians had predicted.[47] French hopes of using Turkish pressure to prevent Russia from acting proved abortive, despite the high regard with which France was then held in Constantinople. The Grand Vizir flattered Villeneuve, and misled him by making contradictory promises to both sides. Turkish options were limited by their conflict with Persia.[48] Furthermore, although Chauvelin wanted an unwritten agreement with the Turks, the latter were determined to have a formal treaty. The hope that Sweden could make a diversionary attack on the Russians in Livonia[49] was far more illusory, but it testified to the continued appeal of the notion of a *barrière de l'est*, an alliance system in eastern Europe.

Given the significance of royal, dynastic and national dignity, honour and pride, considerations frequently advanced in the diplomatic correspondence of the period, it is understandable that Louis should support Stanislaus' candidature, and oppose the attempt to prevent it. In the *Conseil d'État* on 6 May 1733, the bellicose Marshal Villars, who had held senior command positions under Louis XIV, pressed the argument of royal *gloire*.[50] The character of monarchy was at issue. A policy spy reported on 28 May that it was being said in Paris that Fleury did not wish Louis to see fighting, preferring that he hunt, and that France had fallen from her seventeenth-century heights.[51] Fleury was indeed more cautious in 1733 than courtiers such as Villars and ministers such as Chauvelin. Police reports had commented on the bellicosity of Parisian opinion in 1729 when war had seemed possible.[52]

However, as in any explanation of war, there are other factors to consider. A desire to take revenge for the diplomatic isolation of 1731 was important, although it is less clear how far the aggressive French diplomatic strategy of 1733 was related to the domestic political problems of 1732, specifically a very serious dispute between the government and the *Parlement* of Paris. That France went to war probably owed more to a conviction that she must fight for royal honour and to prevent humiliation and isolation, than to any wish to establish her power in eastern Europe. Chavigny, now the bellicose envoy in London, argued that France's friends and enemies would all be affected by the resolution she displayed.[53]

He also offered Friedrich Christian von Plettenburg, the envoy of the Elector of Cologne at the Imperial Diet, an account of French policy that stressed Louis XV's commitment to the public interest of Europe rather than any selfish pursuit of French views. French action was presented as a response on behalf of Europe to Austro–Russian aggression. The fear that Germany would follow Poland was expressed.[54]

Equally, Chavigny, like many other French commentators and diplomats, hoped to use the war in order to restrict Imperial power in Germany and Italy and to thwart the Pragmatic Sanction.[55] The conviction that France was prepared to fight led Philip V and Charles Emmanuel III of Sardinia (ruler of Savoy– Piedmont) to respond to French approaches and to reject attempts to keep them allied to Austria and Britain, and their support further encouraged France to action. On 26 September Charles Emmanuel signed the Treaty of Turin with the French, although the Treaty of the Escorial with Philip V, later known as the First Family Compact, was not signed until 7 November.

On 10 October 1733 Louis XV declared war on Charles VI, unreasonably holding him responsible for the actions of his Russian ally. The latter, however, was not vulnerable to attack. Lorraine was overrun and the Rhenish fort of Kehl seized that year, but the French concentrated their war effort in Italy. A Franco– Dutch neutrality convention of 24 November 1733 prevented the French from attacking the Austrian Netherlands, and concern about the reaction of neutral Britain and the United Provinces may well have limited French operations in the Empire. Despite their hopes, the Jacobites received no support.

The French certainly did not take the opportunity to campaign far to the east of the Rhine. Stanislaus was told that treaties and agreements made any French invasion of Saxony impossible.[56] There was no movement into Bavaria, the essential precondition of any Bavarian action against Austria. Fleury was opposed to such a step, Chauvelin more favourable. Bavaria itself was vulnerable to Austrian attack,[57] and remained neutral despite hopes to the contrary.[58] Count Albert wanted French troops to invade the Empire and thought of them advancing into Bohemia. He urged the French to occupy the Electorate of Cologne and there were rumours that the French were to ally with the Elector and occupy the Imperial free city of Cologne, a Rhine crossing point.[59]

In order to woo neutral opinion, French diplomats – such as Chavigny in London and La Chétardie in Berlin – emphasized the moderation of French objectives and the latter told Frederick William I that the old view that France sought universal monarchy was misplaced.[60] In contrast, French and Sardinian forces easily conquered the Milanese in the winter of 1733–4, and the Spaniards overran Naples in 1734 and then conquered Sicily.

The war saw a major revival of French military and diplomatic power. A small expeditionary force failed to raise the Russian siege of Danzig (Gdańsk) in 1734, the French envoy to Denmark perishing in the attempt, but the French beat off Austrian attempts to reconquer northern Italy in 1734 (battles of Parma – 29 June – and Guastalla – 19 September). The following year, the Austrians were pressed back in northern Italy, but there was no advance towards Vienna comparable to that of Napoleon in 1797 in order to extort favourable terms. Skilful French diplomacy helped to keep Britain and the Dutch neutral,[61] but France had many problems with her allies. Charles Emmanuel III spent much of the war manoeuvring for diplomatic advantage and entered into secret negotiations for a unilateral peace. Underlying the tension over strategy, with France opposed to Spain's plan to conquer Naples and Sicily and leave the defence of northern Italy to the French, was an unsuccessful Spanish determination to hold the diplomatic initiative.

The eventual peace settlement was the product of unilateral negotiations between France and Austria. Fleury avoided both Anglo-Dutch mediation of the conflict and the unilateral Austro-Spanish settlement he had feared. He told the Sardinian envoy that he had turned to the Emperor because of Spanish demands and conduct.[62] The peace left Poland with Augustus, but Don Carlos, Philip's eldest son by his second wife, gained Naples and Sicily, and Stanislaus received Lorraine, with the reversion to France after his death. This gain did not represent a fundamental alteration in the balance of power, a difficult concept to apply with precision anyway. Lorraine had been militarily vulnerable to France for a long time, having been gained by her at the start of every major war. Yet Lorraine in hostile hands was also a threat. It was seen as a potential Austrian route into eastern France. Similarly, in 1737 French interest in Corsica was largely motivated by concern that it might pass from Genoese rule to that by a stronger power.[63]

Austro-French *rapprochement*: 1735–40

The Austro-French *rapprochement* of 1735–40[64] was the greatest shift produced by the war. The preliminary treaty signed at Vienna by the two powers on 3 October 1735, which led to the Third Treaty of Vienna of 1738, produced an entente centred on a French guarantee of the Pragmatic Sanction, although the negotiation of the final treaty was far from easy. French diplomatic support for Austria forced an unwilling Sardinia and, in particular, Spain to accept an Italian settlement less favourable than that which they had militarily secured at the expense of Austria. Austro-French co-operation kept Italy peaceful, although Spanish agreement to evacuate Tuscany was not obtained until December 1736. The aggressively anti-Austrian Chauvelin was dismissed in February 1737.[65] Austrian envoys had complained to Fleury about Chauvelin during the previous period of good relations in 1728–9.[66] His pliant replacement, Amelot, followed Fleury's line. The Spanish envoy, La Mina, made clear Spanish anger at the dismissal of Chauvelin.

Many eighteenth-century wars ended in secret unilateral negotiations, but the terms France accepted in 1735 were completely unacceptable to her allies, and, by abandoning her allies, she destroyed the alliance that had supported her in the War of the Polish Succession; not that Sardinia and Spain had failed to engage in secret diplomacy. The treaty also cut the ground from under the Elector of Bavaria, who was also angered by arrears in his French subsidy.[67] Distrust between the powers that had plotted or acted against Austria in 1732–5 made a successful resumption of such action appear less likely. In 1738 Fleury told the Bavarian envoy, Count Törring, that he knew as little of the views and schemes of Elizabeth Farnese, the influential wife of Philip V of Spain, as he did of those of the distant chief of the Mongols.[68] Indeed difficulties in the Franco-Spanish relationship in 1715–40 were a major limitation in the diplomatic weight of both powers.

When France guaranteed the Pragmatic Sanction she had reserved the prior rights on the Habsburg inheritance of third parties, such as Charles Albert of Bavaria,[69] and on 16 May 1738 the two signed a secret agreement in which France promised to support his just claims. Nevertheless, French conduct in the negotiations in the late 1730s over the succession to the German duchies of Jülich and Berg, ruled by the childless Elector Palatine and claimed by Prussia, did not encourage the Wittelsbachs. In 1737 Austria and France jointly sought to settle the issue. On 13 January 1739 they concluded a secret treaty providing that the Wittelsbach claimant should occupy Jülich–Berg for two years after the death of Karl Philipp of the Palatinate. However, by a treaty of 5 April 1739 with Prussia, France guaranteed her a portion of Berg and promised to persuade Karl Philipp to agree. They sought unsuccessfully to do so via Törring. Fleury had told him that he wanted to block any chance of Prussia allying with Britain.[70] In 1735 Chavigny had pressed the idea of a Franco-Prussian-Wittelsbach alliance.[71] The tentative attempt to negotiate one in 1739 was unsuccessful, but in 1741, thanks to the ambition of Frederick II and Charles Albert, the French were to create such an alliance.

In December 1736 Count Albert suggested that once France had settled her peace with Austria, it would be possible for Charles Albert to approach her. The following year, Törring was sent to Paris as Bavarian envoy to win French support for Charles Albert's claims on the Austrian inheritance. Chavigny urged backing, but he did not enjoy Fleury's favour, and Fleury was unwilling to commit himself in support of Charles Albert's territorial claims.[72] Törring was pessimistic about the possibility of French support while Fleury was in control of policy, and informed him in May 1739 that Charles VI was too closely linked with France to be separated from her. Fleury replied that he could not be sure of future developments, but was adamant that Austro-French ties were limited to friendship.[73] However, the late 1730s did not witness a repetition of the 1731–2 French diplomatic offensive against Austria.

The government did not support the cause of the young Rákoczi, recognized by the Turks in 1738 as Prince of Transylvania, or encourage the Turks to invade Hungary. This policy was advocated by Claude-Alexandre Comte de Bonneval, a French noble who had converted to Islam and pursued a military career in Turkish service. He possibly had links with the anti-Austrian party at the French court, but Fleury, although he refused Austrian requests to detain

Rákoczi when he visited France, was opposed to such adventurism and Villeneuve, the envoy in Constantinople, may in part have been responsible for Bonneval's banishment.[74]

It was in line with his general policy that Fleury responded to Charles VI's death on 20 October 1740 by assuring the Austrian envoy Prince Liechtenstein that Louis XV would observe all his engagements with Austria.[75] Despite Törring's observation to Liechtenstein that it was foolish to imagine that France would not return to her former policies,[76] Fleury was ready to back Charles Albert's candidacy for emperor, but not his claims on the inheritance.

Both in the late 1730s and earlier, Fleury's policies were criticized by some ministerial colleagues, diplomats and commentators, both for being overly cautious and for failing to adopt a more assertive line towards Austria and Britain. Fleury was regarded as unwilling to fight, unprepared in peacetime to spend sufficient on subsidy treaties, and unable to maintain the necessary impression of French power. He was accused of inactivity and criticized in particular for failing to maintain good relations with Spain. Fleury was critical of Spanish policy,[77] and had a low view of the influential Queen of Spain, not least because of her bellicosity.

These criticisms were not simply a matter of debate over policy. Dissatisfied envoys, such as Chavigny, corresponded with prominent figures, such as Belle Isle, one of the leading generals,[78] and in particular, Chauvelin, contributing to a situation in which there appeared to be two different official foreign policies. The rumours that circulated about Chauvelin's fall focused on this issue and on the minister's alleged secret diplomacy. This uncertainty disconcerted other powers, and, although it could be suggested that it left the initiative with Fleury, as the clarifier of policy, the net effect was more one of confusion and uncertainty. France was able to take such a prominent international role thanks to the failings and weaknesses of other powers, rather than an especially skilful diplomacy.

Fleury's age also led to uncertainty about the durability of his policies. Although the Darmstadt agent could report in March 1737 that he had the fitness of a fifty-year-old,[79] there was frequent concern about his health. The time of day was a factor, according to the Sardinian envoy in January 1730: 'in the morning he retains a little bit of good sense . . . in the evening he is like a child'. At the close of the year, the envoy suggested that Bourbon would replace Fleury.[80] Expressing his concern in 1727, the Austrian Chancellor had speculated about the likely replacement: Bourbon, Morville, Torcy, Orléans or Maine.[81] In September 1728 the café report was that Fleury and Chauvelin would be replaced by Maine and Polignac, a change likely to be fatal to the British alliance; in January 1729 it was instead said that Fleury was to retire, indeed that the Austrians had successfully demanded his replacement by Richelieu; and in February 1732 Paris opinion named Chauvelin, Bourbon, Polignac, Noailles, and Villars among the possible replacements and diplomats reported the rumours.[82] They found it difficult to decide who to cultivate. Increasingly, they saw Chauvelin as the influential voice in foreign policy. Thus, in January 1734 the Sardinian envoy reported that he would try to cultivate him.[83]

Most diplomats thought Fleury weak and irresolute, and, although that may have helped him to maintain his position, it created an impression of inaction and failing to grasp the initiative.[84] Fleury was particularly ill in early 1738. This led to a suspension of business before, in the words of one envoy, his resurrection.[85] Thereafter, Fleury's caution seemed redoubled. The bitter Sardinian envoy claimed on 2 May 1738 that Fleury was willing to sacrifice everything to maintain the peace, that he no longer had the mental acuity to follow foreign affairs, that Amelot lacked the credit to determine policy, and that the other ministers were not permitted to take a role. Diplomats speculated about the possibility of Chauvelin's return and the likely views of Philip V on French politics.[86] Yet despite his weaknesses, Fleury settled the War of the Polish Succession successfully, isolated Spain and disgraced Chauvelin. Reports that Chauvelin really ran French policy[87] had proved inaccurate.

Although Fleury negotiated a *rapprochement* with Austria, relations with Russia, broken in 1733, were not resumed until 1739. Fleury was more concerned with Sweden than her stronger opponent, Russia, and the general failure among French policymakers to try seriously to win the support of Russia continued. Indeed in August 1737 Fleury tried to turn Charles VI from his Russian alliance, warning him that Russian gains at the expense of the Turks would destroy the balance of power in Eastern Europe, and suggesting that Austria should only make minor gains from the Turks.[88]

The Danes were pressed at the same time to league with Sweden in order to balance Russia's power in Northern Europe.[89] In March 1738 Amelot noted that the French government would have to see what happened in the war between the Austro-Russian alliance and the Turks before it tried to stir up the Swedes against Russia.[90] The French, however, did in 1738 successfully seek to replace what they saw as a hostile Swedish government by a more friendly one. A French subsidy treaty of December 1738 precluded Sweden from concluding any other alliance without first notifying France and led to Russian fears of a French-financed Swedish naval build-up. The treaty marked a turning point for France after her Polish débâcle. In 1739 a small French squadron appeared in the Baltic, while the Swedes sent troops to Finland.[91]

However, Fleury drew back from pressing Sweden to attack Russia, a course pressed by those hostile to Austria. As a result, French diplomats used different language in Stockholm and Constantinople. In February 1740 the French made clear their opposition to any offensive alliance between Sweden and Turkey because it was then seen as likely to lead Sweden into dangerous steps.[92] The French were willing to make gestures towards better relations with Russia and Fleury was sympathetic to their envoy Cantemir,[93] but the French had no real role in their vision of Europe for a Russia able to use its power to obtain its goals. In the instructions of 2 July 1739 for La Chétardie, the new envoy to Russia, the Austro-Russian alliance was described as very dangerous.

The collapse of Fleury's system

It is far from clear what France might have done had the recently crowned Frederick II – Frederick the Great – of Prussia not attacked Maria Theresa by invading her duchy of Silesia on 16 December 1740. Fleury was already aware that other rulers, especially Charles Albert of Bavaria and Philip V, saw the recent death of Charles VI as an opportunity for territorial aggrandizement. However, Fleury's early plans were restricted to a plan to deny the imperial election to Maria Theresa's husband: Francis of Lorraine, whom she had married in 1736, was now Grand Duke of Tuscany, but the Lorraine background was seen as hostile to France. The pacific Fleury had no apparent intention to eternalize the glory of Louis XV by heeding Providence's call to re-establish a just European balance of power, as Charles Albert suggested.[94] There were elements of continuity between Fleury's problem of knowing how best to deal with the issue of the Austrian succession when he was uncertain of the future intentions of other powers and the dilemma that had faced Louis XIV over the Spanish Succession.

The Prussian invasion of Silesia transformed the situation. Frederick replaced negotiation by action and forced other European powers to define their position. Possibly France would eventually anyway have gone to war with Austria – the opportunity being too good to pass up – but in 1740 she was also moving towards war with Britain, in order to block the latter from possibly conquering Spanish territories in the West Indies.

The War of Jenkins' Ear between Britain and Spain broke out in 1739, essentially over British attempts to trade with Spanish America. As it was a conflict between two powers with whom France then had cool relations it increased her room for manoeuvre and lessened the appeal of both as potential allies for other states, while increasing their need for French support.

However, the French government was closer to Spain for dynastic, geopolitical and commercial reasons. On 26 August 1739 Louis XV's eldest daughter married Don Philip, the younger son of Philip V by his second wife. War between France and Britain was widely anticipated, although Fleury said that it would only be fought at sea, in short that there would be no attack on Hanover.[95] Fearing that the British might attack the French fleet prior to issuing any declaration of war, as they had that of Spain in 1718 and were to do with the French in 1755, Maurepas suggested in the summer of 1739 that the French navy prepare for hostilities.[96] British privateers attacked French shipping the following year, and French public opinion was reported to be very much on the side of Spain and against Britain.[97] Fleury feared war with Britain, but was prepared for it. In August 1740 the French sent a fleet to the West Indies to prevent hostile acts. The admiral, D'Antin, had commanded the squadron sent to the Baltic in 1739, and his new destination could be regarded as symptomatic of a shift in French priorities.

Nevertheless, war with Britain did not break out. The British government chose to regard neither the dispatch of D'Antin's fleet to the West Indies nor the reported French fortification of Dunkirk, in clear breach of treaty obligations, as a cause of war, although they believed it imminent. Despite their concern over British operations, the French did not attack Britain in the West Indies. As in the War of the Polish Succession, when France had taken care to avoid hostilities, so in 1740 an uneasy balance, short of war, was maintained.

The War of the Austrian Succession

Frederick's aggression helped to precipitate a major war in Europe, and in 1756 Maria Theresa was to argue 'that France would not have attacked her, if Prussia had not led the way'.[98] Maria Theresa's refusal to cede Silesia led Frederick to sign the Treaty of Breslau with France on 5 June 1741. He renounced his claim to Jülich–Berg and agreed to support the Imperial candidature of Charles Albert, in return for a French guarantee of Lower Silesia and French promises of military assistance for Bavaria and diplomatic pressure on Sweden to attack Austria's ally Russia, both measures designed to weaken Austria. The settlement of the Jülich–Berg issue lessened the risk of war in the Rhineland and the danger of the strengthening of Prussian power close to France, while enabling France to show that she could deliver benefits to her Wittelsbach allies.

The Prussian alliance also increased French options. It offered an alternative, or addition, to an alliance with the Wittelsbachs. Furthermore, Prussia was increasingly more powerful than Hanover in Germany and without the complications of Hanover's British links. Frederick William I had been willing to present himself as a possible pro-French mediator in the Polish Succession War,[99] but he disliked taking an exposed position and was instinctively more pro-Austrian than French.[100] His son, Frederick II, was far more assertive, and readier to turn to France.

In 1741 France and Frederick encouraged other powers to act, and they did so realizing the opportunities presented by what appeared to be a Europe in flux. If France was to become the most powerful state in Europe, as indeed seemed possible in 1741, she found many rulers willing to support her, rather as Napoleon initially was to do. Amelot claimed in August 1741 that the death of Charles VI gave several princes a legitimate opportunity to advance claims,[101] but no real effort was made to do so peacefully.

The propitious diplomatic situation was rapidly exploited as those who pressed for war, led by Marshal Belle Isle, increasingly took charge. On 15 August 1741, French troops began to cross the Rhine, and on 19 September Belle Isle obtained an offensive alliance between Charles Albert and Augustus III of Saxony. This would have left each with substantial gains from the Habsburg inheritance, but tied to France by the need to retain these gains. This strategy prefigured the Napoleonic attempt to redraw borders in central Europe. The threat of a French invasion of Hanover led George II of Britain–Hanover to abandon his attempt to create an anti–French coalition, and, in a neutrality declaration signed on 25 September 1741, to promise his support for Charles Albert's imperial candidacy.[102] Diplomacy focused on the war or its consequences. French envoys sought to retain allies, divide opponents, encourage neutrals and deal with the details of war, such as the problems over recruitment that affected relations with Zweibrücken.[103]

Conflict with Sweden helped prevent Russian assistance to Austria, a step Fleury feared.[104] This was another example of France's preference for Sweden over Russia and, more generally, the failure – despite the efforts of French diplomats – to develop a positive response to Russia. La Chétardie played a role in supporting the *coup* that had brought Elisabeth to power on 6 December 1741, and she was willing to ally with France, but this opportunity was not taken up. Similarly, nothing came of the Prince of Conti's interest in marriage with Elisabeth. He wished to become Duke of Courland or Tsar. Fleury blocked the scheme.

France seemed dominant, her potential opponents weak, disunited and unwilling to aid Austria. A well-motivated alliance was able to give teeth to French diplomatic conceptions. On 21 October 1741 French and Bavarian troops camped at Saint Polten and Vienna prepared for a siege. A sense of new opportunities affected French policy. Amelot and Belle Isle for example corresponded on whether the Tyrol should become a republic.[105] The return of Stanislaus to Poland, with Augustus III receiving Bohemia in return, was suggested, as was winning the support of Venice by the offer of Mantua.[106]

However, the French war effort in 1741 was affected by a degree of disunity and a related failure to concentrate military resources on achieving decisive victory, that Napoleon was to avoid. Concerned that Augustus III and Frederick II would seize Bohemia, Charles Albert turned north. He captured Prague on 26 November 1741, and was crowned, as Emperor Charles VII, at Frankfurt on 12 February 1742, the first non–Habsburg emperor since 1437.

Thanks in part to the issue of the Imperial succession, German developments were crucial to the diplomacy of the period. However, in addition, the struggle with the Habsburgs was conducted more in Germany than had been the case with the Wars of the Spanish and Polish Succession. In the former the Low Countries and Italy had been more important spheres of conflict than Germany, certainly in 1705–12, and in the latter Italy had been far more important.

The shift in 1741–2 also owed much to the role of Prussia. The French government grasped the nature of the change. Amelot, who distrusted Frederick's ambition and suggested that success for France was the way to retain his alliance,[107] argued that developments in Italy and elsewhere would be greatly influenced by those in Germany, and he pressed the importance of Spain appointing an envoy at Berlin.[108] This shift brought to a close a period in which Italy and the Western Mediterranean had played a leading role in French diplomacy, although it would be misleading to ignore the role of Italy in the warfare and diplomacy of the 1740s.[109] Austria was, thereafter, more clearly seen as a power to be taken into account largely as far as Germany was concerned, while Spain increasingly featured for French policy not as a Mediterranean power but rather in terms of the colonial and maritime rivalry with Britain.

However, France failed in her attempt to create a new territorial order in 1741–2. This was due to a number of factors, including underrated Austrian resilience and Russia's refusal to enter the French system, as La Chétardie, the envoy in St Petersburg, hoped. Unable to dominate Europe militarily, France needed allies, but the very resort to war made it difficult to retain their support. Powers willing to accept subsidies in peacetime proved unreliable, in part because in wartime other states increased their bids for support. Such bids proved more effective as alliances tended to lack any ideological, religious, sentimental, popular or economic bonds.

That was a major problem for French policy. First Frederick, and then Augustus, abandoned France. Frederick had observed in September 1740, before the agreement was negotiated, that an alliance with France was not in his interests, as France alone would derive the benefits, while he would suffer the costs.[110] This was an exaggeration, but Prussia was more exposed than France. The French, however, counted on Frederick, anticipating that they would only need his assistance in a war that they thought would be but short.[111]

Amelot could not see how France could continue without Frederick. He and Fénelon, envoy in The Hague, argued that France had over-committed herself for the sake of her allies,[112] and by June 1742 Amelot could only record that French hopes were founded on the weak basis of better relations with these very allies.[113] There were fears about the reliability of Spain.[114] In March 1740 Count De La Marck, the French ambassador, told his Sardinian counterpart that the Spanish government was primarily motivated by the Italian interests of Don Carlos and Don Philip, Philip V's youngest son, and suggested that this could lead to a reconciliation with Britain.[115] Later that year, France and Spain clashed in the papal election. Nevertheless, Spain remained in the war. Sardinia was rightly distrusted by France.[116]

The French were also badly hit by an Austrian military revival in 1742 and by a more assertive anti-French policy on the part of the new British government. The Austrians seized Linz, Munich and Prague. Walpole was replaced in February 1742 by the more bellicose Carteret, an opponent of France. He was willing to back ideas for winning German support at the expense of France: that Charles Albert join the Anglo-Austrian alliance and, in return, make gains in Alsace.

The changing military and diplomatic situation put great pressure on France. At the request of Fleury, Belle Isle prepared a memorandum in March 1742 in which he warned of the threat that an Austro-British-Dutch force in the Austrian Netherlands would pose to Hainault and French Flanders, and the threat of an Austrian army at Luxembourg to Champagne, Lorraine and the Three Bishoprics (Metz, Toul, Verdun). He also stressed the need to keep the Russians occupied and to limit their influence in Europe and emphasized that it was in France's interest to support Sweden.[117]

The French government was now ready for peace,[118] but the situation had slipped from its grasp. Peace initiatives towards Austria and Britain met with unacceptable responses. Charles Albert pressed Fleury in October 1742 on the need to regain Bohemia for him as the only way for France to weaken Austria and as an issue involving French *gloire*,[119] but such hopes were no longer realistic.[120] Fleury pointed out that the build-up of British forces in the Austrian Netherlands might oblige France to withdraw troops from Bavaria.[121] Furthermore, Bavarian subsidy demands placed a heavy burden on French finances.[122] Charles Albert also demanded command of the French forces in Bavaria.[123] The main French army in Germany was defeated at Dettingen by George II on 27 June 1743. Belle Isle's plans had cost vast sums, led to the loss of much of the army, and failed. France's goals had not been secured and her allies were vulnerable rather than being supports.

In 1744 the accusation that French policy could be seen as renewing the idea of a universal monarchy, produced the response that George II sought to dispose of eastern France like the things in his garden at Herrenhausen.[124] However, the British attempt in 1743, and that of the Austrians in 1744, under Francis's brother, Charles of Lorraine, to make a major impact on France's eastern frontier were unsuccessful. As after Blenheim in 1704, the Austrians dominated the Empire, but the French held their Rhine frontier. They did not need to use the extensive double crownworks added to the fortifications at Metz and Thionville by Louis de Cormontaigne who had become *Ingénieur en Chef* at Metz in 1733. Furthermore, unlike in the War of the Spanish Succession, the French retained the initiative in the Low Countries. The French attempt to invade Britain in 1744 was a measure of their determination to prevent the British from blocking their continental schemes.

Fleury reassessed

By then the elderly Fleury had died, still in office, on 30 January 1743. His notion of graduated war was swept away in 1744 as the neutrality of the Austrian Netherlands collapsed and the French sought to invade Britain.[125] Louis XV declared war on Britain on 15 March 1744, and on Maria Theresa on 26 April 1744. The previous October, by the Second Family Compact, the French committed themselves to help conquer the Milanese, Parma and Piacenza for Don Philip. The limited war that the French had waged north of the Alps (as opposed to in Italy) in 1733–5, and, earlier, against Spain in 1719–20, had been replaced by a more assertive policy.

That was not the sole abandonment of Fleury's legacy. The strong diplomatic position he had created in the late 1730s[126] also collapsed. France had become the most influential foreign power in Sweden and the Turkish Empire. Her allies had risen to power in Sweden in 1738, while the French ambassador, Villeneuve, had mediated the Austro-Turkish Treaty of Belgrade in 1739, winning great prestige for France, leaving Austria weaker and obliging Russia to make peace with the Turks without making gains to match her military success.[127] By 1743 Sweden had been defeated by Russia and a revived Austria had overrun Bavaria. After Fleury's death there was a lack of ministerial coherence that was exacerbated by Louis XV's inability to instill unity and direction. Louis's confidant, Marshal Noailles complained to the king in the summer of 1743 about a failure to create the impression of governmental order and competence.[128]

In some respects the later 1730s were the highpoint of French power and prestige during the *ancien régime*, more so than the early 1680s because French policy was now less distrusted. The hostile diplomatic combinations created in response to Louis XIV had collapsed and Austria was no longer as threatening as she had seemed in the 1710s and 1720s. The revival of Spanish power and pretensions had helped to weaken, and then balance, Austria in Italy and was resisting Britain in the West Indies. Both served French ends, but her policy was not tied to Spain. In addition, the War of the Polish Succession had repeated the success of the War of Devolution of 1667–8: the conflict had been short, the economic and financial strain for France had been limited, and she had obtained results that matched her commitments. There was no equivalent to the conflicts that had gone out of control, in terms of time, resources and number of opponents: the Dutch, Nine Years' and Spanish Succession Wars. As a consequence, government finances were in a good state.

Furthermore, whereas the War of Devolution had ended with a coalition pledged to limit French gains, there was no similar diplomatic result to the War of the Polish Succession. The nearest was the Anglo-Dutch attempt in the winter of 1734–5 to mediate the conflict in order to limit French gains. However, Fleury outmanoeuvred this equivalent to the Triple Alliance and, having obtained his goals, did not attempt after the war to pursue a policy of retribution akin to that of Louis XIV towards the Dutch from 1668. He also avoided the problems posed by incompatible commitments to different powers. In essence, France, in the mid- and late 1730s, was able to discard allies without provoking new conflict. Having taken the initiative, Fleury retained it.

By forebearing to press for immediate territorial gains, Fleury helped to obtain the eventual acquisition of Lorraine. He also made it easier for France to enjoy a diplomatic influence in the late 1730s that was less controversial and less tainted by accusations of surrender to French interests than that of Louis in the mid-1680s. This prominence was accompanied by signs of a more general revival in French power and confidence.[129] The country seemed more stable. The disputes with the Jansenists and the *Parlement* of Paris, that had caused so many problems in 1732–3, eased later in the decade. The succession was more securely established. Success in war in 1733–5 brought a valuable accretion of military prestige.

French policy outside Europe

Outside Europe, French activity revived after the problems of Louis XIV's last years, and the difficulties of the regency when, aside from the collapse of the Mississippi Company, there was serious disorder on Martinique in 1717 and in St Domingue in 1722. Trade grew, especially with the West Indies and in the Near East. From the low base of the close of the War of the Spanish Succession, French Atlantic trade may have increased by 600 per cent by 1744. Bordeaux's imports of sugar, indigo and cocoa from the French West Indies tripled in 1717–20, the beginning of a massive increase in re-exports to northern Europe. Re-exports also brought wealth to Le Havre and Nantes, although the benefit was lessened by the extent to which re-exports were carried on foreign ships, especially on Dutch carriers to the Baltic.

Sugar output from St Domingue doubled in the 1730s, producing profits for Atlantic France as Britain lost out in the sugar re-export trade. French sugar was cheaper, in part because her plantations were newer. French sugar exports grew especially strongly in 1736–43. Tobacco production was badly hit by competition from British North America. In addition, the French colonies provided a market for French goods. In 1741–2 Bordeaux exported over eight million *livres* worth of produce to the French West Indian colonies annually, principally wine and textiles. The comparable figure for 1753–5 was over ten million.[130] Bordeaux had become the leading French colonial port, but other ports, including Marseille, shared in the growth in Atlantic trade.[131] The development of the West Indian colonies greatly encouraged the slave trade from West Africa. Sugar cultivation required more slaves than cotton or foodstuffs. The first slaves reached Louisiana in 1719.

Trade with Asia also increased and the second French East India Company, founded in 1719, was closing the gap on its Dutch and English counterparts.[132] Whereas one ship had been sent to India on average every two years in 1600–64 and three or four annually in 1664–1719, the annual average in 1720–70 was ten or eleven.[133] A major home base was developed in Lorient from 1724 and particularly in the 1730s. In return for imports of cotton, calicoes, pepper, salpetre and wood from India, the French sent alcohol, cloth, gold thread and iron, but the far greater value of the imports had to be made up with bullion, which in 1725–70 was at least half of the value of the cargo from France.

The French were also very active in the Ottoman Empire. They replaced the British as the leading European traders at the foremost port in the empire, Smyrna (Izmir),[134] while the Venetians were hard-pressed commercially in the Morea and the Ionian Islands, and the Dutch faced French competition at Salonica.[135] Marseille merchants backed by the consulate acquired a monopoly of Palestine's external maritime trade.[136] Trading privileges in the empire were renewed in 1740 after the successful mediation of the Balkan conflict. The consular service responded, although war blocked the plan to establish a presence at Isfahan, then the capital of Persia.[137] In the Persian Gulf, the French competed with the British and Dutch at Basra where a vice-consul was appointed in 1738.[138]

Naval effectiveness and strength revived under Maurepas, the active minister of the marine from 1723 until 1749, although, as very few ships were discarded, there was a growing problem of obsolescence.[139] Interest in the wider world helped lead in 1720 to the foundation of an office within the ministry that was responsible for maps, plans and journals.[140] Squadrons were sent to the Baltic during both the War of Polish Succession and in 1739. However, French trade to the region did not match that to the Levant. In 1741–3 ten French ships reached St Petersburg, compared to 315 from Britain and 167 from the United Provinces. French memoranda of 1744 complained about the continued role of Dutch middlemen in the Baltic trade and argued that this hit exports of French manufactures and colonial products.[141]

Naval observation of the Barbary States of North Africa in 1736–9 helped secure France's commercial position in the Mediterranean. More generally, the navy came to play a larger role in French diplomatic and military calculations than had been the case in the 1710s and 1720s, although this in no way compared with the situation in Britain. This greater role owed much to the determination and political skill of Maurepas. The critical Marquis d'Argenson claimed in November 1739 that Maurepas sought war at sea in order to establish the position of his ministry.[142] Due to the role of the Ministry of the Marine in consular and colonial matters, Maurepas was frequently mentioned in the reports of envoys in Paris who were affected by either, for example those of Genoa.[143]

This revival of naval activity was accompanied by more assertive transoceanic policies. The French took a greater role in West Africa, and in the Indian Ocean. In the Senegal valley in West Africa gifts of guns were used to expand French influence, and in 1719 the French fortified Fort St Joseph to protect their trade along the river. They also constructed river boats for trade and protection. However, the French system of forts and boats depended on local co-operation.[144] Further east, Dahomey forces captured the French fort at Whydah in 1728 after blowing up the magazine. Four years earlier, the French and British had clashed over James Island in 1724.

In the Indian Ocean, Port St Louis on the Île de France (Mauritius) was developed as a base and the cultivation of sugar introduced to the island, while coffee was exported from Réunion.[145] In 1725, when French merchants were expelled from Mahé on the west coast of India, where they had established a base in 1721, the French sent a squadron from Pondicherry that forced their return and obtained new commercial benefits.[146] Sent to Chandernagore in 1730, Joseph-Francis Dupleix founded an establishment in Patna which he saw as a base for trade with Tibet and Kashmir. He also thought of an expedition to Australia. Indeed in 1738 the East India Company sent Jean-Baptiste-Charles Bouvet de Lozier and two ships to make discoveries in the southern hemisphere: his discoveries, however, were limited to the South Atlantic. In India, Yanaon became a base in 1731 and Karikal was seized in 1739. Pondicherry had a population of about 120,000 by 1741 and was well fortified, a rampart with bastions on the side facing the land constructed in 1724–35. A new Palais du Gouvernement was built in 1738–52, a rampart on the coast in 1745. Moves against French trade at the coffee port of Mocha in Yemen led to the dispatch of a squadron from Pondicherry in October 1736. Arriving off Mocha the following January, the French bombarded the port, disembarked troops and seized Mocha, leading to a restoration of commercial privileges.[147] The French treaty with the ruler of Mecca was designed to help overcome Turkish opposition to the opening up of the Red Sea to trade.

In North America a new colony was founded at Île Royale (Cape Breton Island) in 1713 as a replacement for the loss of Acadia (Nova Scotia) and Placentia on Newfoundland to Britain. The fisheries remained important to France, with large quantitites of dry cod exported to Europe.[148] Large sums were spent on developing a major military and naval base at Louisbourg on Cape Breton Island, which was founded in 1720.[149] This was designed to support the French presence in the Newfoundland fisheries against the British and to serve as a half-way port between the French West Indies and France.

Far less was spent on fortifications in the North American interior, although Fort Niagara was rebuilt in the 1720s, while in the 1730s Pierre Gaultier de La Vérendrye built a series of posts towards the sea then believed to be in western Canada. Fort St Charles (1732) on the Lake of the Woods was followed by Fort Maurepas (1734) at the southern end of Lake Winnipeg, and Fort La Reine (1738) on the Assiniboine River. Fort Bourbon (1739) took the French presence to the north-west shore of Lake Winnipeg, Fort Dauphin (1741) established their presence on the western shore of Lake Winnipegosis and Fort La Corne (1753) near the Forts of the Saskatchewan, a crucial node of native trade routes first reached by French explorers in 1739–40. These explorations enhanced the French position in the fur trade but did not bring the hoped-for route to the Pacific. In 1738 La Vérendrye set off from Fort La Reine to find the 'great river' reported to run west to the Pacific from near the headwaters of the Missouri. The expedition reached the Missouri near modern Bismarck in North Dakota. In 1742–3 he sent two of his sons on a further search for the Pacific. They crossed much of Dakota before turning back short of the River Platte because their native companions feared attack.[150]

Further south, war with Spain in 1719 led to the capture of East Texas and of Pensacola, the major Spanish base in West Florida, both to surprise attacks. Pensacola was recaptured by an expedition from Havana, before being taken again by the French and their local allies, the Choctaws. The Spaniards regained it at the subsequent peace, while an expeditionary force re-established their position in East Texas in 1721. This encouraged the French to look north from Louisiana. In 1719 Bénard de La Harpe reached modern Oklahoma in his search for native trade and a new route to New Mexico. Further north, interest in the

Missouri and the nearby lands led in 1719 to a treaty-making expedition that reached the Pawnee of southern Nebraska, and five years later to the establishment of Fort d'Orléans on the north bank of the Missouri near its confluence with the Mississippi. A mission westward from there reached the Padouca, possibly the Comanche, in modern central Kansas, in 1724, and found them willing to trade, but the initiative could not be sustained from distant Louisiana, a colony then in difficulties, and in 1728 Fort d'Orléans was abandoned. Eleven years later, a group of nine from New France led by Pierre Mallet crossed Kansas *en route* from the Missouri to Santa Fé. They opened up a precarious trade route, but that was unwelcome to the Spanish authorities.

In the West Indies the French sought to maintain their position, particularly on St Lucia and St Vincent.[151] British settlers were expelled from St Lucia by the Governor of Martinique in January 1723.[152] Far from being a passive responder to British initiatives, the stance of government and its agents led to complaints on the part of Britain, especially over St Lucia, as in 1730. Also in 1730, French warships seized British ships loading timber at the island of St Croix, in order to underline their claim to the island.

The French were dependent on native co-operation in North America. They traded extensively while their settlements relied on local allies, such as the Choctaws near Louisiana. Agreements and alliances, in turn, drew the French into local rivalries, for example supporting the Potawatomi against the Fox tribe of modern Illinois–Mississippi. A series of French–native attacks were launched against the Fox in 1712, 1715, 1716, 1728, 1730, 1731 and 1734. Governor Charles Beauharnais sought to exterminate the Fox. A heavy defeat was inflicted in 1730 and by 1738 the tribe, once 10,000 strong, numbered only a few hundred.[153]

In Louisiana, French territorial expansion was an issue. Fort Toulouse, founded on the Alabama River system in 1717 was designed to limit British expansion from the Carolinas, and the alliance with Britain did not prevent concern about British intentions towards Louisiana, specifically approaches to the native population and the provision of arms. The French competed to win native allies.[154] Similarly, the French and Spaniards competed among the Alabama and the Creek in the late 1710s. Further west, on the Mississippi, upstream from New Orleans, the Natchez initially accepted French trade and expansion and the French were able to establish a fortified trading base at Fort Rosalie (Natchez) in 1716. Nevertheless, in November 1729, a French land fraud led to a Natchez attack in which Fort Rosalie was destroyed and over 200 settlers killed. The Natchez did not receive the support of other tribes and in 1731 were crushed by the French and the Choctaws in a campaign of systematic extermination. The cost hit the colony's proprietor, the Company of the Indies, leading the Crown to resume control of Louisiana in 1731. The rising showed the weakness of the colony as it had been necessary to call in troops from France.[155] Fort Rosalie had been the centre of the tobacco industry, and its destruction greatly harmed attempts to develop economic links with France and the French West Indies. In the 1730s Maurepas supported the development of cotton production in the colony and also sought a revival in tobacco production in order to lessen imports from British North America.[156]

The war with the Natchez led to a spread of French commitments. Having been driven back by the Natchez in an attempt to reach the Arkansas country in 1731, the French established a garrison at Arkansas Post in 1732 in order to keep an eye on the Chickasaws. The remnants of the Natchez had taken refuge with the Chickasaws, rivals of the Choctaw who traded with the British. Their independence concerned the French who in 1736 launched attacks from New France and Louisiana. Both were ambushed and defeated. A large number of French captives were burnt to death. In 1739 a larger force was concentrated, again from both New France and Louisiana. Intimidated, the Chickasaw agreed a truce, but they remained aligned with the British, and in 1749 drove the French from their position at Arkansas Post.[157] The end result was both to place a very heavy financial burden on the government of Louisiana, and to show that the French could use the Ohio valley to move forces from New France to the Mississippi. They followed the route surveyed in 1729 by Chaussegros de Léry, chief engineer of New France.

Such campaigns were far from the concerns of most French policymakers. They were possible because France was not using all her resources in waging war in Europe in this period and, more specifically, as a result of at least acceptable relations with the other European naval powers, especially Britain. In 1735, when war was feared with Britain, the possibility of attacks on Québec and Louisiana was considered.[158] Conflict did not break out. This was to change in mid-century.

CHAPTER FOUR

The diplomatic revolution, its background and consequences, 1743–1774

French foreign policy in mid-century is generally discussed with reference to the 'Diplomatic Revolution', the diplomatic reversals that produced an alignment of Austria and France in 1756. This was indeed important, both then and to the course of French policy up to the outbreak of the French Revolutionary Wars in 1792. However, France's wider position was, if anything, more important. In the 1750s she lost the struggle for position as the leading European power in North America and India. This loss was to be challenged, most obviously with French intervention in the War of American Independence in 1778–83, when, in support of local powers, the French came close to overthrowing the British; but they never succeeded in destroying the lead seized by the British in the 1750s. Rather than treating the latter development as a separate issue to that of French foreign policy, this chapter seeks to discuss both, and to assess the relationship between European and global strategies.

The War of the Austrian Succession II, 1744–8

The broadening out of the conflict in 1744 did not immediately fulfil French expectations. The invasion attempt on Britain was defeated by bad weather, but it was a valuable testimony to the revival in French naval strength and the British had been pushed onto the defensive. The French also made important advances when they invaded the Austrian Netherlands in 1744. In May and June, Menin, Ypres and Furnes fell rapidly. The following year, 'Bonnie Prince Charlie', Charles Edward Stuart, the elder son of the Jacobite Pretender, was transported with French help to the west coast of Scotland. The ensuing Jacobite rising, the '45, greatly assisted the French in the Low Countries. British and British-subsidized troops had to be transported from the Austrian Netherlands to resist the Jacobites, and their failure to defeat the outnumbered prince in late 1745 ensured that they could not be sent back to the continent in time to fight the French at the beginning of the 1746 campaign.

As with the earlier death of the Emperor Charles VI in 1740, a major opportunity appeared to beckon. The prospect of a favourable result in a War of the British Succession led Louis XV to sign the Treaty of Fontainebleau with the Pretender on 24 October 1745. By it, Louis recognized him as King of Scotland, and promised to send military assistance and to recognize him as King of England as soon as this could be shown to be the wish of the nation. An expeditionary force, under the Duke of Richelieu, was prepared at Dunkirk, but delays in its preparation, poor weather, British control of the Channel, and news of the Jacobite retreat from Derby on 6 December 1745 led to its cancellation. Charles Edward was routed at Culloden on 27 April 1746.

This ended the best French chance to knock out one of their leading opponents until the Napoleonic invasion of Austria in 1805. Such opportunities were rare in *ancien régime* warfare, not because goals were limited, but because of the combination of the constraints of distance, and the nature of symmetrical warfare (fighting opponents with similar military systems). France herself benefited from this situation. Even when hard pressed, as in 1675, 1708 and 1792, her centres of power were not taken and no French government fell as a result of invasion until 1814, followed by 1815, 1870 and 1940.

In the 1740s the French had better success in the Low Countries than in Britain. British hopes that the Austrian Netherlands could serve as the base for an invasion of France were wrecked in 1745 when Marshal Saxe won the battle of Fontenoy (11 May) and captured much of the Austrian Netherlands. He was crowned with laurels at the Paris *Opéra* on 18 March 1746. Brussels, Antwerp, Mons, Charleroi and Namur fell in 1746. Saxe defeated his opponents at Roucoux (11 October 1746) and Lawfeldt (2 July 1747). The danger that the United Provinces would be overrun – in 1748 Saxe easily took Maastricht – helped to lead the British to negotiate for peace seriously.

Negotiations had been conducted for much of the war, but most of the powers had fought on, hopeful of success, fearful of the consequences of abandoning their allies, and distrustful of their enemies. In 1745 Charles VII's death broke the impasse in Germany. The Union of Frankfurt, a league of Charles VII, Louis XV, Frederick II, William of Hesse and the Elector Palatine, created in June 1744 and designed to secure Charles's interests,[1] had not shaken Austrian power. The French captured Freiburg, but did not co-operate with Frederick II in overrunning Bohemia. That December, Argenson, the foreign minister, had slapped down Chavigny's schemes for major French commitments and emphasized the need for peace.[2] French strategy became that of forcing Austria to peace.[3] However, Bavaria was overrun by the Austrians in April, and Maximilian Joseph, the new Elector of Bavaria, abandoned France and allied with Austria by the Treaty of Fussen of 22 April 1745.

Determined to exclude the house of Lorraine,[4] France supported Augustus III of Saxony for the vacant Imperial throne, but, on 14 September 1745, Maria

Theresa's husband was elected as Emperor Francis I. As Amelot had predicted in June 1743, an Austro–Bavarian settlement led to more Austrian military pressure in Italy, where the Franco-Spanish army was defeated at Piacenza on 6 June 1746. This weakened the Bourbons' negotiating position.[5] In 1745 Argenson had made secret approaches to Sardinia, leading to a preliminary treaty of 26 December 1745 and an armistice on 17 February 1746; but on 4 March 1746, dissatisfied with French moves, Charles Emmanuel repudiated both. The French had pressed the Spaniards unsuccessfully to accept his demands in north Italy.[6] The French also approached Austria via Saxony in late 1745. They demanded a northern Italian state for Don Philip, as well as gains for France in the Austrian Netherlands. The negotiations collapsed over the French terms for Don Philip.[7] Their failure, and the Austro-Prussian settlement in December 1745, further increased pressure on the French and their allies in Italy, as Argenson had feared.[8]

Saxe's successes in the Low Countries were not speedily translated into a political settlement, although the French made a number of peace initiatives during the war. An approach to Britain in the spring of 1745 was unsuccessful,[9] as was another in May 1746 in which the French proposed the neutrality of the Austrian Netherlands, the cession of Tuscany to Don Philip and the return of captured areas. Argenson rapidly followed up this approach to Britain with another to the Dutch, and in July with a proposal to Frederick II that he try to mediate. Puysieulx was sent to Breda to negotiate peace in a conference that began in October 1746, Argenson hoping that month that Saxe's successes would lead to that end.[10] However, Puysieulx complained that the opposing powers were not pacific and that success in Italy had strengthened their alliance.[11] This was important as French success in peace negotiations had depended on dividing their opponents. The conference was suspended the following spring while both sides awaited the fate of the summer's campaign. The failure of the negotiations helped lead to Argenson's fall on 10 January 1747. He was replaced by Puysieulx.

By late 1747 both Britain and France wanted peace. Despite the capture of Louisbourg in Canada from the French in 1745, the failure of the French expedition sent to regain it and to recapture Acadia in 1746,[12] and naval victories in 1747 (the two battles off Cape Finisterre), the British government was fearful of the consequences of French gains in the Low Countries. The French had invaded the United Provinces in April 1747, storming the major fortress of Bergen-op-Zoom on 16 September.

France, her foreign trade harmed by the British navy,[13] her economy hit by a poor harvest,[14] and her finances by the costly war,[15] was in a parlous state. It had not been easy to adapt to what was a different war, one that had to be fought at sea and in the colonies as well as on land. Government expenditure rose to 300 million *livres* in 1742 and 350 million in 1744, a sum that exceeded those of Austria and Britain combined. Austro-Sardinian forces with British naval support invaded Provence in November 1746, advancing on Toulon, as they had done in 1707; but they were pushed back the following January. Spain, from July 1746 under its new ruler, Ferdinand VI, no longer supported French schemes, despite promises to the contrary.[16] The Spaniards negotiated independently with the British in 1747. The French alliance system had thus collapsed whereas their opponents' alliance remained coherent, although not free from serious tensions.

The French were also concerned at the prospect of British-subsidized Russian intervention on the Rhine.[17] French hopes that Russia could be kept busy by Turkish and Persian commitments and that the Turks could be encouraged to attack Austria[18] proved abortive and the French government became increasingly conscious of Russian strength in Eastern Europe.[19] As a consequence, the French negotiated a defensive alliance with Sweden in 1747 and supported the negotiation of another between Sweden and Prussia in 1746.[20] A triple alliance of France, Sweden and Prussia was concluded at Stockholm on 29 May 1747. The Russians themselves were concerned about French attempts to organize opposition in Poland, the Baltic and Turkey.[21]

As at Utrecht in 1713, it was France and Britain that were responsible for both peace and its terms. The French had delivered terms to the British in August 1747 and negotiations continued under the pressure of French success in the Low Countries. The preliminaries of the Treaty of Aix-la-Chapelle were signed on 30 April and the definitive treaty on 18 October 1748. Aside from relatively minor territorial changes in Italy, including the establishment of Don Philip in Parma, the Pragmatic Sanction was renewed for the remaining Habsburg territories. France regained Louisbourg, and the British East India Company Madras, lost to a French force in September 1746. The disputed Canadian border was referred to commissioners. The French had to agree to recognize the Protestant succession in Britain and to expel Bonnie Prince Charlie. Having refused not to appear in public, the prince was arrested at the Paris *Opéra*.[22]

France made no territorial gains. In August 1745 the French had demanded Furnes and Ypres in a secret peace approach to the Austrians, and Nieuport and Tournai were added a month later, but in 1748, despite reports that France would gain Tournai and Ypres,[23] they agreed to restore the whole of the Austrian Netherlands. Suggestions that France should lose Alsace, Lorraine, Franche Comté, the Three Bishoprics, Roussillon and French Flanders[24] were fanciful.

Like all compromise peaces, that of Aix-la-Chapelle was heavily criticized. In France, there was condemnation of an inglorious peace that had failed to bring any gains.[25] The Earl of Sandwich, one of the British plenipotentiaries, was convinced that his French counterparts sought peace but that the French army had a different view.[26] Peace without conquests was necessary in order to persuade Austria and Britain to terms, and the notion of gaining a slice of the Austrian Netherlands no longer seemed of such value, a source of power and prestige, as had been the case 70 years earlier. Possibly, however, this was a mistake. The notion that the French Revolution could have been averted had victory been obtained in the Seven Years' War or in the Dutch Crisis of 1787, could be extended to the War of the Austrian Succession, for in 1745–8 France enjoyed a military position and a run of successes that was not to be matched or bettered until 1795–7.

She was in a position to make territorial demands, but, however desirable these might have been for domestic reasons, they would have had less happy international consequences, not least by helping to keep alive the hostile wartime opposing coalition. Having failed to recast Europe by partitioning the Habsburg inheritance or installing a client regime in Britain, the French had to work with a less welcoming European system and this was best exploited by not presenting French policy as dominated by territorial aggrandizement. The recent conflict had taught a generation of politicians the danger of leaping into the unknown, of exchanging diplomacy for war. Indeed, in a significant departure from recent policy, Louis Philoxen Brulart, Marquis of Puysieulx, foreign minister 1747–51, sought better relations with Britain and hoped that Anglo–French co-operation would ease tensions, whether in the Baltic[27] or North America, or more generally in Europe.[28] He wished both to defend his allies' interests and to maintain peace, a balance that was difficult to strike.[29] The British envoy argued that Puysieulx was easier to deal with than Maurepas and wrote that his role in negotiating the peace left him determined to maintain it.[30]

The aftermath: 1748–55

This approach was rebuffed by the British in favour of retaining and strengthening relations with Austria, and, after the War of the Austrian Succession, France found herself in a weaker diplomatic situation than she had been after the War of the Polish Succession. It was largely in a misleading hindsight that, in 1773, the Duke of Broglie was able to claim that France had gained in 1748 a brilliant and solid diplomatic position, not least by balancing Prussia and Austria and leaving France able to hold the balance.[31] In fact, although unwilling to accept British priorities, Austria was closer to Britain than to France, and, indeed, in 1748 Puysieulx was uncertain whether Austria would accept what was, like Utrecht, in effect a Anglo–French settlement.[32]

The absence of senior French diplomats in Austria, Britain and Russia at the start of 1749 handicapped French policymaking, and France had totally failed to secure Bavarian interests in the recent conflict. In July 1748 Puysieulx could only press on the Bavarians the need to adapt to circumstances.[33] He was angered, however, by their approach to Austria.[34] Despite French interest in 1750 in maintaining her alliance with Spain, and in co-operating with her to keep the peace in Italy,[35] in 1752 Austria, Sardinia and Spain settled their Italian differences without France.

The French government regarded its principal ally, Frederick the Great, as an unreliable maverick and pointed out that he had twice made peace without consulting France.[36] Having failed to overthrow Austria and Russia in 1741–2 and Britain in 1744–6, the French were left allied to Prussia, a weak, vulnerable and unreliable power, but could not for several years abandon the choice of 1741 and work, instead, at better relations with Austria.[37]

Frederick, in his turn, was very caustic about what he saw as a craven French failure to resist Anglo-Austrian plans in the Empire and the western Mediterranean.[38] He was envious of France's greater strength and frustrated by her policies. Frederick wanted France to be assertive to others and pliable to him. In 1752 he expressed concern over reports of cuts in the French army. Frederick sought to stir French fears, while the French, though promising help if he was attacked, encouraged him to caution and compromise.[39] The two clashed in 1751–2 over policy in Sweden.

Despite France's far from dominant position, she was faced by considerable suspicion, a legacy both of her role in causing war in 1733 and 1741 and of more general concern about her intentions. Puysieulx's successor, François-Dominique de Barbarie, Marquis de Saint-Contest, complained in December 1753 that ambitious views were being falsely ascribed to France by powers that indeed were making plans against her. The previous year, he had noted that the Austrians were making no attempt to bring France into any agreement to maintain the peace of Europe.[40]

In practice, French diplomatic plans were reactive, seeking, in particular, to thwart British initiatives in the Empire and the United Provinces, and to retain French influence elsewhere. In the event of another war with Britain it was important that the Low Countries should be as vulnerable as they had been in 1745–8. The support of Prussia would make them more so, by limiting Austrian assistance. Noailles told the Prussian envoy in January 1750 that Prussia and Sardinia had to be the curb on Austria and that France would be the principal support of the system.[41] The following month, Puysieulx told the British and Austrian envoys that France would come to the assistance of Sweden if she was attacked by Russia, and persuaded Frederick to adopt the same line. In the event of war, Puysieulx planned that the French should overrun the Austrian Netherlands: the best way to intimidate Russia's major ally. He also, however, tried to restrain his allies from taking excessive alarm.[42]

Nevertheless, while seeking to avoid giving automatic credence to fears about Austrian, British and Russian intentions, Puysieulx argued that Russian moves and British support for the Imperial succession scheme gave cause for concern. He was also aware that the Franco-Prussian alliance served to motivate hostile moves by other powers.[43]

In April 1750, Puysieulx sought to create a quadruple alliance with Denmark, Sweden and Prussia, and a league of German princes led by Frederick and subsidized by France. His conviction that a conflict in any part of Europe would rapidly become a general war led him to emphasize the value of a wide-ranging alliance system.[44] In the winter of 1750–51 France signed treaties with Württemberg and the Palatinate, and agreed to pay the subsidies promised by subsidy treaties that Frederick had signed with Brunswick–Wolfenbüttel, Mecklenburg, Bayreuth and Gotha. Puysieulx estimated that the treaties would cost France ten million *livres*.[45]

French diplomacy also ranged more widely. Differences between Denmark and Sweden were settled in 1749 and alliances signed with both in January 1754. There were hopes of alliances between Sweden and Turkey, and Prussia and Turkey, and the anti-Saxon party in Poland was encouraged. These steps were designed to prevent Sweden from becoming as dependent on Russia as Poland was,[46] and to limit Russia, both as a goal in its own right and because that would counteract the close relations between Britain and Russia. Neither Puysieulx nor Saint-Contest sought to use diplomacy to advance any conception of a French-dominated Europe. In December 1753 Saint-Contest cited relations with the Swiss Cantons as an example of the essential passivity of French policy and as an example for the Dutch.[47]

Domestic problems, particularly a crisis in relations with the *Parlement* of Paris, played a major role in French politics, and there was a degree of loss of confidence that is surprising in light of the victories of 1745–8. Always ready to adopt a critical view of his allies, Frederick thought Saint-Contest timid.[48] He was, however, informed by his envoy about French domestic and financial problems and saw them as affecting French policy.[49] French caution helped to restrain Frederick. The Palatine diplomat Wrede noted the belief that France was not in a shape to resist Austrian schemes in the Empire, but Palatine pressure led to French diplomatic support for the satisfaction of her claims as part of any agreement to elect Maria Theresa's eldest son, Joseph, as King of the Romans, heir to the empire,[50] a plan being actively pushed by the British in order to stabilize the Habsburg position in the Empire. The French also pressed the need for unanimity in any imperial election. In January 1753 Saint-Contest emphasized the need for co-operation with Prussia in order to thwart Austria, and suggested the revival of the 1741 system of alliance with Prussia and the Wittelsbachs.[51] French envoys were instructed to co-operate with their Prussian counterparts.[52]

However, the international situation was very different to that of 1741, with Britain, Russia, Sardinia and Spain now closer to Austria, while in France there was little enthusiasm for war. Saint-Contest was also well aware of the limitations of employing diplomatic leverage to settle international disputes,[53] difficulties that helped to block the British-backed Imperial election scheme. He sought to avoid an alarmist approach and had a perceptive grasp of realities. Thus Frederick was told that the British were unlikely to subsidize any Austro-Russian attack on Prussia,[54] no attempt was made to limit the authority of the House of Orange in the United Provinces,[55] and, in October 1753, Saint-Contest responded cautiously to reports from his envoy at The Hague that Britain and Austria would employ force to ensure the election of the King of the Romans. The following January, he was similarly dubious about the possibility of Austro-Russian action.

The French economy benefited from the return of peace. This was especially true of overseas trade. Insurance rates fell and trade resumed as British commerce raiding stopped. In 1749 large quantities of sugar and coffee from the French West Indies reached the great entrepôt of Hamburg,[56] where French trade had been hit very badly during the war and forced to rely on neutral shipping.[57] They continued strong into the 1750s.[58] French exports of luxury goods and wine also resumed. They were harmed by tariffs, although these could also be helpful, as with the replacement of Hungarian by French wine in Silesia as a consequence of Prussian moves against Austrian exports.[59] Trade with Canada and India recovered from wartime disruption.

Austro–French relations

The alliance between Austria and France negotiated in 1756 was less novel than might appear. There had been approaches for good relations over the previous 41 years, largely on the part of France. Aside from Louis XIV's initiative at the close of his reign, and co-operation early in that of Louis XV – not least at the expense of Philip V[60] – Fleury and Sinzendorf, the Austrian Chancellor, developed a good working relationship at the Congress of Soissons in 1728. This, however, led to nothing because the Austrian ministry preferred Prince Eugene's policy of alliance within the Empire and with Russia and Spain.[61]

Fleury and the Austrians co-operated from late 1735 until early 1741, and there had been a number of attempts, for example in December 1745, to settle the War of the Austrian Succession on the basis of an Austro–French understanding. From 1745 the Saxons had sought to create a Franco-Austrian alliance directed against Prussia. Dynastically linked to France by the marriage of the Dauphin to Augustus III's daughter, Maria Josepha, in February 1747, the Saxons sought to turn Louis XV against his Prussian ally, a policy that was to succeed eventually in 1756. Frederick II was worried about the possibility of an Austro-French alliance in September 1747.[62] There was also speculation about a marriage between Augustus III's second son and a daughter of Louis XV in order to improve the chances of the son being elected next ruler of Poland. Saxon talk of the need for a Catholic alliance helped to lead to Austro-French discussions in 1748, but Maria Theresa responded to French advances by making the unacceptable suggestion that Louis abandon Frederick.

The Franco-Prussian alliance was an insuperable barrier to an Austro-French understanding in 1748 and was to hinder efforts to improve relations made by Count Kaunitz when Austrian envoy in Paris in 1750–53.[63] On 21 October 1750, in his first audience with her, Hautefort was told by Maria Theresa that while she was not thinking of retaking Silesia for the present, she could not answer for the future.[64] He was told in 1752 that Prussian intrigues were having an excessive impact on French policy.[65] However, by 1753–4 the alliance was in a weaker state.[66] The varied discussions and negotiations in the decades prior to

1756 indicate the extent to which it is misleading to think of the events of that year as shattering a rigid system.

Indeed, in 1748 Richelieu suggested to Puysieulx that better Austro-French relations would not be too difficult to achieve, even though they would change the system of Europe 'absolument'. He furthermore traced a change in attitude in Vienna, where he had been envoy, to the years after the War of the Spanish Succession.[67] A similar fluidity can be traced in Franco-Russian relations, especially if attention is directed to the period of La Chétardie's embassy, but there were fewer signs of possible reconciliation than in the case of France and Austria.

In November 1753 Saint-Contest informed Aubeterre, the newly-appointed envoy at Vienna, that France would like better relations, but that Austrian actions had to correspond with their expression of good wishes, and that there was no reason to anticipate that they would.[68] The following January, Starhemberg arrived in Paris as the new Austrian envoy without any orders to negotiate an alliance with France.

Trans-oceanic competition with Britain

Despite signs of fluidity in the system, it remained in the same alignments until the chain of events that began in the Ohio valley in 1754 worked itself out. The British and French commissioners – to whom disputes over the Canadian frontier had been referred at Aix-la-Chapelle – had failed to settle them and, as the local agents of both powers jockeyed for advantage,[69] fighting broke out.

The Marquis de la Galissonière, interim Governor-General of New France in 1749–50, pressed for the containment of the British colonies. In 1749 the French had sent a small force into the Ohio Valley, but in 1752–4 they sent more troops, drove out British traders, intimidated Britain's native allies and constructed forts. Both sides were convinced that the other was stirring up native hostility and acting in a hostile fashion.[70] The fur trade interacted with native alliances and a dynamic French strategic policy.[71] The French were also active further north. Their presence north of Lake Superior was marked by the building of Fort-à-la-Carpe on the Albany River in 1751 and the taking of the Hudson Bay Company post of Henley House in 1755. This assertiveness was not simply directed against the British. The destruction of villages and crops forced the Chickasaws to terms in 1752. The French relied heavily on the Quapaws in their fighting with the Chickasaws.

In India, Dupleix, Governor at Pondicherry since 1742, followed an expansionist and interventionalist policy; becoming a player in the volatile situation created by the decline of Mughal power and in particular, the disputes over control of Hyderabad and the Carnatic. This entailed an interaction with Indian potentates in which the French, having proved their prowess, sought to profit from the situation while at the same time they served the purposes of Indian allies. This interpretation, which corresponds with much recent work on the rise of the British in India, can, however, as with the British, be counteracted with another view that stresses the alien character of French expansion and the discontinuities that it caused. This has implications for the perception of Dupleix. The former interpretation makes it easier to present his interventionist policies as an extension to France's coastal presence, while the latter view ensures that they are seen as a departure that was as potentially disruptive within India as they were to be costly to France. The eventual failure of the French intervention ensures that it is difficult to probe this question because the potential implications of Dupleix's policies were not realized, but the Carnatic could well have developed as Bengal rapidly did after the British intervention there is 1757.

In 1746 on the Adyar River, French *sepoys* (Indians trained to fight in a European fashion) defeated the cavalry and elephants of the Nawab of the Carnatic. The French were drawn into the politics of the largest state in southern India, Hyderabad, where a succession struggle had been in progress in 1748. The Nizam (ruler), Nazir Jang, a protégé of the British, was defeated and killed by a mixed French–local force in 1749, and Charles de Bussy became the key adviser of his successors, first Muzzafar Jang and then, more particularly, Salabat Jang, who owed much of their power to French assistance. A French protégé was recognized as the Nawab of the Carnatic, Dupleix was appointed as the Nizam's deputy of the lands south of the Krishna River, the revenues of the Carnatic were allocated to the French, as was control of the crucial trading post of Masulipatnam. Salabat further rewarded the French with the Northern Circars, territory along the coast near Masulipatnam.

Dupleix pressed on to fight the Marathas, defeat of whom he saw as a prelude to an expedition to replace the Nawab of Bengal by a pro-French ruler. On the night of 3–4 December 1751, Bussy led a surprise attack by 411 Frenchmen and the Hyderabadi forces that routed their army. However, Dupleix was wrong to expect a quick war. Instead, it proved difficult to obtain any lasting victory over the Marathas, the lengthy campaign exhausted Hyderabadi finances, and the French were unable to concentrate their own or their allies' forces to fight the British East India Company forces under Robert Clive that undermined the French position in the Carnatic. Dupleix's failure to regain Trichinopoly in 1753 and his demands for men and money led to his recall by the French Company in 1754 and a provisional peace was reached with the British that winter.[72]

In North America, it proved harder for both sides to disengage. Royal authority was more directly involved than in India where it was largely a case of the two East India Companies hiring out troops to rival Indians. In July 1754 a force of Virginia militia under George Washington dispatched to resist French moves in the Ohio Valley was forced to surrender at Fort Necessity. Far from making the British government cautious, as the French hoped, British counter-measures increased tension, and negotiations collapsed on the incompatibility of territorial demands.[73] The largely unsuccessful British attempt to intercept French reinforcements for Canada at sea on 10 June 1755[74] led the French government to order their envoys to leave London and Hanover.[75] Their foreign minister, Rouillé, claimed that the glory of the king, the dignity of the crown, and the protection that Louis XV owed to the life, honour and fortune of his subjects would not allow Louis to overlook the British action.[76] Furthermore, thanks to an influx of funds, the fleet had been built up since 1749. In the early 1750s the design and construction of warships greatly improved, as did naval ordnance production, while arsenals were revived and expanded.[77]

The Diplomatic Revolution

War was not declared until May 1756, but, in the meantime, both powers fought in North America and planned for a wider conflict. Seeking to protect Hanover and fearful of a French invasion of the Low Countries, the British turned to Austria and to Russia. The Austrians were unsympathetic, but closer Anglo-Russian relations in late 1755 led Frederick II, unimpressed anyway by French policy, to accept British proposals to guarantee their respective possessions. France could only offer Frederick the renewal of negotiations for alliances with Denmark and Turkey, neither of which were able to offer effective protection.

The resulting Convention of Westminster of 16 January 1756 – between Prussia and Britain – angered Austria and Russia, and helped drive France towards Austria. Despite Kaunitz's efforts, relations between the two powers had not greatly improved. On 10 August 1755 Starhemberg wrote to Kaunitz that he was certain France would attack Austria as part of the developing international crisis. Three days later, Aubeterre reported that if France attacked Hanover, Austria would act, adding that Maria Theresa would never abandon George II. On 14 September, Rouillé responded sceptically to Austrian assurances that they would not participate in the Anglo-French struggle, asserting that Austria would always depend on Britain, while on 24 September Aubeterre reiterated his view that Austria would never abandon Britain and would help her in the war.[78]

Alongside the formal Austrian approach, there was also private diplomacy: Kaunitz approached Louis through his influential mistress, Madame de Pompadour. Louis indeed was tempted by the idea of dividing Britain from her traditional ally. He also found Frederick an irritating and presumptuous ally. However, it was not clear that Austria would be more reliable, and in September 1755 Pompadour told Starhemberg that Louis and his ministry assumed that British aggression stemmed from their certainty of assistance from their allies.

The suspicion was changed by the Convention of Westminster. Knyphausen, the Prussian envoy in Paris, had warned Frederick in November 1755 that the French government was very worried by reports of Anglo-Prussian negotiations[79] and, indeed, the reports appeared to justify the Austrian claims that month that the Prussian alliance was not a natural one for France.[80]

Frederick did not appreciate the depth of the French reaction, and on 20 January 1756 he told the French envoy, the Duke of Nivernais, who had been sent to renew the Franco-Prussian treaty, that he was keen to do so. In fact, French anger led Louis's council to decide on 4 February not to renew the alliance with Prussia. Knyphausen found himself snubbed by formerly sympathetic ministers such as Belle Isle.[81]

The Convention of Westminster also angered the Austrians, and on 6 March Maria Theresa wrote to Starhemberg that she was ready to accept a French attack on Hanover for the sake of alliance with France. Such an attack was unwelcome, as a measure that might offend other German states, Denmark and Sweden, but the Austrians sought French diplomatic and financial support for war with Prussia. Military assistance was not the issue. The Austrians relied for that on Russia.[82]

On 1 May 1756 Austria and France signed a defensive alliance, known as the First Treaty of Versailles. It specifically excluded the Anglo-French conflict which had escalated on 18 April when French troops under Richelieu landed on the Mediterranean island of Minorca, which had been controlled by Britain since it was captured in 1708. After Admiral Byng failed to relieve the besieged and greatly outnumbered British garrison, it rapidly surrendered. The French declared war on Britain on 9 June.

Austria benefited most from the defensive agreement, because her position made her more vulnerable to attack than France, but France was freed for war with Britain, thus prefiguring the situation during the War of American Independence. She did not have to worry about attack from the Low Countries or northern Italy. The treaty additionally stipulated that, if a British ally should attack France, Austria would support her; but this was unlikely. France was not bound to support Austria in any offensive war to gain Silesia, but was obliged to provide 24,000 men or 288,000 German *gulden* if Prussia attacked Austria. The nature of the French commitment was to be expanded, but it is necessary to judge the First Treaty of Versailles on its own merits, and to appreciate that it was only those terms that the French had accepted at this stage.

The Seven Years' War, 1756–63

Frederick was aware that Austria and Russia were planning to attack. As a preemptive strike, designed to deny them a base, he invaded Saxony on 28 August 1756; Louis XV felt obliged to assist his heir's father-in-law, Augustus III of Saxony, and this added a powerful motive to French antipathy towards Frederick. The invasion of Saxony helped to precipitate an expansion of the Austro-French alliance and a Franco-Russian *rapprochement*. Employing Douglas Mackenzie, a Jacobite *émigré* protégé of the Prince of Conti, the French had already pressed the Russians in the spring of 1756 on the contradictory nature of British treaties with Prussia and Russia. Diplomatic relations between France and Russia, broken in

1747, were resumed, with Douglas named as chargé d'affaires. The First Treaty of Versailles was followed by Austrian efforts to improve relations between France and Russia. On 11 January 1757 Russia acceded to the Treaty of Versailles, although, by a secret convention, the French excepted conflict with Turkey from their obligations to help their new allies in case of war. The new French Ambassador, the Marquis de L'Hôpital, reached St Petersburg on 2 July 1757.

The outbreak of war in Germany gave the French the opportunity in 1757 of overrunning Hanover while acting as an auxiliary of the Empire against Frederick. The French also sought to stir up opposition to Prussia in Germany and Scandinavia. After the Franco-Bavarian Treaty of Compiègne of July 1756, by which Bavaria received subsidies, the Elector was offered more money in order to increase his army,[83] and Rouillé saw the need to improve French diplomatic representation in Germany.[84]

There were still tensions between the powers opposed to Prussia, including Austrian opposition in 1756 to French plans to attack Hanover, French unhappiness about Russian troops operating on Polish territory, and thus limiting Polish liberties, and Elizabeth's anger about France's unwillingness to drop her Turkish alliance. The Turks, however, responded to the new alignments by seeking an alliance with Prussia. Franco-Russian relations remained cool,[85] but, on 1 May 1757, an Austro-French offensive alliance directed against Prussia was negotiated in the Second Treaty of Versailles. France promised an army of 105,000 and a substantial subsidy. Austria was to regain Silesia and then to cede much of the Austrian Netherlands to Louis XV's son-in-law, Don Philip. Don Philip was to return Parma, which he had gained at the close of the War of the Austrian Succession, to Maria Theresa. Once Silesia was conquered, France was to gain Beaumont, Chimay, Furnes, Ostend, Nieuport and Ypres. These acquisitions would consolidate France's position on the North Sea and make it easier for her to threaten Britain and the Dutch. The French were allowed to occupy the ports of Ostend and Nieuport at once.[86]

The situation appeared favourable. The Electorate of Hanover was vulnerable, while initial defeat led Frederick — hopeful that the French still had some feeling for old allies — to seek peace via the Margrave of Bayreuth and France. He planned to send Mirabeau to France in order to bribe Pompadour with 500,000 écus. The French did not respond; and, instead, arguing that Louis XV was too faithful to his allies to negotiate separately, informed the Austrians.[87]

The two conflicts that France was engaged in did not merge. Although France fought Prussia, Austria and Russia never joined France in her war with Britain. As a result, the military and diplomatic histories of the two conflicts were separate, and they ended with different sets of negotiations. For France the major war was that with Britain. Although a French army advanced against Frederick in 1757, it was heavily defeated at Rossbach. The following year, the British moved troops into Germany and, thereafter, the French devoted their military efforts in Germany to the struggle with this force. France remained in occupation of Prussia's Rhenish possessions until the close of the war, but her limited military role ensured that the course of the Prussian war was a matter for Austria and Russia.

The situation was very different as far as Britain was concerned. French and British forces fought in Germany, North America, the West Indies, India and West Africa, and French invasion plans were only ended by British naval victories in 1759. The French were initially successful, capturing Minorca in 1756, as well as several North American forts in 1756–7, and overrunning Hanover in 1757. Richelieu forced the defeated Duke of Cumberland on 8 September 1757 to sign the Convention of Kloster-Zeven which dissolved his army, left Hanover under French occupation and exposed Prussia's western frontier.[88] The Convention, and the imperious manner in which French generals and diplomats proposed to employ their power in north-west Germany, would not have been inappropriate a half-century later, during the heyday of Napoleonic power.[89]

Thereafter, in the Seven Years' War, the fortune of war proved very much against France. By the end of 1760 she had lost Canada as Amherst's successful advance on Montreal finished the task triumphantly carried forward by Wolfe's victory outside Québec on 13 September 1759. On 7 September 1760 the greatly outnumbered French asked for terms, and on 9 September the British occupied Montreal. The British had also captured the French base in Bengal at Chandernagore (1757), the slaving base of Goree in West Africa (1758), and Guadeloupe in the West Indies (1759), while the French forces in Germany and India had been defeated at the battles of Minden (1 August 1759) and Wandewash (22 January 1760).[90] Minden weakened France's chance of acquiring a substantial bargaining counter to exchange for colonial losses in the eventual peace negotiations. Wandewash ruined French chances in India and left their surviving bases vulnerable to attack. Pondicherry, the principal base, surrendered on 15 January 1761. The French were unable to exploit Indian opposition to the British. Lally arrived at Pondicherry in April 1758, after the Nawab of Bengal had been defeated at Plassey by Clive. Lally's alienation of local rulers harmed the French war effort. Law of Lauriston co-operated with the Mughal Emperor Shah Alam but they were beaten by the British at Hilsa on 14 January 1761 and the Emperor soon signed a treaty with the British.

At the same time, the war placed a major burden on the French finances,[91] leading Bernis to argue in June 1758 that peace was necessary.[92] The French financial system lacked the institutional strength and stability of its British counterpart. Silhouette, the controller general of finances, was dismissed on 21 November 1759 at a time of general crisis in the government finances. Choiseul drew attention to the weak state of France's finances when urging Spain in October 1762 to accept peace.[93] Naval finance collapsed in 1759, leading to a failure to build ships and pay wages. It was therefore impossible to recover from the naval defeats of 1759 off Lagos (in Portugal, 18–19 August) and in Quiberon Bay (20 November).[94] The British capture of French seamen was also a major problem, as was the blockade that prevented the shipments of timber to the French dockyards.[95]

War set the pace for French diplomacy. Much of it became a matter of keeping the coalition together and influencing military planning. Defeats in late 1757 destroyed early enthusiasm, leading Bernis at the start of 1758 to see the alliance as a failure. These problems obliged the allies to consider new options. The French government sought, that spring, to persuade Austria to make peace with Prussia,[96] while Austria was determined to fight on, increasingly relied on Russia, and displayed limited interest in the French war. The French defeat at Krefeld on 23 June 1758 ensured that it would not be possible to send an expeditionary corps to help Austria.

The Austrians were irritated by tensions in Franco-Russian relations. Indeed in July 1758 Kaunitz suggested that France should negotiate a separate peace with Britain.[97] Bernis complained in August 1758 that Austria sought to use France only for her own ends, but he acknowledged the following month that France was in a difficult position when he worried that Austria would abandon France and turn to her enemies.[98] This was a repetition of fears expressed about Prussia in 1742. Sweden was seen as a weak ally requiring – rather than providing – help.[99]

Despite these problems, both Louis XV and Bernis emphasized their continued commitment to the Austrian alliance. The French agreed to send 100,000 troops to fight in Germany and to support the election of Joseph as King of the Romans (the scheme they had opposed when Britain had supported it), and the alliance was reaffirmed by the Third Treaty of Versailles, signed on 26 March 1759, but backdated to 31 December 1758. Russia acceded in March 1760.

Nevertheless, attitudes towards Russia remained distant, and in 1760 both Louis XV and Choiseul were concerned about Russian interest in territorial gains from Prussia. French defeats led to a renewed desire for peace. In 1759 Choiseul, who had replaced the exhausted and ineffective Bernis after the latter resigned in November 1758, planned both an invasion of Britain and a continental peace. This was to be achieved by Russian mediation of Austro-Prussian differences, that could be a preliminary to the Russian mediation of the Anglo-French struggle. His terms for the latter were the conditions for the Canadian frontier proposed in 1755 by Britain and a return of British colonial conquests.[100] It was too late, however, for such terms.

Choiseul's plan to use Russia to persuade Austria to abandon her hostility to peace negotiations was not based on any desire for a close alliance. Indeed, Choiseul, who had become the leading minister in 1758, argued in October 1759 that France and Russia were only allies by accident, that the alliance would not last, that Russian power in Scandinavia and Germany was to be feared, and that, owing to trade, Britain and Russia were natural allies. Choiseul was very opposed to Russia retaining conquered East Prussia in any peace settlement.

There were also attempts to widen the Austro-French alliance. Some led to a language that had not been heard for a long while, that of the need for Catholic unity. Britain and Prussia were presented as a Protestant league in Catholic countries such as Spain,[101] although Choiseul was hopeful in 1757 that the successful advance into Hanover would lead to France winning the alliance of two of her Protestant German allies, Brunswick and Hesse–Cassel. This, he felt, would lessen German suspicions about the Austro-French alliance.[102] Bavaria was offered subsidies in 1756.[103] Aside from trying to widen support, there were also attempts to prevent the loss of allied or neutral powers. In July 1757 France signed a neutrality agreement with Denmark. In 1760 French and Austrian promises of help over Holstein helped lead Denmark to reject a British attempt to obtain her backing for Prussia.

Other initiatives were more narrowly focused on the war, ensuring that supplies were obtained[104] or privateering helped. The course of the war affected such efforts,[105] and French envoys had to emphasize victories and create a sense of success. Envoys were instructed to ensure that negative press reports were contradicted and favourable ones inserted.[106]

The French were eventually successful at ending their maritime and colonial isolation. Ferdinand VI (r. 1746–59) had resisted French pressure to act and warnings that the Spanish colonies would follow those of France.[107] His attitude is a reminder of the dangers of adopting a schematic approach to international relations. Far from being driven to align with France by fear of British expansion or by dynastic links, Ferdinand VI was reasonably close to Britain.

Ferdinand's half-brother Charles III, formerly referred to in this study as Don Carlos, who became King of Spain in 1759, was concerned about a fundamental shift of oceanic power towards Britain. Charles III told the French envoy in November 1759 that he was convinced that Spain would be Britain's next victim and he suggested that the French overrun Hanover in order to make Britain more tractable about colonial gains.[108] His attitude both encouraged French firmness in abortive Anglo-French peace negotiations in 1761 and led to co-operation between France and Spain. Choiseul was a keen supporter of alliance with Spain, seeking both a Family Pact and an alliance that other non–Bourbon rulers could join.[109]

On 15 August 1761 the Third Family Compact and a Secret Convention were concluded. France committed herself to cede Minorca to Spain and to support her commercial and colonial disputes with Britain, and Spain promised to declare war by 1 May 1762 if peace had not been concluded.[110] Attacks on Gibraltar, Ireland and Jamaica were discussed, as was pressure on Portugal, a crucial and apparently vulnerable trading partner of Britain, in order to force her to cut her links with Britain, or to make conquests that could be exchanged at the subsequent peace. In the case of Spain and Portugal, France's European and global strategies were closely related. War in Portugal appeared a good idea because, as Choiseul pointed out, however many troops the British sent there, Spain would still enjoy a numerical superiority. Interest in cutting Anglo-Portuguese trade links was an aspect of a strategy that prefigured Napoleon's more sustained and systematic attempt with the Continental System to blockade

Britain. In 1761 the Spaniards also proposed Bourbon action to limit British trade with Livorno and Naples. Choiseul suggested that an attack on Rio de Janeiro should accompany one on Portugal.[111] He also wanted the outbreak of war with Spain to hit British chances of raising the funds necessary to sustain the war through 1762.[112] The French also approached Spain for a large loan, but they were told that Spain was not as wealthy as they believed.[113]

In 1773 Broglie was to claim that Spain's entry into the war had been burdensome to France,[114] but, at the time, it had seemed a diplomatic *coup*. War broke out in early January, but the Spaniards proved far worse prepared than they had assured the French. In the face of British successes against Spanish colonies and the failure of the Franco-Spanish invasion force to overcome Portugal, in August 1762 Choiseul decided that it would be good for Spain if peace could be negotiated, and that the moment had been lost for the conquest of Portugal.

The negotiation of peace

French foreign policy had to confront the problem of ending the war. This was a matter not only of terms and timing, but also of the impact of any negotiations and settlement on France's allies. The pace of negotiations picked up from late 1759 when Spanish mediation was sought.[115] Indeed, at that stage, the need for peace ensured that Choiseul saw Spain's potential entry into the war as more advantageous as a way of intimidating Britain than of helping France in any conflict.[116] He also emphasized the need for Louis XV to consider the internal situation of France. Starhemberg was told by Choiseul on 9 January 1760 that France could not afford to wage her wars on land and sea for another year, and was promised, in the event of peace with Britain, that subsidies to Austria would continue and that France would make her best efforts to obtain Silesia for her.[117] As France's allies were not at war with Britain, her government argued that unilateral negotiations were acceptable.

Choiseul was interested in settling France's conflict with Britain as well as that with Hanover and her allies Hesse–Cassel and Brunswick, and in separating them from the war with Prussia.[118] This willingness, communicated to the British in the spring of 1760, was made more necessary by the Austro-Russian Convention of St Petersburg of 21 April 1760 under which both powers pledged to fight on to obtain Silesia for Austria and East Prussia for Russia. Neither goal was welcome to France. The British, however, sought to include Prussia in the peace, leading Choiseul in August 1760 to decide not to pursue negotiations at The Hague. Frederick himself had made approaches to France in February, but the latter could not commit Austria or Russia. Choiseul was concerned that Britain wanted to divide France from her allies and herself to win the backing of Austria and Russia.[119] The latter two were not prepared to entrust their negotiating position to Choiseul; but that suited him because he was more concerned about relations with Britain and Spain.[120]

The pace of negotiation was stepped up on 31 May 1761 when François de Bussy, who had, earlier in his career as a diplomat and *premier commis*, acted as British agent 101, arrived in London. The French offered the cession of all of Canada bar Cape Breton Island, which was to be retained unfortified so that French fishermen could dry their catches from the valuable Newfoundland fishery. Minorca would be exchanged for Guadeloupe and Goree, the latter giving France a major role in the slave trade.[121] Pitt was unyielding and Choiseul complained that he failed to link the return of colonial conquests to that by France of conquests in Germany. Choiseul also felt it necessary to avoid any suggestion that France had to have peace. Although Pitt's harsh firmness played a role, the negotiations failed once France was certain of Spain. Choiseul wanted peace but the Spanish alliance made it easier to be firm over peace terms.[122]

Anglo-French discussions through Sardinian intermediaries subsequently revived as a reflection of the financial exhaustion of both powers, their desire for an end to the war and their unhappiness with their allies. They led to Preliminaries of Peace, signed at Fontainebleau on 3 November 1762, and confirmed by the Peace of Paris of 10 February 1763. France agreed to restore the territory of Britain's German allies with the exception of Prussia; to return Minorca and to recognize Britain's gains of Canada, Senegal, Grenada, Tobago, Dominica and St Vincent. Britain returned Guadeloupe, Martinique, St Lucia, Goree, Belle Ile and Pondicherry to France and left the French a part of the valuable Newfoundland fishery. Choiseul had proved adamant in the negotiations both on Newfoundland and on the West Indies. The British found him determined as far as possible to protect France's colonial interests. For example, the Earl of Bute noted, 'When Choiseul gives up Senegal and seems facile on Goree, it is with an express proviso that the French be put in possession of a sea port, on the slave coast, and consequently, that they must have some equivalent for the Gum trade'.[123]

France also had to bring a disappointed and defeated Spain into the peace. Choiseul was determined to maintain the alliance with Spain, and claimed to be ready to fight on if Spain wished to do so or if Britain refused to offer Spain acceptable terms.[124] In October 1762 the Spaniards were offered New Orléans and Louisiana west of the Mississippi by France as an inducement, and also advised to cede Florida in order to regain conquered Cuba.[125] Choiseul was angered by Spain's failure to hold onto Havana when it was attacked. The bulk of Louisiana for Spain was a return for Britain's refusal to accept the loss of Minorca. This proved the basis of the eventual settlement. With Florida, Britain gained Louisiana east of the Mississippi.

The territorial clauses reflected the decisiveness of the maritime and colonial struggle. There was no possibility of equivalence, as after the War of the Austrian Succession, when Madras could be seen as matching Louisbourg. These were the greatest losses hitherto experienced by France, far greater than those at Utrecht, and they helped to stamp the mark of failure on what could otherwise be seen as diplomatic successes: the alliances with Austria and Spain. The belated erection in 1763 of a statue in Paris to commemorate Louis XV's glorious role in the War of the Austrian Succession was greeted with derision.[126] A more painful loss was that suffered by the French population of Acadia (Nova Scotia), deported by the British as a security risk in 1755, to be followed, after its conquest, by the population of Île Royale, renamed Cape Breton Island. The population of Pondicherry was ordered to leave in 1761. The French in the St Lawrence Valley and Louisiana had to accept foreign rule. Chandernagore was totally destroyed by the British in 1757, as in 1761 was most of Pondicherry including the churches and the public buildings as well as the fortifications. The conquerors took the loot: pillars and other loot taken from Madras to Pondicherry in 1746 were returned in 1761 when it fell to the British.

War with Prussia was ended by the Treaty of Hubertusberg of 15 February 1763. This brought peace on the basis of the *status quo ante bellum*, a major humiliation for the Austro-French alliance. The failure to crush Prussia underscored the sense of humiliation felt in French army circles over failure at Rossbach. It also provided the backdrop for the developments to come. Prussia played a major role in the Partitions of Poland (1772–95) and the development of the 'Eastern Question', neither of which were welcome to the French government.

The alliance with Austria reviewed

Failure in the war helped to ensure that this diplomatic strategy was not thereafter seen as a success, although there had been criticisms even before the defeats of the Seven Years' War. On 31 January 1757 Starhemberg reported that French public opinion was strongly against Austria and the Austrian alliance,[127] and some French diplomats did not hesitate to criticize the direction of policy. Valory, who did so, also told the Prussian minister Podewils that he, Belle Isle and Nivernais had not been consulted. Choiseul voiced his concern to the Sardinian foreign minister, and even Bernis agreed with the Saxon envoy that France and Austria would clash.[128]

Policy was not set by the public, but the problems that affected the alliance with Austria during the war and concern about post-war developments led to consideration of new options both during the conflict and at its close. At the close of 1759 there was anxiety that the peace would entail a British-arranged reconciliation between Austria and Prussia that would destroy French influence in Germany and Scandinavia. Far from seeking a powerful Austria as a desirable part of the peace settlement, it was argued that Austrian policy might change under Joseph II, that – having destroyed Prussia – Austria could turn to Britain and against France, and that a strong Prussia would be useful in Germany and Italy. A continuation and widening of the Anglo-Bourbon maritime struggle would, it was feared, leave Austria overly powerful in Europe.[129] Belle Isle also argued against the destruction of Prussia.

These themes were to be repeated by French ministers and commentators for the remainder of the century. More particularly, they captured the ambivalence that increasingly affected France's war effort, and the extent to which the Diplomatic Revolution was not seen as a fixed part of the international firmament; indeed, it was specifically contrasted with the Family Compact that linked France and Spain.[130]

However, after the war successive French governments essentially maintained the alliance structure with which France had ended the war. Despite thoughts of turning to Britain, Prussia or Russia, there appeared no better alternative, not least because Frederick was distrusted and Britain seen as overly dominant at sea. Russian plans in Eastern Europe were regarded as hostile. As more generally with bilateral relations, the choice of alliance partners was not simply a matter of policy by and towards France. The improvement in Austro-Spanish relations from 1752 was also very important in helping maintain good relations between France and both Austria and Spain.

This system was not to survive the Revolution, but it is worth noting, as an important aspect of the frequently overlooked successes of the *ancien régime* monarchy. France's influence over her allies, especially Austria, was limited, but she was neither isolated nor essentially reliant on the second-rate and vulnerable, as had been the case for much of the period 1674–1756. British hopes that the Austro-French alliance would disintegrate proved misplaced and, whatever the tensions between the two powers, Austria was unwilling to co-operate with Britain against France until the era of the French Revolution. Diplomatically, France was better prepared to confront Britain; and the absence of continental distractions during the War of American Independence, in which France participated in 1778–83, was an aspect of the success of the Diplomatic Revolution.

Tension with Britain, 1763–74

There was considerable concern in Paris about the policies of Russia and, to a lesser extent, Austria and Prussia in Eastern Europe. This led to occasional suggestions about co-operation between Britain and France, but they were less important than the continued reality of distrust and competition. There was no equivalent to Puysieulx's attempts to improve relations, and France's position was greatly assisted by the continuation of her alliance with Spain, again a contrast to the situation from 1748. Although there were differences, Franco-Spanish relations were largely harmonious and the Spanish foreign minister, Grimaldi, maintained close links with Choiseul.

In both Britain and France it was assumed that the Peace of Paris would not last. Choiseul had begun considering a future war with Britain even before the close of the Seven Years' War.[131] In April 1763 the French began to gather information that might help in an invasion.[132] Choiseul dominated foreign policy in the 1760s, although in 1761–6 it was his cousin, the Duke of Choiseul-Praslin, who was foreign minister, while Choiseul himself was minister of the marine. Choiseul was determined to prepare for a war of revenge, and for him naval reconstruction and diplomacy were both sides of the same coin. Thus, while his cousin was foreign minister, Choiseul remained responsible for relations with Spain, the essential ally in any future struggle with Britain.[133] In the Seven Years' War, the British had benefited greatly from defeating the French navy and capturing many of her colonies before Spain entered the war. Spain's help in any future war was even more necessary because of France's recent colonial losses.

Whereas the Spanish colonies were to a great extent able to sustain their defence from their own resources, the French lacked this capability. This had been true even before the loss of Canada. The warships launched there between 1729 and 1759 were far less numerous and effective than those launched by the Spaniards in Havana.[134] The colonies also depended on troops from France. The situation was even more difficult after 1763, not least as many of the remaining French colonies first had to recover from British occupation.

The British used intimidatory gunboat diplomacy in 1764–5 to defend their position successfully in colonial disputes in West Africa and the West Indies,[135] and Choiseul warned the Spaniards in March 1766 that France could not provide the necessary support for a successful war against Britain for another three years. The French were more successful in thwarting British hostility to their annexation of Corsica in 1768. Charles Emmanuel III of Sardinia had long tried to stir up the British to oppose this step, but Choiseul's decisive actions pre-empted effective opposition.[136]

Two years later, France came to the brink of war, in large part as a consequence of her alliance system. Britain threatened war when Spain expelled a settlement from the Falklands, which was seen as a staging post to the Pacific, an area of Spanish commercial monopoly that the British were increasingly keen to penetrate. Concerned about Russian strength in Eastern Europe, Choiseul initially tried to negotiate a settlement to the dispute, and pressed Spain to moderate her position, but, by the start of December 1770, he saw war both as inevitable and as likely to consolidate his domestic position. Choiseul also felt that a firm stance was likely to secure Bourbon goals and, to that end, he sought to match British naval preparations. Louis XV's unwillingness to fight defused the crisis. Choiseul and his cousin were dismissed on 24 December 1770. Louis thus resolved both the international crisis and the divisions within his ministry. Charles III was notified that France needed peace.[137] This persuaded Spain to reach an agreement with Britain, and also strained relations between France and Spain.[138]

France and Eastern Europe

The Duke of Aiguillon, Choiseul's successor as foreign minister, 1771–4, was primarily interested not in the colonial world, but in shifts within Europe. This represented a continuation of Choiseul's policy from his return to the Foreign Ministry in 1766, and a development of the earlier *Secret du Roi*. This secret diplomacy of Louis XV began in the mid-1740s, with support for a plan that his cousin, the Prince of Conti – grandson of the Conti elected King of Poland in 1697 – become the next king of Poland. Conti was approached in Paris in 1745 by an emissary sent by several leading Poles who did not want the Saxon presence in Poland maintained after the next royal election. Louis XV accepted Conti's request for financial and political support, but also kept the foreign minister and the Council in the dark. Although this owed something to the Polish demand for secrecy, it also reflected a somewhat feline strain in Louis's character.

Conti discovered from the French envoy in St Petersburg that the Russians would not support a French candidate, and he therefore helped to give an additional strand to the anti-Russian character of French foreign policy. Conti's scheme broadened out into a wish to recreate a powerful alliance of Poland, Sweden and Turkey, that could serve French interests against Austria and, especially, Russia, which was seen in France as a disruptive alien force in Europe. Prussia was regarded as an important addition to the alliance. Conti's focus was on Poland and he expected this to be the objective of French policy in Central and Eastern Europe, but, there was an inherent clash with other, wider views of France's interests.[139]

The *Secret du Roi* had to be suspended during the Seven Years' War, when France's supporters in Poland became understandably disillusioned by her willingness to accept Russian pretensions there,[140] while French diplomats who were members of the *Secret* were outraged by the 1757 alliance with Russia. However, the *Secret* was to be revived after the war.

The *Secret du Roi* interacted with a more generalized concern about European international developments that focused in particular on Russia. The sources of this were various and sometimes poorly-formulated, but included a sense of specific concern about France's allies, especially Poland, and a more general unwillingness to accept change, because change appeared to be leading to a more disruptive and hostile environment. The focus of anxiety on Russia was also an aspect of the sense of Eastern Europe as primitive that characterized much Western thought. The Russians appeared as the latest wave of barbarian invaders.

Even during the Seven Years' War, the French had sought to protect their allies from excessive Russian pressure. Thus, in 1756 Rouillé had urged Russia not to intervene in Swedish domestic affairs[141] and had emphasized continued French concern for Poland.[142] Tsarina Elisabeth died in January 1762 and the succession by the pro-Prussian Peter III severed links with France. Peter was replaced by Catherine II – the Great – in July 1762, but Louis XV did not seek to resume the confidential correspondence he had had with Elisabeth.

Policy toward Russia reflected the general direction of French diplomacy. It focused not on developing alliances that could be used against powers with which she was – or was likely to be – at war, but, rather, on creating an alliance system that would bring stability to the Continent and, specifically, counter Russian power. Thus, instead of seeking Eastern European support against the Habsburgs, as she had done prior to 1756, French diplomacy was designed to maintain a static territorial system in Eastern Europe, one that would complement the *status quo* that her alliances with Austria and Spain had brought to the Low Countries, the Rhineland and Italy. A defensive and reactive character to French policy became more marked after 1763, although it was apparent from 1748 and, already in 1756, entry into the European sphere of the Seven Years' War had been in response to an act of aggression.

Financial problems affected the French government. The Seven Years' War had been paid for by borrowing and this left the government with a substantial debt and a recurrent annual deficit. The financial situation both hindered Choiseul's attempt to build up the navy and encouraged Terray, controller-general from December 1769, to favour conciliation in the Falklands dispute.[143]

Attitudes to foreign policy

French policy can also, in part, be related to a climate of thought, specifically the attempts of certain prominent French intellectuals to advocate an international order based on morality and reason; although many were suspicious of the intentions and conduct both of international diplomacy and of French foreign policy, believing them to be manipulative, dishonest and aggressive. In common with natural law theorists, French writers on the subject had little understanding of dynamic elements in international relations, the scope of change and the attempt by certain powerful rulers to match diplomatic developments to their growing power.[144] One of the leading writers, Montesquieu, who regarded war as unnatural and the product of monarchical rule, has been seen as displaying 'a fearful resistance to change'.[145] Most French writers who discussed international relations sought peace.[146]

Just as many natural law theorists came from the federal states of the Empire and the United Provinces, with their stress on legal relationships, and their – in most cases – only limited interest in aggression,[147] so the French writers came from a power that had largely ceased to seek European territorial gains. Their arguments and tone were very different from those of the writers who had applauded Louis XIV's attack on the Dutch in 1672.[148]

The bold and acquisitive aspirations and aggressive methods that had characterized French policy in 1741 were not repeated during the *ancien régime*. In 1752 Hautefort, the envoy in Vienna, stated that 'the maintenance of the peace of Europe' was Louis XV's principal object.[149] In 1745 Argenson had proposed a federation of independent Italian states, a departure from traditional schemes for Valois and Bourbon dynastic aggrandizement. He suggested that Charles Emmanuel become king of Lombardy and ruler of the federation.[150]

Argenson's argument that the Bourbons should exploit the desire of the Italian rulers for liberty against the excessive and tyrannical power of Austria, was countered by Philip V with the claim that the league was impossible or would take many years to negotiate, that it would depend on Bourbon armed support, that any league required a number of near-equal powers which Sardinian power prevented, and that Charles Emmanuel would despoil, not help, Don Philip and other Italian rulers.[151] The French faced the problem that talk of the liberties of Germany or Italy was difficult to separate from the particular interests of Bavaria, Prussia and Sardinia. Furthermore, alliances led to dangerous and excessive commitments. Amelot suggested in February 1743 that any alliance with Sardinia would require a basis of the conquest of all Italy, as only thus would it be possible to reconcile Spanish and Sardinian interests. He noted that this would entail a lengthy war, as Maria Theresa would never accept the loss of all her Italian territories. The Queen of Spain, however, believed it necessary to plan for such an outcome.[152]

The years after the War of the Austrian Succession saw an increase in French emphasis on their pacific intentions and on the opposition to any change in the European system. Justifiably, Louis XV was not seen as a warmonger. Indeed, one diplomat reported in September 1749, 'I am assured at the Council Table with his ministers, he employs himself in writing the names of the dogs he will hunt with the next day'.[153] After 1748, liberties were construed by the French government not (as they had been from 1741) as being incitements for change – against, in particular Habsburg strength and Russian hegemony – but, rather, as part of the existing situation potentially threatened by Austria and Russia. Puysieulx was especially keen on a politics of peace and stability. In 1748 he presented France as Genoa's essential protection against Sardinian expansionism.[154] In November 1750 Puysieulx argued that if Maria Theresa and her allies only sought peace they could count on the backing of France, which, he claimed, was always ready to act against any power that sought to trouble it. If, on the contrary, they had other views, France would block them.[155] In 1751 Puysieulx proposed a French-supported Electoral league of Prussia, Cologne and the Palatinate to maintain the German constitution and to support the case for unanimity in the imperial election. This was a development from France's position as a co-guarantor of the Treaty of Westphalia of 1648 and from proposals advanced over recent decades, for example by Chavigny in 1744, for a league modelled on that of the Rhine.[156]

Opposed to aggressive hegemony on land, French ministers and diplomats also presented their naval and commercial policy as determined by the necessity to put just limits on what Bernis saw in 1758 as the imperial power which Britain wished to exercise on all seas and over all trading powers, a theme repeated by Choiseul in February 1760, and, again, in 1761.[157] In March 1755 Rouillé had argued that Britain sought to destroy the balance of power in the New World,[158] but such arguments were employed to justify an essentially defensive policy, rather than as a prelude to aggression. In November 1759 Choiseul proposed a Spanish-headed maritime association to resist British claims to a right to search at sea, although he was aware that the Swedes, Danes and Dutch were not then in any shape to provide much help.[159]

Once the war had ended, a more aggressive note was sounded and the call for a colonial and maritime balance was employed in order to justify plans for action against Britain.[160] Cutting Britain down to size was seen as a prelude to France taking her rightful place in Europe: the British would be unable to support her opponents.

The image of French policy was not simply presented in re-active and defensive terms, although those were emphasized when the support of other powers was sought. The notion of the king as general arbiter and sovereign protector of 'la tranquilité et liberté publique', to quote a senior French diplomat of 1751,[161] was a notion in which *gloire*, power and this re-active element were all fused, and in which there was no attempt to disguise that the definition of what was acceptable was largely a matter of French choice.

The positive interpretation of French power lent itself to different arguments, although they shared the habit of extending the range of French influence beyond what could be realistically assumed in terms of conventional power politics. The Marquis de Mirabeau, a leading physiocrat, argued in *L'ami des hommes, ou traité de la population* (Avignon, 1757) that the king of France should lead the rest of Europe towards a peaceful and prosperous new economic order of mutual benefit. French ministers expressed similar views to the *philosophes*, Rouillé, for example, differentiating in 1756 between the 'grands principes de la politique' and 'la finesse et l'artifice'.[162]

The French had already abandoned their support for Jacobitism, a policy that – as they knew – had caused unease in Protestant Europe.[163] Such support, with its emphasis on Catholicism and legitimism, seemed anachronistic. Prefiguring the views of the Revolutionaries, Rouillé had argued in 1755 and 1756 that it was only the British 'peuples' who could effect a change in their government.[164] Under the stress of war, invasion had, indeed, been planned in 1759, and was to be again in 1779, but there was no longer any serious commitment to the Stuarts.

D'Aiguillon set out deliberately to make concessions in colonial disputes with Britain, in order to improve French effectiveness in Europe, and in March 1772 he proposed concerted pressure on Austria and Russia in order to dissuade them from partitioning Poland. George III, however, responded coolly, and, when the French-backed Gustavus III staged a *coup* to strengthen monarchical authority in Sweden in August 1772, seizing power from a ministry inclined to Britain and Sweden, suspicion of France increased in Britain.

It was easy for observers to suggest that Britain and France might be able to negotiate an understanding, based on France agreeing not to offend Britain in commercial and maritime matters, but British ministerial suspicion of France remained strong; and, although the British government was concerned about the policies of the partitioning powers, it had no wish to allow France to commit Britain to opposition to them. However poor British relations with the partitioning powers might be, it was more reasonable to hope that they could be improved than that a successful Anglo-French alliance could be created. These attitudes led the British to use threats in 1773 to dissuade the French from deploying their navy against Russia in the Baltic and Mediterranean. Nevertheless, conflict was avoided, as both powers sought peace, both because of their domestic problems, and because they saw no reason to fight.[165]

France and Russia

France, therefore, lacked any effective response to the First Partition of Poland in 1772. It represented a major blow for French assumptions in Eastern Europe, because the French had sought a strong Poland and a strong Turkey as a bar to Russian expansion. In 1762 Louis XV had noted that Poland was the leading object of the *Secret*.[166] The following year, Châtelet, the envoy in Vienna, had expressed concern about what he saw as the despotic intentions of Russia in Poland. France and Austria had discussed joint action to prevent Russia from choosing a pliant successor to Augustus III, and, instead, to support Prince Xavier of Saxony. However, in 1763–4, they proved less determined than Russia and Prussia and were divided over their policy in Poland.[167] The French failed to stir up Turkish opposition, while French policy itself was harmed by Louis XV's irresolution and by differences over which candidate to support. Agents of the *Secret* criticized Praslin's caution, but he was clear that France could not act alone and that powers nearer to Poland had to play the leading role in opposing Russia. The British government made it clear it would not help.[168]

Allied to Frederick, Catherine II was able to impose Stanislaus Poniatowski as the new King of Poland in 1764 (election, 7 September). His secret diplomacy in ruins, Louis was reduced to the impotent responses of refusing to recognize him until December 1765 and of rejecting his request for the hand of the Princess of Orléans,[169] despite the advice of Broglie, the French envoy, that this would help develop French influence.[170] Panin, Catherine's leading adviser on foreign policy, had been bitterly opposed to France while envoy in first Denmark and then Sweden, in 1747–60.[171]

The French became more active later in the decade. Choiseul pursued a markedly anti-Russian policy from April 1766, when he became foreign minister for the second time. He was helped by Turkish disenchantment with Frederick after the Russo-Prussian treaty. Choiseul had Vergennes, whom he saw as insufficiently bellicose, recalled in April 1768, and encouraged Turkey to respond to growing Russian pressure on Poland by declaring war in October 1768.[172]

The French then sought to use the Polish situation to help the Turks. French agents were sent to the anti-Russian Confederation of Bar, Taulès going in 1768. Worried by Russian successes against the Turks, in August 1770 Choiseul chose General Dumouriez as an agent charged with creating a Polish Confederate Army that would, with French help, be able to resist Russia. He was disappointed to find the Confederates divided, badly armed and disciplined, and less numerous than he had hoped,[173] but French plans lent force to the Russian desire to regain control of Poland. Choiseul also tried to revive the policy of the *barrière de l'est* in Sweden. The Count of Modène was sent as ambassador and at the close of 1768 successfully encouraged King Adolf Frederick to limit Anglo-Russian influence in Swedish politics.

Russia recovered control of Poland in 1772 by means of the First Partition, a step that revealed the weakness of the Austro-French alliance. Maria Theresa had opposed the idea of a partition, but the danger that Prussia and Russia might make gains without an Austrian equivalent led to a change of heart, much to the fury of the French. All three powers took a large slice of Poland: D'Aiguillon told Mercy, Austrian envoy in Paris, that the defensive provisions of the Austro-French alliance could not extend to these new gains, while Mercy's counterpart, Rohan, and his government complained about the Austrian failure to consult France.[174]

Anger about the state of the alliance was fuelled by fear concerning the possible consequences of the partition. There was no reconciliation with Russia.[175] In 1773 the Duke of Broglie, then the director of the *Secret du Roi*, a self-confident and difficult aristocrat, warned Louis XV that the consequences of the new alliance would not be limited to the humbling of Poland and Turkey. He warned that Gustavus III of Sweden might be dethroned, Germany brought under Austro-Prussian control, Italy under that of Austria, and all of Europe subject to the influence of the three partitioning powers.[176]

Such fears were exaggerated, not least because the powers rapidly fell out, while, anyway, the use of strength to gain territory without consideration of even tenuous legal claims was not new. However, for the French government, the First Partition was a particular shock because it both represented and underlined the failure of its diplomacy, although some influential intellectuals, such as Diderot and Voltaire, supported the step because they regarded Poland as a less enlightened state than her aggressors. Harnessing the resources and obtaining the backing of the Eastern European states had long been a major theme for their Western European counterparts, particularly after the Austrian defeat of the Turks in the 1680s and the new-found Russian dynamism of the 1690s. In 1756 France appeared to win this struggle, displacing Britain from her Austrian alliance and, through that, acquiring links with Russia that were stronger than those enjoyed by Britain.

Indeed, whereas France had been allied to the weaker 'side' in Central and Eastern Europe from 1742, from 1756 this was, instead, true of Britain. The course of the Seven Years' War had not fulfilled French expectations, but she had exited it in a relatively propitious diplomatic situation, a position encouraged by a more cautious British attitude towards continental interventionism from 1761. After the collapse of the Anglo-Prussian alliance in 1762, it was France, alone, among the powers of Western Europe that had a powerful ally further east.

Choiseul regarded the death of Tsarina Elizabeth that year, and the succession of the pro-Prussian Peter III, as a vindication of the decision to ally with Spain.[177] Austria also was still an ally, although Choiseul feared that her ambitious schemes might bring her into conflict with the Bourbons.[178] Britain had no such option when her alliance with Prussia collapsed the same year. Furthermore, the lessening of tensions in Italy made it possible for France to maintain alliances with both Austria and Spain. Charles III was keen to improve relations with Austria,[179] Choiseul to consolidate a system of Austria, France and Spain.[180]

Mid-eighteenth-century French policy reassessed

It may therefore appear paradoxical that France should be seen by 1774 as having failed: Poland was partitioned, the Turks had been forced by the Russians to accept substantial losses, Austria was clearly not following the French lead, France had no powerful alliance system within the Empire, and approaches to Britain had proved abortive. Yet, in part, this is a matter of perspective and expectations. The degree to which it was realistic to assume that any Western European power could greatly affect developments further east is unclear, but the events of the period 1680–1735 scarcely suggested that their influence would be considerable, unless they had a powerful ally willing to co-operate. This was especially true in wartime. In peace it was possible to have a greater impact, not least if local enmities were finely balanced, but it was difficult to create or maintain such a balance.

The basis of any balance shifted in the eighteenth century. As late as the close of the 1760s it seemed reasonable to hope that Sweden, Poland and Turkey could counteract Russia and Austria, or be part of a system that might achieve such a counteracting. However, such a notion was increasingly supplemented, and, in time, supplanted, by the idea that Prussia or Austria could counteract Russia. Both strategies collapsed in the early 1770s: Turkey and Poland were greatly weakened, to an extent that raises doubts about the wisdom of Choiseul's policies in the late 1760s, while Austria chose to join Prussia and Russia.

These were failures for France, but it is far from clear what she could have done. When Broglie pointed out in 1773 that it was difficult for France to assist the Turks, this was not so much because of the Austrian alliance that he criticized,[181] as because of the inherent problems of intervening successfully in the Balkans. Louis XV frequently stressed the difficulties of helping Poland.[182] Broglie wanted a new alliance with Prussia, but that would have had only a limited impact on the Austro-Russian alignment, and Frederick, anyway, was not willing to accept French views. In many respects the situation repeated that of the mid- and late 1710s with France unable to help Eastern European powers and faced in

Italy and the Empire[183] by a powerful Austria. However, the Seven Years' War had left France with a deep sense of humiliation on land and sea. Memoirs of the period show that this sense was deeply felt in French ruling circles. Revenge on Britain was a major motive in the policies of both Choiseul and Vergennes.

The French government was largely involved in domestic issues, the dispute with the *parlements* that culminated in the 'Maupeou Revolution': a serious clash with the *Parlement* of Paris and the refusal of the latter to yield to Louis's wishes led to the exile of the *parlementaires* and the remodelling of the *parlements*. These political difficulties interacted with, and exacerbated, fiscal problems and encouraged peace. D'Aiguillon wanted to prevent any further growth in Russian strength, but he was also more cautious than Choiseul. This helped the finances. Though Terray undertook a partial bankruptcy in 1770 and failed to balance the budget, in 1771–4 he increased revenues by about 40 million *livres*, cut the deficit and halved the anticipations of future income, establishing a policy of ministerial control over spending that prevailed until 1781.[184]

Furthermore, it is important not to overlook the strengths in her position in 1763–74. France was the most powerful state in Western Europe, and did not need to fight to display or maintain this position. Unlike in the mid-1710s, when the Bourbons had neither territory nor power in Italy, the peninsula now remained under the control of the Bourbons, firmly established in Naples, Sicily and Parma, and the Habsburgs. This effectively kept Italy stable and left the kingdom of Sardinia, Britain's wartime ally for much of the previous 80 years, with little role in international diplomacy. Charles Emmanuel III complained in 1756 that the Austro-French alliance had left him in a 'disagreeable situation'.[185] Two years later, the French envoy in Turin was convinced that Charles Emmanuel was pro-British and only restrained from showing it by fear of Austria and France.[186] In 1762 Choiseul regarded the alliance with Austria as a protection against hostility on the part of Sardinia.[187] A centre of French influence, Parma was protected from Sardinian expansionism.[188]

In 1746 Argenson stated that France did not seek aggrandizement.[189] The abandonment of earlier traditions of French eastward expansion, with their concomitant of an anti-Habsburg alliance system within the Empire, was a necessary cause and consequence of the alliance with Austria. It kept the Low Countries, the Rhineland and the western parts of the Empire peaceful, and ensured that they could not be used as bases from which to attack France. Indeed, France's territorial position improved when she absorbed Lorraine, on the death of Stanislaus Leszczynski in 1766, and purchased and annexed Corsica in 1768–9, a step Choiseul had advocated in 1761.[190] There was, however, no longer any interest in gaining Savoy, as in 1725 and 1732 when it had been proposed to compensate the kingdom of Sardinia in the Milanese,[191] or in acquiring Luxembourg, as in the 1710s, 1720s and 1731, or in dividing the Austrian Netherlands with the Dutch, as had been suggested in 1724.[192] In 1761 Choiseul wrote to Charles III of Spain that it would be helpful for the other branches of the House of Bourbon if his brother, and Louis XV's son-in-law,

Don Philip, gained Luxembourg and Namur, but he proposed to achieve this by means of a negotiated exchange for Philip's Italian possessions, not by war with Austria. Charles III, however, opposed the scheme.[193]

Frontier treaties based on stabilization and equity, rather than aggrandizement and force, were negotiated with her neighbours. In 1750 Louis XV ordered Belle Isle to settle amicably all the disputes over the frontier between Lorraine and the Empire. In 1749 frontier differences with Geneva were resolved by a treaty, with subsequent delimitation agreements in 1752 and 1763. The Convention of Paris of 1718 had left several issues outstanding on the border with Savoy–Piedmont. Negotiations in the late 1750s, culminating in the Treaty of Turin of 1760, marked a major step forward. The French also reached settlements with the Austrian Netherlands (1738, 1769, 1779), the Prince of Salm (1751), the Duke of Württemberg (1752, 1786), Prussia (over Neuchâtel, 1765), the Bishop of Liège (1767, 1772, 1773, 1778), the Prince of Nassau-Saarbrücken (1760), the Duke of Zweibrücken (1766, 1783, 1786), the Canton of Berne (1774), the Elector of Trier (1778), the Prince of Nassau-Weilburg (1776) and the Bishop of Basle (1779, 1785). Long-standing disagreements were settled. The 1769 agreement with the Austrian Netherlands brought to an end a dispute over the Abbey of St Hubert that had lasted since the reign of Louis XIV.

These border treaties were designed to establish a permanent peace as well as to settle disputes. Although the right of the strongest had played a major role in the fixing of frontiers, an entirely different principle had also appeared, that of strict equality between the parties, whatever their respective power, both in the course of the negotiations and in the final agreement.[194] New attitudes towards aggrandizement and frontiers were reflected by the envoy in Berlin in January 1789. He scorned the idea that Louis XVI should wish to gain Geneva, the traditional intellectual core of Calvinism, and argued that if Geneva ceased to be free it would cease to have any particular value.[195]

Expectations of French achievement rose precisely because there were no major conflicts in these regions: no government came to the aid of the Corsicans resisting integration with France. The easy gains achieved by Louis XIV at the expense of Strasbourg and Genoa were not repeated, but this was not a sign of failure. First, it is unclear how far they would have impressed domestic opinion. Secondly, the very avoidance of such action helped to consolidate French influence in Western Europe. This was true not only of Austria and Spain, but also of lesser powers.

The increased strains in Anglo-Dutch relations were one major gain. The two powers had been linked in wartime since 1689, but, in the Seven Years' War the Dutch had been neutral and had complained bitterly about the British attempt to prevent their handling French trade. Relations did not improve subsequently and in the War of American Independence the Dutch were eventually to support France.[196] Improved relations between France and both Spain and – to a lesser extent – the Dutch, helped improve France's naval position in the event of any conflict with Britain. More generally, they also offered possibilities for trans-oceanic co-operation and thus for a revival from the low point reached during the Seven Years' War.

Peace with Britain in 1763 and the return of many of France's colonial losses, made possible a revival of French maritime and colonial activity. Already in 1762 Choiseul had claimed that both required total reorganization.[197] After the war, the fleet was built up, in part thanks to a patriotic subscription,[198] the command structure strengthened and the infrastructure improved. In the early 1770s, however, the fleet deteriorated, primarily as a result of the unhelpful administrative changes of Bourgeois de Boynes, minister of the marine in 1771–4, and, to a lesser extent, due to the fiscal stringency of those years.[199] Other new initiatives after the war included the attempted development and European settlement of the colony at Cayenne, to which about 9,000 colonists were shipped in 1763–4,[200] and the dispatch in 1766 of a nine-ship squadron under Admiral de Bauffremont, designed to intimidate the rulers of North Africa so that they prevented attacks on French shipping.[201] The Cayenne colony was badly hit by disease and poor management. Thousands died and a large debt was accumulated. A comparable effort in Canada in the early 1750s would have had much more of an impact, but it was now too late. The French traders who continued to develop the river routes from the Great Lakes were now working for British entrepreneurs. In 1786 Pierre Vial opened a trail from San Antonio to Santa Fé and in 1792 from there to St Louis, but he was now in Spanish service as Don Pedro Vial. Jean Baptiste Truteau who explored the Missouri valley in 1794 did so for the American Missouri Company.

After 1763, France remained far weaker than Britain in the colonial sphere, but, with the coming of peace, she was now free to pursue her interests. This entailed both the development of the French colonial and commercial system, and attempts to benefit from those of other countries, especially Spain. The latter however was far from easy and there was concern about the Spanish treatment of French trade, for example in 1764. In October 1768 New Orleans rebelled against the Spanish governor, after trade outside the Spanish imperial system or in non-Spanish ships was banned. Having expelled the Spanish Governor and his men, the Louisiana Superior Council appealed to Louis XV to restore French rule. There was support in senior French circles for the idea of Louisiana as an independent republic under French and Spanish guarantee, but, faced with Spanish determination to restore authority, the French did not act and in August 1769 a Spanish force occupied New Orleans and executed the revolt's leaders.

A more assertive attitude was apparent in the Indian Ocean. The Peace of Paris had left France with only five bases in India: Pondicherry, Chandernagore, Yanaon, Karikal and Mahé, all of which were returned to France in 1765. In 1767 Jean-Baptiste Chevalier arrived as Governor of Chandernagore and began to develop plans to expand the French presence in north India.[202] The same year, the government took over control of Mauritius and Réunion and started to improve their defences and increase their garrisons. The islands were developed as bases to support intervention in India. New fortifications were planned for Pondicherry,[203] while French officers sought to make Indian armies better able to resist the British. Colonel Gentil – a French officer who had been hired after the Seven Years' War by Shuja-ud-Daula, the Nawab of Awadh [Oudh], in order to improve his army – became the official French Resident and sought to negotiate a formal alliance between Awadh and France.

France's international position at the close of Louis XV's reign can therefore be seen in the light of her failure to prevent the First Partition, or a less gloomy and more nuanced account can be offered. The latter can focus not on the notion of a general situation in which the interests, strength and success of individual powers can be readily located, but, rather, of particular spheres that they might hope to dominate. This was true of Russia and Eastern Europe, Britain and the North Atlantic, and France and Western Europe.

If France did not have to show and enforce her domination in a fashion akin to Russia, that was a product not of weakness but of a more stable international situation there. It is not clear how far these particular spheres should be aggregated to offer an overall sense of power. That was done by contemporaries, and in the 1760s and early 1770s this process was dominated by the impact of France's defeat in the Seven Years' War. An opportunity to challenge that defeat was soon to be offered.

CHAPTER FIVE

Intervention in America and the policy of Vergennes, 1774–1787

His Majesty . . . is very occupied in seeking to prevent the overthrow that threatens the Ottoman Empire.

Montmorin, foreign minister, 31 August 1787.[1]

In global terms, the fate of Canada and India was the crucial issue in mid-eighteenth century European power politics. In the period 1774–87, the central issue was American independence. France played a major role in helping secure this independence in the face of sustained British attempts to regain control. It is all too easy to see this as an obvious course for France and to overlook the extent to which her government had choices, both as to whether and when to fight Britain, and as to how and with whom to do so. At present, the conventional view is that French policymakers in this period, and indeed from the 1750s, saw Britain as the major enemy, that this stemmed from concern about Britain's maritime power and the financial potential this gave Britain in European power politics, and that this led to a concentration on gaining the support of other maritime powers and on seeking to limit Britain's colonial and commercial growth.[2]

There is considerable weight in this analysis but it is a less than complete account of policy from the 1750s. Firstly, there are methodological problems: as so often, the documents cited are as much evidence of the views of individual ministers as a sign of a transformation in the opinions of the policy-making elite, and, in particular, it is unclear how far Louis XV and D'Aiguillon were as determined on such a policy as Choiseul. Any such analysis has to explain the failure to support Spain over the Falklands and D'Aiguillon's approach to Britain in 1772–3. Furthermore, some of the memoranda are intended to justify or persuade, and are clearly written in the face of contrary views. Secondly, there are problems with suggesting that a new departure, of the type discussed, occurred in the 1750s. It is true that, with the important exception of Corsica,

128

France acted as a sated power in Europe, but that did not make her less concerned about the policies of Austria, Prussia and Russia. Indeed, alongside any stress on maritime competition with Britain, it is possible to point to continued concern about Eastern Europe, specifically Poland: from the succession crisis of 1733 to the *Secret du Roi*, the negotiations of 1763–4, and the response to the First Partition. Similarly, a continuity of interest and activity can be discerned in the case of Sweden and the Turks.

This attention to problems further east can be reconciled with French attention to competing with Britain by arguing that the latter was designed to improve France's position within Europe. Clearly this was believed by some, but it was also a rationalization for naval activity, and for the alliance with Spain, at a time when it was no longer necessary to compete with Austria in Italy. Furthermore, as with many arguments, it was possible to propose and reconcile potentially differing commitments at a time that neither pressed, but when the situation became more difficult it was unclear what priorities would be adopted. In 1778 France went to war with Britain, taking advantage of fortuitous circumstances, but in 1770 it did not, in the late 1770s and 1780 the French were cautious about exploiting Britain's problems in India, and in 1783 Vergennes was more concerned about the Balkans than with fighting on to overthrow the British Empire.

European tensions, 1774–9

Opportunities and problems beckoned France on both sides of the Atlantic, and each opportunity presented the danger of making the wrong choice and thus weakening France's position. Within Europe, there was the possibility of sowing, or benefiting from, dissension among the partitioning powers (Austria, Prussia, Russia). This would probably increase France's influence with each and would offer opportunities for advancing her diplomatic agenda, both by protecting French clients and allies, especially Sweden and the Turks, and by preventing further gains by the powers. Austrian concern about Russian plans was matched by Frederick II's anxiety about the increasingly volatile attitude of the Emperor Joseph II, the son of Maria Theresa and co-ruler with her from 1765 until her death in 1780.

France was seen as a potential player in the jockeying for position among the partitioning powers, because of her interests in Eastern Europe, her influence in Germany and her treaty obligations to Austria. Thus Frederick sought to increase French concern about Austrian intentions. D'Aiguillon's replacement, Charles Gravier, Count of Vergennes, was aware of this strategy and, instead, argued that the Austro-French alliance was mutually advantageous and that the French ought to do everything possible to encourage a distrust between Austria and Prussia.[3]

Frederick II was hopeful that the ambitious views ascribed to Joseph could be used to disrupt the alliance and instructed his envoy in Paris in December 1776 accordingly.[4] The French government was indeed concerned. Having helped to create stability in Germany, the Low Countries and Italy by its own territorial restraint, and as part of a pacific policy, it did not wish to see Joseph alter the situation. The power best placed to block Joseph was France, and conflict with Austria was no longer on the agenda of the French government, a situation Frederick ascribed to the influence of Marie Antoinette and the poor state of French finances.[5] Both were important, but so also was the argument that alliance with Austria weakened Britain by denying her the Continental partner that could most readily distract France, and, more generally, the pacific views of French policymakers.

Louis XVI's views were of great importance. He saw himself not as a warrior king but as a ruler whose policies should reflect and display justice and morality. Louis sought grandeur for France, but it was the grandeur of rational leadership and arbitration. This he thought would ensure peace and thus provide an opportunity for domestic reform. He abandoned the *Secret*, and appointed the moderate and cautious Vergennes as foreign minister. France's most experienced diplomat, Vergennes, also believed in a politics of honesty, restraint and legality.[6] He was concerned to act as the defender of the interests of the second- and third-rank powers. Despite Vergennes' belief that it was necessary to retain the alliance of Austria,[7] there was still much jockeying for dominant position at other courts, such as Naples.[8] He was also concerned about Russian expansion, personally so as most of his diplomatic career had been spent in Constantinople and Stockholm, and he was anxious to avoid a repetition of the Seven Years' War. To him, France's defeat then demonstrated the danger of engaging simultaneously in maritime and European conflicts. It also led him to emphasize the value of the Family Compact with Spain, which he saw as a deterrent to British envy of French colonial development in the West Indies and to British aggression.

The First Partition of Poland in 1772 was the other recent seminal event and warning. To Vergennes it was both the politics of thuggery and a challenge to the pre-eminent position France should enjoy. With his background at Constantinople and Stockholm, Vergennes saw the Partition as a threat to French interests as well as her prestige – not that the two were distinct in his views or those of other French ministers. The ambitions of Joseph II also worried Vergennes, although he did not want to let Austria return to her former alliance with Britain. Vergennes saw better relations with Prussia as a way to block Joseph's expansionist schemes and to keep him concerned about French views, but he did not want to let Frederick dictate French policy. If France was a sated power it was not a satisfied one: it sought not more territory but an international system whose operation better matched French views and the interests of her allies.

Relations with Austria came to a head in 1778. Neither Maximilian Joseph of Bavaria (r. 1745–77), nor his successor, Charles Theodore of the Palatinate, had any direct heirs, and Joseph saw this as an opportunity to gain much of Bavaria. After Maximilian Joseph's death, Joseph reached an agreement with Charles Theodore, by which the latter ceded much of Bavaria, and many of his illegitimate children were found posts in Vienna. This, however, was opposed by Charles Theodore's heir, Charles Augustus of Zweibrücken, and by Frederick II and France, neither of which wished to see the Habsburgs appreciably stronger.

Unwilling to back either side militarily, not least because of her developing commitments to the American cause, France's refusal to support her ally was a serious blow to the Habsburgs, especially as Catherine the Great gave diplomatic backing to Frederick. Frederick attacked in July 1778, beginning an indecisive war that was ended by the Peace of Teschen of May 1779, under which Austria made only small gains.

The peace was concluded under Franco-Russian mediation. This was an important accretion of prestige for Russia, but the French government could afford to be content. France had played a very different, and much greater, role to that in the Partitions of Poland, neither Austria nor Prussia had been able to dominate Germany, and the Austrian territorial gain at the close of the war was modest.[9]

If the peace treaty weakened Bavaria, an important French ally in earlier conflicts, then this was less compromising to her strength than the impact of indifferent Bavarian leadership over previous decades. Furthermore, Bavaria had been shown in the War of the Austrian Succession to be an ally of only limited value. Overrun by Austria in 1742, it had abandoned the war in 1745. Broglie's argument that the Diplomatic Revolution had ended French influence in Germany was credible only if it was assumed that Prussia could be an effective and reliable ally, and the course of Frederick's reign did not invite confidence on that head.

Yet, with the issue of Austrian reliability becoming more acute for France, the German question was being reopened. In 1785 Floridablanca, the Spanish foreign minister, was to suggest that if Joseph II did not abandon his aggressive policies, the Bourbon powers would need to take an assertive stance.[10]

War for America

The American colonists who rebelled against British control were very different allies, and the course by which France came to support them was not an easy one. The new ministry was less inclined than D'Aiguillon to heed British wishes, but they would not have risked war with Britain had it not been for developments in her American colonies. Rebellion broke out in 1775, and the rebels sought the assistance of France.

They found her government unwilling to commit itself publicly, but ready to provide financial and military assistance. Vergennes hoped that the British would lose America and, therefore, that a colonial balance of power, lost in the Seven Years' War, would be restored, enabling the two powers to co-operate in limiting the influence of the partitioning states, and freeing France to redirect expenditure from the navy. Other ministers were more interested in the simple idea of weakening Britain.

The move to war was hesitant, affected by the course of the conflict in North America and by the state of French preparations. The French could anticipate no assistance from Austria and it was far from clear that they would receive any from Spain, the third leading naval power in the world after Britain and France.

French expenditure on the navy more than quadrupled between 1774 and 1778, and, as the condition of the navy improved, so it became more plausible to think of war. Tension over French aid to the rebels – specifically, allowing their privateers to use French ports – led Vergennes to press Louis XVI in the summer of 1777 for French entry into the war. The British failure to defeat the Americans that year led to the treaties of Alliance and Commerce of 6 February 1778 with the rebels. The notification of the Treaty of Commerce to the British government on 13 March led to the recall of the British envoy from Paris, for George III could not accept the recognition of American independence. As neither power wished to appear an aggressor to her allies, hostilities did not begin until June when the struggle to control Channel waters began.[11]

Foreign intervention was to make the perhaps impossible British task of conquering America completely impractical. Until then it had been feasible to imagine that British success might lead to a negotiated end to the war and thus obviate the need for total victory by Britain, but the French role helped make American independence a reasonable goal.

For France the value of the decision to go to war was less clear-cut than it was for her new American allies. High hopes were expressed. Most focused on the destruction of British maritime and colonial predominance, but the possible implications for France's standing in Europe were also teased out by some commentators. Noailles, the envoy in London, wrote to Vergennes in January 1778 of his hope that the division of the British Empire, and thus the loss of British power, would deny France's European rivals their principal help, specifi-cally by ending Britain's capacity to subsidize them.[12] In practice, the war brought France major financial burdens[13] and, in the short term, restricted her possible role in European power politics. By going to war, France, like most eighteenth-century combatants, limited her options and mortgaged her future, but she did so without pressing need. Furthermore, in the long term France did not increase appreciably her influence in Europe or her relative power overseas.

Vergennes was successful in widening the struggle. Spain entered the war on the French side in 1779,[14] a crucial acquisition of naval strength, and the British attacked the United Provinces at the close of 1780, in order to limit the support of their neutral trading to France. The French sent an army to North America in 1780[15] and in India, after their bases were taken in 1778–9, they co-operated with Haidar Ali of Mysore and sent a force, although it was lessened by Vergennes' success in thwarting the bold plans of the ministers of war and the marine, as well as by scurvy and British blockaders.[16]

The French also sought to stir up neutral European powers against British attempts at blockade.[17] Indeed, the maritime and trans-oceanic coalition supporting France was stronger than that in any previous war she had waged, and her own naval effort put the British under great pressure, especially in the West Indies.[18] At the Battle of the Chesapeake on 5 September 1781 the French fleet thwarted an attempt to relieve the British army besieged at Yorktown, leading to the surrender of that army to the blockading American and French force, and the collapse of the British war effort.

However, the results of the coalition effort were disappointing, in part because of the problems of co-ordinating the efforts of the various powers. Thus, Spain pursued in effect a separate war, one in which operations around the Gulf of Mexico were more important than co-operating with the French in the West Indies. The British were defeated in America and also lost Minorca, West Florida and a number of West Indian islands, but the Franco-Spanish attempt to invade Britain in 1779 was unsuccessful,[19] as was the long siege of Gibraltar. Despite a number of victories won by Haidar Ali and an effective campaign by Admiral Suffren, the British held their positions in India. By 1782 British general superiority at sea was established and the Franco-Spanish naval effort was nearing exhaustion toward the end of the war: the French fleet in the West Indies was defeated at the battle of the Saintes on 12 April 1782.

Nevertheless, the earlier surrender at Yorktown led to a change of government in Britain and a willingness to negotiate peace. As Vergennes was anxious to direct his attention to blocking Russian expansion in the Crimea, British readiness to negotiate was matched by that of France.

Bourbon gains in the resulting preliminary agreement of 20 January 1783, and the Peace of Versailles, signed on 3 September 1783, were modest. France received Tobago, Senegal and concessions in the Newfoundland fisheries, as well as the return of St Lucia, while Spain obtained Minorca and East and West Florida. The changed relationship between Britain and France was symbolically demonstrated by the abrogation of the article in the Peace of Paris giving Britain the right to maintain a commissioner at Dunkirk to prevent the rebuilding of its fortifications.[20] Yet the major British territorial loss was to the Americans, not the French, and Britain remained the leading European power in India.

Aside from these specific territorial shifts, there were also wider questions about the impact of the war. Britain remained isolated, but France had failed to destroy the British Empire. Nevertheless, the loss of America was a serious blow and, although France was financially stressed by the conflict and had accumulated a substantial debt, it was possible that she would derive additional benefits once peace was obtained. Her navy had been more effective than in any other war, while the army was recovering from its poor showing in the Seven Years' War.

Postwar Diplomacy

He said we had checked and constrained the French in all the quarters of the world, that he wished for a treaty of peace more just and durable than the last, and that the two principal objects they should attend to were justice and dignity.

Vergennes to British envoy, 9 May 1782.[21]

French foreign policy after the War of American Independence very much bore the stamp of Vergennes, although other ministers also had views and sought to influence the content and conduct of foreign policy. In many respects, Vergennes was a thoughtful and perceptive foreign minister,[22] whose opposition to a politics of aggrandizement accorded with the policies of his predecessor, D'Aiguillon. He has enjoyed a much more favourable scholarly reputation than his predecessors, although there have been criticisms. These include the claim that Vergennes was indifferent to German questions,[23] and the argument that his skill was compromised by his failure to appreciate the domestic costs of his policy, so that unwittingly he helped to precipitate the Revolution.[24] From the perspective of French colonial history, Vergennes has been condemned for mediocrity, lack of vision and failing to support the imperial schemes of Sartine and Castries, naval ministers of the period.[25]

Vergennes wanted Britain to serve French interests in Europe, but he regarded these as based on what was necessary for the continent. Vergennes sought British co-operation in thwarting Russian gains at the expense of the Turks, which he held to be the most obvious sign of the threat to the European system and to the *status quo* posed by the partitioning powers. To the French, Russia appeared especially threatening at this point, not simply because she challenged traditional French protégés, but because she pressed her claims very vigorously. Russia intervened in the Crimea in the autumn of 1782 and annexed it the following April.

In March 1777 Vergennes had already written of the need for Anglo-French co-operation against measures to weaken Turkey.[26] War with Britain did not lead him to abandon this idea.[27] Both during the course of the peace negotiations and subsequently, as the Crimean crisis neared the point when full-scale war between Russia and Turkey – and the danger of the realization of wider Russian ambitions for gains from the Turks – seemed imminent, the French pressed the British for support.[28] Co-operation between Austria and Russia was leading France to new initiatives. This was largely a matter of considering whether steps could be taken with Britain, Prussia and Spain. British political opinion was largely unsympathetic, Charles James Fox sought better relations with Russia, and Frederick II thought Vergennes weak and claimed that no power would ally with France if he remained head of the government.[29]

Despite Joseph II's suggestion that France could gain Egypt from a partition of the Turkish Empire, Vergennes felt that it was in France's interests that the balance of power should not be overthrown by Austrian and Russian gains and that the empire should survive. He claimed that 'if all powers were aware of their interests they would firmly oppose the torrent which threatens Europe', but he was aware that powers tended to pursue their own particular interests.[30]

Vergennes appreciated that any conflict would weaken the Turks,[31] and sought to prevent war and to try by diplomacy either to maintain the *status quo* or to limit Russian and Austrian advances. Vergennes' tactic was to press the Turks to make concessions. Thus, instead of the Turks helping France, as Louis XIV and earlier rulers had sought, France had to protect them. This was a major change in the goals and capability of the French diplomatic system.

For the time being, Vergennes was reasonably successful, even without British help. His efforts to mediate or influence the solution to the Crimean crisis prevented Austria from making any gains, while Russia's gains were kept to a minimum. Vergennes did so by persuading the Turks to accept the loss of the Crimea without fighting.[32] This policy assumed a measure of French influence at Constantinople that would limit the role of the war party there, but such an assumption was risky. In August 1784 Vergennes refused to play any part in Austrian schemes for border negotiations with the Turks because he feared any such role would anger the latter.[33] Vergennes sought to dissuade Austria, Russia and Turkey from aggressive steps,[34] a policy that was not popular with these powers,[35] and in 1787 French efforts to prevent war between Russia and Turkey were to fail.

Already in 1783, the domestic situation within France was far from propitious. The attempt of the *Comité des Finances* to reform the royal finances in 1783 failed, and this entailed an acknowledgement that the king and his ministers alone were incapable of carrying through a meaningful policy of reform. Domestic political and financial stability was never really regained from October 1783, and ministerial divisions contributed powerfully to a sense of political malaise. These divisions affected French policy towards Germany in 1784–5 and in the Dutch crisis of 1786–7.[36]

The Balkan crisis of 1783–4 exemplified the problems of diplomatic influence: France had to reconcile the interests of a traditional ally (Turkey) and a new ally (Austria). This was scarcely novel. In 1733–5, for example, grave difficulties had been faced in preventing differences between Sardinia and Spain from wrecking military operations in Italy. The situation became more difficult in the 1780s, because the problems of reconciling traditional and new allies were exacerbated by the attempt to recruit more powers to the French alliance system. After the recent war, the French sought to create a more permanent relationship with the Dutch. This was challenged in 1784 by Austrian territorial demands on behalf of the Austrian Netherlands in a crisis over the freedom of navigation on the River Scheldt.

Both parties began military preparations and turned to Louis XVI for help. French diplomatic pressure on both powers to be conciliatory was unsuccessful,[37] and, with war seeming inevitable, France prepared to come to the assistance of the Dutch. Calonne, the finance minister, told Frederick II's brother that France would have 60,000 men ready within a fortnight.[38] Kaunitz had warned Joseph II in September 1782 that France would not support him and didn't wish to risk her relations with the Dutch.[39] The crisis, especially Franco–Prussian backing for the Dutch, nearly drove the Austro–French alliance to breaking point. Vergennes considered the prospect, while Joseph II wanted the minister replaced.[40]

France in Europe acted as a satisfied power and a supporter of the *status quo*, and that position was now challenged not only by Russia, as had been the case earlier in the century, but also by Austria, as had not obviously been the case since the 1730s, for Joseph II was unwilling to confine himself to past roles. The Scheldt crisis was to be complicated and superseded by the revival of the Bavarian exchange scheme, the idea that Bavaria should be exchanged for the Austrian Netherlands, a step that would lead to a more consolidated Habsburg state. Joseph II sought to win the backing of French pressure on the Wittelsbachs, both the Duke of Bavaria and his heir. He also sought to influence Louis XVI through his sister, Louis's wife, Marie Antoinette. After an initially promising response in the French Council of State on 1 December 1784, the final decision taken on 2 January 1785 was negative.

All the ministers, bar Vergennes, opposed the scheme, claiming that a rise in Austrian power would lead to a relative fall in that of France.[41] Charles, Marquis of Castries, the dynamic minister of the marine, suggested that France needed to maintain the balance of power against Austria.[42] Such arguments were a reminder of the fragility of the Austro–French connection. It has been claimed that Vergennes was playing a double game,[43] although he informed Noailles, now envoy in Vienna, who was very opposed to the scheme, that he thought the objections were balanced by the advantages.[44]

Louis XVI wrote to Joseph II that the exchange could not take place without Prussian consent,[45] a highly unlikely contingency unless Joseph made concessions. This echoed French policy in the early 1750s towards the Imperial election scheme in which Vergennes and Frederick had been active in thwarting British support for Austrian pretensions. Joseph abandoned the scheme. Vergennes also refused to do anything to dissuade German rulers from entering the *Fürstenbund* (League of Princes), established by Frederick in 1785 to restrict Austrian adventurism, and including George III, as Elector of Hanover, among the members. Vergennes wrote to Noailles that 'the maintenance of the German constitution is the basis of our alliance with Austria'.[46] Vergennes had indeed disproved his critics' claims that French policy was subordinated to Austria and that France had renounced her role in international relations,[47] but that did not stop criticism. Castries urged better relations with Prussia and thwarting Austria. Other ministers also pressed in 1785 for co-operation with Prussia.[48] The following year, Noailles reported that he found a constant jealousy of France on the part of the Austrian government.[49]

France emerged reasonably well from the crises of the period, at least in terms of her international standing, not least because the avoidance of war ensured that her financial weaknesses were not brought to a crisis. There was no sign yet of her diplomatic nullity at the close of the decade. Much to the concern of the British, a Franco-Dutch defensive treaty was signed at Fontainebleau on 10 November 1785 and France successfully mediated Austro-Dutch differences. It was scarcely surprising that Joseph preferred alliance with the France of his despised brother-in-law Louis XVI to the Britain of the equally-despised George III, nor that Frederick II was unwilling to provoke France, nor that in 1786 the British government responded to French pressure to negotiate a trade treaty, the so-called Eden Treaty, signed at Versailles on 26 September.[50] The Dutch were an increasingly important source of investment in France.[51]

The crisis of 1787

The favourable diplomatic situation collapsed in late 1787, both because the 'Patriots', France's Dutch allies, were overthrown and because war broke out between Russia and Turkey. These developments were unwelcome to France and the manner of the first especially so. Both in the United Provinces and in Turkey the French ability to influence allies proved insufficient in crisis situations. Vergennes had favoured restraint on the part of the Patriots towards their Orangeist rivals, and on the part of the Turks towards Russia. Yet in July 1786 the Dutch Estates General removed the command of the Hague garrison from William V of Orange, a provocative step of which the cautious Vergennes disapproved. The French envoy, Vérac, became steadily more involved in Patriot plans, in spite of warnings from Vergennes that he should be careful not to over-commit France in Dutch internal affairs. Yet, Vérac was not replaced.

Similarly, the French mishandled the Balkan question, although, again, the general situation was far from easy. Vergennes undermined his policy – of persuading the Turks to avoid war – by a trade treaty with Russia, signed on 11 January 1787,[52] the news of which was greeted in Constantinople with anger and dismay.[53] The internal coherence of his diplomatic strategy, the desire to keep the Turks calm while, at the same time, improving relations with Russia (and perhaps also restraining her), was destroyed by the interaction of its own contradictions, and by events in Eastern Europe. The latter was most important, although Choiseul-Gouffier, the envoy in Constantinople, reported that the Turks had been affected by reports of a Franco-Russian reconciliation.[54]

Vergennes found his policy opposed by Britain in the Balkans and the Netherlands, and also suspected that the British were trying to block French views elsewhere, for example in Spain.[55] This was ironic as he had made a major effort to improve relations, and that, indeed, was the major reason behind his interest in a commercial treaty.[56] Vergennes' attempt to improve Anglo-French relations was scarcely unprecedented. Dubois, Morville, Puysieulx and D'Aiguillon had all pursued the same goal.

Whereas Dubois, Morville and the other ministers responsible for the negotiation and maintenance of the Anglo-French alliance of 1716–31, had done so within a diplomatic context in which Spain, Russia, and (though to a lesser extent) Austria, but definitely not France, had seemed rising and aggressive powers, unwilling to be restrained by the views of others, and, in various ways, threats to the views of George I and his ministers, Puysieulx had failed in the different context of the late 1740s. By then, France had recovered from her weakness at the end of the War of Spanish Succession, Britain was no longer anxious about Russian strength and was, instead, keen to use Austria and Russia to counteract France and Prussia, while Anglo-French maritime and colonial rivalry had become more acute and, in Britain, politically contentious. Vergennes' failure has to be seen as a repetition of that of Puysieulx, and of D'Aiguillon in 1772–3, rather than as an inability to repeat Dubois's success. Better Anglo-French relations were unlikely while the two powers remained colonial rivals and until Britain became more concerned about the ambitions of another continental power.

Growing French influence in the United Provinces, particularly in the Dutch East India Company, exacerbated relations with Britain in 1786, but it was acceptable to other powers, provided that France could retain influence over her Dutch protégés. In 1786 Prussia preferred to try to influence Dutch affairs by co-operating with France, rather than Britain.

As the Dutch internal situation deteriorated in 1787, however, neither Britain nor France acted purposefully to restrain their envoys' ardent endorsement of clashing Dutch factions, and the policies of both were influenced substantially by their local protégés.[57] French policy, handicapped by internal tensions and by the disruption caused by Vergennes' death on 13 February 1787, was sufficiently interventionist to increase British fears, but had, anyway, been seen as aggressive even when Vergennes was alive, though he sought an amicable settlement of the Dutch crisis.

The conduct and international perception of French foreign policy were complicated by the impact of French domestic difficulties. The financial crisis of the state led to increasing governmental interest in reform and constitutional change. An Assembly of Notables comprised of leading figures nominated by Louis XVI opened on 22 February 1787. It was unclear whether this would produce reform and renewal, as indeed was expected by Vergennes' successor, Armand-Marc, Count of Montmorin.[58] Foreign commentators speculated that reform might come through a national bankruptcy.

The Assembly, in fact, refused to accept the proposals from, first, Calonne, who was compromised by suspicions of corruption, and then Brienne, that the taxation system be reorganized and that both a universal land tax and provincial assemblies elected by landowners be introduced. Instead, the Notables sought government economies and assemblies that were virtually autonomous.[59] Calonne, who saw Britain as a natural enemy, was dismissed on 8 April.

Signs of disunity and financial difficulties in France encouraged the British government to take a more assertive line in the United Provinces. As the province of Holland drifted into anarchy, the French government, increasingly absorbed by its own domestic problems, lost control both of its competing agents there and of the Patriots. Signs of likely British and Prussian military intervention led to talk of French action. A French army was reportedly to be prepared at Givet, able to advance, through the Bishopric of Liège, to Maastricht. The Patriots had indeed sought this step, but the more cautious Brienne was worried about the cost.

Montmorin also sought to prevent war, by offering mediation. His position was weakened by a lack of Austrian support, and the likelihood that France would have to act alone made Montmorin more cautious. Unwilling to follow a French lead, the Patriots appeared a less attractive ally, and Montmorin sought to avoid provoking either Britain or Prussia.[60] On 30 August 1787 Britain and France agreed that neither would increase their naval armaments without informing the other. As an additional, though long-planned positive step, the two powers settled differences over the rights of the French in Bengal. Montmorin pressed Vérac on the need to avoid a Dutch civil war, and finally recalled him.[61]

Nevertheless, the Patriots' unwillingness to heed French advice that they apologize to Wilhelmina of Orange, the sister of Frederick William II of Prussia, and accept foreign mediation, prevented a lessening of international tension, while the British and Prussians were encouraged by signs that France would not act. Indeed, the French response was greatly affected by their domestic difficulties.[62] Calonne, who had taken refuge in Britain, briefed Pitt on the parlous French financial situation.

At the same time as they negotiated, the French continued their preparations to assemble troops at Givet[63] (although they amounted to little in practice), because they hoped that belief in French military preparedness would give her a stronger position in international relations. Ségur, the minister of war, actively sponsored military preparations, and he and Castries, the bellicose minister of the marine, were prepared to call Prussia's bluff and, if necessary, fight, but their enthusiasm was not shared by the bulk of the ministry.[64] The Patriots were sent artillerymen and money. By not totally ceasing to provide support, the French government compromised its position and sowed doubt about its intentions, but the eventual Prussian decision to act owed much to a conviction that France would not respond. Conversely, French hesitation about assisting the Patriots was, in part, attributed to exaggerated fears of Prussian forces.

To the surprise of the French, a Prussian army invaded the United Provinces on 13 September 1787 and the British stepped up naval preparations. The French government was handicapped by division and change and scarcely in a position to act,[65] and French diplomats reported that this was the assessment made by other powers.[66] The refusal of the *Parlement* of Paris on 13 August to ratify new taxes led to its exile to Troyes, and the provincial *parlements* followed by also refusing. The appointment of Brienne as first minister on 26 August exacerbated ministerial rivalries. An angry Castries, who had sought the post, resigned, taking

Ségur with him.[67] Brienne's views on foreign policy are shadowy, but he was opposed to war in 1787 and held responsible for preventing direct action.

France's diplomacy was also in disarray. The Spanish government was unwilling to assist, and Baron Groschlag's mission to Berlin to improve relations was unsuccessful. French forces did not move or impress, a reflection of the decline in military expenditure. France backed down and then disclaimed any intention of seeking, or ever having sought, to intervene.

Arguably, France could not have faced Britain and Prussia alone in 1787. However, she had been outmatched and humiliated in a crisis of brinkmanship. French diplomats felt that they and their government had lost influence.[68] Had Louis XVI acted in 1787 and the Prussians not invaded, possibly he and the French monarchy would have achieved an aura of success and prestige that would have helped to counter the grievances of the period. Starhemberg had told Bernis in May 1758 that unrest within France could be settled only by victories and that the French public never criticized success. Kaunitz had then emphasized the need for France to conquer Hanover.[69] Catherine II told the French envoy on 5 November 1787 that war could end French internal divisions and boost patriotism.[70] The strains produced by earlier participation in the competitive international system, especially the costs of war, particularly the recent War of American Independence, meant that the government had to achieve financial, and thus political, reform, but the likely consequences of such a process were far from clear, there was nothing pre-destined about revolution, and international success would have helped greatly.

The crisis of 1787 marked the failure of French diplomacy. From 1783 a number of influential ministers, including Calonne, Castries and Breteuil, had regarded alliance with the Dutch as very important, but in 1787 it was lost. The Austro-French alignment had been devoid of much meaning in terms of co-operation and shared views for a number of years, but this was made clear in 1787. Spain failed to provide support, hopes of Prussia proved empty, and the commercial treaties with Britain and Russia did not lead to political benefits. Already, prior to the Dutch crisis, the *Conseil d'État* had been told on 28 February 1787 that, without help from Austria and Prussia, France could not effectively aid the Turks. The poor state of French government finances had been emphasized.[71] Later in the year, high-level bankruptcies provided signs of a collapsing financial system.

Empire and trade

The Dutch crisis was not only a serious blow to France's position in Europe. It also gravely affected France's global position, because, with bases in India, Sri Lanka, the East Indies and at Cape Town, the Dutch were a major European power in the Indian Ocean and on the route to the Orient. Benefiting from this presence offered France opportunities analagous to those of seeking to use the

Spanish Empire in the New World. There had been a clear forward direction in French policy outside Europe in the mid-1780s, a continuation of the activity displayed during the War of American Independence. This was shown in a number of areas, including the Black Sea, Egypt, the Indian Ocean and the Pacific. The policy thrust did not come from Vergennes, because he was not greatly interested in India and, instead, sought better relations with Britain.[72] Instead, the Ministry of the Marine, which controlled the colonies, was far more important. Antoine-Raymond-Jean-Gabriel de Sartine, minister in 1774–80, had sought to develop what has recently been termed the 'Mediterranean–Indian Ocean axis'.[73] His successor, Castries, had wanted war to continue in 1783, and had argued that France was then in a very good position in India. He sought to maintain the French navy on a wartime footing in preparation for the resumption of hostilities. There was a major programme of naval expansion that was matched by marked improvements in naval organization, recruitment, supplies and construction. British innovations, such as copper-sheathing of ships' bottoms in order to increase speed and manoeuvrability, and carronades, new powerful short-range cannon, were incorporated. In 1786 the French imposed standard designs of ship construction for their fleet. Construction of an artificial harbour at Cherbourg was begun in 1783. Castries sought to apply scientific knowledge. He instigated research by the Royal Society of Medicine on the preparation and preservation of foodstuffs on board ship, the nutritional requirements of seamen, ship ventilation, and the treatment of illness.[74]

Anti-British, in January 1785 Castries referred to Britain as France's principal and natural enemy. He argued that France should seek to maintain peace and the balance of power in Europe, essentially by not supporting Austria, he claimed that war against the British in India would pay for itself and sought to develop French influence along the route there, particularly in Egypt.[75] Vergennes, in contrast, sought to ease British fears about French schemes in India. He preferred to concentrate on building up good relations.[76]

Ministerial aspirations were given added force by the steep climb in the volume of French trade in the mid-1780s. France's domestic exports were valued at £11.5 million in 1787, while the exports from its colonies to France averaged over £8.25 million per annum between 1784 and 1790. French sugar exports boomed after the return of peace,[77] and the economist Adam Smith favourably compared the production of sugar in the French West Indies with that in the British islands.[78] In 1788 the largest colony, St Domingue, exported 1,634,032 *quintaux* (100 kilograms to a *quintal*) of sugar, more than that from all the British sugar islands. The 1780s was the peak decade for the receipt of slaves by the West Indies colonies: nearly 30,000 slaves annually. The numbers sent to St Domingue rose from 14,000 annually in 1766–71 to 28,000 annually in 1785–9.[79]

Coffee exports expanded greatly, and also indicated the inter-connectedness of the French commercial system. Introduced to Martinique and Guadeloupe in 1725, and St Domingue in 1730, French coffee was more popular than that produced by the Dutch in the East Indies, and it swiftly became the principal global source: 350,000 *quintaux* were produced in 1770 and over 950,000 in 1790. Of the 950,000 *quintaux* imported by French ports in 1790, 794,000 were for re-export, nearly 90 per cent of Marseille's re-exports going to the Turkish Empire. Whereas in 1660 Marseille had imported 19,000 *quintaux* of coffee, of Yemeni origin, from Egypt, in 1785 it imported 143,310 *quintaux*, of which 142,500 came from the West Indies. Trade encouraged shipbuilding. In 1787 the tonnage of French merchant shipping was 729,000, second only to that of Britain at 882,000. The Dutch, whose tonnage had greatly exceeded that of France a century earlier, now had only 398,000 tons, but that was still the third largest in the world.[80]

The situation with the United States was less favourable. Relations deteriorated after the wartime alliance. France proved unable to draw the economic benefits that had been expected from American independence, and that at a time when the financial burdens of her intervention were felt all too keenly. Peace allowed British competitors to re-establish their commercial position and caused a precipitate decline in Franco-American trade. British trade, in contrast, boomed, and – combined with the negative balance of trade between France and the United States – ensured that trade with America moved French capital into the British economy. American success in overcoming French efforts to keep them out of the trade of the French West Indies was an added cause of tension, while the Americans also competed in traditional French markets, such as the Turkish Empire. French officials complained about indifference on the part of American political leaders to their commercial aspirations. A consular convention signed in 1783 was not ratified by the Americans for five years and, in contrast to Britain, they did not respond positively to French approaches for a trade treaty.[81]

The 1786 trade treaty with Britain was to be blamed for problems affecting French industry in the late 1780s. British textile exports were to be especially competitive, while, despite French efforts, the British excluded French silk imports in the treaty. Nevertheless, the French gained one important goal, the reduction of duties on French wines to a rate no greater than that on Portuguese wines, which had enjoyed a marked preference since the Anglo-Portuguese Methuen Treaty of 1703.[82]

The French also sought to increase commerce with Asia via their base at Île de France (Mauritius). This was seen as a way to diversify trade beyond an excessive reliance on the re-export of goods from the West Indies, and as an important support to French power. Exploration was seen in the same light. Knowledge was clearly a means to power when plotting routes across the oceans. The French navy charted the coast of Asia from Suez to Korea in the 1780s. In 1784–9 France sent ten naval expeditions into the Indian and Pacific oceans. A settlement was established on Diego Garcia south of India in 1784, but, as successful cultivation proved impossible, it was evacuated in 1786. The most famous expedition was that of La Pérouse in 1785–8. Having explored the shores of the north-eastern and north-western Pacific, he reached Botany Bay in Australia on 24 January 1788, six days after the British had arrived to found a penal colony there. Although scientific aims played a part in his expedition, political and economic considerations stemming from competition with Britain were also very important.[83]

The range and pace of French activity in Asia increased. There had been French interest in South East Asia since the reign of Louis XIV and it developed in the 1780s. Although the French abandoned their commercial establishment at Rangoon, in 1787 the dynamic ruler of Burma was able to negotiate with the French at their Bengal base of Chandernagore in his search for western arms. However, despite concern about Franco-Burmese links, France played no role in the Burmese attack on Siam in 1786, and the Burmese also purchased firearms from British suppliers.[84]

The French played a larger role in Cochin China, the area around the Mekong delta, where a civil war was in progress. In 1785 Pigneau de Béhaine, Bishop of Adran and Vicar-Apostolic of Cochin China, appealed for help to the Governor of Pondicherry on behalf of one of the claimants, N'guyen Anh. Two years later, N'guyen Anh's son arrived in France. By the Treaty of Versailles of 28 November 1787 with N'guyen Anh, France acquired a claim to bases in Cochin China, and a valuable possibility of increased trade with China opened up. In practice, it proved impossible to implement the treaty because France lacked the resources to send assistance. In place of royal forces, N'guyen Anh received only a small number of Frenchmen, hired thanks to the help of French merchants. With these, however, he was able to train his forces and conquer much of modern Vietnam.[85] In India in 1785 the Nizam of Hyderabad asked Bussy's former aide-de-camp, Michel Raymond, to build up a force trained to fight in European methods, the 'Corps Français de Raymond', that by 1798 was 14,000 strong.

Further west, the French developed their position on their Indian Ocean islands, and also came to play a more active role on the overland route to India, especially in Egypt, and also in the Black Sea. There was an increasing awareness of the strategic importance of Egypt. On 7 February 1785 the French signed an agreement with the beys who wielded most influence in Egypt, opening the Red Sea route to India to overland trade, over the Isthmus of Suez. Marseille merchants sought to exploit the route, although the French East India Company opposed attempts to establish an Egyptian company.[86]

The French were less successful in negotiating alliances with Persia (Iran) and with the Iman of Oman, but they were energetic in both areas. An embassy under the Count of Ferrières-Sauveboeuf was sent to Isfahan in 1784, the same year in which Choiseul-Gouffier, the French envoy in Constantinople, was instructed to seek means to improve French relations with Persia, both for commercial reasons and in order to facilitate trade with India.[87] Ferrières-Sauveboeuf claimed that France was out to develop trade and to limit Russian influence. The making of French–native alliances throughout the Middle East, complementing and supporting that with Mysore, seemed a prospect. The Iman of Oman appeared interested in the idea of joint action against Bombay.[88] British agents in Baghdad, Basra and Shiraz warned in 1784–7 of French activity in Persia and the Gulf, including the arrival of French ships at Basra and Muscat, and anticipated French designs on Bandar Rig and, in 1786, Kharg. Two French frigates arrived at Basra in 1785 with arms and ammunition.[89]

French commercial interests were active. Trade with India revived and in 1785 the French East India Company was refounded.[90] The Turks refused to permit ships flying the French flag into the Black Sea, but Marseille ships flying the flag of Russia were acceptable. In 1785 a French trading company was established at Kherson, at the mouth of the Dnieper. The French government provided a credit of 100,000 *livres* for the purchase of naval stores and a French master mastman organized inspections of timber in Poland and the Ukraine. The route offered the prospect of France gaining a new source of supply for timber and other naval stores from Poland and neighbouring states, and one that was not subject in wartime to British naval control of the North Sea.

These commercial schemes were directly linked to plans for political advantage. To take the Black Sea, in May 1783 Choiseul-Gouffier, who had travelled extensively in the Levant in the late 1770s, submitted a memorandum proposing that France expand her influence there by increasing trade. He argued that it would be possible both to preserve the Turkish Empire and to develop trade with Russia via the Black Sea. In June 1784, by then ambassador at Constantinople, he was given instructions to seek admission to the Black Sea for ships flying the French flag. Louis XVI wrote to the sultan to the same end two months later.[91] Choiseul-Gouffier sailed to Constantinople in a warship under the command of Laurent-Jean-François Truguet who was instructed to prepare charts of the Black Sea and the Nile Delta, and train the Turks in naval warfare.

The sense that France could influence, if not manipulate, developments to her own benefit and that of her allies, clashed with a fear that the Turkish position could not be protected. By the 1780s France had achieved a dominant position in the foreign trade of the Levant and eastern Mediterranean. For both political and commercial reasons, she was the most influential foreign power in the Turkish Empire. In the mid-1780s, experts helped to direct the construction of Turkish warships and of fortifications at the major Black Sea base of Ochakov.

Yet this was challenged by the threat of Russian power. It was unclear whether it would be more in France's interest to join in any partition of the Turkish Empire. An anonymous memorandum of July 1787 suggested that if France joined her ally Austria, and Russia, against Turkey she could hope to acquire Crete and Egypt from the latter. The occupation of Cyprus and Rhodes was also suggested, and the need to prevent Britain occupying Egypt was emphasized.[92]

The sense of competition with Britain lent urgency to the question of French policy outside Europe, while fear of impending war in the Balkans meant that it was necessary to consider the choice between support for Turkey or her potential opponents, or the alternative of French passivity and neglect of French interests by the combatants. Indeed, when war broke out between Russia and the Turks in 1787, the Black Sea trade route was shattered. Ships were seized, cargoes confiscated, and, in the end, the commercial facilities at Kherson had to be closed and the trade suspended.

France appeared to have choices. In India she could seek to develop relations with Hyderabad and Mysore and sustain an anti-British bloc. In the Indian Ocean she could ally with the Dutch. In the Balkans she could seek to strengthen Turkey. Yet, in the first two, France could also try to develop closer relations with Britain, building on the commercial treaty, while in the last she apparently had the option of turning to Austria and Russia.

Policy re-assessed

Any judgement, of the extent to which French policymakers understood the situation and, also, of the intelligence of their direction and management of policy, rests, in part, on the questions of whether choices existed and, if so, of what they were. Was there, for example, a series of stark options: accepting British dominance and/or Russian aggression, or resisting both, possibly unsuccessfully? Or was the situation less clear-cut, and, if so, did French mismanagement play a role in precipitating these options? Such questions can be raised throughout the course of any state's foreign policy, but in the case of France it is particularly important to consider these counterfactual perspectives at this juncture, because of the argument that diplomatic failures played a part in the background to the Revolution. Failure to act in the Dutch crisis led to a general sense of weakness.

The most recent study of the period suggests that much of the pressure for war in 1787 was naïve and that it would have been financially disastrous. This is a valuable challenge to claims that bold action then might have averted the Revolution. Murphy, in contrast, argues that 'Louis XVI and his secretaries of state for foreign affairs were harried statesmen in a painful but necessary retreat from the devastating results of France's overextended position in Europe'.[93] In addition, despite the building of numerous warships, the treasurer of the navy was unable to fund any sustained naval operational activity.[94]

More generally, the decline in the size of the French army from its highpoint in the later years of Louis XIV's reign – in the context of the general peacefulness of Western Europe in 1763-92 – both limited military options and played a role in reducing the opportunities for noble service in France, with arguably serious political consequences. The nature of French public debate over policy suggested that there would be little tolerance of failure if France had intervened militarily without success in the Dutch crisis, and much criticism of any such intervention.

Royal iconography had shifted from the king as a martial leader to a stress on pacific values.[95] *Philosophe* arguments, advanced, for example, by Condorcet, Diderot and Mirabeau, that all people essentially sought peace, that national interests, if correctly understood, were naturally compatible, and that war arose from irrational causes, such as religion and the irresponsibility and self-indulgence of leaders, and from the secret and manipulative nature of *ancien régime* diplomacy, had had an impact. The *philosophes* rejected the claim that they were unpatriotic.[96] They were certainly not bellicose.

Nevertheless, as already suggested, mistaken policies, as well as structures, were at issue. Despite their weaknesses, the French had been able to intervene in the War of American Independence. In 1787 did Montmorin, for example, make too little effort to woo Prussia because he was more interested in closer relations with Austria and Russia? It is too easy to assume the sort of all-or-nothing approach that structural accounts can give rise to: either a power is at the top or not. Instead, to use a modern phrase, it is helpful to consider the notion of punching above one's weight. That was as important for France as it was for other powers.

Punching above one's weight was largely dependent on the maintenance of peace and it required the careful handling of alliances. If such handling was not displayed in 1787, the French were faced by bellicose decision-makers in Constantinople and by Dutch Patriots who were difficult to control. The inability to develop closer relations with Britain and Russia reflected not so much a French failure of perception about European developments as a more general resistance to a simplistic treatment of international relations in terms of building blocks, easily assembled or dispensed with. Aside from suspicion of France – and reluctance to ally with her – within Britain and Russia, there was an understandable concern in France about the idea of discarding allies, however much this might be for present or future advantage. This was not *simply* a matter of an anachronistic refusal to abandon the past; nor *simply* an inability to endorse change comparable to the inability also discerned in French domestic policy.

Instead, as in domestic politics, it is essential to confront the ambivalence of what was, and is, understood by reform. In 1815 France was indeed to accept British maritime and colonial dominance and a comparable Russian position in Eastern Europe, but there seemed little need to face such a situation in 1787. Voronzov, the Russian envoy in London, claimed in October 1789 that 'only two empires really exist: Russia as a power on land and Britain as a maritime power'.[97] Such a situation had seemed less apparent three years earlier, and a protracted period of conflict that was likely to produce such a result did not appear obvious.

Nor did it appear strongly the case in 1787 that either Britain or Russia would accommodate French interests. The possibility that France could benefit from a partition of the Turkish Empire was discussed anew in the winter of 1787–8, but such a role would threaten to destroy France's commercial position in the eastern Mediterranean and would undermine any prospect of her benefiting from links with Poland, Sweden and Prussia. In the case of Britain, there were no insur-mountable obstacles to better relations in the Indian Ocean and South Asia in 1787, but an abandonment of the Patriots by the French scarcely appeared necessary. Similarly, it did not appear appropriate to satisfy Joseph II over the Scheldt crisis and Bavaria in 1784–5.

With the benefit of hindsight, a more managed process of withdrawal from commitments and plans might have been prudent, in order to lessen the shock of the 1787 crisis. However, the aftermath of a successful war is not the best moment to argue weakness and preach restraint. More generally, there was a serious failure to convince the public about the wisdom of government policy, part of a wider crisis in which domestic problems increasingly limited diplomatic options, in which divisions over the latter exacerbated political tensions, and where both international and domestic issues were increasingly seen by the public as interrelated.[98] The initiative passed from France, but it did so in a context in which unforeseen developments challenged the calculations of all the major European powers.

CHAPTER SIX

The impact of Revolution, 1787–1799

Policy and justice are two ideas that have for too long been separated, but the Republic has firmly decided never to separate them.
                    Pierre Lebrun, foreign minister, November 1792.[1]

M. de Maude made a long visit yesterday to the Grand Pensionary, and uttered nothing but classical phrases, natural philosophy, and belles lettres.
                    Lord Auckland, British envoy in The Hague, about his French counterpart, June, 1792.[2]

The path from the Dutch crisis of 1787 first to the outbreak of the French Revolution in 1789 and then to the beginning of the French Revolutionary Wars in 1792 might appear clear, but this was no more the case in foreign policy and international relations than it was in domestic developments. France's prestige and alliance system were gravely weakened in 1787, but it was far from clear that the situation was irreversible, while the likely consequences of the crises of that year, in both the short and the long term, were also obscure. It was, for example, unclear, firstly, whether Britain and Prussia would ally, and, if so, to what end, and, secondly, whether Austria would join Russia against the Turks. An upsurge in the volatility of European power politics might create opportunities for France, or fresh problems.

1787–89

The crisis of 1787 had revealed not that France was without forces, but that she was unwilling to use them in the circumstances of September 1787. France was believed to seek revenge, rumours about her plans circulated, and the likely extent and duration of the French domestic crisis were unclear. The sense of flux that characterized eighteenth-century international relations was accentuated in years of crisis. In the second half of 1787 there was discussion about better relations between France and Prussia, or France and Britain, or France *vis-à-vis* Austria and Russia. In the context of late 1787, each represented a new departure. From August 1787 Montmorin sought to improve relations with Prussia, which was seen as an unreliable power but one that prevented France from having to be dependent on Austria.[3] This led to the dispatch of Groschlag to Berlin, but, in response to the Prussian invasion of the United Provinces, he received less accommodating instructions.[4]

Interest in better relations with Britain was also displayed. Via William Eden, the French government proposed co-operation in protecting the balance of power and in preserving the Turkish Empire from partition, by negotiating and then guaranteeing a peace on the basis of the *status quo ante bellum* [the situation before the war].[5] Given that neither Britain nor France was interested in territorial gains in Europe, it might be suggested that their failure to develop a *modus vivendi* after the Dutch crisis, let alone the 'solid system of friendship and peace' advocated by Eden – and certainly of some interest to the British Prime Minister, William Pitt the younger – was a mistake. The failure obliged Britain to commit herself to Prussia, in short to become involved in the aggressive schemes of the central and eastern European powers.

Eden wanted 'a full and permanent system' with both France and Spain, while the British envoy in Paris, the Duke of Dorset, proposed 'a kind of friendly intercourse' over the Balkan crisis 'especially as there is a disposition here to listen to anything that can tend to secure the peace and tranquillity of, *at least*, Europe'. Colonial rivalry was a major obstacle. Just as the War of American Independence had greatly increased British sensitivity about the strategic situation in Asia, so the Dutch crisis had emphasized the possibility of war and focused attention on naval strength. Colonial and maritime anxiety and competition with France continued and made the British determined to tie the Dutch into their alliance system; while French hopes of winning Dutch naval and colonial support, or, more realistically, of limiting their assistance to Britain, continued.[6] Neither the Anglo-French convention on India signed in August 1787 nor Montmorin's assurances allayed British fears.

In practice, the French were cautious in South Asia and their relations with Indian rulers were not such as to threaten Britain. In 1787 the evacuation of those French troops who were of European origin from Pondicherry was ordered and in 1788 the French government withdrew Residents from Indian courts and abandoned its Cochin China initiative. The Marathas were suspicious of French policy,[7] while Haidar Ali's successor, Tipu Sultan, was less enthusiastic than his father about co-operation with the French.[8] The British were not aware of the tension in the relationship and when, in 1787, Tipu sent an embassy to France in search of military assistance, the British responded with concern. Reaching Toulon in June 1788, the envoys were received by Louis XVI on 10 August

1788. Tipu offered commercial benefits and payment in return for the use of 3,000 troops, but the envoys were sent back with only promises of friendship, much to the displeasure of Tipu.[9]

There were other factors inhibiting any agreement with Britain, reasons that throw light on France's general situation. Distrust was important, specifically the fear that approaches might lead to embarrassing revelations at other courts. The French felt that they could not rely on the British. Until October 1788 the government assumed, as a consequence of the strength of British forces in the Indian Ocean and the West Indies, that conflict was possibly imminent, and took precautions accordingly.[10] Furthermore, the content of any agreement was likely to be unpalatable. There was no incentive for France to commit herself to passivity in the Indian Ocean, as the British required, while Pitt's interest in January 1788 in the idea of France ceding Mauritius and her Indian trading stations, in return for acceptance of gains from the Turks, lacked diplomatic momentum and, if acceptable, was more likely to be furthered by co-operation with Austria and Russia.

Indeed, having failed to prevent Austria from joining Russia against the Turks,[11] in the winter of 1787–8 there was an upsurge in talk about the possibility of a new quadruple alliance – a union of the Franco-Spanish and Austro-Russian alliances, or, at least, a pact of France, Austria and Russia. In a major reversal of policy, the French ministry was willing to support the idea of Austrian and Russian gains, at the expense of their traditional ally Turkey, as the price of an alliance. This was seen as necessary to counterbalance the new Anglo-Prussian alignment, and Montmorin, who had earlier proclaimed France's commitment to the Turkish Empire,[12] now argued that if Austria and Russia made territorial gains it was appropriate for France to do likewise, the thesis of equivalent acquisitions which was used to justify the successive partitions of Poland.[13] There was speculation that France might benefit by gains from the Turks in the Aegean, Crete and Egypt, and, also, that, far from the alliance being restricted to the Balkans, the Bavarian exchange scheme might be revived.

The Russian government pressed France to gain advantages by joining in the Balkan conflict. Montmorin argued that as the Turks had acted without consulting France, she was free to do as she thought best, and was not therefore obliged to support a collapsing empire. He and Ségur, the envoy in St Petersburg, feared that if France did not win the alliance of Russia, Britain would. Ségur thought that an alliance of Austria, France and Russia would create fear in Britain and Prussia, and be a brilliant revenge for the Dutch crisis.[14] Montmorin anticipated that once Austria and Russia had beaten the Turks they would fall out, making France a desirable partner. He argued that the possibility of Franco-Russian co-operation would restrain Austria.[15]

The Spanish government, unhappy about Russian conquests at the expense of the Turks, rejected the idea of the alliance, while the French were unwilling to guarantee the existing status of Russian-dominated Poland. Montmorin was also concerned about the French commercial stake in the Turkish Empire.[16] With a reminder of the uncertainty of international relations, Noailles suggested that, if the Turks defeated the Russians, Catherine II could be dethroned and an alliance negotiated between Russia and Prussia.[17] This did not deter Montmorin, not least because he did not believe in assessing the policy of others in terms that were overly complex, profound and reflective,[18] but it underlined the extent to which the outbreak of war increased the sense of international flux and new opportunities.

Unable to join Austria and Russia against the Turks, France could not gain compensating advantage elsewhere. Prussia allied with Britain in August 1788, and Sweden, a traditional French ally, followed an independent line, beginning a war with Russia in July 1788. This conflict both posed problems for France and revealed its increasing weakness, for it was Britain and Prussia, not France, that persuaded the Danes to agree that October to end their invasion of Sweden. That November, even Karl Eugen, Duke of Württemberg, was ready to abandon his connections with France and Austria and to approach Britain for an alliance. The French government was increasingly unable to influence European diplomacy. Still hoping that relations with Austria and Russia could be improved, Montmorin was not interested in the idea of co-operating with the British in seeking to mediate a settlement in the Balkans.[19]

The very linkage of Austria and Russia was a sign of French failure, and led some French diplomats to regard Prussia with greater favour.[20] Despite what he saw as hostile Prussian policies, Montmorin stressed France's interest in her preservation,[21] a view that reflected ministerial attitudes during the Seven Years' War, when there had been concern that an overly-weakened Prussia would make Austria a difficult ally. In the mid-1780s it was unclear whether Joseph would prefer his Russian ally or the 'alliance of 1756'; in 1787 the decision was clearly taken and it reflected the greater importance of Joseph's alliance with Russia over that with France. This also repeated the situation during the Seven Years' War.

In part, such developments can be seen as a continuation of the general slackening of French diplomatic influence that, to a certain extent, had characterized international relations since the 1680s, and, more markedly, since the mid-1750s. They also reflected the particular dynamics of the international system in 1787-8. French domestic problems were seen as crucial in affecting French policy by many commentators,[22] as well as providing an apparently obvious indication of French strength to foreign observers.

Such a stress on domestic circumstances was traditional. The French Revolution, in its early or 'pre-revolutionary' stages, was seen not as a new development, a product of spreading radicalism, but, rather, as a conventional political crisis, in which a ruler faced serious domestic problems, primarily aristocratic factionalism and financial difficulties. These appeared to affect France's international capability, her ability to wage war or sustain a military confrontation, and her stability as an ally. Thus, for example, in the spring of 1757 one London newspaper reported that the French government needed peace because of the strength of domestic opposition,[23] while it was then believed in diplomatic circles in Turin that the government would have to yield in its disputes with the *Parlement* of Paris.[24]

France did indeed seem weaker in the late 1780s. In terms of the percentage of the French budget spent on the military in the period 1712–88, 1788 was the low point. Post-war demobilization in the army from 1783 was followed by a fresh reduction, and morale was affected badly.[25] In August 1788 payments from the heavily indebted Treasury were suspended and Brienne resigned. The pay of dockyard workers was seriously in arrears. In March 1789 domestic circumstances prevented France from fulfilling plans to send a squadron of observation to sea that would manoeuvre jointly with that of Spain. The Spanish first minister, Count Floridablanca, was very disappointed, as he had hoped that the planned joint manoeuvres would impress the rest of Europe, indicating the continued strength of the alliance. Montmorin could only express the hope that it would be possible to stage joint manoeuvres in 1790.[26]

Such problems were not novel in type, and did not, therefore, necessarily appear insuperable, or likely to provoke a change in the French political system, and it was possible to envisage a revival in French strength. This was to come, eventually, through revolutionary change, but in 1788 and early 1789 it appeared, instead, that a revival, producing a more effective monarchy, would come, either through a solution to the political crisis achieved by traditional means, or thanks to institutional reform and constitutional revival focusing on a new partnership of crown and nation, the path sought by the government and the political nation, and anticipated by Montmorin.[27] In 1782 Frederick II had suggested that a bankruptcy of the French government might permit a process of financial regeneration that left the government with more abundant resources.[28]

Furthermore, in early 1789 France did not appear to be in as poor shape relative to other powers as she had been in early 1788. Joseph II and Catherine II, especially the former, were beset by problems, while Britain was affected by the regency crisis stemming from George III's poor health. France seemed more stable in early 1789 than she had been in the summer and autumn of 1788. The possibility that the Estates General, last called in 1614 and formally summoned on 24 January 1789, would bring renewed vigour to France was credible. It might be able to produce political and fiscal solutions that could offer a guarantee for the national debt. The Count of Aranda, formerly Spanish envoy in Paris, could suggest to Montmorin in January 1789 that the Third Estate would support the crown, in order not to be crushed by the other two estates [clergy and nobility], and that the crown could therefore benefit from a powerful constituency of support.[29] Gustavus III had had considerable success in Sweden in seeking the support of the Third Estate against aristocratic opponents.

The start of the Revolution

After elections in early 1789, the Estates General convened at Versailles on 5 May. Louis XVI's opening speech was interrupted by repeated cries of 'Vive le Roi'. In the opening session Necker pressed the case for reform; but division – over the issue of common voting, a measure that would lessen aristocratic influence, or separate voting, by estate – was serious from the outset. The Third Estate refused to accept the system of orders. Heady oratory, pressure of circumstances and a growing sense of crisis led the Third Estate to declare themselves the National Assembly and to claim a measure of sovereignty on 17 June. The government countered by planning a 'Royal Session' to reassert the authority of Louis XVI. The preparatory prohibition of any meetings by the Estates, however, led the angry deputies, wrongly concluding that a dissolution was intended, to assemble on 20 June in an indoor tennis-court and to pledge themselves not to disperse until reform was complete and France had a new constitution. Eventually held on 23 June 1789, the Royal Session was a failure. Louis XVI's proffered reforms were no longer sufficient, and the Third Estate refused to disperse. Louis backed down, while public order collapsed in Paris. On 27 June the king bowed to the crisis and instructed the clerical and noble orders to join the National Assembly.

In the face of the crisis, Louis XVI was pressed to consider a counter-revolution. On 11 July Necker and his ally Montmorin were dismissed. Whether Louis and the new chief minister, Breteuil, intended to reassert royal authority by force or sought negotiations with the National Assembly, the situation was changed by a popular uprising in Paris.[30] Anger at the Royal Session combined with anxiety about the troops massing near Paris. On 14 July the price of grain peaked in Paris, and the Bastille was seized in an outburst of popular action. Louis was advised that he could not rely on his troops to suppress the Parisians, who had rallied to the support of the National Assembly. Necker was recalled and on 17 July Louis's brother, the Count of Artois, later Charles X, the leading opponent of reform, left Versailles for the frontier.

The return of Necker did not bring stability. The 'October Days' made it clear that the Revolution was not over. Louis's reluctance to accept reform, and rumours of preparations for a counter-revolution, led on 5 October to a march on Versailles by a Parisian crowd, including many women, determined to bring Louis to Paris. After the queen's apartments were stormed by a section of the crowd, the king, under pressure, went to the Tuileries palace in Paris next day. Versailles was abandoned, and the volatile metropolis became even more the centre of power and politics. Montmorin sought to put the best gloss he could on the October Days,[31] but diplomats and other commentators saw royal power as exploded and, as yet, no solid alternative to it.

France was weak, but it was also volatile, and that ensured that diplomatic interest was more sustained than in 1788. This was accentuated by widespread opposition to Joseph II in the Austrian Netherlands that led to revolution there.

Indeed, the prospect of a French role in that revolution ensured that from the outset of the French Revolution, even when the government was very weak, there were still fears that the French might destabilize their neighbours. In August 1789 the Imperial Vice-Chancellor, Prince Franz von Colleredo-Mansfeld, told Noailles that the spirit of disobedience in the Austrian Netherlands was being fanned from France. Noailles replied, with reason, that disturbances had broken out earlier in the Austrian Netherlands;[32] but there was still the danger that they would be exploited either by the current French government or by the unknown quantity of a new one. In 1788 there had been false reports that Joseph II had mortgaged or ceded, part or all of, the Austrian Netherlands to France. The disturbances there could be exploited by France, either to help the rebels or to assist Joseph. The fate of the Austrian Netherlands also raised the issue of which group was in charge of French policy, the government or the radicals of the time.

More conservative elements also sought to influence the situation in France and abroad. They were most vocally represented by the *émigrés* and their foreign supporters. In December 1789 Artois appealed to Pitt for help. He argued that if the French government declared a bankruptcy, it would become a threat to Britain, because there would be an opportunity to start afresh after wiping out accumulated debts, and that, if the Revolution continued, there would be a danger of a general war and of the wrecking of the balance of power. Artois sought a British lead in encouraging other powers to discuss the French situation and suggested, once royal authority was restored, an alliance of Britain, Prussia and France, with Britain compensating herself for her earlier efforts with French colonial possessions. Pitt did not reply.[33]

There was considerable uneasiness about the Revolution from the outset elsewhere in Europe, with efforts to prevent or limit the circulation of news about developments in France, but tacit support for the cause of counter-revolution was equivalent to offering none.

The Nootka Sound crisis of 1790 and the weakness of Revolutionary France

War came close in 1790, not as a consequence of trying to spread revolution or as a product of counter-revolutionary activities, but as a result of French backing for Spain in an unexpected dispute with Britain over Pacific trade and settlement, the Nootka Sound crisis. In origins, the dispute was not dissimilar to that over the Falkland Islands in 1770. The two countries were still united by the Third Family Compact of 1761, and there were suggestions that war might be welcome to some political circles in France, especially the Crown, as it might serve to unite the country. The crisis was both a last gasp of the Anglo-Bourbon *ancien régime* confrontation and a foretaste of what was, in part, a later continuation, the post-1815 struggles between imperial powers for trans-oceanic territory and colonial trading rights, struggles arising from competing interests, not ideologies. Yet the Nootka Sound crisis also revealed the state of uncertainty and flux in interests, objectives and alignments that arose from the revolution in France. Alongside the traditional Anglo–Bourbon element in the confrontation, there were cross-currents suggesting different concerns that might lead to other alignments, joining Britain and France, or Britain and Spain, against the third. Spanish governmental anxiety over developments within France and the possible impact of French revolutionary ideology helped to induce both hesitation about turning to France and post-crisis interest in better relations with Britain.

Uncertainty about French domestic changes affected not only the attitudes of other powers, but also the stages by which the Nootka Sound crisis was played out. In May 1790 Montmorin told the Spanish envoy that fulfilling French obligations to her ally would encounter domestic opposition.[34] Montmorin suspected correctly that the British were trying to divide the Bourbon powers, but by playing on French – not, as in the past, Spanish – fears, a process aided by the emergence in France of the National Assembly as an alternative basis for power to the royal court. Specifically he had suspicions that Spanish armaments were designed to reverse the Revolution.[35]

The transition from the Bourbon Family Pact to a Franco-Spanish alliance reflecting the shifts in power within France created serious strains in the alliance. The rapid speed of changes in France and the absence there of sufficient time, trust and shared views to permit the development of stable constitutional conventions and techniques of parliamentary management, helped to keep the relationship between the royal government and the National Assembly unsettled, but so also did differences over policy. Above all, there was a crucial lack of trust, a justified sense that – if he was able to dispense with it – Louis XVI would not accept the role of the Assembly. Montmorin felt obliged to write to the president of the National Assembly to inform him of Louis XVI's decision to arm 14 ships of the line and of the need to show Europe that domestic developments had not destroyed France's ability to deploy her forces. The Assembly was assured, nevertheless, that Louis would try to settle the dispute by negotiation.[36]

The effect of the decision to arm the ships was greatly lessened on 22 May 1790 by the resolution of the National Assembly, after bitter debates, that the king could not declare war without its approval. These debates reflected a profound division as to the nature of the political community centring on the struggle between different ideas about the relationship between Crown and nation, which developed into a clash of royal versus national sovereignty, with particular reference to the right of declaring war. The eventual decision was a compromise, as it had been argued by some speakers that the monarch should lose the right completely, while others, such as Barnave, had condemned the idea of an armament. Spanish policy had also been criticized bitterly by, among others, Charles de Lameth and Robespierre.[37] The decree appeared to demonstrate not only that France's strength (and therefore the likely response of other powers to her), but also the very process of foreign policy formulation, had been changed dramatically by the Revolution. The pressure for change reflected concern over royal views and the impact of radical writers, such as Rousseau, Mercier de la Rivière, and Condorcet, who argued that reform required the transfer of control over foreign policy from essentially bellicose, irrational and selfish monarchs, to the people who would be led by reason and would love peace.

Such ideas were absorbed, or at least repeated, by French diplomats. Thus, in July 1792 Chauvelin, the envoy in London, wrote of the 'ancien regime which alone caused all the wars that have for too long divided the two nations'. Montmorin himself was convinced that, no matter how the Revolution turned out, the French ruler would never again exercise the unlimited control over foreign policy that he once had; although his reluctance to move the foreign policy prerogative more rapidly into the hands of the popular assembly ultimately doomed him. Perceptive observers predicted that the National Assembly's dismissal of war as an instrument of foreign policy would prove only rhetorical and that 'democratic' states would be as given to aggression as were 'despotic' monarchies.

The Spanish government was concerned in 1790 by signs that France would not provide support. On 16 June a formal demand for French assistance was made, but, in reply, Spain was informed that Louis XVI must submit the request to the National Assembly. Nothing was done until late August, and, until then, it appeared that Spain would receive no aid. Indeed, far from focusing on the alleged threat from British maritime power, the National Assembly was more concerned about the consequences of the Anglo-Spanish crisis for French politics, not least the alleged views of the French envoy in Madrid, Vauguyon, who appealed to Louis XVI for permission to justify himself before the Assembly from charges of having incited the crisis.[38] Links were not only under pressure with Spain. Cooler relations between Austria and France were seen as a problem by Noailles. He warned Montmorin that an alignment between Austria and Britain might lead to opposition to France.[39]

On 26 August 1790 the National Assembly unexpectedly decided to press Louis XVI to negotiate what was termed a national treaty between France and Spain and to authorize the arming of 45 ships of the line and a proportionate number of frigates. The latter step was taken in light of the armaments of other unnamed powers and to provide security for French trade and colonies; Spain was not mentioned. However, the congruence of the authorization of the armament with the pressure for a national treaty, and the nature of Anglo-Spanish relations, made the anti-British objective of the measure readily apparent. The decision was ratified by Louis XVI on 28 August, and on 1 September Montmorin sent word to the Spanish government that the naval armament would be ordered as soon as possible.[40]

This was an early example of the impact of the contents and timing of public politics on French policy. The action of the National Assembly encouraged the British to develop links with politicians there, providing a parallel track to official negotiations with the government. William Augustus Miles was sent to Paris in

July 1790, Hugh Elliot, a friend of Mirabeau, following in late October. Miles made approaches to Talleyrand, Mirabeau and Lafayette, was elected a member of the radical Jacobin Club, and seems to have succeeded in lessening suspicion of Britain among the populist politicians. Elliot explained British policy to a deputation from the Diplomatic Committee of the National Assembly, argued that Spain sought war in order to help the cause of counter-revolution in France, and speculated about the possibility of better Anglo-French relations,[41] only to find that his own government was not interested in such a prospect.

The ending of the confrontation with Spain in October 1790, as Spain climbed down, led to a decline in British governmental interest in France, her politics and policies. Even had the British ministry sought more, the domestic French situation was too unsettled to make negotiations aimed at anything other than immediate objectives worthwhile. Furthermore, whatever her government, France could offer little assistance as an ally, as reports of her recent reported naval armament had indicated. The authorization of a large naval mobilization had not been matched by equivalent activity in the naval dockyards. There were also problems with control over the army. For a power – Britain – preparing in the winter of 1790–91 to confront Russia, France was likely to be not so much an uncertain ally as one so weak, as to have no weight in diplomatic combinations. French weakness indeed had considerably lessened the danger that she would be able to intervene in the Low Countries.

There was a general tendency to refuse to pay taxes in the early revolutionary years, and more direct links between France's domestic situation and her international position, including discontent at the major naval dockyard of Brest. France also worried the Spanish government as a source of subversion: reports from Puyabry, French envoy in Spain, conveyed a sense of the alarm. Frenchmen on Spanish territory were expelled or arrested, measures taken to prevent the spread of French works and ideas.[42] The Franco-Spanish alliance was being dissolved by Spanish concern about domestic French developments and by the determination of French politicians to redefine French policy and to grasp control of it from the Crown. The two powers were to go to war on 7 March 1793.

Thanks also to domestic problems, France could not sustain her recent level of trans-oceanic activity, especially in the Pacific, where the British were making major gains. The French expedition that set off in search of La Pérouse under D'Entrecasteaux in 1791, circumnavigated Australia, named the Kermadecs, discovered the D'Entrecasteaux Islands and explored the Solomons, but the energy that had characterized French activity in the mid-1780s was not maintained, and this activity was cut short by the Revolutionary Wars. D'Entrecasteaux himself died at sea of dysentery in 1793.

A sense of being passed by the British characterized French public debate and affected the government. Although regarding the British conflict with Tipu Sahib of Mysore in 1790–92 as unjust, Montmorin was obliged in February 1791 to deny that France was sending arms to Mysore. She was not in a position to help, a situation very different to that a decade earlier, and in 1792 the Governor of Pondicherry did not respond to an approach from the Sri Lankan kingdom of Kandy for help against the Dutch.[43] Jezzar Ahmed Pasha, Governor of Palestine, used France's loss of prestige following the Revolution to expel her merchants, only inviting them back in 1790 on his own terms. In April 1791, Montmorin was concerned by reports that the British were after an island in the Aegean,[44] an area where French acquisitions had been discussed over the previous decade. He was also worried that in the event of a general war Britain would conquer French colonies or encourage them to seek independence.[45] There was also suspicion that Britain was trying to use French difficulties in order to supplant her trade in the crucial Spanish market. The deputies of the ports had supported naval armaments in the Nootka Sound crisis,[46] and there was a feeling that France had lost out by a failure to assert itself.

The formal renunciation by the National Assembly of war for the purpose of making conquests on 22 May 1790[47] was not an isolated expression of opinion, or even an opinion restricted to the public sphere. A month earlier, France's leading diplomat, Noailles, had written from Vienna to suggest that Europe would be more tranquil if rulers accepted what they had inherited, and concentrated on domestic problems instead of territorial aggrandizement.[48] In June 1790 Luzerne, the envoy in London, criticized the idea that Britain and Spain should fight over Nootka Sound, employing language similar to that of Voltaire when he had condemned the idea of fighting over Canada: 'the horrors of a war for several merchantmen of little value and for the possession of barren territory of no value'.[49]

It would be easy to dismiss such statements simply as a consequence of the acute French weakness discerned by Montmorin,[50] to suggest that the objectives, agenda and course of international relations were essentially set by the distribution and use of power. From this perspective, France did not play an active role when her relative power declined during the early stages of the revolutionary crisis, but in 1792 she returned to take a major part in a system in which she had played a minor role since 1787, and a limited one since the Seven Years' War.

Such an interpretation is excessively mechanistic. French objectives were clearly framed in light of what appeared to be relative capabilities, but they also reflected the conception of the international system held by those who comprised and influenced the government. In this respect, as in much else, there was considerable continuity between the policies of the *ancien régime* French state and those of the politicians of 1789–91. France had essentially abandoned an aggressive continental foreign policy in mid-century, not in 1787 or 1789. Her forces had not campaigned in the Low Countries since 1748, nor had Louis XV or Louis XVI made gains at the expense of the Austrian Netherlands. The essential objective of French foreign policy over the previous half-century, of a stable Europe without aggressive wars, was inherited by the government of Revolutionary France.

This was not surprising. At least initially, the foreign minister, Montmorin, and many of the diplomats were unchanged: it was safer and less contentious to further a view of French interests when in Constantinople than it was in Paris. In addition, a powerful draught of revolutionary enthusiasm contributed to the same end. Aggressive war was as one with feudalism: neither had their place in the best of all possible worlds being created with such alacrity, and both could be safely denounced. Thus, public politics matched governmental priorities.

From Varennes to war with Austria, 1791-2

European diplomatic attention in 1790 and early 1791 was centred on Eastern Europe, not France, but the situation changed in the summer of 1791, owing firstly to a crisis in the position of Louis XVI and, secondly, to a more active stance on the part of Austria. Disenchantment with, and concern about, his position within France led Louis to heed the advice from his wife and others that he should flee Paris. He intended to escape to Montmédy in Lorraine – near the frontier with the Austrian Netherlands and in an area where the military commander, the Marquis de Bouillé, was willing to offer protection – and then to pursue a negotiated restoration of his authority.

It is unclear how far Louis planned to seek international assistance in re-establishing his position. Joseph II's heir, Leopold II, was initially cool about his brother-in-law's plight, but his attitude changed as the situation deteriorated, and as it became clear that Louis would try to flee, thus forcing a crisis. If the king escaped, he would be better able to demand help for counter-revolution, and relations between France and Leopold II would be brought to a head. Had Louis escaped, he would probably have received help from Leopold in re-establishing his power.

Louis was stopped at Varennes and returned to Paris,[51] but the problem of a monarch out of sympathy with developments in his country had not been solved. Having sought in May to calm Artois's zeal for a counter-revolution,[52] Leopold II responded to the flight to Varennes on 6 July 1791 by issuing the Padua Circular, an appeal to Europe's rulers for concerted action to restore the liberty of the French royal family. Such a policy required Prussian support. Catherine the Great of Russia and the virulently anti-revolutionary Gustavus III of Sweden were not in a position to act against France, and Spain and Sardinia were too weak to do so. Indeed, conscious of its military weakness, the Spanish government was unwilling to do much in practice.[53] Frederick William II of Prussia, however, joined Leopold in issuing the Declaration of Pillnitz, on 27 August 1791. It sought to give added force to the principles set forth in the Padua Circular. The rulers made it clear, nevertheless, that they would act to secure the position of Louis XVI only if they gained the support of their fellow sovereigns, which was then unlikely.

France's neighbours had two potentially clashing possibilities: the creation of a security system aimed against any French aggression and support for a counter-revolution in France. The latter was increasingly seen as crucial to international stability in Western Europe. In the short term, this was mistaken. Although French policies and instability challenged her neighbours, a counter-revolution effected by foreign troops could not but be bloody, and might not be successful.

After his unsuccessful flight, Louis XVI had little choice but to accept formally the new constitution on 13 September 1791. Despite Montmorin's hopes, especially about a shift in Austrian and Prussian attitudes,[54] this step did not greatly ease international tension. Instead, signs of French aggression and apparent instability kept the situation volatile. These included in September the annexation of the papal territory of Avignon, seen as an anachronism, growing calls for war against Austria and the German protectors of the *émigrés*, and the distrust between Louis XVI and the new Legislative Assembly which followed his vetoing of the decree against the *émigrés* passed on 9 November 1791.

The war that began with Austria in April 1792 was France's first conflict with a continental power since the Seven Years' War. It began in a very different fashion. France was alone, bar for the backing of foreign radicals, the extent and effectiveness of which was greatly exaggerated. Furthermore, France began the conflict, declaring war on 20 April 1792. She was not drawn in as a result of alliance systems and the action or problems of an ally, as had been the case in 1756. As a consequence, the causes of French policy can be seen to arise largely from domestic circumstances, although these of course were in part activated by the international situation. The move towards war reflected incompatible views on the rights of German princes, both in Alsace[55] and to harbour *émigrés*, but these were made more serious by a mutual lack of sympathy and understanding between Austria and France, and by a shared conviction that the other power was weak and would yield to intimidation.

The increasingly influential Jacques-Pierre Brissot and other leaders of the Girondin faction saw war as a means to unite the country behind them, with Louis either included in this new unity or clearly identified as its opponent. Both these options were regarded as likely to strengthen the Girondins. The move to war divided the radicals. Having initially supported the call for war, Robespierre, on 11 December 1791, condemned it. He feared that war would enhance the power of the executive, while Danton was afraid that it would help his opponent Lafayette who had been given a military command.[56] Brissot's war-mongering tactics in the Legislative Assembly underlined the doubts raised about the debate and decree of 22 May 1790 limiting royal rights in the declaration of war. Politicians were caught up in (and eventually destroyed by) the dynamic of creating policy in a volatile context without stable domestic parameters.

Relations between Revolutionary France and Austria were more acute than those between France and other powers, not so much because of their common frontier in the Low Countries, as because Leopold II was both Emperor and brother-in-law of Louis XVI. In his former role, he had to protect the frontiers of the empire and the interests of the princes threatened by Revolutionary France, whether because they claimed rights in Alsace, or, more seriously, sheltered *émigrés*. On 29 November 1791 the National Assembly called upon Louis XVI to insist that Leopold II and the Elector of Trier disperse the *émigré* forces on their territories. This pressure was more acute because it followed 35 years of generally good relations, or at least of an absence of hostilities. In contrast, there was no element of compromise either in the French demands of late 1791 or in their subsequent policy.[57]

The Archbishop-Elector of Trier, Clemens Wenzelaus, had provided his nephew Artois, who had arrived at his capital Koblenz in June 1791, with the nearby chateau of Schönbornlust. Koblenz had become the centre of *émigré* activity. Another Imperial Elector, Frederick Carl, Archbishop-Elector of Mainz, had appealed for Imperial support against French infringements of his rights, especially his metropolitan (ecclesiastical) rights over the bishoprics of Basle, Speyer and Strasbourg, guaranteed by the Peace of Westphalia, but taken from him by decrees of the National Assembly. In response to French pressure, Clemens Wenzeslaus agreed to expel the *émigrés*, but Leopold, who did not want war, decided that a firm Austrian stance, supported by the threat of military force, seemed the best way to protect the principalities in the region from external and internal threats. He rejected the National Assembly's position on Alsace, and on 21 December 1791 the French envoy was told that action against Trier would lead to an Austrian military response.

Having suppressed the rising in the Austrian Netherlands, the Austrians were in a better position to act in the area. Trier could be easily reached from the fortress of Luxembourg. Presenting the report of the Diplomatic Committee to the National Assembly, Armand Gensonné, a leading Girondin, argued that the Austrian step reflected Leopold's determination to dominate the French government.[58] This was misleading, but, having restored order in Hungary and the Austrian Netherlands, avoided a threatened war with Prussia, and negotiated peace with the Turks, Leopold was now in a better position to defend Imperial interests. The breakdown in relations between Austria and France revived uncertainty about hegemony over France's German borderlands. This was no longer, as under Louis XIV, a matter of unsettled frontiers but, rather, focused on a more 'modern' agenda, specifically ideological subversion and both revolutionary and counter-revolutionary activity and threats. These concerns gave an intensity and urgent paranoia to the situation very different to what might have been anticipated from many of the specific points at issue, especially the feudal rights of German princes in Alsace.

Leopold's role as brother-in-law of Louis XVI was somewhat ambivalent. Although he did not despise him in the robust fashion of Joseph II, Leopold had only limited sympathy for the unfortunate monarch. Furthermore, support for Louis's position was hindered, if not compromised, by the myriad rivalries among the agents of the royalist cause and by the understandable inconsistencies of

Louis's position, exemplified by his switch from flight to Varennes to ostensible support for the new constitution. Leopold sought stability, not war, but miscalculated about how best to use threats to preserve peace.

Misleading expectations about the likely response of the other helped lead both powers to war in April 1792.[59] These suppositions reflected an atmosphere of suspicion and tension. Speakers in the National Assembly returned frequently to the theme of a link between domestic and foreign enemies: each allegedly made action against the other more necessary. The actions of the *émigrés*, the real and rumoured Austrian connections of the royal court, and the obvious hostile sentiments of most foreign monarchs, lent apparent substance to such accusations, as did a strong sense that French interests had been betrayed since 1756 by her Austrian alliance, an alliance for which the fault was held to lie with the Bourbon monarchy. A failure to unite with Prussia was held responsible for unwelcome Austrian actions, for, it was argued, Austria could therefore dare to betray France.[60] Thus, the foreign policy of the *ancien régime* was blamed for the difficult position France was in.

Although condemnation of the Austrian alliance could unite both traditional critics of an alignment that had not lacked enemies under the *ancien régime* and enthusiasts for a new order, not least those who were suspicious of the royal court, it increasingly lent energy to a strong critique of the Crown. Thus, the Girondin Pierre Vergniaud declared in January 1792 – in a vociferous speech in which the threat to the Revolution was stressed and the call 'aux armes' reiterated – 'that the breaking of the treaty is a revolution in the international system as necessary for Europe and for France as the destruction of the Bastille was for our internal regeneration'.[61] Three Girondins gained ministerial office as a prelude to war.

The declaration of war on Leopold's successor, Francis II, on 20 April 1792, was presented as the just defence of a free people against the aggression of a king. It was supported by politicians, such as Louis, Count of Narbonne, the minister of war, who hoped that a successful war would rally support for constitutional royalism within France, and by others, pro- and anti-royalist, who imagined that success or failure would serve their ends, by leading to the defeat of the Revolutionaries, as Marie Antoinette hoped, or by discrediting the monarchy.

The Revolution and French foreign policy

The Revolution had brought changes of great consequence to the tone of French policy. Confidence in France's ability to confront and overcome the domestic and international world of established privilege and traditional rules was expressed fervently in the somewhat millenarian atmosphere of the debates in the National Assembly. This affected aspects of continuity in policy objectives. For over a century, French policy had focused on the need to avoid the development of a powerful opposing coalition, and this had interacted with a sense of caution, for example, to limit territorial objectives in 1733–5 and 1741–3. Some French politicians and diplomats still urged this course in 1792. They hoped to win the support, or at least neutrality, of Britain, Prussia and the United Provinces, the apparent alternative to Austria. Narbonne, minister of war from December 1791 to March 1792, and Charles-François Dumouriez, the anti-Austrian foreign minister from 15 March to 13 June 1792, both sought to win Prussian neutrality. A French mission, whose most prominent member was Talleyrand, arrived in London in search of better relations in January 1792. He saw his mission as parallel to one in Berlin.[62] Brissot claimed in January 1792 that the collapse of the Austro–French alliance was a guarantee of Prussian neutrality and urged his audience to recall the Anglo–French alliance of 1716.[63] Frederick William II, however, fulfilled his defensive alliance with Austria and declared war on France on 21 May 1792.

Brissot's speech was but one instance of the common habit of speakers in the National Assembly of ranging widely over French policy that century with scant suggestion that past episodes were irrelevant because of subsequent domestic or international changes. This ahistoricism was related to a habit of arguing from first principles, a practice that also paid little heed to the views of others.

The new nature of the discussion, formulation, and execution of French policy ensured that the suggestion that allies be sought was not pursued consistently, that it was compromised by attempts to inspire political change elsewhere, if not also political and social radicalism, and that the new universalist rationale of the French policy, its mission and ideology, made *ad hoc* attempts at compromise and at the retention of aspects of the *ancien régime* diplomatic system unconvincing. Once unconvincing, there was little mileage in them, for a degree of certainty about the intentions and consistency of a partner in negotiation was as important as the apparent nature of those intentions.

Yet, alongside a new public attitude there were still attempts to prevent war with the whole of Europe. Due to the pressure of public politics and the accompanying risk of denunciation, and the established requirements of secret diplomacy, these attempts were secretive and frequently obscure. However, they were important both to attempts to bring a measure of consistency to French policy and to the views of foreign governments, and they can be traced throughout the 1790s. To give an example, in the summer of 1792 Scipion-Louis-Joseph, Marquis de Chambonas, who was briefly foreign minister, made approaches to Prussia and (though to a lesser extent) to Austria, in an effort to limit, if not end, the war; and he also approached Britain, suggesting that Austro-Prussian co-operation had destroyed the balance of power in the empire, and that the two powers ought to align accordingly. The Elector of Mainz was approached with the same warnings about Austria and Prussia, while, in May, Dumouriez had instructed the newly accredited envoy to Naples to seek Neapolitan neutrality.[64]

Chambonas's approaches met with no response, and can be seen as evidence of improbable hopes and desperate fears. War with Austria and Prussia was a more serious prospect than those that had faced France at the beginning of wars earlier in the century. Once the hopes of Prussian non-intervention had been shown to be naïve, the French radicals in 1792 were mostly driven into a bunker mentality with a hostility to the outer world, sometimes shot through with implausible hopes of alliances. Chambonas's political position was less radical. His approaches to other powers also reflected a desperate opportunism, and too much weight should not be placed on individual arguments at such a juncture.

As with other analyses of the international situation, that by Chambonas has to be set in context. Thus, reasons had to be advanced to support the approach to Britain. Accepting this caveat, the approach on the eve of a major period of conflict in Europe is interesting for its echo of earlier suggestions, most recently by D'Aiguillon in 1772–3, by Vergennes after the War of American Independence, and by Montmorin in late 1787. All assumed that Britain should be an ally in opposing unwelcome steps by all, two or any of the Partitioning powers. This cut across the argument that France's interests were bound up with a struggle with Britain for maritime supremacy. Such an argument meant little during the struggle for survival in 1792. Chambonas's suggestions are important in indicating the extent to which efforts were made to maintain or create links in 1792, and suggest the volatility of French policy at this juncture. Chambonas was one of the five foreign ministers in 1792: revolutionary politics put a major strain on the conduct of foreign policy.[65]

These efforts were to be hindered, and yet also given new energy, by the pressure of domestic change. Louis XVI's dismissal on 13 June 1792 of the Girondin ministers appointed on 10 March had both created a sense of new diplomatic possibilities and helped to unite and radicalize his opponents. Marseille volunteers marched into Paris on 30 July, singing the *War Song* written by Rouget de Lisle. Such volunteers were keen to fight against the enemies of the Revolution, and, increasingly, ready to identify them with the occupants of the Tuileries, where the Girondin press claimed that an 'Austrian committee' was meeting with the support of the queen. The poisonous effects of paranoia brought denunciations and violence to Paris. On 25 July the advancing Prussian commander, the Duke of Brunswick, issued a declaration setting out the aims of Frederick William II and Francis II. They claimed to seek the re-establishment of Louis XVI's legislative authority and, to that end, Brunswick warned that Paris would be subject to exemplary vengeance if the king was harmed.[66]

News of the declaration caused outrage in Paris, helping precipitate the crisis on 10 August in which the Tuileries was stormed. The monarchy was suspended by the Legislative Assembly, and on 13 August Louis XVI was in effect imprisoned in the Temple keep. The theory and, to a limited extent, practice of popular sovereignty was thrust to the fore. Surrender of frontier fortresses – Longwy on 23 August and Verdun on 3 September – to the advancing Allied forces, led in Paris to the September Massacres, as 1,100–1,400 people accused of treason, including Montmorin and his successor, Lessart, were killed.

The practice of authority was similarly disrupted in the French colonial world. In Mauritius and Réunion popular assemblies seized power and in November 1790 a mob killed the Count of Macnamara, commander of the French squadron in the Indian Ocean. More generally, the breakdown of authority in France and the French colonial world gravely weakened the navy.[67] The Revolution divided the French adventurers in India, who having developed westernized forces for Indian princes served as foci for French interests and hopes, especially in Hyderabad and northern India. In the West Indies, the Revolution encouraged slave aspirations for a new order and led to a total breakdown of authority and colonial control with a major rebellion in St Domingue.

Diplomats had been accredited to Louis XVI and the collapse of his government led in August 1792 to a break in formal diplomatic relations. The British, Danish, Dutch, Polish, Spanish, Swedish and Venetian envoys left. However, the new revolutionary government wished to maintain relations, and indeed hoped for an alliance with Britain, Prussia and the Dutch, a favoured scheme of the new foreign minister, Lebrun,[68] a former journalist. Danton wished to restrict the war to Austria. The attacks on Montmorin in the Legislative Assembly on 21 and 31 August 1792 had centred on his failure the previous year to take advantage of what was seen as a good opportunity to negotiate a Franco-Prussian alliance.[69]

From Valmy to war with Britain, 1792–3

Diplomatic might-have-beens were overtaken by military success. The Prussian advance on Paris was blocked by a larger French force at Valmy, about 108 miles from Paris, on 20 September 1792. The Prussians had already encountered serious problems with the intractable terrain of the Argonne, logistics, the effect of rain on the roads, and sickness, especially dysentery. They were not prepared for a major campaign, and the very presence of a numerous, well-prepared French army was sufficient to check them. Negotiations between Dumouriez and the Prussians for a cessation of arms began on 23 September and lasted for a month. The French government hoped for a separate Franco-Prussian peace as a possible prelude to a quadruple alliance of the two powers, Britain and the Dutch. What they obtained was a Prussian withdrawal from France.

Brunswick abandoned Verdun on 8 October and Longwy on 22 October. Meanwhile, on 22 September the French Army of the Alps invaded Savoy. Chambéry fell on 24 September, Nice on 29 September. In the Rhineland, French troops advancing on Brunswick's flank, captured Speyer on 30 September, Worms on 4 October, Mainz on 21 October and Frankfurt on 22 October.

On 23 October the celebratory salvoes of the cannon of General Kellermann's Army of the Moselle proclaimed that all foreign troops had been driven from the Republic. Following a victory over a smaller Austrian army at Jemappes on 6 November, the Austrian Netherlands were rapidly overrun. Brussels fell on 13 November, Ostend on 16 November, Liège on 27 November, Antwerp on 29 November and Namur on 2 December.

On 16 November 1792 the Executive Council decreed that the Austrians should be pursued wherever they retreated, a threat to neutrals such as the Elector of Cologne and, more particularly, the Dutch, and that the estuary of the Scheldt was to be open to navigation, a clear breach of the Peace of Westphalia of 1648. Four days later, these decisions were ratified by the National Convention, which had come into being on 21 September 1792 after the overthrow of the constitution of 1791. The logic of their new ideas and their rejection of the past made the French radicals unwilling to accept the apparent denial of the natural right of the Belgians to trade, which had been enforced by the closure of the Scheldt.

Asserting the importance of the independence of nations, Lebrun argued that he was not seeking to harm the right of the Dutch, who had insisted on the closure of the Scheldt in order to benefit their own trade, but that the Belgians were not obliged to maintain engagements made by their former Habsburg masters, whose yoke had now been rejected.[70] This argument indicated Lebrun's wish to dramatize the breach between *ancien régime* and revolutionary diplomacy, as did his offer of Tobago to Britain with the caveat that the consent of its inhabitants was necessary.[71] The dispatch of warships up the Scheldt would also enable the French to put pressure on the garrison in Antwerp, then still resisting the French.

French decrees individually and collectively helped to raise international tension and increase suspicions. On 19 November 1792, in response to appeals for help from radicals in Zweibrücken and Mainz, the National Convention passed a decree declaring that the French people would extend fraternity and assistance to all peoples seeking to regain their liberty.[72] As a general principle, this was subversive of all international order; it was also unrealistic and was revoked by the Convention on 14 April 1793, Danton pointing out that it would oblige the French to assist a revolution in China. In specific terms, the decree challenged the Dutch government, for Dutch 'Patriot' refugees in Paris continually pressed for action on their behalf, as indeed did refugees from all over Europe. Citizenship was given to a number of European radicals.

On 27 November 1792 conquered Savoy was incorporated into France – a consequence of the decree of 19 November; on 3 December the decision was taken to try Louis XVI, and on 15 December a decree to ensure that the *ancien régime* be swept away in territories occupied by French forces was promulgated. Elections were to be held to create a new order, but the electorate was restricted to adult men ready to swear an oath to be 'faithful to the people and the principles of liberty and equality'. It was anticipated that people thus 'freed' would support and seek 'union' with France, where elections entailed an oath of loyalty to the Revolution. French pressure on Geneva led to the creation there of a new-model francophile government in early December, while the threat of naval attack later in the winter made the Neapolitan government agree both to acknowledge the French republic and to be neutral.[73] Lebrun argued that any treaty by which people were obliged to submit to harmful systems of government was void,[74] a view that challenged the principles and practice of Russian intervention in Poland and Sweden.

Absorbed by the trial of Louis XVI, the atmospherre and strains of which made compromise in foreign policy very difficult, and affected by the rhetoric and experience of success, the French government failed to appreciate the impact of its policies and statements on neutral powers, especially Britain and the United Provinces. Negotiations in the winter of 1792–3 were hampered by mutual suspicion and incompatible views and principles. The Dutch decision not to resist the passage of French ships up the Scheldt, and the French order of 13 December to Dumouriez to respect Dutch neutrality and to move into winter quarters, served to defuse immediate tension over Dutch security; but the general context was of steps that made the overall tenor of relations worse and the atmosphere more charged and bitter. The Executive Council and many French politicians sought peace with Britain and the Dutch, but not at the price of returning all France's territorial gains. Lebrun's response to a Neapolitan suggestion for Austro-French negotiations scarcely suggested any prospect of peace. He made it clear that a breach between Austria and Prussia would be a necessary preliminary to any agreement, and that Austria could then seek compensation for the loss of the Austrian Netherlands in the conquest of Silesia.[75]

The expulsion of the French envoy from London after the execution of Louis XVI on 21 January 1793 was received with fury in Paris. The political atmosphere there was not conducive to any abandonment of ideals, statements and conquests. Though some politicians were worried about the prospect of expanding the war, they were not strong enough to force through the concessions demanded by Britain. Influential speakers in the National Convention were convinced that Britain was weak and that the people, especially in Ireland and Scotland, would support France. Secret peace negotiations were meaningless without the political will and ability to win support for any agreement, and, under pressure from the Jacobins, their rivals were in no position to run the risk of being accused of making concessions, let alone actually to make any.[76]

On 1 February 1793 the National Convention decided unanimously to declare war on Britain and the Dutch. Making novel use of the notion that war was declared on sovereigns, and, thus, that aggression was not being committed against other peoples, the Convention also agreed to a motion that the British people be asked to rebel by an address composed by, among others, Tom Paine, a prominent radical who was a member of the Convention.[77] War on Spain was declared on 7 March 1793.

The foreign policy of the republic

The willingness of the French to sponsor or encourage discontent and sedition was seen as an indication both of the essential objectives of French policy and of the means by which they sought to effect them. In May 1791 Montmorin, noting the belief that the French wished to force 'tout l'univers' to adopt their new regime, had, instead, argued that it was up to each nation to judge what was best for itself. Eighteen months later, it was credible to argue that the French had bridged the two propositions by defining other nations in terms of revolutionary and pro-French populaces, and, indeed, the support of such elements compromised French diplomacy.

The French government might complain of misleading and hostile images spread by *émigrés*,[78] but the course of the Revolution appeared to justify them. The policy of French agents in this respect was a crucial source of distrust. The interception of Maulde's dispatches revealed that his protestations of good intentions towards the Dutch government did not inhibit his encouragement of sedition.[79] Such action suggested that no French envoy or approach could be trusted. If individual French agents, or indeed ministers, differed in private from the more alarmist aspects of French policy, as many did, that was of limited consequence because they were unwilling and unable to stop it in the electric public forum that was now so crucial to its development.

Far from French intentions being secondary to the fact of power, these intentions were the issue. It was not a matter of suspicion, for hostile intentions were proclaimed in France without hesitation or equivocation. Furthermore, rapid changes in the government of France made it appear dangerous, sinister, violent and radical. French statements and demands made the revolutionary threat apparent and concrete. French declarations and the debates they sprang from reflected the application of philosophical idealism to international relations with all the cant and self-righteous response to the views of others that was to be anticipated. The new society that was being advocated and created in France was not essentially designed to be formed with reference to the concept of the territorial state. In so far as the new politics and ideology illuminated the policy of French governments, they did not encourage the limitation of policy aspirations nor compromise with the interests of territorial states.[80] Diplomatic instructions revealed an unwillingness to accept the validity of other perceptions and there was no consistent willingness to compromise with other states to any serious extent.

Nor was there any sustained attempt to explain the views of other powers to the National Assembly and the Convention. The creation of these institutions was part of a political culture that encouraged both the public expression of specific views on foreign policy and attempts to influence policy with these. Ministers and politicians who wished to fight were encouraged; their more hesitant colleagues became cautious about expressing their opposition and lost the ability to push through their own ideas. The fevered nature of the crucial debates, the declamatory style and extravagant arguments of the speakers and the frequent interventions of the spectators on the side of action and against compromise, all combined to produce a context within which it was difficult to conduct not just diplomacy as conventionally understood, but also any negotiations in which mutual comprehension and concessions were to play a role. The reading of dispatches in the National Assembly angered French diplomats and their contacts.[81] There was also anger that their dispatches appeared in the French press.[82] Envoys worried about the negative impression created by instability within France.[83] They found it difficult to adapt the convention that internal disorder created a bad effect abroad (previously applied to other countries) to new circumstances in France,[84] and, more generally, to learn to cope with the discussion of foreign states in both the French press and the National Assembly.[85]

Problems were also created for foreign powers. In April 1792 Lord Grenville, the British foreign secretary, wrote to Earl Gower, the envoy in Paris, concerning a recent clash between frigates off India. 'You will observe that my dispatch is drawn with a view to public discussion, as I imagine that considering the present state of things in France, *that* can hardly be avoided, however desirable it would have been'. In this case, however, a crisis was avoided. The French were then far more concerned about the breakdown in relations with Austria. The Earl of Elgin, another British diplomat, then in Paris, heard, and was pleased by, the minister's report on the episode to the National Assembly.[86]

Even if the 1780s and 1790s can be seen in large part in terms of continuity, of the tensions of the early-modern period, even if parallels can be found in the Reformation, the Revolution still represented a break from *ancien régime* diplomacy. The revolutionaries thought of themselves as acting in a new fashion, an important aspect of novelty in response to a culture that was primarily reverential of, and referential to, the past. In 1792 Lebrun sought to free France from 'miserables querelles d'etiquette'[87] and argued that the phrase '*pacte de famille* doit etre effacé du vocabulaire de la politique françoise; la Republique ne connoit plus de famille que la grande famille de l'Etat'.[88] Chauvelin referred to 'lettres de créance signées au nom de 24 millions d'hommes libres et vainqueurs'.[89]

Diplomatic relations, procedures and personnel were all disrupted and this also affected the consular service.[90] Relations with the Papacy collapsed.[91] Avignon became French and the position in Alsace altered not in response to international treaty, but as a result of what were held to be popular will and natural rights. The argument that treaties entered into by rulers could not bind people was subversive. The subordination of foreign policy and the foreign minister to control by a committee of a popular assembly was new: control passed from the executive to the legislature.[92]

Particular episodes over the previous century prefigured some of the experience of the revolutionary period. The Revolution was still different because it affected France, the most populous state in Western Europe, the paradigm of

European monarchy and the most important western European participant in continental international relations, because the radicalization of the Revolution was unprecedented for any large polity, and because the French Revolutionary Wars involved and affected all of Europe. The Revolution released, energized and directed French resources, so that the country was able and willing to play a more forceful role in international relations.

Nevertheless, the willingness of powers to negotiate with a regicide regime was striking. The Treaties of Basle between France and Prussia, the United Provinces and Spain (1795) were followed by the Franco-Sardinian Armistice of Cherasco (1796), the Franco-Austrian treaties of Campo Formio (1797) and Lunéville (1801),[93] and the Anglo-French Treaty of Amiens (1802). Furthermore, traditional interests and objectives can be stressed in the international relations of the 1790s. Continuity can also be emphasized if an effort is made to distinguish clearly between on the one hand revolutionary ideologies and ideals, and, on the other, actual policies, what ministries in Paris did or tried to do. However radical the speeches made by revolutionary orators, many of the presuppositions underlying government policy were to a large extent traditional. Ideas about France's traditional allies, notably the Turkish Empire and the Poles, were largely as they had been under the *ancien régime*. In the winter of 1792–3 the French offered sympathy to the Polish patriots, one of whom, Tadeusz Kościuszko, visited France in early 1793. Later that year, the French tried to revive their alliance with Turkey.

The hostility of the revolutionaries to the Austrian alliance had deep pre-revolutionary roots;[94] and the tendency to look to Prussia as a possible or likely ally went back to the 1740s. The idea of closer relations with the German states, other than Austria and Prussia, was also revived, as was interest in splitting Catalonia from Spain, a policy supported in the 1640s.[95] It can, therefore, be argued that, although revolutionary emotion altered much of the tone of French policy, it had much less effect on its substance, and thus the situation after 1792–3 was one of the pursuit by greatly expanded means of aims which were not in themselves new.

Against this must be set the new element of distrust in relations that the Revolution introduced, a distrust that was paranoid, linked alleged domestic and foreign threats, and echoed the fevered anxieties of Reformation relations. Britain was accused of stirring up disaffection within France, and the prospect of more energy being devoted to such a policy, led Montmorin in February 1791 to worry about the prospect of peace in Europe.[96] The distrust, which characterized the Revolutionaries, and their opponents, as well as neutral powers, affected the content and character of policy and foreign relations. Louis XIV had aroused considerable distrust elsewhere in Europe, but posed less of a threat to the affairs of other countries than the Revolutionaries.

Similarities have been found between *ancien régime* and revolutionary policy, both in terms of French goals[97] and of the application of reason.[98] Chambonas's argument in July 1792 that rivalry between Prussia and Austria was a guarantee of the independence and liberties of the empire, that any alliance between the two was dangerous, and that Russia's policy towards Poland made it suspect, would have been familiar to many earlier foreign ministers.[99] Nevertheless, revolutionary ideals and the logic of domestic politics pushed France towards war in a fashion that was totally different from the impact of domestic pressures elsewhere. It had proved possible to avoid war over the Scheldt in 1784, and in the Dutch crisis in 1787. Such a process of compromise was not possible in 1792–3. Basle, Cherasco, Campo Formio, Lunéville and Amiens were very much the products of military exhaustion, failure or defeat.[100]

The course of Revolutionary foreign policy and the response of other powers both greatly reflected the fortunes of war. Defeat at Neerwinden on 18 March 1793 and the loss of Belgium to the Austrians led to a more cautious approach to annexation and the spread of revolution, and led to stronger interest in peace. Brissot and the Girondins fell in June 1793. The Jacobin coup gave power to Danton, who sought a return to more conventional diplomacy. The Girondin foreign minister, Lebrun, was imprisoned and then executed.

In order to obtain peace, Danton tried to create a powerful league. Prussia, Sardinia, Switzerland and Tuscany were offered terms that were designed to weaken the relative position of Austria and Britain. Danton sought a negotiated peace with Britain in late 1793, but French objectives were scarcely those that would satisfy her or Austria. The situation was transformed by the victories of the Revolutionary armies in Belgium in 1794. The army was given new force by the *levée en masse*, able new commanders, and more effective organization. The *levée en masse* entailed an obligation on all to serve in the war, and all single men between 18 and 25 being called upon to join the army. The armies raised were both larger than those deployed by France hitherto, and enabled her to operate effectively on several fronts at once, to sustain casualties, and to match the opposing forces of much of Europe. Initially, at least, Revolutionary enthusiasm was an important element in French capability, helpful in providing the morale required for effective shock action, for crossing the killing ground produced by opposing firepower.

The outbreak of war increased the paranoia of French public culture and helped the Revolutionaries to associate themselves with France. Demonizing their opponents, they waged war by the brutalization of subjects and the despoliation of foreigners. An extension of government power helped mobilize resources. In 1793–4 alone, nearly 7,000 new cannons and howitzers were cast. The exploitative nature of French rule abroad led to a crucial increase in resources that complemented France's domestic mobilization, but the exploitation helped to limit the popularity of the Revolution outside France. Victory gave war prestige and discouraged compromise, as did the Terror within France. The government, military and generals required continued warfare in order to fund their activities.[101]

Thermidor and the Peaces of Basle

This remained true of the Thermidorean regime that succeeded the Terror on 27 July 1794. Expropriation and exploitation generated resistance,[102] but Austria, Prussia and, particularly, Russia were increasingly concerned about Eastern Europe. The Second Partition of Poland in 1793 was followed by the Kościuszko rebellion and then by the Third Partition in 1795. Having overrun the Low Countries in 1794–5, the French were able to negotiate peace with an exhausted Prussia. Under the Peace of Basle of 5 April 1795, Prussia accepted French occupation of the left bank of the Rhine, France promised compensation on the right bank and accepted a Prussian-led neutrality zone in northern Germany. This abandonment of the coalition covered France's position in the Low Countries and led other powers to follow. The conquered Dutch on 16 May 1795 accepted satellite status as the Batavian Republic, a massive indemnity, the cession of Maastricht, Venlo and Dutch Flanders, a French army of occupation until a general peace was negotiated, and a loss of control over the navy. The creation of new sister republics, of which this was the first, epitomized the use of power to make revolutionary changes elsewhere in Europe. Natural limits and small republics had indeed been aspects of the Girondin plan for Europe,[103] but they were to be introduced under the shadow of a dominant and exploitative France.

Although Bilbao and Vitoria were captured by the French in 1795, Spain had not been overrun. The Catalans had ignored French suggestions of a French-backed independent republic. Spain was also tangential to the principal spheres of French strategic and territorial interest. By its Peace of Basle of 22 July 1795, Spain only ceded Santo Domingo, its half of Hispaniola, to France. The following year, Spain allied with France. As a result, the British fleet was outnumbered in the Mediterranean and withdrew from it in late 1796. These treaties improved France's position towards Austria and Britain, neither of which were seriously interested in accepting French gains, and the French invaded southern Germany and northern Italy in 1796. War would continue.

The foreign policy of the Directory, 1795–9

The idea that domestic change within France could be accepted so long as she renounced foreign gains was not credible, because not enough French politicians were willing to accept it and fight for it. French policy did not reveal a consistent willingness to accept limits that were acceptable to others. Furthermore, war as a means to blunt the hostility of others proved counter-productive, for it encouraged fresh ambitions on the part of France and a fearful desire for her defeat and for revenge from her opponents.

The government of the Directory (1795–9) believed war necessary in order to support the army, to please its generals, and, for these and other reasons, to control discontent in France, not least by providing occupation for the volatile commanders, the views and ambitions of many of whom were not limited to the conduct of war. At every level, the processes of diplomacy were designed to serve the cause of war. In 1796 the residence of the consul general in Morocco was transferred from Salé to Tangier, so that he would be able to report on naval movements in the Straits of Gibraltar.

Interest in peace was not pursued with great energy. The Alsatian Jean François Reubell, who was the most influential in foreign policy of the five Directors, sought a peace that would guarantee what were presented as natural, and, therefore, rational frontiers: the Rhine and the Alps. Such frontiers appeared a counterpart to the redrawing of boundaries within France, as long-lasting provinces were replaced by the new *départements* and their supposedly more rational boundaries. This rationalization also entailed a significant expansion of French power into Germany and the Low Countries. Reubell saw this also as a reasonable compensation for the gains made by Austria, Prussia and Russia through the Partitions of Poland.[104]

In northern Italy, initial French victories led to pressure for further conquest, in order to satisfy political and military ambitions and exigencies.[105] Napoleon rose to prominence through his successful operations as commander of the French Army of Italy in 1796–7, and because his successes contrasted with the failed invasions across the Rhine in 1795 and 1796. Napoleon's victory at Mondovi in 1796 knocked the kingdom of Sardinia out of the war, and his triumphs at Lodi, Bassano and Arcola in the same year, and at Rivoli in 1797 brought triumph over the Austrians, apparently compensating for some of the costs of war.

It proved difficult to fix success. The brutal exploitation of Lombardy in 1796 led to a popular rising that was harshly repressed. There was also a serious popular rising in Swabia and Franconia, evidence of the fragile basis of French gains. In Italy, Napoleon managed to regain the initiative, a characteristic feature of his imaginative generalship and opportunistic approach to international politics. Marching to within 70 miles of Vienna, he forced Austria to accept the Truce of Leoben on 18 April 1797.

Napoleon's victories had already destroyed the Directory's initiative earlier in the year, of peace on the basis of the gain of Belgium, with Austrian possessions in Italy returned. His victories ensured that the Directory, which was primarily interested in the annexation of the left bank of the Rhine, and saw Italian gains as negotiable for Austrian consent, had, instead, to accept the Leoben terms, and the accompanying French commitment to Italy. Austria agreed to cede Belgium to France, and the Milanese to a newly-formed French satellite republic, the Cisalpine Republic, and was to receive the Veneto (Venice's possessions on the Italian mainland) in return. Venice would be compensated with Bologna, Ferrara and Romagna, territories seized by France from the pope in the Treaty of Tolentino of 19 February 1797. The principle of compensating victims at the expense of others, one established in *ancien régime* international thought, but less so in practice, was now being applied with both ruthlessness and energy. Napoleon was to become a master of the technique.

Napoleon also planned to seize the Ionian Islands, Venetian possessions that would improve France's position in the Mediterranean. They were occupied in June. The Directory, angered by Napoleon's failure to secure the left bank of the Rhine, hoped for additional gains in the Rhineland that cut across any idea of real compromise with Austria in Germany. Seeking a peace that would allow France to retain wartime gains, the Directory proved aggressive and expansionist, although the Directors claimed that gains were necessary in order to redress the impact of the Partitions of Poland on the balance of power.

France therefore sought to be central to power in both Germany and Italy, a position not attempted since the first half of the century. In June 1797 Napoleon remodelled much of Northern Italy into the Cisalpine and Ligurian Republics. This pro-active position was increased by the *coup* of 18 Fructidor (4 September 1797), when the two moderate Directors – Barthélemy and Carnot – were removed by their more assertive colleagues: Barras, Reubell and La Revellière. This 'Second Directory' also denied the French right the gains made in the elections of March 1797. The different prospects offered by a royalist France had been thwarted by the failure of attempts to overthrow the Directory in 1795.[106]

To avoid the resumption of war, Austria was obliged to accept the Treaty of Campo Formio on 18 October 1797. The location of the treaty's signing, at a village near Udine, in what is now north-east Italy, was a testimony to the range of Napoleon's advance. France's gain of the Ionian Islands, Venetian Albania, the major north Italian military base of Mantua, and the prospect of most of the left bank of the Rhine, as well as Austrian recognition for the Cisalpine Republic, exceeded the hopes of Louis XIV and Louis XV. France was left the dominant power in Italy and Germany, although Austria received Venice, the Veneto, Salzburg, and the likelihood that it would benefit from the congress that would be held to negotiate peace between France and the Holy Roman Empire. The cession of Venice to Austria was condemned by Jacobins as a betrayal of revolutionary ideals.[107]

The Congress, held at Rastatt, agreed to the cession of the left bank of the Rhine to France, with the secular rulers compensated at the expense of the ecclesiastical states, the terms outlined by Napoleon when he visited Rastatt in November 1797. As the ecclesiastical states had been great supporters of the Imperial system, these terms augured the end of the Holy Roman Empire, and thus helped to create a vacuum beyond the Rhine. They also exemplified the process of seeking the support of the defeated at the expense of others, the technique of divide and rule that the French were to employ so successfully.

Although there was a popular desire for peace, this was not the end of French expansion. Military convenience, lust for loot, the practice of expropriation, ideological conviction, the political advantages of a successful campaign, and strategic opportunism, all encouraged aggressive action both before and after Campo Formio, as with the occupation of Venice in 1797, the Papal States in February 1798 and Piedmont in December 1798, and the invasion of Switzerland in February 1798.

Furthermore, the traditional Bourbon claim that Britain's maritime and colonial position subverted any balance was repeated. On 19 August 1796 France and Spain signed the Treaty of San Ildefonso, creating an offensive alliance aimed at Britain, and her ally Portugal. Spain declared war in October, a triumph for French diplomacy that repeated the Bourbon achievement in 1761. The British sought direct peace talks with France at Lille, but their demand for a mutual return of conquests, akin to that of Choiseul in 1759, was unacceptable and in December 1796 the French brought the negotiations to a close. A French invasion force appeared off southern Ireland in December 1796, and another invasion army was prepared a year later. The Irish rising of 1798 led to the landing of a small force in western Ireland, but it was quickly defeated.[108] French schemes to overthrow Britain included plans to invade Jamaica and instigate slave risings there. However, Britain's position improved with victories over the Spanish and Dutch fleets at St Vincent and Camperdown.

Italy was not the limit of Napoleon's range and ambition. Having decided that an invasion of England would fail, Napoleon, supported by the foreign minister, Talleyrand, pressed the case for an invasion of Egypt, in order both to retain his own military position and for France to be better able to challenge the British in India. Thus the interest expressed in the 1780s was to be followed up. Napoleon put Piveron de Morlat, Resident at the Mysore court in 1778–86, on his staff. The Directors were keen to keep Napoleon out of France.[109]

Mounted in 1798, this invasion of Egypt was a major independent initiative on the part of Napoleon. It revealed a characteristic absence of the sense of mutual understanding that is crucial to the successful operation of the international system. He assumed that the Turks, the imperial overlords of effectively autonomous Egypt, could be intimidated or bribed into accepting French action, which, indeed, followed a whole series of provocative acts. These assumptions were coupled with a contempt for Turkey as a military force. Napoleon's sense of grandiloquence and his belief that the Orient was there to serve his views emerged from his recollection:

In Egypt, I found myself freed from the obstacles of an irksome civilization. I was full of dreams . . . I saw myself founding a religion, marching into Asia, riding an elephant, a turban on my head and in my hand the new Koran that I would have composed to suit my needs. In my undertakings I would have combined the experiences of the two worlds, exploiting for my own profit the theatre of all history, attacking the power of England in India and, by means of that conquest, renewing contact with the old Europe. The time spent in Egypt was the most beautiful in my life, because it was the most ideal.[110]

Reality was to be otherwise. Having first easily overrun Malta, a vulnerable military target then ruled by the Knights of St John, Napoleon's army landed in Egypt on 1 July 1798. He defeated the Mamelukes, the *de facto* rulers of Egypt, at Shubra Khit (13 July) and Embabeh, the battle of the Pyramids (21 July), spectacular victories for defensive firepower over shock tactics. These gave the French control of Lower Egypt.

The Turks, however, resisted in alliance with Britain and Russia. The French cultural supposition of superiority and arrogance of power had led to a lack of sensitivity that caused the war. Although it was Sultan Selim III who in September 1798 declared war on France, there was no viable alternative response to the invasion of Egypt. Napoleon had almost casually caused war with the Turks, and driven them to ally with his opponents. Egypt was to prove the graveyard of the bulk of the army and navy he took there. Nelson destroyed the invasion fleet in Aboukir Bay, in the Battle of the Nile on 1 August 1798. The following year the British overran Mysore, France's likeliest ally in India, and Napoleon was repulsed at Acre. With British naval support, Acre was defended by a Turkish garrison under a French *émigré*, Colonel Antoine Le Picard de Phélypeaux, just one instance of the way in which French domestic policies helped her opponents. After Napoleon had evaded the British fleet and returned to France in the autumn of 1799, the French army left in Egypt was eventually defeated by the British in 1801.

More immediately, the French, again, as in 1741, discovered that the use of force to extend their power produced unexpected responses which France could ill afford. Furthermore, force increasingly defined their relations with other powers. Paul I, who became tsar in November 1796, had initially abandoned his predecessor's plans to send a British-subsidized army to oppose the French in Western Europe,[111] but he was increasingly doubtful about the willingness of the French to limit their expansion and concerned about their ideological agenda. The French occupation and then annexation of the Ionian Islands in 1797, and their occupation of Malta in 1798, accentuated Paul's doubts about both the geopolitics and the legitimacy of French power. He was unprepared to see France expand into the eastern Mediterranean.

The Egyptian expedition led in 1798 to a move by Paul I and by Ferdinand IV of Naples into the anti-French camp, and in 1799 to a Russo–Turkish capture of the Ionian Islands. As the two powers had been bitter enemies, this remarkable co-operation was a testimony to the unexpected consequences of Napoleon's aggression.

The Neapolitans attacked French-occupied Rome in November 1798, although they were rapidly repulsed. Occupying Naples in December 1798, the French established the Parthenopean Republic, another satellite regime, just as they had set up the Helvetic Republic when they conquered Switzerland earlier in the year. However, these new governments were unpopular and compromized by their links with expensive and meddlesome French occupation. Risings in 1798–9 were crushed, but they were a warning about the need to find a broader base for a French system. At a more minor level, the Egyptian expedition led Algiers, Tunis and Tripoli to break off relations.

The War of the Second Coalition began in 1799, with Austria, Britain, Naples, Portugal, Russia and Turkey opposed to France. Distrust, rather than the specific points at issue, similarly proved the crucial element in leading France and Austria to renew hostilities in 1799. The Austrians also sought revenge. The French were defeated by the Austrians in Germany in March at Ostrach and Stockach and driven back across the Rhine, and also expelled from most of Italy by Austrian and, in particular, Russian forces, and from Switzerland by the Austrians. With Poland partitioned out of existence and Russia at peace with Turkey, the Russians were able to intervene effectively in Western Europe.

Anglo-Russian plans to overthrow the Republic and restore the Bourbons exaggerated the scope of the divided Coalition's power. The Directory was able to rally French strength, helped by the failure of their opponents to disrupt seriously the French home base, but it was unpopular, discredited by division, and unable to manage the army. A change seemed necessary.

A *coup* in Paris on 18 June 1799 was followed by a more vigorous prosecution of the war that helped to exacerbate differences in the opposing coalition. Paul I and the Austrians fell out, while an Anglo-Russian amphibious invasion of Holland failed. Paul withdrew from the Second Coalition. The French were helped throughout the period by divisions among their opponents, and these divisions strengthened whether France did well, leading her opponents to fear that they would be left behind in their allies' rush for peace, or did badly, leading to a dispute over spoils. Nevertheless, the strains on France of a conflict – the War of the Second Coalition – that owed much to Napoleon's folly helped to provide the opportunity for his seizure of power.

CHAPTER SEVEN

The foreign policy of Napoleon, 1799–1815

Napoleon's seizure of power on 9–10 November 1799 (the *coup* of 18–19 *Brumaire*), as the Directory was replaced by the Consulate, might seem to reflect a return to *ancien régime* patterns of diplomatic activity. The inexorable scope of Napoleon's ambition and his vainglorious capacity to alienate others can be seen to repeat those of Louis XIV. Just as Napoleon's regime marked a limitation of radicalism within France, so it can be seen as reflecting and sustaining an abandonment of revolutionary objectives and methods in international relations. Open diplomacy was replaced by pragmatism,[1] and fraternity by the restoration of slavery in Guadeloupe and Martinique in 1802 and the prohibition of entry to France for West Indian blacks and mixed race people.[2] This would, therefore, suggest that a fundamental divide in foreign policy came, not with the final fall of Napoleon and the Vienna peace settlement of 1815, but, rather, with his rise to be First Consul (1800) and then Emperor (1804). Such an approach can be taken further by suggesting that there was, therefore, a fundamental continuity throughout the nineteenth century: Napoleon III (President of France 1848–51, Emperor 1852–70) could, justifiably, look to the example of Napoleon I.

Such a continuity, however, did not mean that the return of France to a monarchical system under Napoleon I entailed a return to an *ancien régime* system of international relations. Instead, a characteristic feature of warfare, both in the Revolutionary/Napoleonic period and subsequently, was a degree of popular mobilization, that was greater than that of the pre-revolutionary eighteenth century, and one that owed much to measures to obtain a favourable public opinion. This focused on nationalism, understood both as a positive force for identity and cohesion and as a negative xenophobic response to others, both other nation states and incorporating international forces, most obviously Napoleonic France. This response led to violent episodes that could be presented as incidents justifying hostilities or the threat of war. Thus, in 1797, the French embassy in Rome was occupied by papal police during a riot, and a French general killed, while, the following year, the flag of the French embassy in Vienna was insulted by a crowd, leading to a demand for satisfaction.

The political changes of the 1790s both created major internal problems and led to a governmental fear of revolution, a fear that played a role in foreign policy. The need for domestic support in wartime encouraged not only propaganda, but also an explanation of conflict that would appear acceptable. Combined with the contemporary emphasis on the nation, this led to explanations that hinged on the defence of national interests and honour, but such a defence could well be advanced and presented in aggressive terms.

Napoleon's foreign and military policies were not only a continuation of those of the 1790s in the reliance on popular mobilization. There was also a similar unwillingness to accept compromise, a desire, at once opportunistic, brutal and modernizing, to remould Europe, a cynical exploitation of allies, and a ruthless reliance on the politics of expropriation that had led not only to gains by Revolutionary France, but also to the three Partitions of Poland.

The calls for national risings for liberty that, albeit often cynically, had characterized the 1790s became far less common. Napoleon called on the Hungarians to rise for independence from Austria in 1809, talked of an Italian national spirit in the Kingdom of Italy, and sought to profit from Polish nationalism in the Grand Duchy of Warsaw, but, in general, he avoided international populism. A bully in negotiations, Napoleon sought agreements that were provisional in one direction: containing clauses that enabled him to make fresh demands. Thus, in 1807 Napoleon followed up the Treaty of Tilsit by continuing to occupy Prussia and by trying to make Russia invade Sweden, accept a French gain of Silesia if it seized Moldavia and Wallachia, and grant French companies monopoly privileges. The Russian envoy in Paris, Tolstoi, saw such demands as part of an inexorable aggrandizement driven by Napoleon's personality and his reliance on his large army.

Weaker powers, whether allies or defeated, were victims, their possessions and resources to be used for the benefit of Napoleon's diplomatic and military calculations. Thus in 1806, in his peace negotiations with Britain, Napoleon did not consult his ally Spain, even when proposing to cede the Balearic Islands to Ferdinand of Naples, and in 1808 Florida was offered to the United States as a bribe for alliance, again without considering the integrity of the Spanish Empire. The same year, the French agreed, by the Conventions of Paris and Elbing, to end their onerous occupation of Prussia, but at the cost of the cession of Magdeburg and Prussia west of the Elbe to France, the permanent occupation of the major fortresses in eastern Prussia, a massive indemnity, a network of French military roads across Prussia, the limitation of the Prussian army, Prussian support in any conflict with Austria and the free transit of French goods. Given territory at the expense of Austria in 1809, Bavaria was obliged to cede land to Württemberg and the Kingdom of Italy.

Napoleon showed himself unwilling and unable to maintain peace. He sought triumphs in war in order to consolidate his power, most obviously after he seized power in November 1799. Thus Napoleon did not want Austria to accept the peace he offered in February 1800 until he had had another opportunity to defeat her, as he did at Marengo on 20 June, a victory that consolidated his position in France and lessened the likelihood of a *coup* against him.

Napoleon then successfully divided his foreign opponents. The Austrians would have preferred no peace without Britain, but further French victories, especially by Moreau at Hohenlinden on 3 December 1800, led on 25 December to an armistice and, on 9 February 1801, to the Treaty of Lunéville with Austria. Based on Campo Formio, this included Austrian recognition of French annexation of the entire left bank of the Rhine. The earlier annexation of Belgium was confirmed, and the Emperor, Francis II, also recognized the French satellite republics.

France had achieved a territorial settlement that exceeded Bourbon expectations, a settlement that Austria and most of Germany and Italy were willing, albeit grudgingly, to accept; and in 1800 Paul I had abandoned his conflict with France. Britain was isolated. Early in 1801 Paul I sent a mission to Paris to discuss co-operation against Britain, only for his envoys to discover that Napoleon sought co-operation simply on French terms. Paul's assassination on 22 March ended the alliance negotiations.[3]

The French were also checked by the defeat of their army in Egypt on 21 March 1801 and the British naval victory off Copenhagen on 2 April, but the French-supported Spanish invasion of Portugal in April 1801 forced the latter to break with Britain, which became more isolated. However, Napoleon characteristically sought to deny any benefit to Spain and succeeded in alienating her support. France could not defeat the British at sea, but the latter had to accept French hegemony in Western Europe.

Lunéville and the Treaty of Amiens with Britain (25 March 1802) were followed on the part of Napoleon not by any serious attempt to control disputes, but by military consolidation and political aggrandizement, including an attempt to regain control of St Domingue, that were rightly perceived as threatening. Napoleon broke treaties as and when it suited him; for example, the clause of the Treaty of Amiens in which he had agreed to respect the neutrality of the Batavian Republic, formerly the United Provinces. This was crucial to Britain, given the strategic importance of the Dutch colonies, especially the Cape of Good Hope, which the British had returned at Amiens, as they had also all their colonial gains from France. It was also foolish to alienate the British, because at Amiens they had accepted French dominance of the Continent. This removed from the equations of continental power the paymaster of opposition to France.

Napoleon's will to dominate

Napoleon was happiest with force; his character, views, ambitions, and ambience did not lend themselves to accommodation, other than as a short-term device.

He was in a position not only to act as an innovative general, but also to control the French military system and to direct the war effort. Enjoying greater power over the French army than any ruler since Louis XIV, Napoleon was in many respects also more powerful than Louis. His choice of commanders was not constrained by the social conventions and aristocratic alignments that affected Louis, and both armies and individual military units were under more direct governmental control than had been the case with the Bourbons. Furthermore, Napoleon was directly in command of the leading French force throughout the wars of his reign. French resources were devoted to the military with a consistency that the Revolutionary governments had lacked.

In his generalship, Napoleon was fired by the desire to engage and win. He confronted grave problems, not least the number and fighting quality of his opponents, the difficulty of establishing their positions, let alone intentions, the primitive communications of the period, and the need to raise the operational effectiveness of his conscripts. In response, Napoleon developed an effective military machine, even as he undermined it by the strains of near-continuous warfare, and eventually overwhelmed it in 1813–14 by failing to end a multi-front struggle. Able, even in 1813–14, to adapt rapidly to changing circumstances, Napoleon had a remarkable ability to impose his will upon war. He won close to 50 battles in his career, including the largest, most complex engagements hitherto seen in the gunpowder age.

Napoleon's will to dominate was both personal and a continuation of that of the Revolution. It ensured that peace treaties were imposed, and that, once they were made, the French sought further benefits, while their defeated opponents felt only resentment and a determination to reverse the settlement. This, in turn, led to further conflicts. Whereas the European peace treaties of 1763 – Hubertusberg and Paris – had been followed by over a decade of peace between the former combatants, and that of Vienna in 1814–15 ushered in a longer period of peace, 1795–1814 was a great age of peace treaties, but repeatedly saw them broken.

This was not only because of the sense that the French position was unacceptable and that Napoleon could know no limits, but also because of the conviction on the part of opponents that the French could be held and even beaten: war was unavoidable and victory possible. This inspired not only the attack on France in 1792 but also subsequent coalitions. If Napoleonic France could not be incorporated into the balance of power politics, and could not be accepted as a hegemonic state, it had to be brought down.

Although French propaganda presented Napoleon as always in favour of peace, the Napoleonic regime celebrated power, not least the power of victory, as in Baron Gros's battle paintings, such as *Napoleon at the Battle of Eylau*.[4] A quasi-mystical emphasis on the cult of the warrior can also be seen in the celebration of the mythical Celtic poet Ossian, for example in the decorations of Josephine's palace at Malmaison. Napoleon took further the increased tendency to employ soldiers in diplomatic roles and as heads of missions abroad, a tendency that already could be seen in the 1790s.[5] This contributed to an increasing militarization of the conduct of French policy. Thus, for example, General Andréossy was sent to Austria to enforce a diplomacy of bullying after Prussia had been defeated at Jena in 1806. General Savary, the envoy sent to St Petersburg in 1807 after the Peace of Tilsit, was arrogant and difficult. Savary was sent to Madrid in 1808, in order to prepare for the French seizure of power. Another general, Lauriston, succeeded Caulaincourt in St Petersburg in 1811, and failed to maintain the latter's careful and cautious approach to relations with Russia. The use of generals was an important aspect of a failure to appreciate that an effective diplomatic service must produce reports and ideas that might be challenging. It was not of course new. The Bourbons had employed generals as diplomats, as had their Revolutionary successors. Bernadotte fought the Austrians before being sent to Vienna in 1798.

The settings of the Napoleonic regime were not those that might encourage moderation. Indeed, the looting of Europe's artistic treasures to glorify its new centre encapsulated the apparent benefits of aggression. Begun by the National Convention in December 1793, the policy of looting art treasures had been implemented in Belgium in 1794 and Germany in 1796, and comprehensively developed by Napoleon in Italy in 1796.[6] The spoils of aggression were also shown by the Senate's proclamation of him as Emperor of the French on 18 May 1804. That December, Napoleon crowned himself with the Crown of Charlemagne. The following year, he followed by becoming King of Italy and crowning himself with the Iron Crown of Lombardy. His family was rewarded with kingdoms.

Napoleon's views contributed strongly not only to repeated breakdowns of compromise peace treaties but also, more generally, to a sense that he could not be trusted, a sense that, in turn, affected the attitudes of other rulers to his specific demands. This distrust exacerbated more general problems of misperception. A recent study of the outbreak of war between Britain and France in 1803 argues that the two powers went to war reluctantly as a result of a combination of misperceptions:

> Although the decisive misperception was the British conviction that Bonaparte was planning to send a second expedition to Egypt, the difficulty in maintaining amicable Anglo-French relations owed less to geopolitics and more to misperceptions based upon divergent cultural traditions governing the law and the powers of the state.[7]

This affected French views of the British failure to act as Napoleon wished against critical *émigré* writers. In turn, the British were unwilling to mould their laws to suit the French government. Each side became certain of the other's hostility. The nature of Napoleonic government, at once authoritarian and radical, greatly increased the chances of such cultural misperceptions.

Napoleon's unwillingness to accept limits for any length of time stemmed from his personality, but also from a related assessment of a Europe in which the hegemony of one power – himself – was unconstrained by any outside force. This was the international politics of imperial China, or of the twentieth-century USA towards Latin America. It created far more problems in Europe, with its traditions of multipolarity. There was a widespread reluctance to accept his perspective, a reluctance that reflected the strength of political identities across much of Europe. Equally, Napoleon's precarious new imperial system enjoyed only limited support, especially in Iberia, southern Italy, and Eastern Europe with the exception of Poland, and attempts to encourage consistency, coherence and co-operation fell foul of existing attitudes, habits, practices and interests, as well as of policy contradictions. For all his egocentric ambition, Napoleon was genuinely interested in a certain kind of rational modern administration and government that he sought to promote in the Europe he controlled. He introduced some worthwhile features of government, but his ideas of rational modernity were often crude, for example his views on economic and financial matters, and he undermined his efforts by his rapacity, militarism and neo-feudalism.[8]

The Napoleonic system and psyche required force. Napoleon did not understand compromise, and rejected the excellent advice he received, but even without these character flaws he faced formidable obstacles. Napoleon initially benefited from the operational and organizational advantages that the French enjoyed over their opponents in the 1790s, but these relative advantages were eroded in the 1800s as other states absorbed many of France's developments. Across much of Europe, the modernization of political structures and administrative practices was influenced by French occupation or models, or by the need to devise new political and administrative strategies to counter the French. The changes introduced in the Prussian army and society after defeat by Napoleon in 1806 are an important example, although there was also considerable continuity with the enlightened reforms of the pre-Revolutionary period.

The end of peace, 1802–5

Napoleon needed to command. Thus, he rapidly ignored the limits agreed with Austria at Lunéville in 1801, and quickly violated the assumptions on which Russia made peace at Tilsit in 1807, while, having signed the Treaty of Amiens with Britain in 1802, a treaty which included provision for the French evacuation of Egypt, Napoleon sent Colonel Horace Sébastiani to report on the possibility of a reconquest. His positive report was published in the official *Moniteur* on 30 January 1803. The French gain of Louisiana from Spain in 1801, their creation of a new pro-French political system in Switzerland in 1803, their attempts to acquire Florida and to build up their navy, and moves to increase their presence in Algiers and Muscat, also worried the British. This was not the conduct of a ruler willing to accept territorial or procedural limits on his hegemony, and it exacerbated British distrust, leading to a Russian-backed refusal to evacuate Malta despite having agreed to do so. On 18 May 1803 Britain declared war.[9] Two months later, General Decaen, Governor of Île de France, arrived off Pondicherry with 1,250 men mostly intended to train *sepoys*. Finding the British in control, he sailed back.

The most recent detailed study of the international relations of the period, by Paul Schroeder, repeatedly compares Napoleon to Hitler. Schroeder argues that French hegemony was not the issue, that, in fact, the continental powers had been brought by defeat to accept such hegemony, but that Napoleon was unwilling to allow others any independence.[10] In short, he was intent on reversing the multipolarity that had been a defining feature of the European international system for centuries, and intent on replacing it by an empire to which only obedience and tribute could be offered; somewhat akin to the position of imperial China during the same period. Napoleon sought not to adjust the balance of power politics, but to abolish them. The British were to create and dominate such a system at sea, but that was less controversial than Napoleon's programme of continental empire. He not only adopted the title and imagery of empire; he also sought the reality of imperial power. Victory was followed by major transfers of territory.

Napoleon sought satisfaction, not as part of a process of negotiation and conciliation, but as something to be seized. He had no real idea of how to turn strengths and successes into lasting and acceptable solutions. As a result, he wrecked the hopes of those who had hoped for partnership, or at least co-operation, with France, such as Alexander I of Russia, in 1803 and 1807, or the Austrians, who in March 1807 produced a plan for a general peace that would have left Napoleon in control of the Low Countries and much of Italy.

Alexander's peace plan of 1803, a plan produced in response to Napoleon's request for mediation of his differences with Britain, was curtly rejected, because it would have required France to evacuate Hanover, Italy, Switzerland and the United Provinces. Alexander and his ministers were offended by the contemptuous way in which they were continually treated, and concerned by the onward march of French policy. They were anxious about France's views for the Ionian Islands and worried about French intentions in the Balkans. The kidnapping from Baden of the Duke of Enghien, a Bourbon prince believed to be conspiring against Napoleon, and his trial and execution in March 1804, led to a marked deterioration in relations. France rudely rejected the Russian protest, and relations were broken in August 1804.[11] The Russians then stepped up their efforts to persuade Austria to take a prominent role in an alliance against France, efforts that had already led to refusals in December 1803 and April 1804. Napoleon meanwhile wooed Prussia. The Russians allied with Britain in the spring of 1805, but Alexander sent a peace mission to Paris, only to abandon it when Napoleon annexed Genoa to France in June.[12]

In the early 1800s, the Austrian government sought to accommodate itself to French power, and adopted a conciliatory approach towards extensions of

Napoleon's power in Germany and, in particular, Italy where Napoleon annexed Elba and Piedmont in 1802 and had himself elected President of the Italian Republic (as the Cisalpine Republic was now called). Despite this, in August 1805, Napoleon demanded that Austria demobilize and formally declare its neutrality, in other words surrender its capacity for independent action. This drove Austria to co-operate with Britain and Russia. Austria declared war on France and invaded her ally Bavaria.

In peace as well as war, Napoleon devoted much energy to improving France's military position. Occupied areas, satellite states, such as Switzerland and the Ligurian Republic, allies, such as Spain, and neutrals, were all expected to provide troops, ships or resources to help. Once war had been renewed with Britain in 1803, Napoleon brought the Batavian and Italian republics and Switzerland into the conflict on his side. Spain was obliged to provide subsidies. This led to a British attack on Spanish treasure ships, and in January 1805 to a Spanish declaration of war. This did not, however, enable Napoleon to win his naval struggle with Britain, a struggle that had to be won if Britain was to be invaded and the Mediterranean left free for the projection of French power. At Trafalgar, on 21 October 1805, Nelson destroyed a Franco-Spanish fleet.

The costs of such co-operation discredited alliance with Napoleon, just as it had earlier weakened the satellite republics. The burdens of war also helped to cripple reform initiatives in the territories of German allies, such as Bavaria. The army of the Kingdom of Italy grew from 23,000 in 1805 to 90,000 in 1813. The majority of those sent from it to fight in Spain, Russia and Germany died.[13] The Grand Duchy of Warsaw had to man a 30,000-strong army, much of which died in Russia in 1812. French economic control was disruptive and could also be harsh.

War with Austria, Russia and Prussia, 1805–7

The War of the Third Coalition that began in 1805 opposed Austria, Britain, Naples and Russia to Napoleon. Having invaded Bavaria, the Austrians halted and were successfully counterattacked by the French. Decisive victories at Ulm (20 October) and Austerlitz (2 December) completely changed the situation. The French had benefited from the years of peace on the Continent from 1801 in order to train their infantry, increase their artillery and cavalry, and produce better balanced corps. The earlier years of war had provided experienced troops and an officer corps sifted by merit.

In 1805 the Austrians were preparing for an attack from the west through the Black Forest, but they were outmanoeuvred by the rapid advance of the French from the middle Rhine to the Danube in their rear. The overly cautious Austrian response left an army bottled up in Ulm and, after it surrendered, Napoleon overran southern Germany and Austria. This brought him closer to the advancing Russians. At Austerlitz Tsar Alexander I and an 85,000-strong Austro-

Russian army attacked the 75,000-strong French. A powerful assault on Napoleon's right was held and, in a surprise attack, the French turned the weak flank of this Russian attack in order to win. The French were better able than their Russian counterparts to use numerical superiority at the point of contact they had sought. Aside from Napoleon's superior generalship, the French command system proved better able to integrate the different arms effectively.

Austria left the war by the Treaty of Pressburg of 26 December 1805. This cost her Venetia, Istria, Dalmatia, the Voralberg and the Tyrol and a massive indemnity, terms that made it difficult to support Napoleon in Vienna other than on the basis of expediency. Germany seemed securely under French leadership. Frederick William III of Prussia had refused to support the Third Coalition and, instead, by the Treaty of Schönbrunn of 15 December 1805, secured Hanover from Napoleon.

However, Napoleon's exploitative treatment of Prussia, French bullying, threats, and infringements of the Prussian neutrality zone, and Prussian opportunism, led to war in 1806. The poorly-commanded and outmanoeuvred Prussians were rapidly defeated at Jena and Auerstädt on 14 October. At Jena, massed artillery and substantial numbers of skirmishers inflicted heavy losses on the Prussian lines. Jena persuaded the Danes that Napoleon could not be resisted; and led the Sultan, Selim III, to move towards a French alliance. The French envoy, Sebastiani, now a general, was given a magnificent reception at Constantinople on 9 August 1806.[14] The Turks declared war on Russia on 24 December 1806.

In a politics of trickery and bullying, meanwhile, neutral powers were exploited and attacked by Napoleon. Peace became war by other means. Naples and Hanover, potential allies of Britain, were both occupied in 1803; the Hanseatic cities and much of the Papal States following in 1806, and Rome in 1808. The French position in the Baltic was strengthened when the Swedish German possessions of Stralsund and Rügen were seized in 1807. Etruria (Tuscany and Parma) was annexed in 1808, Rome in 1809. This was the culmination of a process of bullying that led to Napoleon's excommunication by Pius VII, a step countered by the arrest of the pope.[15] Switzerland lost the Valais, while the Canton of Ticino was occupied. The Kingdom of Holland was annexed to France in 1810,[16] as were Hamburg, Lübeck, Bremen and Oldenburg.[17] Having intervened in Spain in 1808, Napoleon allocated Spain north of the Ebro to four military governorships, as a stage towards annexation. Opposition within Napoleonic Europe was repressed, 48,000 troops being committed to suppress the rebellion that began in Calabria in 1806.

Once Austria had been defeated, Napoleon reorganized Germany, creating in July 1806 an institutional basis for French intervention, the *Rheinbund* or Confederation of the Rhine. This league linked France and 16 South and West German states, the largest of which were Bavaria, Württemberg and Baden. Territorial gains helped make these rulers allies. Napoleon was to be their Protector. This alliance was designed to limit Austrian and Prussian influence, represented a rejection of the Russian intervention in German politics under the Peace of Teschen of 1779, and was intended to give Napoleon control over the forces and resources of the members of the Confederation. All the *Rheinbund* backed Napoleon against Prussia later in 1806. He had the Emperor, Francis, dissolve the Holy Roman Empire, so that Francis now became only Emperor of Austria, a title he had assumed in October 1804. The Austrians were forced to accept this when Napoleon moved the entire Grand Army into Upper Austria. They even handed over the imperial crown. In 1806 Napoleon also had Saxony made a kingdom, part of his strategy of building up an ally in east-central Europe capable of opposing Russia.

Control over Germany was a crucial prelude to the continued prosecution of the war with Russia. This conflict, brought to an end by the Treaty of Tilsit of 7 July 1807, was punishing, but it further vindicated the quality of the French military machine. The fighting of 1805–7 had indicated the superiority of the French corps and divisional structure over the less coherent and less co-ordinated opposing forces. French staff work, at army and corps level, was superior to that of both Austria and Russia, and this helped to vitiate the numbers France's opponents put into the field. The quality of French staff work enabled Napoleon to translate his wide-ranging strategic vision into practice, to force what might have been a segmented war into essentially a struggle in one major theatre of operations where he could use the *Grande Armée* effectively.

War with Britain, Spain and Austria, 1806–9

No serious effort was made to settle differences with Britain, foolishly so, as the resources of worldwide British trade financed opposition to France. Negotiations in 1806 were designed by Napoleon only to isolate Britain, preparatory to an eventual new French attack. The British were prepared to accept French hegemony in Europe west of a Russian sphere, but Napoleon was not ready to make such hegemony even vaguely palatable. While peace was not on offer, war was to be total. The Berlin decree of 21 November 1806 – its place of issue under French occupation since 25 October – decreed a blockade of Britain, the confiscation of all British goods and the arrest of all Britons. The decree was for France's allies as much as France. The former were pressed to develop their navies for use against Britain.

The assault on British trade – Napoleon's Continental System launched in 1806, and expanded by the Edict of Fontainebleau (1807) and the two Decrees of Milan (1807) – was a unilateral policy formulated and executed without consultation with client states, allies and neutrals. It hit long-established trades, infringed sovereign rights, and created enormous hostility.[18] An economic policy centred on French interests meant that Napoleon's effort to anchor his new dynasty in Europe found no popular roots. Alliance with France was revealed as costly and humiliating. Action against Britain could have been rendered more popular if Napoleon had been willing to abandon some of his hegemonic goals.

Believing that everything was possible for him, Napoleon 'lost touch with reality'.[19] Portugal was invaded in 1807, despite its attempts to appease Napoleon, because he insisted on closing it to British trade and saw its conquest as a way to increase the French military presence in Iberia. Once conquered, there was no attempt to conciliate the Portuguese. Increasingly imperious and unwilling to listen to critical advice, Napoleon dismissed his experienced, independent-minded foreign minister, Talleyrand, in August 1807. In 1808 Napoleon used the disputes between Charles IV and Crown Prince Ferdinand – who succeeded Charles as Ferdinand VII – in order to replace the Bourbon monarchy in Spain by a Bonapartist one, that of his brother Joseph: an alliance amounting to indirect control was not enough, and Charles and Ferdinand were tricked and bullied into handing over the Kingdom to Napoleon.

However, a nationalist rising in Spain (from 2 May) and Portugal led to the Peninsular War, creating a military and political problem that was to challenge Napoleon for the remainder of his period of office. British troops were sent to Portugal in 1808 and, after several years campaigning, eventually overcame the French in Spain in 1813. In the meanwhile, France also had to fight Spanish regulars and guerrillas, operations that absorbed large numbers of troops.[20] Spanish naval strength had also been lost, greatly limiting Napoleon's post-Trafalgar attempt to rebuild his navy in order to challenge Britain anew. The invasion of Spain also gave Napoleon a new war aim. Under the treaty with Alexander signed at Erfurt on 12 October 1808 that essentially confirmed Tilsit, no treaty was to be made with Britain unless she recognized the Bonapartist position in Spain, terms that would have entailed French dominance of Latin America.

The Bonapartist *coup* in Spain gave an edge to Napoleon's bullying of Austria. In December 1808 the Austrian government again decided on war, because it felt its safety threatened by French policy, which included a demand for disarmament, and because it feared a recurrence of the *coup* method already staged against Spain. Once armed, the finance minister warned that the armaments could not be long sustained, thus increasing the pressure for action. There was a sense that there was no choice, that French policy anyway threatened to impose the consequences of defeat, and that war was the sole alternative.[21]

Austria got both war and defeat in 1809. Francis declared war on 9 April, and Napoleon found Austria a tougher opponent than in 1805, although the Austrians were handicapped by poorly-conceived war aims, inadequate and divided central leadership, and a foolish strategy. At Aspern-Essling (21–22 May 1809), Napoleon's bold attack on a superior Austrian force was repelled and he had to abandon the battlefield in the face of a serious Austrian advance and better Austrian generalship. At Wagram on 5–6 July, however, Napoleon proved the better general and the French corps commanders were superior to their Austrian counterparts. Napoleon's counter-attack drove the Austrians from the field, but it was no Austerlitz. The French victory was essentially due to leadership and to their overall superiority in troops and material in what was a battle of attrition.

The Austrians received no help from Frederick William III of Prussia or the other German rulers, and the diversionary British attack on Walcheren was both too late and unsuccessful. Now allied with France and pursuing its own interests, Russia offered no support to Austria and, instead, attacked her. The Treaty of Schönbrunn of 14 October not only awarded Austrian territory to France and Bavaria, but also left the Duchy of Warsaw, a French client state in Poland, with gains from Austria. Austria was left landlocked, with a large indemnity and with its army limited. In 1810 Napoleon married the Archduchess Marie Louise, a spoil of war designed to cement Austria's new relationship with France. Until the summer of 1813 the Austrians sought peaceful partnership with Napoleon.[22] The rivalry and mutual distrust of Austria and Russia was important to Napoleon's success.

Relations with Russia, 1807–12

By the Treaty of Tilsit of 7 July 1807, Alexander I had reached an agreement that left Napoleon dominant in western and central Europe. This was an acceptance of French hegemony that previous tsars had refused to signal. Indeed in 1735 and 1748 Russian armies had moved into Germany in order to put pressure on France. Such an acknowledgement was especially important, given the rise of Russian power in the closing decades of the eighteenth century with the partition of Poland and the defeat of the Turks. Signature at Tilsit, on the Russo-Prussian frontier, was a testimony to the range of Napoleon's power.

The Treaty of Tilsit applied the principle of the partition of Poland to the whole of Europe. Russia lost little territory and gained a small portion of Poland, but her policy was now intertwined with that of Napoleon. Alexander agreed not only to deliver his Mediterranean base, the Ionian Isles, to France, but also to join with her in offering Britain peace terms. If these were rejected, Alexander was obliged to go to war with Britain and to coerce Austria, Denmark, Portugal and Sweden into doing the same. Frederick William III was abandoned by his Russian ally: Prussia was to lose her territory west of the Elbe, lands that contained nearly half Prussia's population. In return, France agreed to fight Turkey if she rejected the peace with Russia that Napoleon was to seek to obtain. If so, the Turks were to lose most of the Balkans, thus creating the need for a Franco-Russian *entente* over the fate of what would be a fatally weakened Turkish Empire.

Yet, despite his experience of Russian fighting quality at the battles of Eylau (8 February 1807) and Friedland (14 June 1807), Napoleon could not sustain this accommodation and these mutual guarantees, and thus concentrate his forces against Britain, let alone turn Tilsit into a strong partnership. His development of the Grand Duchy of Warsaw as a French client state, nominally ruled by the pliable King of Saxony, challenged Russia's position in Eastern Europe.[23] For over 250 years Polish weakness had been a condition of Russian strength. Napoleon's refusal to accept a draft convention, negotiated in January 1810 by his ambassador to Russia, guaranteeing that the kingdom of Poland would not be revived, greatly increased Russian distrust about Poland and much else, and ensured that French actions were viewed through this prism. There was no true peace. Although Tilsit greatly harmed Franco-Turkish relations,[24] the French were unenthusiastic about supporting Russian ambitions in the Balkans. Matters were made worse in December 1810 by the French annexation of the north-west German Duchy of Oldenburg, which had dynastic links with the Romanovs and had been guaranteed at Tilsit in 1807.

At the end of 1810, Russia left the French economic camp, when it abandoned the Continental System which was proving ruinous to the Russian economy. Such a unilateral step threatened the cohesion of the French system and challenged Napoleon's insistence on obedience and his treatment of allies as servants.[25]

Napoleon responded to Russian independence, first with bluster, but also by greatly stepping up the military preparations for possible war with Russia, preparations already begun in October 1810 – although, at this stage, they were designed for intimidation, not conflict. He did not respond positively to Russian diplomatic approaches the following spring. From October 1811 French military preparations were accelerated and in January 1812 France's position in the Baltic improved with the occupation of Swedish Pomerania.

Having assembled a powerful coalition against Russia, forcing an isolated Prussia to accept an offensive alliance treaty against Russia on 24 January 1812, Napoleon invaded on 24–25 June 1812, the logic of his system demanding the curbing of his victim. Marquis Armand de Caulaincourt, formerly ambassador to Alexander, and now a leading courtier, told Napoleon, 'Undoubtedly your majesty would not make war on Russia solely for the sake of Poland, but rather that you should have no rival in Europe, and see there none but vassals'.[26] There was no formal declaration of war.

Napoleon's closest advisers opposed the invasion, which was as unnecessary diplomatically as it was foolish militarily. But for the invasion, the French might well have beaten their Spanish opponents, and then been better placed to defeat the British expeditionary force. As with his earlier attacks on Austria, Prussia and Spain, and his planned invasion of Britain in 1805, Napoleon resolved to strike at the centre of his opponent's power, thus gaining the initiative and transferring much of the logistical burden of the war to his enemy.

Napoleon invaded with half a million men, most of whom were allied troops, principally German, Italian and Polish. The Russians, however, fell back, denying Napoleon a decisive battle. Russian scorched-earth and guerrilla activity hit supplies, and the French lost men through hunger, disease and fatigue. Finally, at Borodino on 7 September, the Russians sought to stop the advance on Moscow.

In a battle of attrition that involved 233,000 men and 1,227 cannon, the Russians resisted successive attacks and were driven back without breaking. Russian casualties were heavier, but Napoleon lost a quarter of his army. Napoleon followed up Borodino by entering an undefended Moscow, but the city was set ablaze, probably by the Russians. The enormity of the task, logistical problems and the endurance of the Russian foes had defeated Napoleon militarily before the difficulty of securing any settlement could thwart him politically. He had no terms to propose, faced an opponent who would not negotiate, and could not translate his seizure of Moscow into negotiations.

This was equally true once he had retreated from Russia with very heavy casualties. Due to heavy snowfalls, supply breakdowns and Russian attacks, especially as the French crossed the Berezina River on 26–27 November, the retreat turned into a nightmare. Thereafter, there was no real attempt to accept the military verdict and offer Russia terms that would assuage its hostility. Napoleon could neither conceive of a new ethos in French foreign policy or a new system in Eastern Europe. This greatly contributed to Russia's determination to implement the decision in December 1812 to press on against France, and thereby put Prussia, which Napoleon had instructed to raise another 30,000 men, in the front line. The failure on 23 October of the attempted *coup* in Paris by ex-General Claude-François Malet was scant consolation.

Defeat in Germany, 1813

The other states that Napoleon had bullied into providing troops and resources were quick to abandon him as soon as he faced failure, although some, such as Austria – which sought peace – took a while before attacking France. A wave of francophobia in the army and parts of the populace in early 1813 led Prussia to declare war on Napoleon in March, beginning the collapse of his grip on central Europe where he had long struggled to establish dominance and had come close to succeeding in 1809–12. In January 1813 Napoleon had harshly rejected Prussian terms and ordered the continuation of exactions.

Napoleon fought back hard in Germany, aided by concerns about Russian and Prussian intentions among the German rulers. He rebuilt his army to a force of over 400,000 plus his artillery, but the new recruits were more like the fresh troops of 1792 than the veterans of his earlier campaigns, and, unlike in 1792, France's opponents were not outnumbered. In addition, Napoleon was unable to create a new cavalry to match the troops lost in Russia. New levies, both French and German, helped Napoleon drive his opponents out of Saxony in May 1813, winning victories at Lützen (2 May) and Bautzen (20–21 May), and North Germany did not rise against him as had been anticipated. Saxony rallied to Napoleon in May, and Denmark in July. Concerned about their intentions, Austria refused to join Russia and Prussia but, instead, stopped fighting Russia, became neutral, mediated the armistice of Pleswitz on 4 June 1813, sought to mediate peace, and proposed an independent central Europe, neutral towards both France and Russia. Metternich, the Austrian foreign minister, was hostile to Prussia and Russia, and hoped to reach an agreement with Napoleon, in order to secure a partnership that would secure Austrian interests. He offered Napoleon the left bank of the Rhine, co-guarantorship of a neutralized *Rheinbund*, non-interference over Spain, and diplomatic support over colonial concessions from Britain.

The response was unhelpful. Napoleon declared all France's annexations inalienable and began military preparations against Austria. Defeat had not curbed his instinctive bellicosity. Napoleon's refusal to negotiate peace, or to understand that it entailed compromise, delivered in person by an angry Emperor to Metternich in Dresden on 26 June, led Austria finally to join the anti-French camp: she declared war on 11 August.

The league of the partitioning powers had been re-created but, unlike in 1772, their target was a France that refused any limitations on its power. The French were also heavily outnumbered. Austrian, Prussian, Russian and Swedish forces exceeded 600,000, while Napoleon's total field army was only 370,000, in part because some of the members of the Confederation of the Rhine did not provide their full quota of troops. The allies adopted the Trachenburg Plan: battle with Napoleon was to be avoided while independent forces under his subordinates were to be attacked. The plan reflected the Allies' respect for Napoleon's generalship. The Prussians defeated detached French forces at Grossbeeren (23 August), on the Katzbach River (26 August) and at Dennewitz (6 September); and the Austrians won at Kulm (30 August).

By failing to concentrate his forces during the campaign, Napoleon had allowed their attenuation, and this had preserved neither the territory under French control nor the strategic advantage. Only at Dresden (27 August) was Napoleon victorious. Threatened with Austrian invasion, Bavaria, long a stalwart of French interests,[27] allied with Austria in October, repeating their alignment of 1745. On 16–19 October, in the major battle of the year, the heavily outnumbered Napoleon was defeated at Leipzig. Germany was lost. Napoleon was no longer in a position to assist and exploit Frederick August of Saxony, whose territories were now occupied by Prussia and Russia. The *Rheinbund* collapsed.

Both then, and in 1814, Napoleon failed to offer terms that would divide his assailants, despite the fact that Austria distrusted Russia and Britain, and would have liked to retain a strong France, while the Russians sought a strong France in order to balance Britain. Their definitions of strength included a France territorially more extensive than in 1789 and, at least initially, they were willing to accept a continuance of Napoleon's rule, but his instinctive refusal to accept limits or half measures wrecked such schemes. Furthermore, repeated French assaults on other states for two decades had led them to adopt reforms that enhanced their ability to mobilize their resources. Thus, Napoleonic policies helped to close the capability gap between France and other states and to end the subservient acceptance on which his imperial rule depended.

The collapse of the Napoleonic empire, 1813–14

There were also changes in the international system in response to Napoleon. If Napoleon was immensely destabilizing in terms of established notions of international relations, he also represented a culmination of the politics of 'grab' exemplified by the Partitions of Poland. Indeed, Tilsit was in some respects another partition treaty with a different cast. Partly in reaction to the chaos and incessant conflict of such 'diplomacy', a concept and culture of international relations emphasizing restraint developed. It was seen in operation in the negotiations that led to and accompanied the anti-French coalition in 1813–15, in the Congress of Vienna, and in the post-war attempt to maintain peace and order by the Congress system. Napoleon could not be encompassed in this new system, and his system and methods were made redundant by it.

He was abandoned by former allies in 1813–14, losing for example Württemberg and Naples to Austrian alliances in 1813 and January 1814. Napoleon accepted the loss of Spain and made a peace treaty with Ferdinand VII, but refused to surrender the Kingdom of Italy, the Rhineland and Holland as the price of a more general peace, and, instead, planned to invade Italy. However, the French forces abandoned Holland in November 1813, and Napoleon's attempts to divide the alliance, for example his response to the Austrian proposals of November 1813, failed. In France, Napoleon was affected by falling tax revenues, widespread draft avoidance, a serious shortage of arms and equipment, and a marked decline in the morale and efficiency of officials. The economy was in a parlous state, hit by British blockade and by the loss of continental markets.

In early 1814, the Allies invaded France. Initially successful – so that Napoleon discovered a willingness to negotiate, abandoning his earlier demands for a Rhine frontier and much of Italy – the Allies were checked in mid-February as Napoleon manoeuvred with skill in order to destroy the most exposed Austro-Prussian units. He then returned to his demands of the start of the year. These, however, were unacceptable to Austria, the power most willing to negotiate and to leave Napoleon in power. After Napoleon's attitude to diplomacy had ruined the chance to use the negotiations at Châtillon in February to bring peace, the Allies on 1 March agreed at Chaumont not to conclude any separate peace with Napoleon and, instead, to continue the war and then join in maintaining the peace (the agreement was announced on 9 March 1814).

On 15 March 1814 Caulaincourt presented Napoleon's counter-proposal to the Châtillon offer, a proposal that would have left France with the left bank of the Rhine, her colonies, and control over the Kingdom of Italy. Such unrealistic responses weakened the chance that the Allies would fail to ensure the end of Napoleon. Napoleon was no longer willing even to read Caulaincourt's letters, because his minister insisted on offering unwanted advice.

Numbers told in the war. In place of the 80,000 opposing troops Napoleon had anticipated, there were about 200,000, and his own army was 70,000 strong, not the 120,000 men he had anticipated. As the Allies advanced on Paris, Napoleon's control over both regime and army crumbled. A provisional French government deposed Napoleon and, with his marshals unwilling to fight on, Napoleon abdicated on 6 April.

Louis XVIII returned to France on 24 April. Already, under the Treaty of Fontainebleau of 11 April, Napoleon had been given the title of Emperor, the small Mediterranean island of Elba as a principality, and a revenue from the French government. Under the armistice signed on 23 April, the Allies agreed to evacuate France.

The Congress of Vienna

German hopes of regaining Alsace were not fulfilled in the Peace of Paris of 30 May 1814. Instead, France got her frontiers of January 1792, with some important and favourable border rectifications. She kept Avignon. She also received back all her colonies, bar Tobago, St Lucia and the Seychelles, all of which went to Britain. These were generous terms designed to help Louis XVIII. Under an armistice signed in Italy on 16 April, the French had already evacuated the peninsula. However, both Louis and Talleyrand sought a more prominent role for France in the subsequent peace negotiations at Vienna. As in 1667, 1678, 1713, 1735, 1748 and 1783, peace offered an opportunity for new alignments. Russia sought co-operation with France against Britain, but Louis preferred an informal relationship with the British, designed to ensure that France played a role in the German and Italian issues. As a consequence, France had a part in the Vienna discussions.

The Congress established a *barrière de l'ouest* designed both to reward powers and to limit France. The kingdom of Sardinia was strengthened with the acquisition of Genoa. Opportunities for French expansion or influence in northern Italy were further lessened with Lombardy–Venetia becoming part of Austria, and Parma and Tuscany a Habsburg secondogeniture. The Austrian Netherlands and the United Provinces were joined as the kingdom of the United Netherlands under the pro-British William V of Orange. Prussia gained much of the lower Rhineland, including Cologne. Geneva and the Valais became Swiss cantons, Baden and Württemberg were both strengthened, and in the Mediterranean Britain was left in control of Malta and the Ionian Isles.

These territorial changes helped mark the end of an era. Unlike Louis XIV, Napoleon left a smaller France, and one with fewer opportunities for further expansion. The Congress also helped set a new agenda for the next century down to 1914. This agenda was initially built partly around the Congress system of dispute settlement, but over the longer term owed much in Western Europe to a slow realization of French decline and to the replacement of Britain by Germany as the major French enemy. French relative decline owed much to French politics, specifically the heavy loss of life in the French Revolutionary and

Napoleonic Wars. Over a million Frenchmen died as a result. The Revolution itself was less bloody, but a combination of civil war and emigration both led to heavy losses and disrupted family life and peacetime reproductive strategies. Partly as a consequence, France's population grew by less than 50 per cent in 1750–1850 while that of England nearly tripled. This contrast can in part be attributed to a fall in the French birth rate arising from the spread of birth control in the late eighteenth century, but repeated choices for war were also important.

Talleyrand took a prominent role at Vienna in opposing Russo-Prussian pressure for the Prussian annexation of Saxony. His co-operation with Austria and Britain on the issue was designed to replace the alliance that had defeated Napoleon, and whose continuation would have left France with only a limited role, by a new diplomatic order in which France could have greater influence in Europe, as well as specific benefits on her frontiers. Count Blacas, the personal representative of Louis XVIII, advocated a league against Russia that initially would unite Britain, and her protégé the United Netherlands, with the Bourbon powers, and then be widened to include Austria and Prussia. Good relations were sought with Sultan Mahmud II. A politics of interest was linked to a sense that France was rightfully the arbiter of Europe and an accompanying suspicion of aggrandizement by others. Louis and Talleyrand disliked Russian predominance in Eastern Europe and tried to limit Austrian power and influence in Italy. In addition, Louis sought to recreate a Bourbon Family Compact with Spain and to restore the Bourbons to Naples.[28]

From Elba to Waterloo, 1815

Louis, however, was overthrown when Napoleon returned from Elba. Landing in southern France on 1 March 1815, he advanced on Paris, Louis fleeing before his arrival. Napoleon was able to reimpose his authority relatively easily. The Vendée rose again but the rising was crushed at the battle of Rocheservière. Napoleon promised to observe existing treaties and affirmed peace with the rest of Europe, but his rhetoric within France was hostile and bellicose. Caulaincourt, again foreign minister, was ordered to create a new league with the lesser powers, including Spain, Portugal, Switzerland and the minor German and Italian states, a testimony to Napoleon's lack of realism.

Napoleon's return united the powers. On 25 March 1815 they renewed their alliance to overthrow the restored Emperor. Had he not been defeated by British, Dutch and German forces at Waterloo on 18 June, other Allied armies would probably have rapidly defeated him. At Waterloo, defensive firepower beat off successive French frontal attacks. Flank attack or yet more frontal assaults might have succeeded, but the arrival of the Prussian forces on the French right spelled the end.

France was then invaded and occupied. Napoleon surrendered to a British warship and was exiled to distant St Helena, a British possession in the South

Atlantic, to return to France only as a corpse. Louis XVIII returned to Paris on 8 July. The Second Treaty of Paris of 20 November stipulated an occupation of northern France for five years, a large indemnity of 700 million francs, and the cession of Beaumont, Bouillon, Saarlouis and Landau. The loss of the Saar and Sambre coalfields has been seen as a serious blow to France's industrial development.[29] By the Quadruple Alliance of 20 November 1815, the four great powers – Austria, Britain, Prussia and Russia – renewed their anti-French alliance for 20 years, a step designed to limit the chances of France disrupting the alliance. Napoleon had failed, totally.

CHAPTER EIGHT

France and the world

Napoleon and the loss of overseas empire

In European terms, Napoleon failed. He did not create a lasting dynasty, his empire collapsed, and, under the terms of the Treaty of Vienna, France was constrained territorially, especially with the establishment of Prussian power on her German frontier. The acquisition of Belgium by the House of Orange and its restoration in the Netherlands was designed to create a powerful pro-British state on France's north-eastern border, and to provide a reliable axis linking Britain with the continent. Napoleon III (President 1848–52, Emperor 1852–70), the reviver of Bonapartist monarchy, had to attempt to overthrow a European order that provided no opportunities for French expansion.

There was also a failure of France as a global power. In the 1780s British politicians had worried about France's global ambitions, especially in the Indian Ocean and the Middle East. There had been fears that the French would overthrow the British in India, as they had earlier done in North America. France's trans-oceanic empire, trade and possessions were, however, hit with the outbreak of the French Revolutionary Wars as the British from 1793 captured many of the imperial bases. Napoleon I got these possessions back under the Treaty of Amiens of 1802, and the treaty was followed by a revival in France's Atlantic trade, including the slave trade, both of which had been badly hit by war and British naval mastery in the 1790s. However, this revival was cut short by the resumption of war with Britain in 1803.[1] This resumption also hit French diplomacy. Bernadotte had been appointed envoy to the United States in January 1803, but was unable to assume that duty. Instead, he commanded I Corps of the *Grande Armée* in the Ulm–Austerlitz campaign of 1805.

Like the Revolutionaries before him, Napoleon also failed to hold on to the French world. He could not, despite initial successes, recapture Haiti, losing large numbers of troops to yellow fever; he had to accept the collapse of French hopes in the Middle East; and he was unable to prevent the British defeat of the Marathas in India in 1803–5. Mysore, the state in Southern India most ready to look to France, had already been conquered in 1799, and the Nizam of Hyderabad's French-trained force had been disarmed by the British the previous year. Indeed, fears about Napoleon helped to drive a British forward-policy in India, and the success of this policy made Britain the dominant power there and, therefore, in South Asia.

Furthermore, benefiting from their naval power and their skill in amphibious operations, the British took the leading French bases – Martinique (1809), Réunion (1810), and Mauritius (1810) – after war resumed in 1803, as well as the bases of France's client states, such as Cape Town (1806) and Batavia (1811) from the Dutch, although they were unsuccessful when they attacked Buenos Aires. In addition, having gained Louisiana from Spain in 1800 by the Treaty of San Ildefonso, Napoleon sold what was then France's most extensive overseas possession to the Americans in 1803, thus ending France's options in North America. Having persuaded Charles IV of Spain to hand over his territories in 1808, Napoleon planned to take over the Spanish Empire, not only in the New World, but also the Philippines. These hopes were thwarted by Spanish resistance, and would, anyway, have been inhibited by British naval power.

Napoleon's global ambitions essentially arose from seeking to thwart Britain, a power that opposed France in Europe, and these ambitions were blocked by Britain, albeit with the important assistance of Napoleon's inability to sustain co-operation with Russia and Spain. Partly as a consequence, he pursued his colonial plans within (rather than outside) Europe, although – like Hitler – his world view, anyway, was largely focused on Europe, especially on territories to the east. After the Egyptian expedition of 1798, Napoleon's interest in, let alone commitment to, the world outside Europe was episodic. Furthermore, it essentially arose from interest in harming European rivals, rather than from any sense of France's role in an expanding Western world.

British influence rested in large part on trade. This was true not only of Asia but also of the New World, both the newly-independent United States and the Iberian colonies. Napoleon did not greatly understand either how to further trade, or the dynamics of commercial activity and its relation with public finances. This failing, serious enough in Europe, was of even greater consequence beyond the bounds of French power. Napoleon's replacement by Louis XVIII was greeted with enthusiasm in the leading trading ports, such as Bordeaux and Marseille, but far less so in Toulon, which relied on its role as a naval base.

The Napoleonic legacy was not only a weaker France in Europe, and a European international system that left few options for France, but also a European overseas world dominated by Britain. France's colonies in 1815 were only those allowed them by Britain. Britain dominated the Western world and France was in a weaker trans-oceanic position, both absolutely and relatively, than had been the case both before and after the peace treaties signed in 1697,

1713, 1748, 1763 and 1783, and indeed than in the nadir of Revolutionary weakness, division and defeat in 1793. Despite imperial expansion from 1830, especially in North Africa (Algeria) and, later, West Africa and Indochina, France was never to reverse that loss.

Empire and resources

A major reason for France's failure was the lack of resources devoted to colonial development. Such a remark may appear unreasonable given the range of French activity during the period. It is easy to present the extent and pace of colonial development as impressive. For example, in the new colony of Louisiana, Fort Maurepas (Biloxi) was founded in 1699 to guard the access to the Mississippi. It had four bastions constructed of logs, three of them mounted with cannon. The following year, more artillery was added and Fort Mississippi was constructed, and in 1702 Fort Louis (Mobile) was laid out with bastions and batteries.

Yet, the commitment of resources was slight, not least in comparison with the deployment of forces in Europe. Fort Mississippi had only a 15-man garrison with a small cannon on an elevated bank, had no real fortifications, and was abandoned in 1706–7. Fort Maurepas had 12 cannon and 12 swivel guns by the end of 1700, but was also abandoned. The entire garrison of disease–ridden Louisiana was no more than 45 in 1706, suffered from the absence of a hospital and of fresh meat, and from insufficient swords, cartridge boxes, nails, guns and powder, from demoralization and desertion, and its survival rested on acceptance by the native population. In 1710 the woodwork at Fort Louis was so rotten with humidity and decay that the cannon could not be supported.

Further north, the French in 1715 sent a garrison of only 20 to Michilimackinac, and planned only ten for Detroit. Four years later, the French force that captured the Texan mission of San Miguel de los Adaes from Spain was only seven-strong; the opposition a single soldier unaware that the two powers were at war. Pierre Petit de Coulange established the post on the Arkansas River in 1732 with only 12 soldiers.[2] More generally, after the failure of Law's bold plans for the Mississippi Company in 1720, there was a loss of interest in Louisiana among both officials and the public. This led to the less regular dispatch of supplies, with consequent shortages of food and manpower. There were 242 soldiers in the colony in August 1730 and most were of low calibre. Instead of the 600 troops requested to deal with the Natchez rising, only 150 men were sent.[3] Elsewhere, the numbers deployed by France were also limited. The squadron sent to Siam (Thailand) in 1687 carried 1,361 people. Of the 636 troops on board only 492 reached Siam and many died soon after arriving.[4] By the time the 1,400 reinforcements *en route* for India reached Mauritius in July 1782, 1,032 were ill with scurvy. Many others had died on the voyage.[5] At Cuddalore in June 1783 Bussy had 2,200 French troops, rather than the 10,000 he was supposed to have, and 2,000 sepoys. He still defeated the 12,000-strong British East India Company force.[6]

Such modest resources help to explain the setbacks the French encountered in trans-oceanic activity, although it would be misleading to suggest that greater numbers or more persistence would necessarily have brought success. Further-more, despite the small numbers sent there, the French presence in Louisiana expanded.

Eighteenth-century successes and failure

Elsewhere, there were setbacks as well as successes. Plans in the late 1660s to develop a colony on Madagascar had been thwarted by a hostile environment and local population,[7] and the French, instead, had concentrated on smaller islands in the Indian Ocean that were easier to control: Réunion and Mauritius. They were driven from Fort Dauphin, their principal base on Madagascar, in 1674. The French re-established a base at Fort Dauphin in 1748 and laid claim to the island in 1768, but that had little impact. The island was not controlled from the posts of Fort Dauphin and Ile Ste. Marie, although the French had staked a claim to a possible base on the route to the Orient. Madagascar was not conquered until 1894–5.

Further east, the French were expelled from Burma in 1757, when Alaunagpaya occupied Pegu. The French arms and advisers that played a role in Vietnam from the late 1780s did so to the benefit of the expansionist schemes of Nguyen Anh – who had conquered all of Vietnam by 1802 – rather than in order to advance French control. Nearer home, in 1741, the Bey of Tunis seized the offshore island of Tabarca, which the French had purchased from the Lomellino family, defeated a counter-attack by a small French force in 1742 and sacked the French Africa Company's base at Cape Negre. A French attempt to land at Larache in Morocco in 1765 failed in the face of heavy fire.

Such failures were not unique to France, and are a reminder of the limitation of European military systems in their confrontations with non-Europeans. The British, for example, also failed in Burma. Indeed, as far as non-Europeans were concerned, the French did reasonably well. If in 1706 the Governor of Pondicherry avoided Mughal attack by making a large present, Pondicherry by then was a major base and the English at Bombay had fared worse from the Mughals in 1686, as the Portuguese were to do, at the hands of the Marathas, in the late 1730s. In the 1720s a threatened attack on Pondicherry by the Nawab of the Carnatic was also bought off, but in 1740–41 the French gained great prestige when Pondicherry did not yield to Maratha threats.[8]

Initially, in the late seventeenth and eighteenth centuries, France was the European power that geographically expanded most vigorously in North America. Whereas the British colonies were bound more closely to the Atlantic seaboard and to the frontier of settlement, the French projected their power along the great rivers of the interior, especially the Mississippi, following trade routes and seeking to link Québec and New Orleans in a bold undertaking.

Much of this expansion did not involve force. As the French sought trade, not land, it was often possible to reach an accommodation with the native population. Any emphasis on conflict is misleading, as it ignores the general ability of the French to maintain their position without war, an ability that would have been enhanced had the British not stirred up opposition, as with the Miami in the Ohio valley in 1747–51.

A lack of emigrants

The absence of large-scale settlement distinguished the French from the British in North America; although not in India or West Africa, as neither power had much settlement there. This was paradoxical, as France had the largest population in Western Europe and was the most densely populated of the major European states. Neither Louisiana nor the St Lawrence valley were as promising for settlement as many of the British colonies, particularly for the cultivation of grain, but the element of opportunity was as much set by the more liberal attitude of successive British governments to the composition of the emigrant population. The British were especially tolerant of religious groups outside the established churches. This was noted by anxious French envoys. Guerchy commented in 1763 and 1764 on emigration to North America by French Protestants travelling via Britain.[9] Durand had urged the government in 1750 to pay attention to the large number of emigrants going to British North America.[10]

New France, France's principal settlement colony, contained some Protestant and Jewish merchants, but it was overwhelmingly Catholic.[11] Huguenots were not allowed to settle there, and, instead, went to British North America. Religious exclusion played a major role in Louis XIV's attitude to colonialism and colonial trade,[12] institutionalizing a strong Catholic presence, and this attitude affected the subsequent history of New France. France lost many talented people among the Huguenots who emigrated. Many of them, and their descendants, joined the English and Dutch East India Companies. François Martin's *Mémoires* mentions the obstinate hatred for France of those he encountered. French colonial policy was to found Catholic colonies in North America. The fur trade was envisaged only as a way of paying for that colonizing purpose.

In the early 1660s there were only about 3,000 French inhabitants of French North America. By the end of the seventeenth century the number had risen to about 10,000, but there were about 210,000 Europeans in British North America. This was despite the fact that Britain's population was only about a quarter that of France and that much of the French population migrated within France. In Britain there was a willingness to emigrate or act as an entrepreneur in distant areas which was much more limited in France. This contributed to the dynamic of British expansion in North America and India.

The disparity with Britain became more marked during the eighteenth century. Canada had about 56,000 inhabitants of French origin in 1740, British America nearly a million people of European background. Religious refugees were particularly encouraged in Georgia, enabling the fledging colony to anchor Britain's presence between Carolina and Florida, and to develop strong links with the Native Americans of the south-east of the modern USA. The French proprietary companies that administered Louisiana from 1717 until it reverted to Crown control in 1731 sought to encourage immigration. John Law saw this as crucial to the prosperity of the colony and there was both voluntary and forced immigration. The former, however, proved largely unsuccessful as far as French settlers were concerned, although there was an important German immigration.[13] By 1763 there were about 4,000 whites and 5,000 blacks in the colony. Only about 11,370 French people settled in Canada between 1608 and 1759.[14] About six or seven people per million left France for Canada each year. Most of the indentured labourers who were sent to work in Canada went back to France at the close of their service.[15] The climate was discouraging as was the shortage of readily cultivable land and neither Canada nor Louisiana had positive connotations in the minds of the French people. The colonies were associated with indentured labour, hostile environments and savage natives. The situation was different as far as North America and the British were concerned. The overall disparity in numbers between British and French North America had obvious implications for the size of forces that could be raised locally and for the extent of the local market.

The alternative to European immigration was a demographic strategy based on assimilation, whether by enculturation and intermarriage with Native Americans, as was in small part attempted in Canada and Louisiana, or, more controversially, by seeking to incorporate free Africans as subjects, as with Louis XIV's *Code Noir* of 1685 and with the abolition of slavery in 1793–4.[16] These strategies were controversial and their impact varied. They were more successful in creating a situation open to loyalism and French cultural influences in Canada and Louisiana than in St Domingue, where the French presence was so heavily associated with slavery,[17] but, in all three cases, French control collapsed when the French state was unable to sustain it.

Government control and empire

Limited immigration ensured that there was no expansionist demographic dynamic comparable in scale to that which encouraged the spread of British settlement and activity in North America. As a consequence, the French colonial presence was dependent on a metropolitan government that was concerned about colonial costs and, at times, ambivalent about expansion.[18] A similar argument has been made about the French in India. Dupleix has been presented as untypical of a French East India Company essentially motivated by trade and commercial profit,[19] and attention has been drawn to the strength of anti-colonialism in French public debate.[20] The French government has been seen as anxious after the Seven Years' War to replace British control and influence in India with a restoration of independence by local rulers, not with French control.[21] This has been linked to French respect for Indian culture,[22] although the strength of Indian rulers was clearly also important.

Lally's instructions in 1757 were to destroy the English East India Company, not to replace it. In the midst of protests and criticisms from vested interests and 'colonial' lobbies, Bussy and Suffren similarly proclaimed in the early 1780s that the king's instructions were to liberate India, not to replace the British hegemony with a French one. Souillac – the Governor of Île de France (Mauritius), who had sent Duchemin with his troops immediately to India in 1780 – was, in contrast, a proponent of a strong, colonial policy. In the absence of specific instructions from Versailles, he ordered Duchemin not to co-operate with Haidar Ali unless a treaty had been signed between them allocating parts of India to France. Haidar Ali was unimpressed, as these areas had not yet been conquered. Souillac was heavily reprimanded for these instructions by Castries who told him that French policy was to liberate Indian territories and return them to their legitimate sovereigns.

The regulation of migration to North America and elsewhere was but part of the general regulatory framework within which the French colonists and merchants were expected to operate. Church and State weighed heavily on passengers and shipping to the colonies, with controls and restraints. The impact of this regulation is a matter of controversy. It has led to claims that government heavy-handedness hindered entrepreneurialism, a charge focused on the case of monopoly chartered companies, seen by successive governments as ways to harness and control private enterprise. In the absence of reliable statistics and an effective state machinery for regulation, French government created or turned to existing bodies, rather than establishing a general supervisory regime and permitting free trade within it. The most recent comparative study of European commercial enterprise in pre-colonial India suggests of the French that 'in so far as state support involved state management to a degree not encountered in the case of any other East India Company, it constituted in the long run more of a liability than an asset and may perhaps legitimately be held largely responsible for the eventual failure of the French enterprise in Asia'.[23] It has also been argued, however, that private merchants were more dynamic and less constrained by the regulations than is generally appreciated.[24]

Furthermore, it would be misleading to suggest that merchants were necessarily opposed to regulation. Far from advocating free-trade policies, the deputies of the Council of Commerce established in 1700, who were selected by the leading commercial towns, were protectionist in outlook, and their pleas for liberty were based on the traditional support of rights and privileges. Believing in the importance of the balance of trade and of maintaining large reserves of bullion, the deputies sought to achieve these objectives collectively through a symbiotic relationship between government and commerce, and individually by obtaining state support for specific privileges.[25]

Then, and more generally, the ambiguities latent in any symbiotic relationship were exacerbated by the continual struggle by interested parties for privileges. In 1700 only six French ports were allowed to trade with the French West Indies. The existence of a vast network of interests, institutions and corporative regulations made it necessary for industrial and commercial concerns, especially new ones, to seek privileges.

The French fur trade has been extensively studied. It was far more regulated than that of Britain in North America. From 1632 until 1681, travel in the Canadian interior without permission was prohibited, leading to the illegal trade of the *coureurs de bois*, unlicensed fur traders. Monopolistic practices and taxation were a burden on the fur trade, making French products in Canada more expensive. The interior trade was not liberated until 1681, although it was still regulated thereafter by means of a system of permits. Liberalization led to a large supply of beaver in Montreal, and the response was more regulation. In 1696 a royal edict closed most interior trading posts and ended the permit system. The angry *coureurs de bois*, unable to trade with Montréal, instead sold their furs to the British. The permit system was restored in 1716, a liberalization in French terms, but one that restricted the fur trade and made it easier to force the traders to pay taxes to support the French military presence.[26] A mercantilist regime and ethos also prevailed in Louisiana. These regimes were shot through with profiteering and clientage by officials. Although that can be seen as free enterprise and as a way to harness individual energy and private resources, it was potentially detrimental to both government and trade.[27]

Taxes and monopolies also led to problems and protests in other parts of the French commercial system. In 1718 Jean-Baptiste Poussin, envoy in the major entrepôt of Hamburg, pressed the need for a cut in export duties. He repeated merchant views that a cut in tariffs would lead to an increase in trade and a rise in revenues.[28] In the 1730s French cloth manufacturers at Amiens and Rouen frequently complained that Marseille enjoyed a monopoly on French trade with the Ottoman Empire that obliged them to purchase Turkish yarns at a higher cost than if they had been permitted to import them from Dutch merchants. They therefore requested the end of the monopoly and the freedom to purchase raw materials from the Dutch.[29] British trade with Salonika, one of the leading ports in the empire, was held to benefit from lower dues on commerce and more freedom than that of France.[30] More generally, the British commercial system was freer than that of France to act as the focus for multiple networks of capital formation.

The state of the fur trade was important because it dominated Canadian exports. However, Canada's limited economic potential can be gauged from the fact that, once conquered by Britain, it provided less than 5 per cent by value to British trade with North America in the 1770s. Louisiana was also of limited value. In his *Description de la Louisiane* (Paris, 1688), Louis Hennepin, a missionary who had accompanied La Salle, had described Louisiana as the future bread-basket for the French Empire, a fertile area able to produce wine and foodstuffs for the French West Indies. Reality proved otherwise. From the 1700s explorers had been sent up the Missouri to exploit copper mines and along the Red River in order to find silver and gold deposits or benefit from the Spanish ones in New Mexico, but hopes that Louisiana would be a mineral colony, or would serve as a base for trade with the Pacific or, to any extent, with New Mexico, proved abortive. Furthermore, the route to New Orleans was poor by all navigational criteria. Nevertheless, the Spaniards were concerned, as they had been when La Salle landed in Texas in 1684.[31]

With its major production of sugar and coffee, the West Indies was far more important to the French colonial (and metropolitan) economy than Canada. In the West Indies, the control of European immigration and settlement by the colonial authorities was less harmful to the French presence than it was in North America. It was also not an issue in India. In both India and the West Indies, naval strength was crucial to the French position. Their bases were dependent on maritime links with Europe and those, indeed, were the reason for their exist-ence. In contrast, Spanish America was less vulnerable to blockade or invasion, not only thanks to the tropical diseases that debilitated attacking forces, but also because it was far more populous and much less reliant for defence and finances on trade with the homeland.

Although war with other European powers was not important to the expan-sion of the French (and Spanish) colonial and maritime presence, it was crucial to their retention. Britain and France were at peace between 1713 and 1744, and, in those years, French trans-oceanic activity and commerce were able to develop without being concerned with conflict with European powers, with the exception of the short war with Spain in 1719–20. The situation was very different, however, in 1744–63, in much of which period France was at war. Trade with Asia fell in that period, hitting the accumulation of profits necessary to encourage and finance fresh activity.[32] Trade with the West Indies was also hit in wartime. In 1748 Philippe Lagau, the consul at Hamburg, a crucial entrepôt for re-exports to Northern Europe, complained that, due to British obstacles to French colonial trade, the price of goods from Martinique was very high.[33] This lessened their competitiveness, and also the ability to finance imports into France.

The Anglo-French struggle for empire

For both Britain and France, the major fault-lines of colonial conflict were those between the two powers. With the benefit of hindsight, the course of the conflict appears all too clear. France would be on the defensive, increasingly pressed by a power that was stronger at sea and thus able to take the initiative. With the support of North American colonies that were far more heavily populated than their French counterparts, the British were therefore bound to win there.

In practice, the situation was far more complex. It was not inevitable that the British would dominate the oceans or take the initiative, or that, if they did take it, that they would necessarily be successful. British attempts on Québec in 1690 and 1711 failed. In the War of the Austrian Succession, France took the initiative in India, capturing Madras in 1746, and then holding off a British offensive in 1748 against their base Pondicherry. The French were also able to send a large expedition to North American waters in 1746 in a fruitless effort to regain Louisbourg. The subsequent peace treaty in 1748 brought no colonial gains for either power, and also failed to settle their differences. Both states contained influential figures, especially in their colonies, convinced of the inexorable ambitions and schemes of their rivals, in North America, the West Indies and India, although direct hostilities were avoided until 1754.

The Seven Years' War is generally seen in terms of a string of British successes, but there were also serious British failures. These included the successful French–Native ambush of General Braddock's larger army at the battle of the Monongahela on 9 July 1755, the loss of Forts Oswego, George, and William Henry to French advances from Canada in 1756–7, the abortive British plan to capture Louisbourg in 1757, the heavy losses in the poorly managed and unsuccessful British frontal attack on Carillon (Ticonderoga) in 1758, the French victory at the battle of Sainte-Foy over the British army outside Québec in April 1760, and, in India, the French capture of Fort St David in 1758.

British failures serve as a reminder that the French were helped by the difficulties of the British task, not least the complications of amphibious operations, the problems of operating in the interior of North America, the need to allocate limited resources across a number of schemes, logistical problems, and the resourcefulness of the leading French commanders: Lally in India and Montcalm in Canada. Major British successes were frequently only obtained with considerable difficulty. Thus, the capture of Québec in 1759 followed a frustrating two months in which the natural strength of the position, French fortifications, and the skilful character of Montcalm's dispositions, had thwarted the attacking British force under James Wolfe.

The relatively small forces involved in trans-oceanic operations, and the close similarity of their weapons and methods of fighting, put a great premium on leadership, an ability to understand and exploit terrain, morale, and unit cohesion and firepower. The British were generally adept at all of these, but so also were the French, and sometimes more so. Montcalm made effective use of French troops and native allies and understood how best to operate in the interior of North America. He was particularly successful in 1756–7.

The duration of the struggle was also significant. Had the Seven Years' War ended in 1758, or even the end of April 1760, then it would not have been anywhere near as successful for the British. The interconnectedness of the war was also as important as the conflicts in particular areas. The British were able to move forces within their imperial system. Louisbourg fell in 1745 to 3,000 Massachusetts militia, transported by New England ships and supported by the small Leeward Islands squadron of the British navy. In 1762 French colonies in the West Indies fell to British troops sent from North America, rather than distant Britain. The French force that temporarily captured St John's in Newfoundland that year had to come from France, while the British force that drove it out came from North America.

Naval predominance and success in European waters meant an ability to grasp the initiative outside Europe. That was the crucial interconnectedness of British power. It was not so much that the French lost Canada in Germany – that the concentration of French effort there from 1757 deprived Montcalm of men – as that the British conquered Canada off Brest. The blockade of the leading French naval base, a blockade that led ultimately to victory in Quiberon Bay in 1759, made it difficult for France to retain the initiative in North America, or, indeed, to send substantial reinforcements to their colonies, or to maintain important trade links with them. French insurance premiums for ships to Québec rose from about five per cent in 1755 to 50 per cent or more in 1758 and were seldom obtainable in 1759, a year in which many of the merchantmen sent to Canada were captured.[34]

The French imperial system collapsed before the British captured the colonies. The control and organization of maritime links was vital for demographic, economic, organizational and military factors.[35] Without a large hinterland, French colonies were vulnerable, while, thanks to British naval strength, French attacks on British positions, such as Lally's siege of Madras in 1758–9, or the siege of Québec in 1760, could be more readily thwarted. Whereas the French conflicts with Spain, Austria and Prussia in 1667–1763 were those of a continental against continental powers, especially the last two, and in Europe the British struggle with France was that of a maritime versus a continental power, outside Europe it was a war between two maritime powers that the British won in the 1750s, crucially in 1759.[36]

The French also deployed fewer resources in North America than the British. In 1745 the garrison of Louisbourg was only 1,300 strong. In 1758 the British had 24,000 regulars and 22,500 provincial troops in North America, the French 6,600 *troupes de terre*, 2,900 *compagnies franches de la marine* and about 15,000 militia. Even these numbers pressed hard on food supplies which were themselves hit by a series of poor harvests, caused serious inflation in Canada, and led to an enormous increase in expenditure on the province that helped to cause the financial crisis of October and November 1759.

The size of the respective forces was not the sole determinant of success. The Canadian militia was very good and had more experience in wilderness warfare than their New England opponents, the large British armies faced logistical problems, and, in the operations near Québec in 1759–60, it was not numbers alone that were crucial. Furthermore, British naval strength did not prevent the arrival of six battalions in Canada in 1755, two in 1756, two in 1757 and another two in 1758. Numbers were not the issue when the British attacked Martinique in 1759. They rapidly retreated in the face of a local militia able to take effective advantage of the difficult local terrain. Nevertheless the exceptionally large resources devoted to the struggle in Canada by the British in 1758–60 stacked the odds against New France.[37]

After the war, France was very much in the position of challenger, but, unlike after the Wars of the Spanish and Austrian Succession, she was helped by close relations with Spain. Thanks to much shipbuilding in the late 1760s and 1770s, especially by Spain, then one of the most dynamic states in Europe, France and Spain combined had a quantitative superiority in naval tonnage over Britain of about 25 per cent by 1780.

Partly as a result, when conflict resumed in the War of American Independence, the British were unable to repeat their success of the Seven Years' War. Their navy gained control of neither European nor American waters, and in 1778 was unable to defeat the French before Spain entered the war. The British concentration of naval strength on defending home waters enabled the unblockaded Toulon fleet to sail to American waters. In 1779, when France and Spain sent a fleet into the Channel, their attempt to invade Britain was thwarted by disease and poor organization, not British naval action. It was not until the Battle of the Saintes on 12 April 1782 that there was a decisive British naval victory to rank with Quiberon Bay in 1759, and it was a testimony to the rising importance of colonies and transoceanic operations, and the British failure to maintain an effective blockade, that this battle was fought in the Caribbean, south of Guadeloupe, not in European waters. In 1782, the British were concerned about a possible Bourbon attack on Jamaica, not – as in 1759 – with blocking an invasion of Britain.

Naval strength was crucial to colonial operations in the War of American Independence. Besieged British positions that were relieved, such as Gibraltar, were held, while those that were not relieved, such as Yorktown in 1781, were lost. French success in blockading the Chesapeake in 1781 was crucial to the course of the war in North America, and is a reminder of the limitations of assuming any structural determinism in eighteenth-century military history, not least of arguing from total fleet size and the supporting political, administrative and financial infrastructure, to inevitable results. The British navy was more successful in helping prevent the overthrow of the British position in India. Bussy had far fewer troops than the 10,000 men he had requested in 1778, in part because of the ships that were prevented from sailing or were intercepted by the British navy. Had Bussy reached India, as Rochambeau did America in 1780, without delay, with healthy troops and with all his artillery, he would have been more likely to achieve his objectives, not least because Suffren was a better naval commander than de Grasse, his counterpart off North America.

Without assured naval dominance, the articulation of the British military system was weak and the success of the individual parts limited, but the loss of British dominance did not mean that the Bourbons had gained it. Instead, the war was messy, in large part because neither side was able to predict the likely success of initiatives. This remained the case in the post-war naval race between Britain and France, and, subsequently, in their renewed conflict until Trafalgar (1805). With the support, voluntary or coerced, of Spain, France could challenge the British at sea.

Such a challenge was central to France's ability, as a European trans-oceanic power, to hold its own against other European transoceanic powers, but it was less important to her ability to make gains at the expense of non-European powers when she was at peace with European powers. Here it is the weakness of the French colonial drive in the decade 1783–92 that is most notable. Colonialism was weak, both in French policy-making circles and in public debate. There was a desire for naval strength and a marked interest in both trade and exploration, but not a strong pressure to plant the flag on distant shores.

This can also be seen in the Napoleonic period. Napoleon toyed with the idea of French hegemony on the Mediterranean–India axis, but it was a hegemony to be gained with the assistance of other powers – Russia or Persia – not by replacing them. This matched French policy towards India in the 1780s and 1790s. The French then sought to work with local rulers, although their efforts were greatly handicapped by the Revolution. They were not able to build up anything comparable to the substantial politico-military control and tax-raising powers that the British already possessed in Bengal and the Carnatic, and that they further expanded in this period. As a result, the French lacked a strong anchor to their political and commercial presences in South and East Asia. Mauritius and Réunion were important French bases, but they did not produce the goods and silver to trade with China that the British gained from India and its trade. Egypt was seen as a source of cotton, rice and coffee, and as a base for French commercial expansion, but Napoleon was unable to retain control after the initial success of his invasion in 1798.

France and the Spanish Empire

More generally, a co-operative approach was central to France's approach within the Atlantic world, albeit a co-operation framed by French power and interests, and dependent on the expropriation and sufferings of others, not least slaves from Africa. During the century the French colonies obtained 1,015,000 slaves from French sources, and in 1788 the French West Indies contained 594,000 slaves, many harshly treated. In 1687 St Domingue contained 4,500 'whites' and 3,500 'blacks', in 1789 28,000 'whites', 30,000 free 'blacks' and 406,000 slaves.[38]

In the Atlantic world in the eighteenth century, France sought power essentially as the beneficiary of the Spanish system, rather than by replacing it. With the exception of brief moments, France and Spain were not at war after 1697.

These moments indicated the potential for French expansion. The French capture of Pensacola in Florida in 1719 was especially important, as in strategic terms it was the Spanish presence in the Gulf of Mexico that offered a target to the French, not that of Britain.

The same was true in the West Indies. The tempting targets were not the British islands, but the large Spanish possessions, such as Santo Domingo, the other half of Hispaniola. In 1678 Philippe de Villette-Mursay, a French naval captain, was amazed by the wealth of Cartagena, one of the leading Spanish ports on the Caribbean coast of South America.[39] After 1697, conquests from Spain were not an option, although Spanish concern about French expansion from Louisiana continued, and was expressed during the negotiation of the Third Family Compact in 1761.[40] Nevertheless, the French did not seek to undermine the Spanish position in their colonies. The fleet sent to the West Indies in 1702 was instructed to protect the Spanish treasure fleet, not seize it. Suggestions for expansion, such as that made in 1718 by a Frenchman in Buenos Aires, and the idea floated in 1715 and 1717 that France ask for Santo Domingo in lieu of Spanish debts, were not followed up.[41] Alliances made with native tribes served to protect Louisiana, rather than to serve as a basis for the conquest of nearby Spanish possessions.[42] In June 1777 France and Spain settled their differences over boundaries on Hispaniola.[43]

French policy was intertwined: alliance with Spain, maintenance of her colonial empire against Britain, naval combination with Spain, and trade with Spanish America via Spain. Rather than drawing straight lines of causality, it is more appropriate to present these as mutually reinforcing.

The New World was a crucial market for the French. In the Orient, the taste for European manufactures was limited, but the European colonies in the New World had a large population of European origin and with relatively high wage rates. They were able to purchase European manufactured goods in return for their bullion and plantation crops. The struggle to supply goods to the Spanish Empire was as sharp as that to sell colonial goods in Europe. For French manufacturing towns such as Elbeuf, Spain and the Spanish Empire were important markets.[44] The population of Nantes rose considerably after 1730 as the New World market for its cheap silks grew. In 1762 Choiseul feared that if the Seven Years' War continued and the British conquered Mexico it would provide a market for their manufactures and ruin much of France's.[45]

The limited population of Canada and Louisiana restricted the markets there, that of British North America was closed by protectionist legislation and consumer preference, and Portuguese Brazil was part of the British economic system, thanks to economic and financial links that had developed when Britain and Portugal were closely allied. Puysieulx thought it 'natural' that Britain should replace France as Portugal's ally once the Bourbons had acceded to the Spanish throne.[46] Although the French had a commercial role there,[47] Portugal and its Brazilian empire took significant quantities of British products, particularly textiles, paying for them with Brazilian gold, which helped to keep the British financial system buoyant and to finance British trades that showed a negative balance. This encouraged French, or French-supported Spanish, invasions of Portugal in 1762, 1801 and 1807.

Britain was more successful in obtaining colonial markets for her manufactures. This was partly due to political factors. The French were disappointed by the unwillingness of their Spanish allies to open up their empire to French commercial penetration. The French also faced stiff competition. In 1715–35 their dominance of the Spanish linen market was broken by Silesian linens shipped from Hamburg. The outbreak of plague in Marseille in 1720 hit trade with Spain and was exploited by British and Dutch merchants.[48] In 1726, when Austria and Spain were newly allied, there was worry about Spanish trade concessions to merchants from the Austrian Netherlands.[49] In 1734 more than twice as many British as French ships entered Cadiz (596 to 238).

As the French essentially traded with Spanish America through Cadiz, they were keen to prevent direct British and Dutch trade with the Spanish colonies. This entailed not only opposition to legal trade, particularly British and Dutch attempts to gain and retain the *asiento*,[50] but also support and encouragement for Spanish attempts to prevent illegal trade. This was also true of periods when Britain and France were allied, as in 1726.[51] In such periods French ministers took the view, as Chauvelin put it to Magnan, envoy in Russia, in 1729, that co-operation did not extend to commercial privileges.[52] More generally, they did not want Britain and Spain too close to each other.[53]

The French hoped to benefit commercially from closer relations with Spain from 1733. A project for a commercial treaty was produced the following year.[54] However, they found that Spanish interest in developing their imperial economy restricted French opportunities and required careful management. There were repeated complaints about the treatment of French trade, and the privileges of French merchants were frequently ignored.[55] In the Atlantic the French could try to develop a Franco-Spanish system, but in the Indian Ocean they were in a weaker position; both because they lacked allies and because their opponents were allied. Britain and the Dutch were close allies in 1689–1748; and for much of the rest of the period, particularly in 1748–74, they were disinclined to push their differences. The British concentration on India and that of the Dutch on Sri Lanka and the East Indies reduced tension. This lessened the opportunities available to France, and other European powers proved no substitute.

Co-operation with the Portuguese had been sought by Colbert in 1669–70, but it was rejected by the Portuguese in favour of neutrality in the forthcoming Franco-Dutch struggle. Although Spain controlled much of the Philippines, it was not an Indian Ocean power, and the Philippines could not serve as the basis for Franco-Spanish co-operation in the Western Pacific. In the Indian Ocean, France was obliged to pursue hopes of alliance with native powers that lacked maritime strength – Siam (Thailand) in the 1680s, Hyderabad, the Carnatic, Mysore and the Marathas each for at least part of the period 1746–1799, Burma in the 1750s and Cochin China in the 1780s – and to seek to turn co-operation with Britain (as in 1672–4) or the Dutch (as in 1780–7) to profit in the region. Neither policy served France's goal of creating an effective and reliable maritime position from which French strategic and commercial goals could be pursued. In 1672–4 the English East India Company refused to help the French, while in 1672 Charles II turned down the idea of the dispatch to the Indian Ocean of a joint Anglo-French fleet. The possibilities of Franco-Dutch co-operation in 1780–87 and 1795–1814 were greatly limited by vigorous British counter-measures.

Empire and the Revolution

There was no radical change in France's maritime position until the French Revolution. The collapse then of the Family Compact encouraged ideas that France could benefit from the overthrow of Spanish colonial rule, either directly, or by using the possibility to win better relations with Britain,[56] or, indeed, the United States.[57] War with Spain led to the gain of Santo Domingo in 1795, and the stronger France was able to insist on the return of Louisiana under the Treaty of San Ildefonso of 1800. The idea of agreed action against the Spanish Empire, floated in 1792 as a lure to the British, was abandoned when war broke out in 1793 and not revived with the Treaty of Amiens of 1802. The attempt to use the Spanish Empire in order to secure better relations with the United States, led to Napoleon's sale of Louisiana in 1803. Napoleon gained little, but had he not sold New Orleans the British might have captured it: the French defenders lacked the resources available to Andrew Jackson when he successfully defended the city against British attack in 1815. A British presence in Louisiana might well have inflamed Anglo-American relations prior to 1812 or have made it harder to negotiate a settlement to the Anglo-American War of 1812–15. Either outcome would have benefited France.

With the Revolution, the French were forced back on their own resources. They lost their allies, and a combination of domestic instability and international enmity disrupted French commercial and financial networks. Their European trade was badly hit. The percentage of the total value of St Petersburg's overseas commodity trade controlled by French merchants fell from 2.7 in 1768–79 and 2.0 in 1781–92 to 0.7 in 1795–8 and zero in 1800–01. The comparable British percentages were 44.4, 32.6, 49.2 and 45.8.[58] The situation further afield was also bleak. Having earlier backed the Spanish Bourbons in Spanish America, lost Canada, and supported the independence of the United States, France could only benefit from the New World indirectly. Even this process was compromised by the international impact of the political shifts within France of the 1790s. The violent, radical and atheistical course of the Revolution greatly weakened sympathy for France in the United States. The Revolutionary and Napoleonic crisis also destabilized Spain, and the subsequent collapse of the Spanish Empire in the New World did not benefit France. Instead, countries like Argentina became part of the British trading system. In the short term, Napoleon's exploitative and insensitive treatment of Spain lessened and eventually destroyed its value as an ally, and thus gravely compromised France's opportunities as a global power.

The problem of limited options in the New World from the 1780s is an aspect of what may be termed a turn to the east, a notion that has played a controversial role in discussion of British imperial policy after the loss of the Thirteen Colonies.[59] Such a turn can be seen in French interest in the Near and Middle East and Indian Ocean in the 1780s, but the Dutch crisis of 1787 had severely shaken such hopes. Furthermore, in 1790–92 France did not act to support its major Indian ally, Tipu Sultan of Mysore. The garrison of Pondicherry was withdrawn.

Militarily weak, the French turned to idealistic hopes. In January 1792 the attention of the National Assembly was directed by its Colonial Committee towards Madagascar:

> not to invade a country or subjugate several savage nations, but to form a solid alliance, to establish friendly and mutually beneficial links with a new people . . . today it is neither with the cross nor with the sword that we establish ourselves with new people. It is by respect for their rights and views that we will gain their heart; it is not by reducing them to slavery . . . this will be a new form of conquest.[60]

Such hopes came to nothing, although previous French schemes in Madagascar had been little more successful. In October 1794 the National Convention was told that France would gain influence in India, if it stood for justice and liberty; but that year Tipu, who had received no help when he fought the British in 1790–92, was not interested in an alliance.[61] The French found that there was no substitute for power, but British successes in 1798–9 over the French navy and Tipu Sultan – at the Battles of the Nile and Seringapatam respectively – followed by their victories over the French army in Egypt in 1801, made it clear that France would not be able to project her power successfully along the Egypt–India axis. Seringapatam, like other fortresses in Mysore, had been fortified with help from French engineers.

Aside from being unable to expand her power – as Britain did not only at the expense of European powers and in India, but also in Australasia – France also lost her colonies. The most profitable, St Domingue, suffered a major slave rebellion in August 1791. Troops were sent in 1792 and slavery abolished in the colony in 1793 (and in all the French colonies the following year), but, greatly assisted by the impact of yellow fever on French troops, the determination of the black population not to remain under French rule ultimately prevailed. In 1793 Spain went to war with France and provided aid to the rebels. British troops intervened in 1794 only to withdraw in 1797, leaving the black forces in control.

They were defeated by a French force of 20,000 men under Napoleon's brother-in-law, Charles Leclerc, sent in 1802, in part because their leader, Toussaint L'Ouverture, was treacherously seized during negotiations.

Napoleon hoped that St Domingue would be part of a French Empire in the west that would include Louisiana, Florida, Cayenne, Martinique and Guadeloupe. However, resistance continued, and in 1803 the resumption of war with Britain led to a blockade of St Domingue's ports. Their food supplies cut, the French lost the initiative and were pushed back. Driven back to Le Cap, the French force, now under General Donatien Rochambeau, agreed a truce with the black army under Toussaint's successor, Jean-Jacques Dessalines, and in November 1803 was transported by British warships to Jamaica. The surviving white settlers fled to Cuba. The independence of Haiti, the second independent state in the New World, was proclaimed on 1 January 1804.[62]

The French army had included 5,000 Polish troops who had fought for the French in Italy in the 1790s. Most of those sent to Haiti died of yellow fever. Like the later use of Irish troops in Central Europe, rather than against the British, the deployment of the Poles reflected the degree to which the national interests of France's allies were subsumed to Napoleonic imperialism.[63] The expeditionary force also included a large number of Swiss conscripts.

Napoleon made a number of efforts to expand French power to the east. In 1798 he asked Piveron de Morlat, who had served as French agent in Mysore in 1778–86, to join his staff in Egypt and sought to win the alliance of the Pasha of Acre by promising help against Turkey. Napoleon's secretary, Louis Antoine Fauvelet de Bourrienne, thought that the general wished to repeat the triumphs of Alexander the Great by marching overland against India.

Failure in Egypt checked but did not end thoughts of the East. In 1803 General Decaen sailed from Mauritius to try to reoccupy Pondicherry. His squadron carried some 1,250 men, many young officers intended to continue France's earlier policy of raising and training forces for native rulers. They could not land at Pondicherry, however, because it was occupied by the British, and that year General Lake destroyed the 'Brigades françaises de l'Hindoustan' of de Boigne and Perron in North India.[64]

Pierre-Amédée Jaubert, who was sent to Persia in the spring of 1805, arrived in Teheran in 1806. His instructions included an offer of military help, and his embassy was followed in 1807 both by the arrival of a Persian envoy to visit Napoleon and by the dispatch of a French military mission that was charged with reorganizing the Persian army. The two powers signed the Treaty of Finkenstein of 7 May 1807, but their priorities were different. The Persians wanted help in driving the Russians out of Georgia, while Napoleon wished to see Persia exclude British influence and hoped that it could be a base against British India.

Tilsit wrecked the chance of the alliance developing, although it could be argued that the contradictory expectations of the partners anyway limited the possibilities. Relations were breached and it was to Alexander I that Napoleon in February 1808 proposed a joint advance towards the Persian Gulf in order to threaten British India. In 1810–11 Georges Outrey was sent as a new envoy to Persia, but his instructions were ambiguous and the high hopes held earlier not repeated.[65]

Attempting to negotiate alliances at a great distance was far from easy. Jaubert left Teheran on 14 July 1806 and did not reach Paris until 21 June 1807. The same difficulty had affected Louis XIV's hopes of alliance with Siam (Thailand), and also eighteenth-century plans for co-operation with Indian rulers. Different cultural suppositions and political practices were also a problem, as the British discovered when they sent the Macartney mission to China in 1793. So also was the response of other European powers. Earlier, Catherine II had been angry about the French mission to Persia in 1784, while French diplomatic pressure in 1786 against the presence of Russian forces in Georgia had been neither welcome to the Russians nor central to French interests.[66]

At war with Britain, the leading maritime power, for most of the Napoleonic period, France was unable to enjoy the benefits of the European hegemony she had gained. The colonial empires of her European allies were outside her (and their) control, and the resources that Napoleon deployed could not be used to project French power. This was a failure that was not inherent in France's position, but one that reflected the relatively low priority of maritime as opposed to continental activities, and the successes of the British navy. Like Louis XIV, Napoleon wanted colonies and a strong navy, but, under pressure, the army came first. Had they occurred, naval victories by France and her allies might, however, have led to different conclusions about the appropriateness of French priorities.

The failure to sustain trans-oceanic trade hit French re-exports to Europe and revenues, and reduced the ability of France to subsidize her allies. In the 1740s France had subsidized Bavaria, Sweden and Don Philip, and in 1757–62 Austria. Napoleon, in contrast, used France's allies as a source of support, helping greatly to lessen the acceptability of his policies. The loss of trade also encouraged de-industrialization and accentuated the already-powerful value and values of land ownership.

The character of empire

The rebellion on St Domingue, and slavery in general, serve as reminders that France's global presence was as part of an appropriating European expansionism. Land was grabbed and colonized, people bought and seized, cultivation, drainage, settlement and terrain organized and understood for the benefit of the French state and French interests, and with scant response to other concerns. Towns, including native areas, were laid out on European-imposed grid plans. French missionaries followed the French state. The Jesuits arrived at Pondicherry in 1690 and they built a large church there in 1699. Mapping was designed to serve French interests by facilitating territorial claims, military control and economic exploitation.[67] When Martinique and Guadeloupe were mapped after the Seven Years' War, their maps recorded the plantation system of a sugar, coffee and cotton colony and were also designed to provide information in the event of another war with Britain. Mapping was carried out by engineers and linked to a policy of fortification. On the maps, the names of owners were marked on plantations.[68]

The understanding of place, space and people in terms of France and the French was a typical feature of European expansion. Slaves lost their names and their identity was challenged.[69] The brutal treatments meted out to disobedient slaves was a far blunter instance of the same cruel process, as was the practice of burning prisoners alive that began in New Orleans after the Natchez rising of 1729.[70] Difficulties experienced in Christian proselytism led in the late seventeenth century to a harsher attitude towards Native Americans that also served to justify imperial expansion.[71] Mercier's description in his novel *L'An 2440* of a monument in Paris depicting a coloured man, his arms extended, a proud look in his eye, surrounded by the pieces of 20 broken sceptres, and atop a pedestal with the inscription 'Au vengeur du nouveau monde', was utopian.

CHAPTER NINE

Conclusions

Was it the French victory at Minden in 1759 or in the Mediterranean in 1798, or Napoleon's triumphant entry into London in 1805 that put paid to the idea that France's geopolitical position was such that she could be the dominant power on the landmass of Western Europe, but would fail to be the leading European colonial and maritime power? To buy peace in each case, Britain had to return colonial gains, as she had also done in 1748. In each case France was able to assert her position in the world, both in her own right and in conjunction with her allies, especially Spain. The claims of domestic and foreign critics that particular aspects of French society and the French state made them less likely to prevail over more mercantile, tolerant and populist Britain seemed redundant.

France of course did not win these wars, but the fancy outlined above directs attention to the question whether her failure was inherent or the product of contingency and chance. If inherent, it is necessary to consider both how far it is appropriate to think in terms of inevitability and how far the inherent characteristics altered during the period. Were there, for example, factors particular to *ancien régime* France that were swept away by the Revolution? If so, what were they?

Resources, government and public culture

One obvious answer is that the Revolution released, energized, organized and directed French resources.[1] More specifically, it can be argued that *ancien régime* France was resource-rich, both in wealth and population, and regarded as such by foreign diplomats.[2] However, the nature of society, politics and political culture, specifically the role of private financiers and the implications of venality (private ownership and sale) of office-holding, made it very difficult for the government to tap these resources. Reliance on a small number of privileged money-lenders did not provide security or predictability for government finances and confidence or investment for the economy. Britain's state financial credit system was superior to that of France, in part for constitutional reasons. With the atrophy of the Estates General, there was no equivalent in France to the Westminster Parliament. The *Parlement* of Paris was no equivalent in terms of creating a culture and practice for eliciting a workable system of consent and co-operation between government and society.

In 1748 Frederick II contrasted the wealth of France with the disorder of its badly administered finances. The *taille*, the basic land tax, suffered from problems of assessment, exemption and political control. Assessments were often out of date or dependent on valuation by the owner. There was no systematic income tax. Much wealth was tied up in venal offices, many of which brought tax exemption. Just as levels of personal taxation were below those of Britain,[3] so also, in another crucial aspect of resources, there was no conscription to compare with the situation in Russia.

Limited taxation increased the pressure on government finances, leading both to higher debt and greater borrowing. This was especially a problem given the competitive nature of the international system, and the resulting costs. In late 1758 French naval debts were reckoned at over 42 million *livres*, and in 1759 the navy spent 20 million more than it received, leading to a collapse in its credit system. Naval expenditure rose from 20 million *livres* in 1774 to 200 million in 1778, as France moved towards war with Britain. By 1789 the French government was using 60 per cent of its revenues just to pay the interest on its debts. Financial problems were cited when excusing unwelcome steps. On 4 April 1784 Louis XVI told Suffren that the war in America had so hit French finances that it had not been possible to fight on in Asia.[4] In this case, however, such a continuation did not accord with Vergennes' concerns about Russian aggrandizement, and, once American independence had been secured, France had obtained her major war goal. To fight on to weaken Britain in India would have been to commit French policy to uncertain objectives and unpredictable allies. By 1783 Tipu Sultan was isolated in India.

Public finances also had to confront a very uncertain income stream. The extensive crop failures in 1770 and the consequent economic and financial crisis, were probably partly responsible for the government's support for reform and attempt to increase taxes in 1771. In the 1780s, a number of poor harvests cut tax revenues, hitting finances already weakened by the cost of intervention in the American War of Independence. Nevertheless, war, rather than poor harvests, was the major fiscal calamity. Whereas a rescheduling and partial repudiation of debts in the 1660s and 1710s had lessened the long-term burdens created by the conflicts in 1628–61 and 1688–1714, and had facilitated fresh military activity, there was no comparable process after the wars of 1741–8 and 1756–63. There was no *Chambre de justice* to fleece the financiers as there had been in the 1660s and 1716–17.[5] In 1763–4 the *parlements* thwarted an attempt to produce a general survey of land ownership, designed to serve as the basis for a more rational system of taxation.[6]

The government then was neither sufficiently strong nor in a bad enough state of crisis to lead to major change. There was no political discontinuity capable of serving as the basis for, and in part requiring, major governmental changes, comparable to that of the Glorious Revolution of 1688 in Britain. Nor from the 1760s, when the need for change was increasingly grasped was there a constitutional consensus behind any particular process of change. Thanks in part to disputes over Jansenism, there was a significant level of distrust between Crown and the *parlements*, and the latter could not readily serve as intermediate institutions capable of forwarding an acceptable consensus. As a consequence, the reforms introduced by particular ministers were dependent on court faction and there was a serious lack of consistency in policy. This was readily apparent in attempts to improve financial administrations and in the general operation of state finances, neither of which were foredoomed to failure.[7]

Structural limitations influenced the character and development of overseas as well as metropolitan France. The French Empire was greatly affected by the 'confluence' in the seventeenth-century of the French counter-Reformation, the 'Bourbon administrative monarchy' and the development of trans-oceanic trade and colonialism.[8] In combination, these could be seen as more harmful to mercantile enterprise and demographic growth than the English legacy, although the success of the eighteenth-century Spanish Empire, which similarly drew on the energies and precepts of the Catholic Reformation and of Bourbon administrative monarchy, encourages caution on this head.

Structural problems were a matter of social mores as well as political culture. The stiffness and pride of the French nobility, and its contempt for commoners, were emphasized during the 'réaction nobiliaire' that reached its peak in the 1760s and 1770s. French Jesuits in early eighteenth-century India had already been struck by the similarities between French and Indian societies, the caste system, and the hierarchical distinctions and psychological barriers of societies of orders. These divisions limited the talent available and affected particular operations. Duchemin, the army commander in India in 1780, was betrayed by his subordinates, who told Haidar Ali that he was an outcast in French society while they belonged to the highest military caste, and that therefore Haidar could only negotiate with them since they alone had any real power in the army. Suffren had to dismiss several captains who refused to fight under his orders and did not attack when he sent the signal. Other captains preferred to take sick leave. The captains refused to acknowledge Suffren's seniority because of his inferior titles of nobility.

This conduct affected the course of the battles between Suffren and Hughes. But for it, Suffren might have achieved naval supremacy in the Bay of Bengal, and Madras would have been in great peril. Bussy mistrusted the French 'adventurers' in India, those enterprising individuals who took service with local rulers, as a rabble of commoners and miserable treasure-seekers. His social attitude also affected his view on Indian politics, and was the principal reason why he totally mistrusted Haidar Ali and Tipu Sultan. Bussy saw them as upstarts, illegitimate rulers despised by the Nizam and by everybody who 'mattered' at that time. He wrongly assumed that Mysore, the most powerful ally the French had in India, would be soon destroyed by a coalition of the great, natural powers of the land, and this disastrous attitude greatly harmed operations against Britain.

Within France, problems with public finance were related to other structural difficulties affecting the French economy, such as the internal tariff barriers that increased transport costs and limited regional economic specialization. In place of a national economy, there were only a number of weakly-connected regional and local economies. Such barriers were part of a culture of privilege that limited shared interests and common action. At the beginning of the century, Bordeaux's sugar refiners enjoyed the right of transporting their product to much of France without paying many of the internal tolls of which their rivals at La Rochelle, Marseille and Nantes complained. In contrast, in England, there were no such barriers and a 'transport revolution' helped to integrate the economy and also to further a sense of British national identity. Transport was not simply a matter of tariff barriers. The major role of government in the French system ensured a failure to respond promptly to economic needs that contrasted with the situation in Britain. There, also, a stabler system of public finance encouraged long-term private investment. The French government intervened where it could be of little service, and did not play a role where it could have really helped.[9] More generally, both within Britain and in their colonies, British governments appear more receptive than their French counterparts to co-operation with – indeed dependence upon – entrepreneurial, ambitious and expansionist individuals and groups.[10] This was important not least because France had both a larger economy than Britain and had had a long-term process of industrial growth since the sixteenth century. For Britain to compete effectively it had to support enterprise and encourage growth.

Limitations in the French system were increasingly serious because other states were becoming more successful in overcoming financial and other problems. Britain's debt was greater per capita than France's, but it was funded on a public, national and systematic basis, and was thus less of a problem. More generally, the ability of most European states to continue borrowing was striking, and financial difficulties did not prevent major warfare in eastern Europe in 1787–92, nor much of Europe from fighting France from 1792. This reflected demographic and economic growth from mid-century, and, in part, a general tendency towards the legalization, unification, centralization, commercialization and funding of public debt.

Thus, it was not simply a question of the structural problems that were faced by France in the attempt to mobilize resources but also of the extent to which these were becoming more serious, as other states improved their administrative capability in a competitive system. This was revealed clearly in the case of naval administration and finance during the Seven Years' War. The British were better able to equip and supply their ships, and to pay their sailors and dockyard workers. The French were weaker both in particulars and as operators of a responsive administrative system. For example, French iron-foundries had great difficulties in producing guns for the very much expanded navy, a problem exacerbated by the state's inability to pay them. The navy had to accept many guns that were of inferior quality and which normally should have been rejected.[11]

The issue of relative capability in the sphere of military service can be presented in a number of ways. The absence of conscription for regular troops during the *ancien régime* can be seen as success or failure. If the former, it can be argued that France raised the necessary forces with a minimum of disruption. In the early 1750s the section of the army composed of French troops, 130,000, was only slightly more than 0.5 per cent of the population. There were also 40,000 non-French troops, mostly from Switzerland, together with other units from Germany and Italy. During the subsequent Seven Years' War, men under arms, including the navy, at any one moment totalled 2.5 per cent, while the need to replace losses ensured that, despite what has been described as 'a manpower crisis',[12] in total nearly a million Frenchmen – about four per cent of the population – served.[13] This was achieved with relatively minor economic effects, suggesting that recruits were men whose labour could be reallocated with least difficulty, thanks to the significant underemployment of the rural population.[14]

Thus, the absence of anything equivalent to the conscription introduced in Spain in 1704, Russia in 1705 or Austria in 1771, and to the cantonal conscription system organized in Prussia in 1727–35, should not necessarily be seen as a source of failure. France had a smaller army than Austria, Prussia and Russia in the 1760s, 1770s and 1780s, but this reflected the requirements of her international situation, just as the expansion with the *levée en masse* and Napoleonic conscription were to do.

It was not only in failing to introduce conscription that the French made military choices. In the inter-war period of 1748–56, the army neither matched developments in those of Austria and Russia, nor prefigured the period of change it was itself to experience after 1763. The *École Militaire* in Paris was founded in 1751, but a need for French military reform was in the main perceived only after her defeats in the Seven Years' War. The French did better than is generally allowed in that conflict, especially in Westphalia, and their reputation was excessively tarnished by the success of the Prussian surprise attack at Rossbach in 1757, but an avoidance of defeat and a repetition of Saxe's triumphs in 1745–8 would have offered vital prestige.

This emphasis on choice is instructive, for it helps explain how an account of France's 'failure' to become *the* great European world power can be related to foreign policy. First, it is necessary to be sceptical about attempts to explain developments in a structural fashion. The international system comprised not only the range of interests and issues that divided and united states, but also the attitudes that affected the conduct of policy, or, rather, the attitudes whose furtherance the policies were designed to obtain. The system can also be seen as having a dimension that was less directly a product of the views and acts of individuals, still less under their ready control. This dimension can be usefully discussed in terms of structural – in other words, inherent – characteristics of the state system of the period, provided only that it is not adopted as a mechanistic or reductionist analysis.[15]

A major problem with systemic/structural approaches, however, is that they can employ such an analysis and argue in terms of inevitability. Interests can appear clear-cut, alliances predictable, conflict bound to arise. This is not, however, appropriate. None of the last three postulates is supported by empirical research. Interests were not clear-cut, and even when powers were separated by hostile interests that did not have to lead to war. This was true for example of France and Russia in 1726–56 and 1763–87. In addition, periods of peace between recent rivals were not simply opportunities to prepare for a fresh war. They could witness close co-operation, as between France and Britain from 1716 to 1731, or France and Austria in 1757. The co-operation did not have to be so close, but it could be such as to make it unclear that conflict was bound to occur. If political differences drove Louis XIV to invade the United Provinces in 1672, they did not prevent close co-operation between him and William III of Orange in replanning the map of Europe and the New World in the Partition Treaties of 1698 and 1700. This can be seen as a short-term agreement, a prelude to a bitter war; but, to take another case, France attacked Austria in 1733, 1741 and 1792 and was allied to it in 1756–91. More generally, France in 1700–60 fought Austria, Britain, the Dutch, Spain and Prussia, but, far from this being a case of taking on the world in a struggle for hegemony, she also had important alliances with each of these powers for at least part of the period, and can be seen as a 'sated' or 'satisfied' power, willing to accept the restraints and limits of her position, certainly in Europe in 1748–90.

Aside from a general scepticism about structural interpretations of international relations, caution also arises from the difficulty of establishing how a system is supposed to work. If a system and its development are defined, then it is all too easy to assume that events that correspond to the system are explained by it and prove it, and that those that do not are due to deviations from the model. This is intellectually flawed. In the case of international relations, such deviations can be explained in terms of the personal idiosyncracies of particular rulers. Such an interpretation was employed in eighteenth-century Europe when accounting for the descriptive and prescriptive limitations of the leading theory of international relations, that of the balance of power which drew heavily on the concept of natural interests. Thus, the alliance with Austria from 1756 was blamed on Madame de Pompadour. Such specific interpretations might or might not have been true – and they had, and have, the merit of leaving a major role for contingencies and individuals – but they suffer from the assumption that there was a core policy that was necessary and should have been obvious. In the eighteenth century the notion of natural interest was as central to polemic about foreign policy as it was to diplomatic analysis.

One of the more worrying aspects of the use of structural theories and models is that they were, and are, sometimes employed by those who clearly have little interest in the surviving evidence concerning the conduct of affairs, evidence understood in terms of records of the views and policies of contemporaries. In recent scholarship, a neglect of archival evidence may owe something to the impact of economic reductionism, or to the view of politics as epiphenomena, matters of limited and essentially transient significance, or to a sense, most recently inspired by postmodernism, but of longer genesis, that contemporaries were unaware of the factors dominating and determining international relations.

Policy and choice

This prescriptive approach is unhelpful, as it neglects the uncertainties of the past, the role of choice, and the difficulties of choosing. Furthermore, in the case of foreign policy, it is necessary to focus on the attitudes of those who took decisions. Concepts such as glory and honour, or ideas such as natural interests, were not uniform, or unchanging in their impact. It is important to ascertain what they meant to specific individuals or groups at particular moments.[16] Such specificity subverts long-term models and is difficult to incorporate into them.

It is unclear, for example, how far the factional character of French ministerial politics from the 1740s to the 1780s can be related both to particular social circles and to policies. It is possible to discern a Choiseul 'party' of high aristocrats keen on military glory and to contrast them with more cautious ministers, many of a robe background.[17] This can be taken forward into the 1780s and related to differences between Ségur, Castries and the queen on the one hand and Vergennes and Calonne on the other. A similar tension between Belle Isle and the secretaries of state can be seen in the 1740s. Yet, the extent to which social differences drove policy or were related to policy options is unclear. Individual ministers, such as Choiseul, had contrasting priorities at particular stages of their career. Furthermore, the call for an assertive position in the Dutch crisis of 1787 was very different to the schemes of 1741 for re-ordering Europe. It may be more appropriate to counterpoint ministers who were focused on financial issues with those concerned with diplomatic and/or more assertive activity, and to suggest that this contrast was institutional and/or psychological as much as social in its dynamic.

Concern about systemic and structural accounts returns attention to the specific and the individual. It offers the opportunity to join policy to circumstance, not with the former dictated by the latter, but in an interactive and dynamic relationship in which policies are chosen and in which debates over policy have weight and meaning. This ensures that consideration of the details of diplomacy is not redundant and permits a discussion of France's successes and failures, at least in part, in terms of foreign policy.

This is more obviously the case if alliances are considered. Rather than taking their composition and chronology as obvious, it is worth addressing both facets in terms of choice, by France and by other powers. Furthermore, an understanding of France's conflicts and peacetime position, at least in part, in terms of the strength, determination and dynamics of alliances directs attention to these alliances. In short, in so far as France failed, did it do so because, in general, it preferred to look to Poland and Turkey rather than Russia, Bavaria rather than Prussia, and Spain rather than Britain? The role of choice on the part of France was naturally circumscribed by the attitudes of other powers and by French commitments to particular allies, but choice there was, sometimes sharply so, as (for example) in 1668–72, 1678–88, 1713–16, 1718, 1728–9, 1733, 1735, 1741, 1744, 1756, 1763–4, 1772, 1776, 1787, 1792–3, 1805, 1812, 1813 and 1814.

Choices were linked to conceptions of France's natural policy and conduct. Both indeed are bound up in the question of how far France failed. Aside, for example, from 'prudential' considerations about Russia's limitation as a reliable ally, there were also notions of traditional obligation towards the Poles. The Wittelsbachs were able to appeal to the same, and, indeed, Puysieulx referred to them in 1748.[18]

Such attitudes and arguments can be dismissed as anachronistic, but alternative alliances might not be possible or desirable. Russia was scarcely a 'satisfied' power, and the British did not appear to act like one, certainly not in North America or on the high seas. Choiseul was striving for effect when he pressed Spain in 1761 on the need for joint measures 'to put a limit on Britain's maritime ambition and greed'.[19] Nevertheless, such remarks – and his policies – also drew attention to the difficulty of conceiving of a *modus vivendi* in which France could accept Britain's position. This difficulty, even reluctance, was not the same as support for a pre-ordained struggle for world mastery between Britain and France. French reluctance to accept the real or apparent pretensions of other major powers did not mean that French governments necessarily sought hegemony or dominance, but rather that it was difficult to conceptualize a satisfactory stable response towards other states that were seen as naturally expansionist.

This difficulty was not simply a matter of cultural politics on the part of French governments, their definition of an international order and set of French goals within which it would be possible to pursue allies. It was also necessary to consider how French policies would be understood by foreign powers and how this would affect their willingness to consider France as an ally. The French sought to affect these understandings, by both force and diplomacy. The latter should be understood both in conventional terms and with reference to other attempts to influence perceptions, for example the declamatory rhetoric of

Revolutionary assemblies and propaganda. The willingness of other states to accept French perceptions was both the goal and a means of French power-projection. This was a process that was neither unchanging, nor dictated by France. It also implies that contemporary presentation of French governments as aggressive and/or untrustworthy was important. Far from dismissing such presentations as an aspect of a polemical debate that is irrelevant to any account of French foreign policy and great-power status, or only relevant as a misinformed consequence, it is best to understand the extent and character of the discussion of French policy as an aspect of its success and failure.

This argument cannot be pushed too far. Concern about French intentions and methods did not necessarily prevent co-operation with France, and could, indeed, encourage it. This was particularly seen under both Louis XIV, as in 1670–73, and Napoleon. It could be a matter of shared benefit or fear, and the two could also be reconciled in a willingness to accept the hegemonic pretensions of France.

If a 'realist' interpretation of international relations, with its emphasis on innate conflict, is adopted, then it is relatively immaterial whether acceptance and co-operation were gained by persuasion or fear. If a more 'idealistic' emphasis is followed then it is more appropriate to consider contemporary debates and the ideological dimension of France's international stance.

In the latter case, it is necessary to note that responses elsewhere in Europe were not uniform. This was not simply a matter of responses to specific policies, for example France's attitude towards Lorraine or support for the *barrière de l'est*. It was also the case that the language and ethos of French policy were perceived very differently in particular milieus. An emphasis upon an abandonment of territorial aggrandizement had contrasting impacts in The Hague and Moscow. Such considerations affected French policy, but concern with the foreign response to French policy was least pronounced at the height of Louis XIV's power in the 1680s and again under Napoleon. In some cases, such as the Revocation of the Edict of Nantes in 1685, contrasting responses on the part of other powers were anticipated. In general, particularly during the pre-Revolutionary eighteenth century, there was no desire to alienate the wide range of European opinion. If such an alienation was achieved in 1792–3, this was only as part of a conscious rejection of the European elites. At other times, there was no comparable social, political or ideological alienation of opinion.

Alliance possibilities and alliances were constricted as much by opinion as by interest, and it was difficult to ensure a positive response on the part of other powers. This was especially so if French policy apparently stood for change. That situation was not a particular reaction to France, but was also directed against other rulers, dynasties and states that sought to make major gains. It took a century for Russia to force the Poles and Swedes to accept its hegemony. The French faced a similar situation. By 1740 their dominance of Alsace, Lorraine, Franche-Comté, Artois and French Flanders was largely accepted by France's neighbours, but it had been a long process. A new moderation in French aggrandizement was one key to the acceptance. After the War of the Spanish Succession, further gains in the Low Countries were not pursued. There were no attempts to reconquer what had been lost at Utrecht or to recover the position in 1684. Namur and Luxembourg remained outside French power. The same was true on the Rhine frontier, and in Italy: Breisach and Casale were not to be regained.

Success and failure

This situation was not a cause or sign of failure. The French were more influential in Italy in the eighteenth century than they had been in the seventeenth. This reflected very different relations with Spain and Austria than hitherto and, also, a greater degree of caution on the part of French governments in their treatment of other powers, whether allies or not, than had been the case with Louis XIV. In 1748 Puysieulx urged Richelieu to have patience over the problems he had encountered in dealing with Spain. He claimed that Spain 'had always treated France in the bizarre fashion of a self-willed and despotic woman', specifically a reference to Philip V's second wife, Elizabeth Farnese.[20] Nevertheless, relations were generally closer than they had been in the seventeenth century. In Germany, the French were able to find allies for successive attempts to challenge Habsburg influence in 1715–56 and, thereafter, could consider Prussia an option if they were to fall out with Austria.

The situation on the global scale was similar, but the consequences were less fortunate for France. In 1661–1700 the French had pursued maritime predominance and colonial gain at the expense of Spain, England and the Dutch, although there had also been brief periods of co-operation: with the Dutch in 1665–7 and with England in 1672–4. Nevertheless, rivalry had culminated in 1689–97 with France simultaneously at war with all three.

This situation was not to recur until 1793–5, and, then, only under the disruptive strains created by the impact of the French Revolutionary War. In the meanwhile, with Spain there had only been a very brief war in 1719–20, and with the Dutch no conflict after 1748. Indeed, Spain had allied with the French in fighting Britain in 1702–13, 1744–8, 1762–3 and 1779–83, and the Dutch – neutral in the Seven Years' War – had also, albeit unwillingly, fought Britain in 1780–83. These periods of Dutch and Spanish co-operation with France against Britain can be seen as prefiguring the alliances of the period 1795–1813, although there was a major element of compulsion in the latter.

There was a major shift between the late seventeenth century and the first half of the eighteenth, and, even more, with 1750–90. France was no longer isolated. Her arguments were acceptable, and her foreign policy had important successes in widening the French alliance system, so that it encompassed much of the European world. This is underrated, because Britain was not beaten; but the absence of any naval ally for Britain between 1748 and 1787 is, in part, an instructive comment on French success. France was also the major power in Western Europe. The Western Question had been settled, with the Bourbons dominant in Western Europe, and France clearly the major power in the region. From 1756, she was linked to the crucial alignment in Eastern Europe, that of Austria and Russia.

French governments were also more at ease with the international situation. The Habsburg–Bourbon struggle for mastery changed greatly when Philip V was established on the Spanish throne in 1700, and, even more, because the Bourbons were established in Italy from Don Carlos' arrival in Parma in 1732. The acquisition of Lorraine also made a great difference, both in strategic terms and by weakening Austrian interest in the empire west of the Rhine. Opportunity and strength ensured that France and her allies were the aggressors against Austria in 1733 and 1741. Furthermore, throughout the century, the Austrians did not intervene in French domestic politics, as the Spanish Habsburgs had done, while the exploitation of tensions by foreign powers within the French royal family became far less marked, unless the rivalry with Philip V is to be seen in part in that light. France benefited from a transformation in Austrian policy. Prussia, not France, was Austria's principal opponent in 1744–5 and from 1748.

The global perspective

Such an account is Eurocentric, in that it concentrates on the global dimension of French policy from the perspective of France's relations with other European powers. That is, indeed, accurate as far as the bulk of French governmental attention and activity were concerned. Furthermore, relations with non-Europeans, whether Native American tribes or Indian rulers, the Miami or Mysore, were largely motivated by rivalry with other European powers.

Changes in France's relations with European powers, especially with Spain, affected the relative capability of French power within the range of European power, but not farther afield; unless France itself was at war and, thus, unable to deploy military resources at the expense of non-European powers. Nevertheless, in peacetime it was necessary to consider the sensitivity of other European states. Spain was opposed to French expansion from Louisiana and, owing to Spain, French hopes of Florida had long been quashed. Thanks to Spain and Portugal, French opportunities in South America were limited, and, aside from ecological and environmental factors, Cayenne could not become another Louisiana.

Yet there was still West Africa, the Indian Ocean, India and the Pacific. In each case, however, there was only a limited opportunity to create a great-power status. As the Dutch had discovered on Formosa (Taiwan) in the 1660s, the East Asian powers were capable of repelling European advance; and the Portuguese had shown on the Zambezi in the 1690s that the same was true of penetration into the African interior. The French were similarly unsuccessful in Madagascar.

In India, several Frenchmen pursued successful military and political careers, but this depended on co-operation by local rulers, and could not be set to an agenda drawn up in Paris. The same was true of the French presence in Indo-China in the last three decades of the period.

The Indian sub-continent can be treated alongside Europe as another sphere for the conduct of foreign policy, but, owing to distance and the nature of the French presence, specifically the roles of commercial interests, comparisons are of limited value. Nevertheless, as in Europe, it was difficult to persuade other powers to accept French priorities. The most knowledgeable reports sent by French agents in India in the late 1770s claimed that religious, political and caste rivalries among the native powers would prevent a coalition of the three major states (Mysore, Hyderabad and the Maratha Confederacy) against the British. If the French made any treaty with one, it would throw the other two into British arms. Despite these warnings, the French decided to strike in India on a scale similar to their intervention in North America.

As far as France's trans-oceanic relations with other European powers were concerned, the decisive developments were two-fold. First, at the start of the period, France's presence in the New World, the prime area of European expansion, was not in the areas most attractive to European settlement or – although this was less marked – economic exchange. This could not be easily rectified. Like the British state, the French government found it difficult to raise revenue in its North American colonies,[21] but, in the case of the French, this was largely a matter of the nature of the local society and economy, rather than the political culture. Unlike the British colonies, there was little substitute for government resources. Despite Louis XIV's 1689 plan for the conquest of New York,[22] and successful inland offensives against British forts in 1746–7 and 1756–7, the conquest of New England, the Middle Colonies and Virginia, was scarcely more an option than that of New Spain would have been. The 1689 plan itself required a fleet from France, as well as forces from Canada.

The diplomatic situation was crucial. From 1689 France was at war with Britain, but earlier they had generally been allies, or at least not opponents, and periods of confrontation were brief. This provided only fleeting opportunities for colonial gains from Britain, as in 1665–6 when, then in alliance with the Dutch, the French overran English St Christopher and occupied parts of Antigua and Montserrat. French and Dutch forces captured Surinam. There were more opportunities at the expense of the Dutch, who had taken over New Sweden in the Delaware valley in 1655, but the Dutch possessions were seized by the English in both the Second and the Third Anglo-Dutch Wars, and definitively ceded to England in the peace treaty of 1674. Thus, French options in North America were constrained by the alliance with Charles II in 1672–4, and Louis XIV failed to benefit from the vulnerability of the Dutch in North America. The fleet of ten ships of the line that Estrées took to the West Indies in 1676 could not have been sent instead against New Amsterdam; the town had been renamed New York.

Secondly, the course of eighteenth-century conflict was such that France's gains from her alliance with Spain and, eventually, from the short-lived alliance with the rebellious British colonists in North America, were offset by Britain's successive maritime and land victories. In the end, foreign policy could only achieve so much. Britain had been isolated, but not overcome. At this point of failure, it is worth emphasizing the role of military chance, seen most clearly in the contrasting verdicts at Yorktown (1781) and the Saintes (1782).

Yet, there were also choices in foreign policy. French policy-makers put Europe first for much of the period. They were able to maintain their leading position in Western Europe, but not to gain a comparable one in the expanding European world. It is not idle counterfactualism to wonder how far this could have been different. Could Louis XIV have devoted more resources to trans-oceanic activity in the 1660s and 1670s, or forced the Dutch and Spaniards to accept such a situation? Could he have prevented Anglo-Dutch co-operation in 1689–1713, either by thwarting William III's invasion of 1688 or by retaining the Dutch support he had enjoyed earlier?[23] Could greater effort have sustained and strengthened the promising French positions in India and North America in the early 1750s? Could the promise of the period 1783–6 – expanding trade, alliance with Spain and the Dutch, and an isolated Britain – have been developed? Could Napoleon have maintained the Tilsit agreement, successfully incorporated Iberia in his system, and then forced Britain to terms that left France a major role outside Europe?

Such scenarios should not be dismissed with reference to structural limitations in French finances or other similar factors, although it is clear that the character of French political culture, especially the relatively limited concern with commercial interests during the reign of Louis XIV, affected the perception of options. Rulers living in Versailles were much less exposed to the dynamic forces of European economics and overseas activities than a government and parliament located in London, a growing centre of world trade. When the Count of Broglie, father of the Broglie who directed the *Secret du Roi*, arrived in London as ambassador in 1724 he was astonished by the innumerable quantity of shipping in the Thames.[24] For geographical, cultural and political reasons, France was different to Britain as an economy, a society and a state.[25] This affected, but did not determine, policy choices, resource availability, and international responses. There may have been no need to choose between European and global roles. A Jacobite Britain might have accepted, or had to accept, a North Atlantic world dominated by France. The past was far from fixed and we will only misunderstand it if we pretend otherwise.

Notes

Chapter 1: Introduction: A European and world power

1. J.M. Black, *European Warfare, 1660–1815* (London, 1994).
2. H. Vyverberg, *Historical Pessimism in the French Enlightenment* (Cambridge, Mass., 1958), p. 229.
3. BL. Add. 61573 fol. 139.
4. AE. CP. Prusse 93 fol. 293, Suède 272 fol. 20.
5. AE. CP. Aut. 165 fol. 129.
6. AE. CP. Prusse 210 fols 9–10; *Sbornik*, 75, 189, 289; PRO. SP. 78/331 fol. 441. cf., *re* Spain, AN. B7 292, 28 June 1728; *re* Britain in 1728, AE. CP. Ang. sup. 8 fol. 54; *re* Turks in 1735, BN. NAF. 6834 fol. 58; and *re* Saxons in 1763, AE. CP. Aut. 295 fol. 11.
7. AE. CP. Russie 116 fol. 13.
8. P.W. Schroeder, *The Transformation of European Politics, 1763–1848* (Oxford, 1994).
9. B. Trigger, *Natives and Newcomers: Canada's 'Heroic Age' Reconsidered* (Montreal, 1985).
10. AN. KK. 1402 p. 228.
11. J.H. Shennan, *Philippe, Duke of Orléans* (London, 1979).
12. M. Antoine, *Le Conseil du Roi sous le règne de Louis XV* (Geneva, 1970), p. 3; J.C. Rule, 'The king in his council: Louis XIV and the *Conseil d'en haut*', in R. Oresko, G.C. Gibbs and H.M. Scott (eds), *Royal and Republican Sovereignty in Early Modern Europe* (Cambridge, 1997), pp. 216–41.
13. PRO. SP. 78/223 fol. 138.
14. AE. CP. Bavière 114 fol. 47.
15. F.E. Phipps, *Louis XV: A Style of Kingship, 1710–57* (PhD, Johns Hopkins University Baltimore, 1973); M. Antoine, *Louis XV* (Paris, 1989).
16. Munich KS 17190, 23 Feb.
17. J. Hardman, *Louis XVI* (New Haven, Conn., 1993).
18. A. Beer (ed.), *Joseph II, Leopold II, und Kaunitz* (Vienna, 1873), p. 191.

19. E. Boutaric, *Correspondance Secrète inédite de Louis XV sur la politique étrangère* (2 vols, Paris, 1886) I, 214, 216; II, 368.

20. F. Bluche, *Louis XIV* (Oxford, 1990).

21. Marquis de Vogüé (ed.), *Mémoires du maréchal de Villars* (6 vols, Paris, 1884–1904), V, 72; AE. CP. Ang. sup. 8 fol. 14.

22. Arsenal, MS Bastile 10157 fols 143, 152.

23. AST. LM. Francia 170, Solaro, 23 Feb. 1734.

24. A. Baudrillart, *Philippe V et la cour de France* (5 vols, Paris, 1890–1901), III, 361–3.

25. HHStA. Frankreich Varia 11 fol. 456.

26. Vogüé, *Villars* V, 165, 167.

27. AE. CP. Bavière 114 fol. 149.

28. For example, J.C. Rule, 'King and minister: Louis XIV and Colbert de Torcy', in R. Hatton and J.S. Bromley (eds), *William III and Louis XIV* (Liverpool, 1968), pp. 213–36.

29. P. Sonnino, *Louis XIV and the Origins of the Dutch War* (Cambridge, 1988).

30. P. Sonnino, 'The dating and authorship of Louis XIV's *Mémoires*', *French Historical Studies*, 3 (1964), pp. 303–37, and 'Louis XIV's *Mémoires pour l'histoire de la guerre de Hollande*', ibid., 8 (1973), pp. 29–50.

31. On the organization see J. Baillou (ed.), *Les Affaires Étrangères et le Corps Diplomatique Français. I De l'ancien régime au second empire* (Paris, 1984), and, for specific periods, C.-G. Picavet, *La diplomatie française au temps de Louis XIV (1661–1715): institutions, moeurs et coutumes* (Paris, 1930); H. Doniol, 'Le Ministère des Affaires Étrangères de France sous le comte de Vergennes', *RHD*, 7 (1893), pp. 528–60; F. Masson, *Le département des Affaires Étrangères pendant la Révolution, 1787–1804* (Paris, 1877). An excellent example of the process of policy formation is provided by J.C. Rule, 'Colbert de Torcy, an emergent bureaucracy and the formulation of French foreign policy, 1698–1715', in R. Hatton (ed.), *Louis XIV and Europe* (London, 1976), pp. 260–88. See also C. Frostin, 'L'organisation ministérielle sous Louis XIV: cumul d'attributions et situations conflictuelles, 1690–1715', *Revue historique de droit français et étranger*, 58 (1980), pp. 201–26.

32. AE. CP. Ang. 437 fol. 367.

33. [Mouffle d'Angerville], *Vie privée de Louis XV* (4 vols, London, 1781), II, 42–3; C. Piccioni, *Les premiers commis des Affaires Étrangères au XVIIe et au XVIIIe siècles* (Paris, 1928); J.P. Samoyault, *Les bureaux du Secrétariat d'État des Affaires Étrangères sous Louis XV* (Paris, 1971), pp. 41–2.

34. J.C. Batzel, *Austria and the first three Treaties of Versailles, 1755–1758* (PhD, Brown University, 1974), pp. 466–7, 456–7.

35. AG. A1. 2643 no. 40.

36. S. Horowitz, *Franco-Russian Relations, 1740–1746* (PhD, New York University, 1951), pp. 350–55.

37. BVC 40 fol. 108.

38. B. Auerbach, *La France et la Saint Empire Romain Germanique depuis la Paix de Westphalie jusqu'à La Révolution Française* (Paris, 1912), p. 269 fn. 1.

39. AE. CP. Aut. 263 fol. 54.

40. M. Antoine and D. Ozanam, 'Le Secret du Roi et la Russie jusqu'à la mort de la Czarine Elisabeth en 1762', *Annuaire Bulletin de la Société de l'Histoire* (1954–5), pp. 80–81. For another secret diplomacy of the period by Louis XV, see R. Butler, 'The secret compact of 1753 between the kings of France and of

Naples', in Oresko, Gibbs and Scott, *Royal and Republican Sovereignty*, pp. 551–79, e.g. p. 561.

41. Vogüé, *Villars*, V, 87–90.

42. *Polit. Corr.* 10, 180.

43. Boutaric, *Correspondance secrète* II, 504.

44. E. Cruickshank, *The Factions at the Court of Louis XV* (PhD, London, 1956).

45. H. Schlitter (ed.), *Correspondance secrète entre le comte A.W. Kaunitz-Rietberg, ambassadeur impérial à Paris, et le baron Ignaz de Koch, sécretaire de l'impératrice Marie-Thérèse, 1750–1752* (Paris, 1899), p. 167; *Polit. Corr.*, 9, 43, 452, 14, 212, 15, 377–8, 391; BL. Add. 6843 fol. 59.

46. Munich, Gesandtschaft Paris 218, 27 Nov. 1754.

47. Antoine and Ozanam, *Correspondence secrète du comte de Broglie avec Louis XV, 1756–1774* (2 vols, Paris, 1956–61) I, xxxix–xli; J. Flammermont, *Les Correspondances des agents diplomatiques étrangers en France avant la Révolution* (Paris, 1896), pp. 102–3.

48. Flammermont, *Correspondances*, p. 194; *Polit. Corr.* 46, 423, 460, 557.

49. *Recueil . . . Danemark*, p. 146.

50. J. Heidner (ed.), *Carl Fredrik Scheffer. Lettres particulières à Carl Gustaf Tessin, 1744–1752* (Stockholm, 1982).

51. R. Mettam, *Power and Faction in Louis XIV's France* (Oxford, 1988).

52. B.S. Trotter, 'Vauban and the question of the Spanish succession', *PWSF*, 21 (1994), p. 62; PRO. SP. 80/52 fols 92–3.

53. AE. CP. Esp. 506 fol. 225; AN. KK. 1401, p. 563.

54. J. Richard (ed.), *Histoire de la Bourgogne* (Toulouse, 1978), p. 274; G. Livet, *L'intendance d'Alsace sous Louis XIV, 1648–1715* (Paris, 1956).

55. P. Leon, 'Un épisode de la main mise de la France sur le Comtat Venaissin: la guerre économique franco-comtadine (1730–1734), *Actes du 77e congrès des sociétés savantes* (Grenoble, 1952).

56. P. Blet, 'Louis XIV et le Saint Siège', *XVIIe Siècle*, no. 123 (1979), pp. 137–54.

57. L. Dollot, 'Conclaves et diplomatie française au XVIIIe siècle', *RHD*, (1961), pp. 124–35; P. Paul, *Le Cardinal Melchior de Polignac* (Paris, 1922), pp. 268, 313–16; M. Boutry, *L'Abbé de Tencin, chargé d'affaire à Rome, 1721–24* (Paris, 1901).

58. Paul, *Polignac*, p. 310.

59. AE. CP. Esp. 488 fol. 9; AN. KK. 1393, 8 July, 28 Sept., 23 Nov. 1776.

60. L. de Voinovitch, *La monarchie Française dans l'Adriatique. Histoire des relations de la France avec la république de Raguse, 1667–1789* (Paris, 1917), pp. 101–6.

61. AE. CP. Ang. 397 fols 109, 113.

62. D.F. Allen, 'Charles II, Louis XIV and the Order of Malta', *European History Quarterly*, 20 (1990), pp. 324–5.

63. AST. LM. Francia 163, Maffei's reports, 26, 29 Ap.

64. AE. CP. Allemagne 373 fols 50, 129.

65. AE. CP. Esp. 537 fol. 185.

66. AE. CP. Aut. 251 fols 101, 110–23, 135. For Cambis's entry at Turin in 1725, MF. 7149, pp. 211–20.

67. A. Vandal, *Une ambassade française en Orient sous Louis XV: la mission du marquis de Villeneuve 1728–41* (Paris, 1887), pp. 3–4; BN. MF. 7185 fols 6–10; *Recueil . . . Danemark* (1895), pp. 142–3.

68. BVC. 30 fol. 93; AE. CP. Ang. 451 fols 240–41.

69. M. Degros, 'Les consulats de France sous la Révolution. Les états barbaresques', *RHD* 105 (1991), p. 117.

70. BVC. 58 fols 120–22; AN. KK. 1400, p. 271; *Polit. Corr.* 10, 161.

71. Diary of James, 1st Earl Waldegrave, 2 Dec. 1727, Chewton House, Chewton Mendip, Somerset, Waldegrave Papers; Paul, *Polignac*, p. 295.

72. HHStA. Frankreich Varia 11 fol. 456.

73. *Sbornik* (1897), p. 38.

74. M. Giraud, *A History of French Louisiana. II: Years of Transition, 1715–1717* (Baton Rouge, Louisiana, 1993), pp. 185, 200.

75. BL. Add. 32780 fol. 29, 32782 fol. 194; PRO. SP. 80/46, 23 Jan. 1722, 92/41, 8 June 1737.

76. AE. CP. Aut. 349 fols 281–2, 318–19.

77. L. Bély, *Espions et ambassadeurs au temps de Louis XIV* (Paris, 1990); J. Rule, 'Gathering intelligence in the age of Louis XIV', *International History Review*, 14 (1992), pp. 732–52.

78. Vogüé, *Villars*, V, 118; Rochefort (Hamburg) 15 Jan. 1723, AN. AM. B7 282.

79. Vogüé, *Villars*, V, 327; AE. CP. Turquie 175, Russie 121.

80. BN. MF. 7186 fol. 302, NAF. 14914 fol. 83, NAF. 14196 fols 138, 218–19.

81. *Sbornik* 64, 365.

82. L. de Laigue, 'Le comte de Froulay, ambassadeur à Venise (1733–1743) d'après les archives du ministère des affaires étrangères', *RHD*, 24 (1910), pp. 117–40, 428–61; *RHD*, 27 (1913), pp. 65–138.

83. Vandal, *Villeneuve*, iv; G.F. Broche, *La République de Gênes et la France pendant la guerre de la succession d'Autriche, 1740–48* (Paris, 1936), p. 13.

84. AN. KK. 1400, p. 58; AE. CP. Aut. 252 fol. 59.

85. AE. CP. Ang. 582 fol. 9.

86. AE. CP. Ang. 582 fols 80, 111, 586 fol. 343.

87. A. Mezin, 'Le consul Charles Flüry: de l'ambassade de Choiseul-Gouffier à la Restauration', *RHD* (1997), pp. 273–90.

88. O. Connelly, *Napoleon's Satellite Kingdoms* (New York, 1966).

89. K. Malettke, *Opposition und Konspiration unter Ludwig XIV. Studien zu kritik und Widerstand gegen System und Politik des französischen Könings während der ersten Hälfte seiner persönlichen Regierung* (Göttingen, 1976), pp. 137–42, 182–94, 287–97; F. Piétri, 'La conspiration de Cellamare', *RHD* (1960), pp. 198–207; P.M.F. Labracherie, *La conspiration de Cellamare* (Paris, 1963).

90. Thomas Robinson to George Tilson, 17 Sept. 1732, PRO. SP. 80/90.

91. Arsenal 10162 fol. 196.

92. J.D. Woodbridge, *Revolt in Prerevolutionary France: The Prince de Conti's Conspiracy against Louis XV, 1755–1757* (Baltimore, 1994).

93. A. Cobban, 'The British secret service in France, 1784–92', *English Historical Review*, 69 (1954), pp. 226–61.

94. *Sbornik*, 64, 126, 131.

95. AN. KK. 1400, p. 341.

96. AE. CP. Ang. 538 fol. 203.

97. Dresden 2676 II fol. 59.

98. AE. CP. Aut. 348 fols 129–30.

99. AN. AM. B7 304.

100. Dresden 2733 fol. 97; PRO. SP. 78/188 fol. 128.

101. AE. CP. Ang. 582 fol. 109.
102. L. Boles, *The Huguenots, the Protestant Interest, and the War of the Spanish Succession, 1702–1714* (New York, 1997).
103. AE. CP. Ang. 583 fol. 26.
104. BL. Add. 32802 fol. 3.
105. Nancy 3F 87 no. 27.
106. J.B. Wolf, *Louis XIV* (London, 1968), pp. 203, 220–22, 239–43, 460.
107. C. Pincemaille, 'La guerre de Hollande dans le programme iconographique de la grande galerie de Versailles', *Histoire, Economie et Société*, 4 (1985), pp. 313–33.
108. AE. CP. Aut. 63 fol. 42.
109. J. Cornette, *Le Roi de Guerre: Essai sur la Souveraineté dans la France du Grand Siècle* (Paris, 1993); P. Burke, *The Fabrication of Louis XIV* (New Haven, Conn., 1992); K. Ahrens, *Hyacinthe Rigauds Staatsporträt Ludwigs XIV. Typologische und ikonologische Untersuchung zur politischen Aussage des Bildnisses von 1701* (Worms, Germany, 1990).
110. R.W. Berger, *A Royal Passion. Louis XIV as Patron of Architecture* (Cambridge, 1994), p. 118; C. Mukerji, *Territorial Ambitions and the Gardens of Versailles* (Cambridge, 1997).
111. J. Dewald, *Aristocratic Experience and the Origins of Modern Culture. France, 1570–1715* (Berkeley, Cal., 1993), p. 207.
112. J.-P. Labatut, 'Patriotisme et noblesse sous le règne de Louis XIV', *Revue d'histoire moderne et contemporaine*, 29 (1982), pp. 622–34.
113. G. Rowlands, *Power, Authority and Army Administration under Louis XIV: the French Crown and the Military Elites in the Era of the Nine Years' War* (D.Phil., Oxford, 1997).
114. AE. CP. Esp. 419 fol. 67.
115. Arsenal MS Bastille 10158 fol. 340.
116. A. de Boislisle (ed.), *Lettres de M. de Marville, lieutenant général de police au Ministre Maurepas, 1742–1747* (3 vols, Paris, 1903–5); S. Pillorget, *Claude-Henri Feydeau de Marville, lieutenant-général de police de Paris, 1740–1747* (Paris, 1978). For French sensitivity to café opinion in 1719, Hanover Cal. Br. 24 Nr. 1987 fol. 11.
117. J. Klaits, *Printed Propaganda under Louis XIV. Absolute Monarchy and Public Opinion* (Princeton, N. J., 1976); B. Köpeczi, *La France et la Hongrie au debut du XVIIIe siècle* (Budapest, 1971), p. 375; C.G. Picavet, *Diplomatie Française au temps de Louis XIV*, pp. 311–22.
118. K.M. Baker, 'Politique et opinion publique sous l'ancien régime', *Annales*, 42 (1987), pp. 41–71; A. Farge, *Subversive Worlds: Public Opinion in Eighteenth-Century France* (Cambridge, 1994); D.K. Van Kley, 'In search of eighteenth-century Parisian public opinion', *French Historical Studies*, 19 (1995), pp. 215–26.
119. A. Beer (ed.), *Joseph II, Leopold II und Kaunitz* (Vienna, 1873), p. 136.
120. P.R. Campbell, *Power and Politics in Old Regime France, 1720–1745* (London, 1996), pp. 29, 91–2, 304; J.M.J. Rogister, *Louis XV and the Parlement of Paris, 1737–1754* (Cambridge, 1995), pp. 233–4.
121. P. Boyé, *Un roi de Pologne et la couronne ducale de Lorraine: Stanislas Leszczynski et le troisième traité de Vienne* (Paris, 1898), p. 375.
122. B.R. Kreiser, *Miracles, Convulsions and Ecclesiastical Politics in Early Eighteenth-Century Paris* (Princeton, 1978).
123. C. Aubertin, *L'Esprit public au XVIIIe siècle* (Paris, 1889).

124. Flammermont, *Correspondances*, p. 359.

125. *Polit. Corr.* 46, 422.

126. *AP* 37, 89.

127. AE. CP. Esp. 533 fol. 38.

128. Matlock, Derbyshire Record Office D 2375 M/76/186; Edinburgh, Scottish Record Office GD 267/7/20; Picavet, *Diplomatie*, p. 322.

129. H. Kurz, *European Characters in French Drama of the Eighteenth Century* (New York, 1916), p. 276.

130. M. de Lescure (ed.), *Journal et mémoires de Mathieu Marais, avocat au Parlement de Paris . . . , 1715–1737* (4 vols, Paris, 1863–5), e.g. III, 507, 512.

131. BN. NAF. 9513, p. 318.

132. Arsenal, MS Bastile 10158 fol. 261.

133. Arsenal, MS Bastile 10158 fol. 11.

134. The limited role of oceanic interests and identities is apparent in X. de Planhol, *An Historical Geography of France* (Cambridge, 1994).

135. AE. CP. Bavière 41 fols 69, 88.

136. A. Cherel, *Fénelon au XVIIIe siècle en France* (Paris, 1917), pp. 152–3.

137. E.J.B. Rathéry, *Le Comte de Plélo. Un gentilhomme français au XVIIIe siècle, guerrier, littérateur et diplomate* (Paris, 1876).

138. C.W. Cole, *Colbert and a Century of French Mercantilism* (2 vols, New York, 1939); J. Meyer, *Colbert* (Paris, 1981); G.J. Ames, *Colbert, Mercantilism and the French Quest for Asian Trade* (Dekalb, Illinois, 1996).

139. J.F. Bosher, 'The Paris business world and the seaports under Louis XV. Speculators in marine insurance, naval finances and trade', *Histoire Sociale/Social History*, 12 (1979), pp. 281–97.

140. H. Robert, 'Les traffics coloniaux du port de La Rochelle au XVIIIe siècle, 1713–1789', *Bulletin de la Société des Antiquaires de l'Ouest* (1949), pp. 135–79; P. Butel, *Les négociations bordelais, l'Europe et les Iles au XVIIIe siècle* (Paris, 1974).

141. D. Miquelon, *Dugard of Rouen: French trade to Canada and the West Indies, 1729–1770* (Montréal, 1978).

142. J. Clark, *La Rochelle and the Atlantic Economy during the Eighteenth Century* (1982).

143. T.J. Schaeper, *The French Council of Commerce, 1700–1715: A Study of Mercantilism after Colbert* (Columbus, Ohio, 1983); H.T. Parker, *An Administrative Bureau during the Old Regime: the Bureau of Commerce and its Relations to French Industry from May 1781 to November 1783* (Cranbury, New Jersey, 1993).

144. On which see O. Teissier, *La Chambre de Commerce de Marseille* (Marseille, 1892) and C. Carrière, *Négociants marseillais au XVIIIe siècle* (Marseille, 1973).

145. AE. CP. Ang. 354 fols 111, 195, 209; AE. CP. Ang. 360 fols 263–6; AE. CP. Ang. 362 fols 14–29; AN. AM. B7 288, 7 Sept. 1726, 294.

146. AE. CP. Ang. 455 fol. 38.

147. D. Ozanam, 'La colonie française de Calais au XVIIIe siècle', *Mélanges de la Casa de Velazquez*, 4 (1968), pp. 259–347.

148. Chewton, Waldegrave diary, 6 Jan. 1728.

149. Arsenal, MS Bastile 10157 fols 228, 239.

150. Chewton, Waldegrave diary, 3 Jan. 1728.

151. J. Voss, *Universität, Geschichtswissenschaft und Diplomatie im Zeitalter der Aufklärung: Johann Daniel Schöpflin, 1694–1771* (Munich, 1979), pp. 316–18.

152. Voinovitch, *Monarchie Française dans L'Adriatique*, p. 89.

153. A. Mézin, *Les Consuls de France au Siècle des Lumières, 1715–1792* (Paris, 1997), pp. 42–3.

154. AN. AM. B7 299, 301, 1 Dec. 1729, 21 Mar. 1730; H.D. Rothschild, 'Benoît de Maillet's Leghorn letters', *Studies on Voltaire* (1964), pp. 353, 366, 372; BN. MF. 7195 fols 1–9.

155. C. Roure, 'La réglementation du commerce français au Levant sous l'ambassade du marquis de Villeneuve, 1728–41', in J.P. Filippini (ed.), *Dossiers sur le commerce français en Méditerranée Orientale au XVIIIe siècle* (Paris, 1976), pp. 34, 37–76, 89.

156. *Recueil . . . Turquie*, xlvi–xlviii; BN. NAF. 7192 fols 98–107.

157. AN. AM. B7 343, 30 May, 6 June 1740; Mézin, *Consuls*, p. 146; BN. NAF. 7192 fols 1, 3.

158. AN. KK. 1393, 5 Oct. 1776.

159. AN. KK. 1393, 8 July, 31 Aug., 12, 19 Oct., 2, 23 Nov. 1776, 3, 10, 17 May, 2, 30 Aug. 1777, 7, 21 Mar. 1778. See, more generally, R. Romano, *Le Commerce du Royaume de Naples avec la France et les Pays de l'Adriatique au XVIIIe Siècle* (Paris, 1951), eg. pp. 13–14, 57.

160. D. Pilgrim, 'The Colbert–Seignelay naval reforms and the beginnings of the War of the League of Augsburg', *French Historical Studies*, 9 (1975–6), pp. 235–62; For a more positive view, J. Meyer, 'Louis XIV et les puissances maritimes', *XVIIe Siècle*, 123 (1979), p. 170.

161. G.J. Ames, 'Colbert's Grand Indian Ocean Fleet of 1670', *Mariner's Mirror*, 76 (1990), pp. 236–9.

162. PRO. SP. 80/61 fols 63–4.

163. AE. CP. Ang. 445 fol. 21.

164. R.R. Crout, *The Diplomacy of Trade: The Influence of Commercial Considerations on French Involvement in the Anglo-American War of Independence, 1775–78* (PhD, Georgia, 1977).

Chapter 2: Louis XIV and Europe, 1661–1715

1. R.M. Hatton, 'Louis XIV and his fellow monarchs', in *Louis XIV and the Craft of Kingship*, J.C. Rule (ed.) (Columbus, Ohio, 1969), pp. 155–95, reprinted in *Louis XIV and Europe*, Hatton (ed.) (London, 1976), pp. 16–59; Hatton, 'Louis XIV: Recent gains in historical knowledge', *Journal of Modern History*, 45 (1973), pp. 277–91; Hatton, 'Louis XIV et l'Europe: Eléments d'une revision historiographique', *XVIIe Siècle* (1979), pp. 109–35.

2. Particularly interesting works appearing since Hatton's 1969 essay include R. Place, 'The self-deception of the strong: France on the eve of the War of the League of Augsburg', *French Historical Studies*, 6 (1970), pp. 359–73; R.D. Martin, *The Marquis of Chamlay, Friend and Confidential Adviser to Louis XIV: The Early Years, 1650–1691* (PhD, University of California, Santa Barbara, 1972); P. Sonnino, 'Louis XIV's *Mémoires pour l'histoire de la guerre de Hollande*', *French Historical Studies*, 8 (1973), pp. 29–50, and 'Arnauld de Pomponne, Louis XIV's minister for foreign affairs during the Dutch War', *PSWF*, 1 (1974), pp. 49–60; A.S. Szarka, *Portugal, France, and the coming of the War of the Spanish Succession* (PhD, Ohio State University, 1975); J.T. O'Connor, *Negotiator out of Season. The Career of Wilhelm Egon von Furstenberg* (Athens, Georgia, 1978); C.J. Ekberg, *The Failure of Louis XIV's Dutch*

War (Chapel Hill, North Carolina, 1979); 'Louis XIV et L'Europe', special issue of *XVIIe Siècle*, 123 (1979); B. Neveu, 'Tricentenaire des traités de Nimèque', *Revue des travaux de l'Académie des Sciences morales et politiques et comptes-rendus de ses séances*, 132 (1980), pp. 355–80; J. Bérenger, 'Strasbourg au XVIIe siècle ou l'impossible neutralité', *Revue historique des armées* (1981), pp. 7–34; P. Sonnino, 'The origins of Louis XIV's wars' in *The Origins of War in Early-Modern Europe*, J.M. Black (ed.) (Edinburgh, 1987), pp. 112–31; L. Bély, *Espions et ambassadeurs au temps de Louis XIV* (Paris, 1990) and *Les rélations internationales en Europe, XVIIe–XVIIIe siècles* (Paris, 1992); R. Babel (ed.), *Frankreich im europäischen Staatensystem der Frühen Neuzeit* (Sigmaringen, 1995); K. Malettke, 'Ludwigs XIV Aussenpolitik zwischen Staatsräson, ökonomischen Zwängen und Sozialkonflikten', in H. Duchhardt (ed.), *Rahmenbedingungen und Handlungsspielräume europäischer Aussenpolitik im Zeitalter Ludwigs XIV* (Berlin, 1991), pp. 43–72; K. Malettke, 'Grundlegung und Infragestellung eines Staatensystems: Frankreich als dynamisches Element in Europa', in P. Krüger (ed.), *Das europäische Staatensystem im Wandel. Strukturelle Bedingungen und bewegende Kräfte seit der Frühen Neuzeit* (Munich, 1996), pp. 47–68.

3. W.J. Roosen, *The Age of Louis XIV: The Rise of Modern Diplomacy* (Cambridge, Mass., 1976); *Les Affaires Etrangères et le Corps Diplomatique Français*, ed. J. Baillou (Paris, 1984), pp. 53–241.

4. A. Lossky, '"Maxims of State" in Louis XIV's foreign policy in the 1680s', in R. Hatton and J.S. Bromley (eds), *William III and Louis XIV* (Liverpool, 1968), pp. 7–23.

5. D. Parrott, 'The causes of the Franco-Spanish War of 1635–59', in *Origins of War*, ed. Black, p. 106.

6. A.E. Zanger, *Scenes from the Marriage of Louis XIV. Nuptial Fictions and the Making of Absolutist Power* (Cambridge, 1998), e.g. pp. 39–44.

7. H. Lonchay, *La Rivalité de la France et de l'Espagne aux Pays Bas, 1635–1700* (Brussels, 1896), pp. 196–7.

8. G. Hanlon, *The Twilight of a Military Tradition. Italian Aristocrats and European Conflicts, 1560–1800* (London, 1998), p. 185; Szarka, *Portugal, France*, pp. 83–5, 89.

9. J.A. Lynn, 'A quest for glory: The formation of strategy under Louis XIV, 1661–1715', in W. Murray, M. Knox and A. Bernstein (eds), *The Making of Strategy: Rulers, States and War* (Cambridge, 1994), pp. 184–7.

10. P. Sonnino, *Louis XIV's View of the Papacy, 1661–1667* (Berkeley, Cal., 1966), pp. 30–53.

11. P. Bamford, *Fighting Ships and Prisons: The Mediterranean Galleys of France in the Age of Louis XIV* (Minneapolis, 1973), p. 23.

12. J.J. Jusserand, *A French Ambassador at the Court of Charles the Second* (London, 1892), pp. 123–6.

13. S.L. Mims, *Colbert's West Indian Policy* (New Haven, 1912).

14. L. Codignola, 'Laurens Van Heemskerk's pretended expeditions to the Arctic, 1668–1672', *International History Review*, 12 (1990), pp. 514–27; G.J. Ames, 'Colbert's Grand Indian Ocean Fleet of 1670', *Mariner's Mirror*, 76 (1990), pp. 230–31.

15. J. Bérenger, 'An attempted *rapprochement* between France and the emperor: The secret treaty for the partition of the Spanish succession of 19 January 1668', in *Louis XIV and Europe*, ed. Hatton, pp. 133–52; E. Lainé, 'Une tentative de renversement

des alliances sous Louis XIV, le Baron de Mandat', *Revue des Études Historiques*, 100 (1933). See, more generally, H. Weber, 'Die französische Rheinpolitik zwischen dem Westfälischen Frieden und dem Renversement des Alliances', in H.W. Hermann and F. Irsigler (eds), *Beiträge zur Geschichte der frühneuzeitlichen Garnisons und Festungsstadt* (Saarbrücken, Germany, 1983), pp. 74–86.

16. John de Stuers, *Étude historique sur les droits successoraux de la reine Marie-Thérèse de France née Infante d'Espagne et les causes et les résultats des guerres de dévolution, 1667–1668, et de la succession d'Espagne, 1701–14* (Geneva, 1949).

17. N. Buat, 'Louis XIV arbitre de l'Allemagne: la sentence de Heilbronn et l'intervention de la France dans la querelle du Wildfang (1660–1674)', *RHD* (1996), pp. 4–24.

18. M. Braubach, 'Um die "Reichbarriere" am Oberrhein. Der Frage der Rückwinnung Erlas um die Wiederherstellung Lothringens während des Spanischen Erbfolgerkrieges', *Zeitschrift für Geschichte des Oberrheins*, 50 (1936), pp. 482, 489.

19. K.H.D. Haley, *An English Diplomat in the Low Countries: Sir William Temple and John De Witt, 1665–72* (Oxford, 1986).

20. R. Hutton, 'The making of the Secret Treaty of Dover, 1668–1670', *Historical Journal*, 29 (1986), pp. 297–318.

21. Szarka, *Portugal, France*, pp. 103–4.

22. J. Glete, *Navies and Nations. Warships, Navies and State Building in Europe and America, 1500–1860* (Stockholm, 1993), pp. 190–91, 195, 199, 204, 211.

23. G. Pagès, *Le grand électeur et Louis XIV 1660–1688* (Paris 1905), p. 217.

24. P. Sonnino, *Louis XIV and the Origins of the Dutch War* (Cambridge, 1988).

25. C.J. Ekberg, *The Failure of Louis XIV's Dutch War* (Chapel Hill, North Carolina, 1979); Sonnino, 'Arnauld de Pomponne', pp. 49–60; K.P. Decker, *Frankreich und die Reichsstände, 1672–1675. Die Ansätze zur Bildung einer 'Dritten Partei' in den Anfangsjahren des Holländischen Krieges* (Bonn, 1981).

26. E. Laloy, *La révolte de Messine, l'expédition de Sicile, et la politique française en Italie, 1674–1678* (Paris, 1929).

27. G.J. Ames, 'An elusive partner: Portugal and Colbert's projected Asian alliance, 1669–1672', *Revista Portuguesa de História*, 28 (1993), pp. 33–57, and 'Colbert's Grand Indian Ocean Fleet of 1670', pp. 235–40; S.P. Sen, *The French in India: First Establishment and Struggle* (Calcutta, 1947), pp. 321–51; A. Martineau (ed.), *Mémoires de François Martin, fondateur de Pondichéry* (3 vols, Paris, 1931–4).

28. N.M. Crouse, *The French Struggle for the West Indies, 1665–1713* (New York, 1943).

29. J.B. Collins, 'The role of Atlantic France in the Baltic trade; Dutch traders and Polish grain at Nantes, 1625–1645', *Journal of European Economic History*, 13 (1984), pp. 239–89.

30. P. Boissonnade and P. Charliat, *Colbert et la Compagnie de Commerce du Nord, 1669–1677* (Paris, 1930).

31. R.W. Unger, 'The tonnage of Europe's merchant fleets, 1300–1800', *American Neptune*, 52 (1992), p. 261.

32. J.A.H. Bots (ed.), *The Peace of Nijmegen, 1676–1679* (Amsterdam, 1979).

33. M.O. Piquet-Marchal, *La Chambre de Réunion de Metz* (Paris, 1966); P. Harsin, *Les relations extérieures de la Principauté de Liège sous Jean Louis d'Elderen et Joseph Clément de Bavière* (Liège, 1927), p. 169, 190–91.

34. K. Malettke, *Frankreich, Deutschland und Europa im 17. und. 18. Jahrhundert. Beiträge zum Einfluss fransösischer politischer Theorie, Verfassung und Aussenpolitik in der Frühen Neuzeit* (Marburg, Germany, 1994).

35. O.N. Gisselquist, *The French Ambassador, Jean Antoine De Mesmes, Comte d'Avaux, and French Diplomacy at The Hague, 1678–1684* (PhD, University of Minnesota, 1968).

36. J.R. Jones, 'French intervention in English and Dutch politics, 1677–88', in Black (ed.), *Knights Errant and True Englishmen: British Foreign Policy, 1660–1800* (Edinburgh, 1989), pp. 1–23.

37. Martin, *Marquis of Chamlay*, pp. 146–55.

38. A. Lossky, *Louis XIV, William III, and the Baltic Crisis of 1683* (Berkeley, Cal., 1954).

39. J. Bérenger, 'La politique ottomane de la France dans les années 1680', in Babel (ed.), *Frankreich*, pp. 87–101.

40. C. Boutant, *L'Europe au Grand Tournant des Années 1680. La Succession palatine* (Paris, 1985); L. Hüttel, 'Die Beziehungen zwischen Wien, München und Versailles während des Grossen Türkenkrieges, 1684 bis 1688', *Mitteilungen des Österreichischen Staatsarchivs*, 38 (1985), pp. 81–122.

41. Martin, *Chamlay*, pp. 172–3.

42. W.J. Eccles, *Frontenac: The Courtier Governor* (Toronto, 1959), pp. 157–72.

43. AE. CP. Esp. 75 fols 222–3.

44. D.G. Pilgrim, *The Uses and Limitations of French Naval Power in the Reign of Louis XIV: The Administration of the Marquis de Seignelay, 1683–1690* (PhD, Brown, 1969).

45. *Il Bombardamento di Genova nel 1684* (Genoa, 1988).

46. AE. CP. Esp. 75 fol. 84.

47. D. Van der Cruyse, *Louis XIV et le Siam* (Paris, 1991), pp. 406–7; M. Jacq-Hergoualc'h, 'La France et le Siam de 1680 à 1685: Histoire d'un échec', *Revue française d'histoire d'Outre-Mer* (1995), pp. 257–75.

48. Szarka, *Portugal, France*, p. 32.

49. AE. CP. Allemagne 323 fol. 139; Jacques Solé, 'La diplomatie de Louis XIV et les protestants français réfugiés aux Provinces-Unies, 1678–1688', *Bulletin de la Société de l'Histoire du Protestantisme Français*, 115 (1969), pp. 625–60.

50. J. Bérenger, 'La Revocation et Les Habsbourg', *Bulletin de la Société de l'Histoire du Protestantisme Français*, 132 (1986), pp. 301–6; Hatton, 'Louis XIV and the Revocation of the Edict of Nantes', *Proceedings of the Huguenot Society of London*, 24 (1986), pp. 296–302.

51. Vogüé, *Villars*, I, 399, 401–2; R. Place, 'Bavaria and the collapse of Louis XIV's German policy, 1687–1688', *Journal of Modern History*, 49 (1977), pp. 369–93.

52. *The Negotiations of Count d'Avaux* (4 vols, London, 1755), IV, 246; AE. CP. Hollande 157 fols 230, 243.

53. AE. CP. Hollande 156 fols 172–4.

54. AE. CP. Aut. 63 fols 84–6, Hollande 156 fol. 237; Martin, *Chamlay*, p. 222.

55. AE. CP. Aut. 63 fols 103–4.

56. AE. CP. Esp. 75 fol. 84.

57. Martin, *Chamlay*, pp. 197, 203; AE. CP. Saxe 14 fols 100–05.

58. AE. CP. Aut. 63 fols 216–17, 335; A. Lossky, *Louis XIV and the French Monarchy* (New Brunswick, New Jersey, 1994), p. 234; G. Symcox, 'Louis XIV and the

outbreak of the Nine Years' War', in Hatton (ed.), *Louis XIV and Europe*, pp. 179–212.

59. For example, Lossky, *Louis XIV, William III, and the Baltic Crisis of 1683*, p. x, and 'The general European crisis of the 1680s', *European Studies Review*, 10 (1980), p. 193; Ekberg, *Louis XIV's Dutch War*, pp. 56, 178.

60. AE. CP. Esp. 75 fols 290–91.

61. C. Storrs, 'Machiavelli dethroned: Victor Amadeus II and the making of the Anglo-Savoyard alliance of 1690', *European History Quarterly*, 22 (1992), pp. 347–81.

62. H. Duchhardt (ed.), *Der Friede von Rijswijk, 1697* (Mainz, 1998); A. Blanchard, *Vauban* (Paris, 1996), p. 443; Puysieulx to Richelieu, 22 July 1748, AN. KK. 1372; AE. CP. Esp. 75 fol. 290.

63. J. Garret, *The Triumphs of Providence: The Assassination Plot, 1696* (Cambridge, 1980).

64. D.J. Sturdy, 'Le ménage à trois. Les relations entre l'Irlande, l'Angleterre et la France, 1660–1690', in C. Smith and E. Dubois (eds), *France et Grande-Bretagne de la chute de Charles Ier à celle de Jacques II, 1649–1688* (Oxford, 1990), pp. 35–45; R. Pillorget, 'Louis XIV and Ireland', in B. Whelan (ed.), *The Last of the Great Wars. Essays on the War of the Three Kings of Ireland, 1688–91* (Limerick, 1995), pp. 1–16.

65. C. Buchet, *La Lutte pour l'Éspace Caribe et la Façade Atlantique de l'Amerique Centrale du Sud, 1672–1763* (2 vols, Paris, 1991).

66. W.J. Eccles, 'Frontenac's military policies, 1689–1698. A reassessment', *Canadian Historical Review*, 37 (1956), pp. 201–24; G. Lanctot, *Histoire de Canada. Du régime royal au Traité d'Utrecht, 1663–1713* (Montréal), 1963); W.J. Eccles, *Canada under Louis XIV, 1663–1701* (Toronto, 1964).

67. A.F. Williams, *Father Baudoin's War: D'Iberville's Campaigns in Newfoundland, 1696, 1697* (St John's, Newfoundland, 1987).

68. E.B. Osler, *La Salle* (Don Mills, Ontario, 1967); M. de Villiers du Terrage, *L'Expédition de la Salle dans le Golfe du Mexique* (Paris, 1931).

69. J.C. Rule, 'Jerome Phélypeaux, comte de Pontchartrain, and the establishment of Louisiana', in J.F. McDermott (ed.), *Frenchmen and French Ways in the Mississippi Valley* (Urbana, Illinois, 1969), pp. 179–97.

70. N.M. Belting, *Kaskaskia under the French Regime* (Urbana, Illinois, 1948).

71. J. Delumeau, *Le Mouvement du port de Saint Malo, 1681–1720* (Rennes, 1966).

72. Szarka, *Portugal, France*, pp. 123–61.

73. AE. CP. Ang. 175 fol. 30.

74. AE. CP. Ang. 174 fols 139–47.

75. AE. CP. Ang. 180 fol. 37.

76. AE. CP. Ang. 180 fols 135–6.

77. D.A. Gaeddart, *The Franco-Bavarian Alliance during the War of the Spanish Succession* (PhD, Ohio State University, 1969), pp. 191–2.

78. Many of the French documents are published in H. Reynald, *Succession d'Espagne, Louis XIV et Guillaume III. Histoire des deux traités de partage et du testament de Charles II d'après la correspondance inédite de Louis XIV* (2 vols, Paris, 1883) and A. Legrelle, *La Diplomatie française et la succession d'Espagne* (2nd edn, 6 vols, Braine-le-Comte, France, 1895–9). Useful work in English includes M.A. Thomson, 'Louis XIV and

the origins of the War of the Spanish Succession' in Hatton and J.S. Bromley (eds), *William III and Louis XIV* (Liverpool, 1968), pp. 140–61 and W. Roosen, 'The origins of the War of the Spanish Succession', in Black (ed.), *Origins of War*, pp. 151–75.

79. E. Boka, 'Le Marquis Charles de Ferriol, ambassadeur de France à Constantinople, 1699–1703', *Acta Historica Hungaricae*, 31, pp. 87–112.

80. Gaeddart, *Franco-Bavarian Alliance*, pp. 32–3.

81. J.S. Gibson, *Playing the Scottish Card: The Franco-Jacobite Invasion of 1708* (Edinburgh, 1988).

82. E. Taillemite, 'Une Marine pour quoi faire? La Strategie navale de Louis XIV', in *Guerre maritime, 1688–1713* (Vincennes, 1996), pp. 93–102.

83. C. Sturgill, *Marshal Villars and the War of the Spanish Succession* (Lexington, Virginia, 1965); D.G. Chandler, *Marlborough as Military Commander* (London, 1973); D. Francis, *The First Peninsular War, 1702–13* (London, 1975).

84. Boles, *Huguenots*.

85. H. Mercier, *Une Vie d'Ambassadeur du Roi Soleil* (Paris, 1939), pp. 217, 220.

86. AE. CP. Ang. sup. 4 fols 150–51.

87. PRO. SP. 78/154 fols 358–9; Bolingbroke to Shrewsbury, 17 Feb. 1713, New York, Montague collection vol. 10.

88. B.K. Király and P. Pastor, 'The Sublime Porte and Ferenc II Rákóczi's Hungary. An episode in Islamic–Christian relations', in A. Ascher, T. Halasi-Kun, and Király (eds), *The Mutual Effects of the Islamic and Judeo-Christian Worlds: The East European Pattern* (New York, 1979), pp. 145–6.

89. P. Sonnino (ed.), *Louis XIV. Mémoires for the Instruction of the Dauphin* (New York, 1970), p. 87.

90. AE. CP. Lorraine 81 fol. 95.

91. H. Baumont, *Études sur le règne de Leopold Duc de Lorraine et de Bar* (Nancy, 1894); F.A. Maure, *Recherches sur les negociations diplomatiques préparatoires au Traité de Paris de 1718* (Diplôme d'Etudes Supérieures d'Histoire, Nancy, 1965), pp. 54–5, 98; J. P. Segondi, *Les relations diplomatiques entre le Royaume de France et le Duché de Lorraine après le Traité de Paris, 1718–21* (Diplôme, Nancy, 1971), pp. 2–3; V. Tapié, 'Territoire et dynastie: la maison de Lorraine et la France au XVIII siècle', *Annuaire bulletin de la Société de l'Histoire de France* (1966–7), pp. 29–37; G. Livet, 'La Lorraine et les relations internationales au XVIIIe siècle', in *La Lorraine dans l'Europe des Lumières* (Nancy, 1968), pp. 15–48; D.H. Pageaux, 'Les relations hispano-lorraines au XVIIIe siècle', *Annales de l'Est*, 20 (1969), pp. 155–78; J. Voss, 'La Lorraine et sa situation politique entre la France et l'Empire vues par le Duc de Saint-Simon', in J.P. Bled, E. Faucher and R. Taveneaux (eds), *Les Habsbourg et la Lorraine* (Nancy, 1988), pp. 91–9.

92. L. Dussieux and E. Soulié (eds), *Mémoires du Duc de Luynes sur la Cour de Louis XV* I (Paris, 1860), pp. 2–3.

93. L. de Piepape, *Histoire des princes de Condé au XVIIIe siècle* (Paris, 1911).

94. AN. KK. 1393, 10, 24 May, 1 Nov., 27 Dec. 1777, 17, 31 Jan., 7, 14 Mar., 25 Apr. 1778.

95. AE. CP. Aut. 251 fols 18–19, 26, 31–40.

96. Mercier, *Une Vie d'Ambassadeur*, p. 203.

97. J.C. Rule, 'Royal ministers and government reform during the last decades of

Louis XIV's reign', *Consortium* (1973), pp. 1–35; A.N. Hamscher, *The Conseil Privé and the Parlements in the Age of Louis XIV: A Study in French Absolutism* (Philadelphia, 1987).

98. Lossky, *Louis XIV and the French Monarchy.*
99. AE. CP. Allemagne 323 fols 176, 193.
100. W. Roth, 'L'affaire de Majorque', *RHD*, 96 (1972), pp. 21–53.
101. AE. CP. Rome 538 fols 219, 228, 245.
102. AE. CP. Rome 538 fol. 367.
103. S.J. Klingensmith, *The Utility of Splendor. Ceremony, Social Life, and the Architecture at the Court of Bavaria, 1600–1800* (Chicago, 1993).
104. T.J. Schaeper, *The French Economy in the Second Half of the Reign of Louis XIV* (Montreal, 1980).
105. P. Butel, 'France, the Antilles and Europe in the seventeenth and eighteenth centuries', in J.D. Tracy (ed.), *The Rise of the Merchant Empires* (Cambridge, 1990), pp. 153–73; J. Delumeau, 'Le commerce extérieur française au XVIIe siècle', *XVIIe Siècle*, 71–2 (1966), pp. 81–105; C. Frostin, 'Les Pontchartrain et la pénétration commerciale française en Amérique espagnole, 1690–1715', *Revue Historique*, 245 (1971), pp. 307–36; C. Huetz de Lamps, *Géographie du commerce de Bordeaux à la fin du règne de Louis XIV* (Paris, 1974).

Chapter 3: Foreign policy under the regency, Bourbon and Fleury, 1715–43

1. AST. LM. Francia 163.
2. A. Baudrillart, 'Les prétentions de Philippe V à la couronne de France', *Séances et travaux de l'Académie des Sciences Morales et Politiques*, 127 (1887), pp. 723–43, 851–97; J.M.J. Rogister, 'Philippe V, successeur de Louis XV? Les démarches secrètes de 1724–1728', in Y. Bottineau (ed.), *Philippe V d'Espagne et l'Art de Son Temps* (2 vols, Paris, 1995), II, 141–67.
3. J.H. Shennan, *Philippe, Duke of Orléans, Regent of France 1715–1723* (London, 1979).
4. Baudrillart, *Philippe V* (5 vols, Paris, 1890–1901), III, 478.
5. Mercier, *Vie d'Ambassadeur*, p. 221.
6. A. Manno, E. Ferrero and P. Vayra, *Relazione Diplomatiche dalla Monarchia di Savoia della prima alla seconda Restaurazione. Francia, periodo 3* (3 vols, Turin, 1886–91), II, 44, 52, 55, 41, 51.
7. *Ibid.*, II, 41, 65, 120, 151, 187.
8. BL. Add. 32812 fol. 139; L. Wiesener, *Le Régent, l'Abbé Dubois et les Anglais* (3 vols, Paris, 1891–9); E. Bourgeois, *Le Secret du Régent et la Politique de l'Abbé Dubois* (Paris, 1907).
9. H. Legoherel, *Les Tresoriers Generaux de la Marine, 1517–1788* (Paris, 1963), pp. 179–80.
10. HHStA. Frankreich Varia 10 fol. 185.
11. BN. MF. 7149, p. 223.
12. AE. CP. Ang. 339 fol. 181.
13. PRO. SP. 90/15, 14 Oct. 1721.

14. AE. CP. Ang. 323 fol. 86.

15. AE. CP. Prusse 73 fols 4, 51.

16. J. Dureng, *Le Duc de Bourbon et l'Angleterre 1723–1726* (Paris, 1911).

17. M. Langrod-Vaughan, 'Le mariage polonais de Louis XV', *Revue Internationale d'histoire politique et constitutionelle*, new series 17 (1955).

18. J.F. Chance, *The Alliance of Hanover* (London, 1923).

19. Fleury to Richelieu, 4 June 1727, A. de Boislisle (ed.), *Mémoires authentiques du maréchal de Richelieu* (Paris, 1918), p. 26; HHStA. Frankreich Varia 11 fol. 453, Nachlass Fonseca 12 fol. 14; Vogüé (ed.), *Villars*, V, 112. The best study of Fleury's foreign policy remains A.M. Wilson, *French Foreign Policy during the Administration of Cardinal Fleury 1726–1743* (Cambridge, Mass., 1936). See also Black, 'French foreign policy in the age of Fleury reassessed', *English Historical Review*, 103 (1988), pp. 359–84. The most recent treatment of the domestic situation is P.R. Campbell, *Power and Politics in Old Regime France, 1720–1745* (London, 1996).

20. AE. CP. Allemagne 375 fol. 12.

21. AE. CP. Allemagne 374 fol. 272; AE. CP. Allemagne 375 fol. 123; AE. CP. Brunswick-Hanovre 47 fols 114–15, 139, 160, 163, 188.

22. AE. CP. Brunswick-Hanovre 47 fols 94, 121.

23. BVC. 30 fol. 227; J. Dureng, *Mission de Théodore Chevignard de Chavigny en Allemagne* (Paris, 1912).

24. HHStA. Frankreich Varia 11 fol. 25, Nachlass Fonseca 21 fol. 408.

25. HHStA. Nachlass Fonseca 13 fol. 187.

26. HHStA. Nachlass Fonseca, 13 fol. 90.

27. Nancy 3F 86 no. 37.

28. AN. AM. B7 296, 24 Mar. 1729.

29. Baudrillart, *Philippe V*, III, 506.

30. AE. CP. Brunswick-Hanovre 47 fol. 134.

31. Chewton, Journal of James, 1st Earl Waldegrave, British envoy in France, 7, 20 Aug. 1730, Chewton Mendip, Chewton House.

32. Dureng, *Chavigny*.

33. AE. CP. Hesse 7 fols 20–21.

34. AE. CP. Prusse 95 fol. 85.

35. BN. MF. 7149, p. 102.

36. BVC. 31 fol. 181.

37. BVC. 32 fols 92–3.

38. Black and A. Reese, 'Die Panik von 1731', in J. Kunisch (ed.), *Expansion und Gleichgewicht. Studien zur europäischen Mächtepolitik des ancien régime* (Berlin, 1986), pp. 69–95.

39. Vogüé (ed.), *Villars*, V, 321, 324.

40. AE. CP. Allemagne 379 fols 138–9, 154, 174, 177.

41. Albert to Törring, 21 Apr. 1732, Munich KS 17122; Münster NA 47 fol. 37.

42. E.V. Puttkamer, *Frankreich, Russland und der polnische Thron 1733* (Königsberg, 1937); E. Rostworowski, *O Polska Korone – Polityka Francji w latach 1725–1733* (Cracow, 1958), French summary, pp. 330–47.

43. *Sbornik* 81, pp. 534, 537.

44. *Sbornik* 75, 410.

45. *Sbornik* 64, 81, 133.

46. G. Lebel, *La France et Les Principautés Danubiennes du XVI siècle à la chute de Napoléon 1er* (Paris, 1955), p. 49.

47. AE. CP. Bavière 84 fols 40–43.

48. M.L. Shay, *The Ottoman Empire from 1720 to 1734 as revealed in Despatches of the Venetian Baili* (Urbana, Illinois, 1944), pp. 37, 147–88; BN. MF. 7179 fols 180–84, 190–91, 222–3, 228, 242–3, 249, 401, 404; BN. MF. 7196 fols 68, 82.

49. AE. CP. Pologne 206 fol. 338, Ang. 382 fol. 28.

50. Vogüé (ed.), *Villars*, IV, 309–10.

51. Arsenal, MS Bastille 10163 fol. 225.

52. Arsenal, MS Bastille 10159 fols 48, 89.

53. AE. CP. Ang. 379 fols 158–9.

54. Münster, NB 104 fols 47–9; AE. CP. Ang. 380 fol. 65.

55. AE. CP. Ang. 381 fols 358–60.

56. P. Boyé, *Un Roi de Pologne et la Couronne ducale de Lorraine: Stanislas Leszczynski et le troisième Traité de Vienne* (Paris, 1898), pp. 197–8; AST. LM. Francia 170, 27 Apr. 1734.

57. AE. MD. Allemagne 74 fol. 5.

58. AE. CP. Bavière 84 fols 100–02.

59. Albert to Törring, 29 Jan., 5 Feb. 1734, Munich KS 17132; AE. MD. France 446 fol. 92, CP. Cologne 72 fol. 110; Anon. to anon., 27 Feb. 1734, Munich Bayr. Ges. Paris 87; F. Deybeck, *Die Politik Bayerns in der Zeit des Polnischen Thronfolgerkrieges* (Munich, 1897).

60. AE. CP. Ang. 382 fol. 22, Prusse 95 fols 85–6; Wolfenbüttel, Staatsarchiv, 1 Act 22 nr. 588 fol. 40.

61. P. Vaucher, *Robert Walpole et la Politique de Fleury, 1731–42* (Paris, 1924).

62. AST. LM. Francia 172, 31 Oct. 1735.

63. AE. MD. France 505 fols 4–5; Münster NA 148 fol. 346. For the importance of Lorraine's roads, G. Livet, 'Strade e poteri politici nei "Pays d'entre deux": Il modello Lorenese (secc. xv–xvii)', *Quaderni Storici*, 22 (1987), pp. 81–110; T.E. Hall, *France and the Eighteenth-Century Corsican Question* (New York, 1971), p. 34.

64. M. Braubach, *Versailles und Wien* (Bonn, 1952), pp. 276–345.

65. E. Driault, 'Chauvelin, 1733–1737: Son rôle dans l'histoire de la réunion de la Lorraine à la France', *Revue d'histoire diplomatique*, 7 (1893), pp. 31–74; J.M.J. Rogister, 'New light on the fall of Chauvelin', *English Historical Review*, 83 (1968), pp. 314–30, and 'A minister's fall and its implications: The case of Chauvelin, 1737–46', in D.J. Mossop, G.E. Rodmell and D.B. Wilson (eds), *Studies in the French Eighteenth Century presented to John Lough* (Durham, 1978), pp. 200–17; L. Bély, 'Schoepflin et Chauvelin, l'historien et le ministre: étude comparative de deux visions des relations internationales', in B. Vogler and J. Voss (eds), *Strasbourg, Schoepflin et l'Europe au XVIIIe siècle* (Bonn, 1996), pp. 225–42, esp. p. 241.

66. HHStA. Nachlass Fonseca 13 fol. 91.

67. Albert to Elector Charles Albert, 16 Jan., Albert to Törring, 22 June, 28 Sept., 5 Oct., 5 Nov., 7, 10 Dec. 1736, Munich KS 17142–3.

68. Munich, KS 17190, 3 Jan. 1738.

69. A. Broglie, 'Le Cardinal de Fleury et la *Pragmatique Sanction*', *Revue Historique*, 20 (1982), pp. 257–81.

70. Törring to Charles Albert, 9 May 1739, Munich KS 17194.
71. Haslang to Törring, 22 Aug. 1735, Munich KS 17210.
72. Albert to Törring, 14, 24 Dec. 1736, Törring to Charles Albert, 10 Nov., – Dec. 1737, 3 July 1738, Munich KS. 17143, 17189, 17191; AE. MD. France 457 fol. 76.
73. Munich, KS 17194, 9 May 1739.
74. S. Gorceix, 'Bonneval Pacha et le jeune Rákoczi', in *Mélanges offerts a M. Nicolas Iorga* (Paris, 1933), pp. 347–61.
75. M. Sautai, *Les Préliminaires de la Guerre de la Succession d'Autriche* (Paris, 1907); P.C. Hartmann, *Geld als Instrument europäischer Machtpolitik im Zeitalter des Merkantilismus. Studien zu den finanziellen und politischen Beziehungen der Wittelsbacher Territorien Kurbayern, Kurpfalz und Kurköln mit Frankreich und dem Kaiser von 1715 bis 1740* (Munich, 1978).
76. Munich KS 17194, 4 Jan. 1739.
77. L. Dussieux and E. Soulié (eds), *Mémoires du Duc de Luynes sur la cour de Louis XV*, 17 vols (Paris, 1860–65), III, 366–7.
78. See, for example, AG A1 2643 nos. 13, 40, 2677 nos. 11, 55, 70.
79. Darmstadt, Staatsarchiv EI M14/3.
80. AST. LM. Francia 164, 23 Jan. 1730, 165, 25 Dec. 1730. See also 172, 28 Apr. 1735.
81. HHStA. Fonseca 11 fol. 441.
82. Arsenal, MS Bastille 10158 fols 153, 341–2, also 10159 fols 15, 23, and 10161 fols 90–7, 187; Nancy, 3F 87 no. 7; AE. CP. Prusse 91 fol. 140; Dresden, 2735 IV, fols 24–6.
83. AST. LM. Francia 170, 5 Jan., 16 Feb. 1734.
84. For example, Solaro, Sardinian envoy, 12 July, 6 Sept. 1738, AST. LM. Francia 177.
85. AST. LM. Francia 176, 1, 11, 18, 29 Mar., 12 Ap. 1738, Munich KS 17190, 3, 14, 17, 23, 28 Feb. 1738; Trevor to Keene, 6 Mar. 1738, Aylesbury, Buckinghamshire County Record Office, D/MH vol. 11.
86. AST. LM. Francia 176.
87. AST. LM. Francia 172, 9 Feb. 1735.
88. K.A. Roider, *The Reluctant Ally: Austria's Policy in the Austro-Turkish War, 1737–1730* (Baton Rouge, Louisiana, 1972), p. 121.
89. *Recueil . . . Danemark*, pp. 148–50.
90. Amelot to St Severin, 20 Mar. 1738, British intercept, Iden Green, Kent, Weston papers.
91. C. Nordmann, *Grandeur et liberté de la Suède, 1660–1792* (Paris, 1971), pp. 252–4.
92. W. Holst, *Carl Gustaf Tessin* (Lund, 1931), pp. 418–19.
93. AE. CP. Ang. 394, fol. 171.
94. Sautai, *Préliminaires*, pp. 475–6; M. Doeberl, *Geschichte Bayerns* (3 vols, Munich, 1928) II, 195.
95. AE. CP. Prusse 105 fol. 237.
96. R.D. Bourland, *Maurepas and his administration of the French Navy on the eve of the War of the Austrian Succession* (PhD, Notre Dame, Indiana, 1978), pp. 309–10.
97. AE. CP. Prusse 105 fol. 265; PRO. SP. 78/223 fol. 289.
98. PRO. SP. 80/197 fol. 110.
99. AE. CP. Prusse 91 fol. 209.
100. AE. CP. Prusse 93 fol. 293, 95 fols 157–8, Ang. sup. 8 fol. 212.

101. AE. CP. Brunswick-Hanovre 49 fol. 54.

102. AE. CP. Brunswick-Hanovre 49 fols 99–100, 144–6, 149–50, 161–4; AE. MD. Brunswick-Hanovre 9 fols 164–250.

103. Duke of Zweibrücken to Wernike, envoy in Paris, 12 May 1743, Munich Ges. Paris 216.

104. *Recueil . . . Russie* I, 344.

105. AE. CP. Bavière 94 fol. 223.

106. AE. CP. Esp. 470 fol. 26.

107. AE. CP. Bavière 94 fols 292–3.

108. AE. CP. Esp. 470 fols 28, 61–2, 153.

109. G.E. Broche, *La République de Gênes et la France pendant la guerre de la Succession d'Autriche, 1740–48* (Paris, 1936).

110. *Polit. Corr.* I, 49.

111. AE. CP. Bavière 102 fol. 78.

112. AE. CP. Esp. 470 fols 15, 23, Hollande 443 fol. 261.

113. AE. CP. Hollande 443 fol. 68.

114. AE. CP. Esp. 475 fols 75–6.

115. AST. LM. Spagna 69, 7 Mar. 1740.

116. AE. CP. Esp. 475 fols 75–6.

117. AE. CP. Bavière 97 fols 245–6.

118. AE. CP. Hollande 442 fol. 92.

119. AE. CP. Bavière 100 fol. 271.

120. AE. CP. Bavière 102 fol. 78.

121. AE. CP. Bavière 101 fol. 419.

122. AE. CP. Bavière 101 fols 333, 398.

123. AE. CP. Bavière 103 fols 58–9.

124. AE. CP. Bavière 110 fol. 71.

125. F. McLynn, *France and the Jacobite Rising of 1745* (Edinburgh, 1981).

126. H. Duchhardt, *Balance of Power und Pentarchie* (Paderborn, 1997), pp. 287–303.

127. A. Vandal, *Une Ambassade Française en Orient sous Louis XV: La mission du Marquis de Villeneuve, 1728–41* (Paris, 1887).

128. C. Roussel (ed.), *Correspondance de Louis XV et du maréchal de Noailles* (2 vols, Paris, 1865), I, 147–8; II, 61.

129. T. Besterman (ed.), *The Complete Works of Voltaire* (Toronto, 1969), II, 464.

130. J.R. McNeill, *Atlantic Empires of France and Spain: Havana and Louisbourg, 1700–1763* (Chapel Hill, North Carolina, 1985), p. 180; R. Stein, 'The French sugar business in the eighteenth century: a quantitative study', *Business History*, 22 (1980), pp. 6, 10, 12.

131. C. Carrière, *Négociants Marseillais au XVIIIe siècle* (2 vols, Paris, 1970), I, 332.

132. O. Prakash, *European Commercial Enterprise in Pre-Colonial India* (Cambridge, 1998), pp. 255–6.

133. P. Haudrère, 'The Compagnie des Indes Orientales', in R. Vincent (ed.), *The French in India* (Bombay, 1990), p. 37.

134. M. Morineau and C. Carrière, 'Draps du Languedoc et commerce du Levant au XVIIIe siècle', *Revue d'histoire économique et sociale*, 46 (1968), pp. 108–21; E. Frangakis-Syrett, *The Commerce of Smyrna in the Eighteenth Century, 1700–1820* (Athens, 1992).

135. Erdbrink, *On the Threshold of Felicity* (The Hague, 1975), pp. 166, 177–9, 182–3.

136. A. Cohen, *Palestine in the Eighteenth Century* (Jerusalem, 1973).

137. BN. MF. 7186 fol. 25.

138. A.A. Amin, *British Interests in the Persian Gulf* (Leiden, 1967), p. 22.

139. Bourland, *Maurepas and his administration of the French Navy*; J. Glete, *Navies and Nations*, pp. 256–8, is sceptical about the relative strength of France's navy.

140. E. Taillemite, 'Les Archives de la Marine des origines à la fin du XIXe siècle', *Revue Historique des Armées*, 171 (1988), p. 61.

141. AN. AM. B7 349.

142. E.J.B. Rathery (ed.), *Journal et mémoires du marquis d'Argenson* (9 vols, Paris, 1859–67), II, 304–5.

143. For example, ASG. LM. Francia 44, reports of 1733.

144. A. Delcourt, *La France et les établissements français au Sénégal entre 1713 et 1763* (Dakar, 1952); J.F. Searing, *West African Slavery and Atlantic Commerce, 1700–1860* (Cambridge, 1993).

145. P.D. Hollingworth, *A Study of the Policy of La Bourdonnais 1735–47* (MA., Durham, 1957).

146. La Farelle, Chevalier de, *Mémoires sur la prise de Mahé*, ed. E. Lennel de La Farelle (Paris, 1887).

147. Abbé Desfontaines, *Relation de l'expédition de Moka en l'année 1737* (Paris, 1739).

148. J.F. Brière, *La pêche française en Amérique du Nord au XVIIIe siècle* (Montreal, 1990).

149. J.S. McLennan, *Louisbourg from its Foundation to its Fall, 1713–1758* (Sydney, 1957); M. Filion, *La pensée et l'action coloniale de Maurepas vis-à-vis du Canada, 1723–1749, l'âge d'or de la colonie* (Ottawa, 1972); F.J. Thorpe, *Rémparts Lointains: La politique française des travaux publics à Terre Neuve et à l'île Royale, 1695–1758* (Ottawa, 1980); D. Miquelon, *New France, 1701–1744: A Supplement to Europe* (Toronto, 1987).

150. Y.F. Zoltvany, *Philippe de Rigaud de Vaudreuil. Governor of New France, 1703–1725* (Toronto, 1974); L.J. Burpee (ed.), *Journals and Letters of Pierre Gaultier de Varennes de la Vérendrye and his Sons* (Toronto, 1927).

151. AE. CP. Ang. sup. 7 fols 56–60.

152. For French complaints, see AE. CP. Ang. 370 fols 339–46.

153. R.D. Edmunds and J.L. Peyser, *The Fox Wars. The Mesquakie Challenge to New France* (Norman, Oklahoma, 1993).

154. AE. CP. Ang. 369 fols 89–94; M. Giraud, *A History of French Louisiana. II: Years of Transition, 1715–1717* (Baton Rouge, Louisiana, 1993), pp. 162–79.

155. P.D. Woods, 'The French and the Natchez Indians in Louisiana, 1700–1731', *Louisiana History*, 19 (1978), pp. 413–35; M. Giraud, *A History of French Louisiana. V: The Company of the Indies, 1723–1731* (Baton Rouge, Louisiana, 1991).

156. J.M. Price, *France and the Chesapeake. A History of the French Tobacco Monopoly, 1674–1791, and of its Relationship to the British and American Tobacco Trades* (Ann Arbor, Michigan, 1973), p. 342.

157. P.D. Woods, *French–Indian Relations on the Southern Frontier, 1699–1762* (Ann Arbor, Michigan, 1980), pp. 111–46; M.S. Arnold, *Colonial Arkansas, 1686–1804* (Fayetteville, 1991), pp. 31, 99–106.

158. Louis XV to M. de St Ovide, 10 May 1735, AN. AM. B 63.

Chapter 4: The Diplomatic Revolution, its background and consequences: 1743–1774

1. BN. NAF. 14914 fol. 43.
2. AE. CP. Bavière 114 fol. 149.
3. AE. CP. Bavière 114 fol. 282.
4. AE. CP. Bavière 119 fol. 22.
5. AE. CP. Esp. 491 fol. 11.
6. AE. CP. Esp. 488 fols 65, 136–46.
7. BVC. 40 fols 76–8.
8. AE. CP. Esp. 488 fols 48, 128.
9. AE. CP. Ang. 421 fols 7–9, 13–18, 30, 47.
10. AE. CP. Hollande 462 fols 4–6.
11. AE. CP. Hollande 462 fols 22–3.
12. J. Pritchard, *Anatomy of a Naval Disaster. The 1746 French Expedition to North America* (Montreal, 1995).
13. E. Taillemite, 'Une bataille de l'Atlantique au XVIIIe siècle; la guerre de Succession d'Autriche, 1744–1748', *Guerres et Paix* (Vincennes, 1987), pp. 131–48.
14. Intelligence from Lyons, PRO. SP. 84/445 fol. 73.
15. Puysieulx to Richelieu, 23 Jan., 22 July 1748, AN. KK. 1372; C.M. Desbarats, 'The cost of early Canada's Native alliances: reality and scarcity's rhetoric', *William and Mary Quarterly*, 3rd series, 52 (1995), p. 625.
16. Baudrillart, *Philippe V* (5 vols, Paris, 1890–1901), V, 456.
17. Puysieulx to Richelieu, 20 Feb. 1748, AN. KK. 1372.
18. Gorceix, 'Bonneval-Pacha', p. 363.
19. PRO. SP. 78/331 fol. 440 (an Argenson intercept); BVC 40 fol. 126.
20. BVC. 40 fol. 126; R.N. Middleton, *French Policy and Prussia after the Peace of Aix-la-Chapelle, 1749–1753: A Study of the Pre-History of the Diplomatic Revolution of 1756* (PhD, Columbia, 1968), pp. 7–8.
21. Horowitz, *Franco-Russian relations*, pp. 574, 580–81 (re 1746).
22. Broglie, *La Paix d'Aix-la-Chapelle* (Paris, 1895); R. Lodge, *Studies in Eighteenth Century Diplomacy, 1740–1748* (London, 1930); C. Baudi di Vesme, *La Pace di Aquisgrana, 1748* (Turin, 1969).
23. BN. NAF. 14917 fols 218–19.
24. PRO. SP. 84/433 fols 358–9.
25. Puysieulx to Belle Isle, 17 June 1748; Broglie, *La Paix d'Aix-la-Chapelle* (Paris, 1895), p. 260.
26. PRO. SP. 84/434 fol. 83.
27. AE. CP. Ang. 425 fol. 406.
28. AE. CP. Brunswick-Hanovre 50 fol. 223; AE. CP. Esp. 503 fol. 286.
29. AE. CP. Esp. 506 fols 150, 171.
30. Windsor Castle, Royal Archives, Cumberland Papers 43/208; BL. Add. 35355 fols 69, 116.
31. E. Boutaric, *Correspondance secrète inédite de Louis XV sur la politique étrangère* (2 vols, Paris, 1886) II, 497–8; II, 122–4.
32. AE. CP. Bavière 129 fol. 30.
33. AE. CP. Bavière 129 fol. 106.

34. AE. CP. Bavière 129 fols 157, 186, 188–9.
35. AE. CP. Ang. 429 fol. 278; AE. CP. Esp. 506 fols 251, 288.
36. Middleton, *French Policy and Prussia*, passim.
37. M. Antoine and D. Ozanam, 'Le Secret du Roi et la Russie jusqu'à la mort de la Czarine Elisabeth en 1762', *Annuaire Bulletin de la Société de L'Histoire de France* (1954–5), p. 71.
38. *Polit. Corr.* 6, 381; 9, 36, 54, 56, 61–2, 71; Podewils to Palatine diplomat Wrede, 22 July 1752, Munich KB 9/23.
39. AE. CP. Prusse 171 fols 225, 238–9, 260–61, 275–8, 283, 307.
40. AN. KK. 1400, pp. 390–91; AE. CP. Aut. 251 fol. 57. See also AE. CP. Ang. 432 fol. 207.
41. *Polit. Corr.* 7, 243.
42. AE. CP. Aut. 247 fol. 11.
43. AE. CP. Aut. 248 fols 25–6; AE. CP. Ang. 429 fols 310–11, 353–4.
44. AE. CP. Ang. 429 fol. 191.
45. Middleton, *French Policy and Prussia*, p. 149.
46. T. Bussemaker (ed.), *Archives ou Correspondance Inédite de la Maison d'Orange-Nassau*, 4th ser., 1 (Leyden, 1908), p. 604.
47. AN. KK. 1400, pp. 390–91.
48. *Polit. Corr.* 9, 45, 67.
49. *Polit. Corr.* 10, 63–4, 148.
50. Elector Palatine to Louis XV, 31 May 1752 and reply, 15 June, Saint-Contest to Baron Wachtendonck, 11 June, Baron Grevenbroek to Wachtendonck, 20 May, 12 June, Wrede to Elector, 26 June, Wrede to Wachtendonck, 30 June 1752, Munich KB 9/11, 12, 19, 20; AE. CP. Palatinat 78 fol. 5.
51. AE. CP. Prusse 171 fol. 40.
52. AN. KK. 1400 p. 30; *Polit. Corresp.* 10, 149; G. de Bourge, 'Le Comte de Vergennes, ses débuts diplomatiques en Allemagne auprès de l'électeur de Trêves et de l'électeur d'Hanovre', *Revue des questions historiques*, 44 (1888), pp. 92–166; O.T. Murphy, *Charles Gravier, Comte de Vergennes* (Albany, New York, 1982), pp. 19–50.
53. AE. CP. Prusse 171 fols 414–15.
54. *Polit. Corr.* 10, 143; AN. KK. 1400, p. 330; AE. CP. Aut. 253, fol. 21.
55. AE. CP. Ang. 432 fol. 224.
56. AN. AM. B7 375, 5, 26 Jan. 1750.
57. AN. AM. B7 350, 10 Apr. 1744; PRO. SP. 82/69 fol. 45.
58. AN. AM. B7 384, 3, 31 Jan. 1752.
59. AE. CP. Aut. 254 fols 37–8.
60. *Relazioni diplomatiche . . . Francia* II, 102.
61. D. McKay, *Prince Eugene of Savoy* (London, 1977), pp. 218–19.
62. *Polit. Corr.* 5, 476, 498.
63. L. Schilling, *Kaunitz und das Renversement des Alliances* (Berlin, 1994).
64. AE. CP. Aut. 247 fol. 346.
65. AE. CP. Aut. 251 fols 71–2.
66. AE. CP. Ang. 438 fols 413–14; Middleton, *French Policy and Prussia*, pp. 310–11.
67. AN. KK. 1372, 8 July 1748.
68. AE. CP. Aut. 252 fols 269–70.

69. L.H. Gipson, *Zones of international friction: North America, south of the Great Lakes region, 1748–1754* (New York, 1937).

70. AE. CP. Ang. 437 fols 294–6.

71. W. Eccles, 'The fur trade and eighteenth-century imperialism', *William and Mary Quarterly*, 3rd. ser. 40 (1983), pp. 341–62. For the native perspective, R. White, *The Middle Ground: Indians, Empires, and Republics in the Great Lakes Region, 1650–1815* (Cambridge, 1991).

72. P.J. Marshall, 'Reappraisal: the rise of British power in eighteenth-century India', *South Asia*, 19 (1996), p. 75; G.B. Malleson, *History of the French in India* (London, 1886, Delhi, 1986), pp. 231–82; V.G. Hatalkar, *Relations Between the French and the Marathas, 1668–1815* (Bombay, 1958), pp. 87, 274; G. Bodinier, 'Les officiers français en Inde de 1750 à 1793', in *Trois siècles de présence française en Inde* (Paris, 1995), pp. 69–89.

73. T.R. Clayton, 'The Duke of Newcastle, the Earl of Halifax and the American origins of the Seven Years' War', *Historical Journal*, 24 (1981), pp. 571–603; A. Reese, *Europäische Hegemonie und France d'outre-mer. Koloniale Fragen in der französischen Aussenpolitik, 1700–1763* (Stuttgart, 1988), pp. 249–89.

74. J. Aman, *Une campagne navale meconnu à la veille de la Guerre de Sept Ans: l'escadre de Brest en 1755* (Vincennes, 1986).

75. AE. CP. Ang. 439 fol. 255; AE. CP. Brunswick-Hanovre 52 fol. 16.

76. AN. K 1351 no. 91; AE. CP. Ang. 438 fol. 249; BL. Add. 35480 fols 32–4, 59–60.

77. Glete, *Navies and Nations*, pp. 265–6.

78. Batzel, *Treaties of Versailles*, p. 72; AE. CP. Aut. 254 fols 254–7, 319, 279–81, 330.

79. *Polit. Corr.* 11, 408–9.

80. Batzel, *Treaties of Versailles*, p. 102.

81. *Polit. Corr.* 13, 8, 73; J. Flammermont, *Les correspondances des agents diplomatiques étrangers en France avant la Révolution* (Paris, 1896), p. 47; L. Perey, *Un petit neveu de Mazarin* (3rd edn, Paris, 1890), p. 369.

82. Batzel, *Treaties of Versailles*, pp. 82–139.

83. *Polit. Corr.* 14, 7.

84. AE. CP. Bavière 134 fol. 362.

85. L.J. Oliva, *Misalliance: A Study of French Policy in Russia during the Seven Years' War* (New York, 1964).

86. G. De Boom, *Les Ministres Plénipotentiaires dans les Pays-Bas Autrichiens principalement Cobenzl* (Brussels, 1932), pp. 275–85.

87. *Polit. Corr.* 15, 187, 218, 25, 256; AE. CP. Prusse 186 fols 65, 80; AE. CP. Brunswick-Hanovre 52 fol. 145.

88. W. Mediger, 'Hastenbeck und Zeven. Der Eintritt Hannovers in den Siebenjahrigen krieg', *Niedersachsisches Jahrbuch fur Landesgeschichte*, 56 (1984), pp. 137–66.

89. AE. CP. Brunswick-Hanovre 52 fols 119, 130–31. For examples from the correspondence of Richelieu, BVC 58 fols 86, 100–01, 109–10, 135, and BVC 59 fol. 101.

90. Black, *Britain as a Military Power, 1688–1815* (London, 1999).

91. J.C. Riley, 'French finances, 1727–1768', *Journal of Modern History*, 59 (1987), pp. 209–43, and *The Seven Years' War and the Old Regime in France: The Economic and Financial Toll* (Princeton, New Jersey, 1986).

92. Batzel, *Treaties of Versailles*, pp. 454, 467–9, 471.

93. AE. CP. Esp. 537 fol. 260.

94. J.F. Bosher, 'Financing the French navy in the Seven Years War: Beaujon, Goosens et Compagnie in 1759', *Business History*, 28 (1986), pp. 115–33; J. Pritchard, *Louis XV's Navy, 1748–1762: A Study of Organization and Administration* (Kingston, Ontario, 1987).

95. T.J.A. Le Goff, 'Problemes de recrutement de la marine française pendant la Guerre de Sept Ans', *Revue Historique*, 203 (1990), pp. 215–33.

96. Batzel, *Treaties of Versailles*, pp. 405, 428.

97. Batzel, *Treaties of Versailles*, pp. 402, 412, 429, 473–4.

98. Batzel, *Treaties of Versailles*, pp. 479, 486.

99. AE. CP. Esp. 526 fol. 62.

100. AE. CP. Esp. 527 fol. 11.

101. AE. CP. Esp. 522 fol. 520; AE. CP. Esp. 523 fols 15, 18.

102. BVC. 58 fols 20–21.

103. AE. CP. Bavière 134 fol. 362.

104. AE. CP. Allemagne 597 fol. 221; R. Boudard, *Gênes et La France dans la deuxième moitié du XVIIIe siècle, 1748–1797* (Paris, 1962), pp. 67–8.

105. AE. CP. Esp. 523 fol. 3.

106. BVC. 59 fols 249, 251.

107. AE. CP. Esp. 517 fols 26, 28, 192–3, 281–5; A. Bourguet, *Le Duc de Choiseul et l'Alliance Espagnole* (Paris, 1906), pp. 6–7, 25.

108. AE. CP. Esp. 526 fols 7, 13, 17.

109. AE. CP. Esp. 532 fols 235–6.

110. The Family Pact and Secret Convention, AE. CP. Esp. 533 fols 270–85, 290–4; L. Blart, *Les rapports de la France et de l'Espagne après le pacte de famille, jusqu'à la fin du ministère du duc de Choiseul* (Paris, 1915), pp. 205–17.

111. AE. CP. Esp. 533 fol. 452.

112. AE. CP. Esp. 533 fol. 475.

113. AE. CP. Esp. 533 fols 322–3, 355, 382–3, 446–7, 472.

114. Boutaric, *Correspondance secrète* II, 216–17.

115. AE. MD. Ang. 41 fols 295–404; AE. CP. Ang. 442 fols 275–80; Bourguet, *Choiseul et l'Alliance Espagnole*, p. 50.

116. AE. CP. Esp. 526 fol. 238; AE. CP. Esp. 527 fol. 136.

117. AE. CP. Aut. fols 19–26.

118. Bourguet, 'Le Duc de Choiseul et l'Angleterre', *RHD*, 17 (1903), p. 543.

119. AE. CP. Esp. 532 fol. 221; AE. CP. Ang; AE. CP. Ang. 445 fol. 17.

120. AE. CP. Ang. 445 fol. 12.

121. AE. CP. Ang. 443 fol. 337; AE. CP. Ang. 445 fols 21–3.

122. AE. CP. Ang. 445 fols 17–19; W. Grant, 'La Mission de M. de Bussy à Londres en 1761', *RHD*, 20 (1906); K.W. Schweizer, 'Lord Bute, William Pitt and the peace negotiations with France, April–September 1761', in Schweizer (ed.), *Lord Bute* (Leicester, 1988), pp. 41–55; AE. CP. Esp. 533 fols 35–6.

123. BL. Add. 36797 fol. 1.

124. AE. CP. Ang. 446 fol. 56; AE. CP. Esp. 537 fols 160–61, 209, 216.

125. Blart, *Rapports*, pp. 41–2; A.S. Aiton, 'The diplomacy of the Louisiana Cession', *American Historical Review*, 36 (1931), p. 78; E.W. Lyon, *Louisiana in French diplomacy, 1759–1804* (Norman, Oklahoma, 1934).

126. S. Rombouts, 'Art as propaganda in eighteenth-century France: the paradox of Edme Bouchardon's Louis XV', *Eighteenth-Century Studies*, 27 (1993–4), pp. 255–82.

127. Batzel, *Treaties of Versailles*, p. 271.

128. C. Bréard (ed.), *Correspondance inédite du Général-Major de Martange* (Paris, 1898), p. 32.

129. AE. CP. Esp. 626 fols 252–8.

130. AE. CP. Esp. 626 fol. 255.

131. AE. CP. Esp. 536 fol. 32; AE. CP. Esp. 537 fol. 224.

132. Boutaric, *Correspondance secrète*, I, 361; M.C. Morison, 'The Duc de Choiseul and the invasion of England, 1768–1770', *Transactions of the Royal Historical Society*, 3rd ser., 4 (1910), pp. 83–115.

133. F.P. Renault, *Le Pacte de Famille et l'Amérique. La politique coloniale franco-espagnole, 1760–1792* (Paris, 1922); R.E. Abarca, *Bourbon 'Revanche' against England: The Balance of Power, 1763–1770* (PhD, Notre Dame, Indiana, 1965), and 'Classical diplomacy and Bourbon "revanche" strategy, 1763–1770', *Review of Politics*, 32 (1970), pp. 313–37; H.M. Scott, 'The importance of Bourbon naval reconstruction to the strategy of Choiseul after the Seven Years' War', *International History Review*, 1 (1979), pp. 17–35; M.M. Escott, *Britain's Relations with France and Spain, 1763–1771* (PhD, University of Wales, 1988).

134. J. Mathieu, *La Construction Navale Royale à Québec, 1739–1759* (Québec, 1971).

135. N. Tracy, 'The gunboat diplomacy of the government of George Grenville, 1764–65', *Historical Journal*, 17 (1974), pp. 711–31.

136. T.E. Hall, *France and the Eighteenth-Century Corsican Question* (New York, 1971); P. Da Passano, *Histoire de l'annexion de La Corse* (Le Coteau, 1990).

137. E. Daubigny, *Choiseul et la France d'outre-mer, après le Traité de Paris* (Paris, 1897), pp. 252–84; Blart, *Rapports*, pp. 143–202; M. Antoine, *Louis XV* (Paris, 1989), pp. 923–4; Scott, *British Foreign Policy in the Age of the American Revolution* (Oxford, 1990), pp. 140–56.

138. A.S. Aiton, 'Spain and the Family Compact, 1770–73', in A.C. Wilgus (ed.), *Hispanic American Essays* (1942), pp. 135–49.

139. Antoine and Ozanam, 'Le Secret du Roi', pp. 89, 91, and *Correspondance secrète du Comte de Broglie à Louis XV* (2 vols, Paris, 1956); Vandal, *Louis XV et Elisabeth de Russie* (3rd edn, Paris, 1896); H. Stiegung, *Ludvig XV's Hemliga Diplomati och Sverige, 1752–1774* (Lund, Sweden, 1961), French summary; G. Perrault, *Le Secret du roi* (Paris, 1996).

140. AE. CP. Brunswick-Hanovre 52 fol. 141.

141. BN. NAF. 22010 fol. 30.

142. BN. NAF. 22010 fols 76–8.

143. J.F. Bosher, 'The French crisis of 1770', *History*, 57 (1972), pp. 17–30.

144. A.D. Hytier, 'Les Philosophes et le problème de la guerre', *Studies on Voltaire* (1974), pp. 243–8; R. Niklaus, 'The pursuit of peace in the Enlightenment', *Essays on Diderot and the Enlightenment in Honour of Otis Fellows* (Geneva, 1974), pp. 231–45; H. Meyer, 'Voltaire on war and peace', *Studies on Voltaire* (1976); H. Mason, 'Voltaire and war', *British Journal for Eighteenth-Century Studies*, 4 (1981), pp. 125–38.

145. M.L. Perkins, 'Montesquieu on national power and international rivalry', *Studies on Voltaire* (1965), p. 76.

146. I.O. Wade, *The Structure and Form of the French Enlightenment* (2 vols, Princeton, New Jersey, 1977) I, 317–33. See, more generally, E.V. Souleyman, *The Vision of World Peace in Seventeenth and Eighteenth-Century France* (1941).

147. F.S. Ruddy, *International Law in the Enlightenment. The Background of Emmerich de Vattel's Le Droit des Gens* (Dobbs Ferry, New York, 1975).

148. N. Ferrier, 'Les écrivains français et la conquête de la Hollande en 1672', *XVIIe Siècle*, 93 (1971), pp. 112, 114.

149. AE. CP. Aut. 251 fol. 72.

150. E. Zévort, *Le Marquis d'Argenson et la Ministère des affaires étrangères du 18 Novembre 1744 au 10 janvier 1747* (Paris, 1880).

151. AE. CP. Esp. 488 fols 65, 139–41.

152. AE. CP. Esp. 475 fols 76, 116.

153. M. Antoine, *Louis XV* (Paris, 1979), p. 403; Windsor, Royal Archives, Cumberland Papers 43/311.

154. Puysieulx to Richelieu, 4 June 1748, AN. KK. 1372.

155. AE. CP. Aut. 248 fol. 26.

156. AE. CP. Bavière 109 fol. 195.

157. AE. CP. Esp. 523 fols 6, 15, 18; AE. CP. Esp. 527 fol. 235; AE. CP. Esp. 532 fol. 334.

158. AN. KK. 1351 no. 88.

159. AE. CP. Esp. 526 fols 62, 74–6.

160. AE. MD. Ang. 56 fols 21–31.

161. AE. CP. Ang. 432 fols 207–8.

162. BN. NAF. 22010 fol. 40.

163. AN. KK. 1402 p. 234.

164. AE. CP. Ang. 438 fol. 349; AE. CP. Hollande 488 fol. 170; AN. KK. 1402 p. 257.

165. B. du Fraguier, 'Le Duc d'Aiguillon et l'Angleterre', *RHD*, 26 (1912), pp. 607–27; Scott, *British Foreign Policy*, pp. 181–90.

166. Boutaric, *Correspondance secrète*, II, 284.

167. AE. CP. Aut. 295 fol. 8; D. Lerer, *La politique française en Pologne sous Louis XV, 1733–72* (Toulouse, 1929); Scott, 'France and the Polish throne, 1763–64', *Slavonic and East European Review*, 53 (1975); J. Staszewski, 'Le "Secret du Roi" sans mystères', *Acta Poloniae Historica*, 51 (1985), pp. 123–31.

168. AE. CP. Aut. 295 fols 140, 261.

169. S.K. Padover, *Prince Kaunitz and the First Partition of Poland* (PhD, Chicago, 1932).

170. E. Rostworowski, 'La France de Louis XV et la Pologne', *Acta Poloniae Historica*, 22 (1970), pp. 74–5.

171. D. Ransel, *The Politics of Catherinian Russia* (New Haven, Conn., 1975), pp. 17–33.

172. H. Dehérain, 'La mission du Baron de Tott et de Pierre Ruffin auprès du Khan de Crimée de 1767 à 1769', *Revue de l'histoire des colonies françaises* 15 (1923); V. Aksan, 'Ottoman-French Relations, 1739–1768', in S. Kuneralp (ed.), *Studies on Ottoman Diplomatic History I* (Istanbul, 1987), pp. 56–7; Scott, 'Russia as a European Great Power', in R. Bartlett and J.M. Hartley (eds), *Russia in the Age of Enlightenment* (London, 1990), pp. 20–22.

173. Padover, *Kaunitz*, pp. 49–50.

174. Flammermont, pp. 66–7; M. Boutry, 'L'Ambassade du Prince Louis de Rohan à Vienne (1772–1774)', *RHD*, 17 (1903), pp. 229, 241.

175. C.I. Andriescu, 'La France et la politique orientale de Catherine II (d'après

les rapports des ambassadeurs français à St Petersbourg)', *Mélanges de l'Ecole roumaine en France*, 5 (1927), pp. 3–155; L.-H. Labande (ed.), *Un diplomat français à la cour de Catherine II, 1775–1780: Journal intime du chevalier de Corberon* (Paris, 1901).

176. Boutaric, *Correspondance secrète*, II, 497–8.

177. AE. CP. Esp. 535 fol. 149.

178. AE. CP. Esp. 536 fol. 29.

179. AE. CP. Esp. 535 fol. 168.

180. AE. CP. Esp. 536 fol. 174; AE. CP. Esp. 537 fols 31, 147.

181. Boutaric, *Correspondance secrète*, II, 93, 466–7.

182. Boutaric, *Correspondance secrète*, II, 368–9.

183. *Relazioni diplomatiche . . . Francia* II, 187, 195, 209.

184. J.F. Bosher, *French finances, 1770–1795* (Cambridge, 1970); D. Echeverria, *The Maupeou Revolution* (1985).

185. Earl of Bristol to Henry Fox, 7 July 1756, PRO. SP. 92/62.

186. AE. CP. Sardaigne 229 fols 2–3.

187. AE. CP. Esp. 536 fol. 171.

188. H. Bédarida, *Parme et la France de 1748 à 1789* (Paris, 1928) and *Parme dans la Politique Française au XVIIIe siècle* (Paris, 1930).

189. PRO. SP. 78/331 fol. 448.

190. AE. CP. Esp. 532 fol. 43.

191. BN. MF. 7149 p. 102; Vogüé (ed.), *Villars*, V, 371.

192. BVC. 31 fol. 183, Vogüé (ed.), *Villars*, V, 300; BL. Add. 32740 fol. 45.

193. AE. CP. Esp. 532 fols 274–5, 358–62, 367, 384, 387–8.

194. AE. CP. Sardaigne 229 fols 99, 102, 435–6; AE. CP. Aut. 295 fols 54, 251–2; *Relazioni diplomatiche . . . Francia*, II, 146–8; P. de Lapradelle, *La Frontière: étude de droit international* (Paris, 1928), p. 45 n.1; J.F. Noel, 'Les problèmes des frontières entre la France et l'Empire dans la seconde moitié du XVIIIe siècle', *Revue Historique*, 235 (1946), pp. 336–7; N. Jecko, 'L'abbaye de Saint-Hubert et la rivalité politique et économique entre la France et la Maison d'Autriche, 1697–1769', *Annales de l'Institut Archéologique du Luxembourg*, 95 (1965); G. Livet, *Recueil . . . Trèves* (Paris, 1966), pp. 58, 228–46, 254–6, 278–93; P. Waeber, *La Formation du Canton de Genève* (Geneva, 1974), pp. 42–3; H. Ammerich, 'Die Grenzverhandlungen zwischen Frankreich und Pfalz-Zweibrücken in der zweiten Hälfte des 18 Jahrhunderts', *Mitteilungen des Historischen Vereins der Pfalz*, 77 (1979), pp. 231–52; N.G. D'Albissin, *Genèse de la frontière franco-belge. Les variations des limites septentrionales de la France de 1659 à 1789* (Paris, 1979); J. Pallière, 'Le traité du 24 mars 1760 et les nouvelles frontières de la Savoie', in Société Savoienne d'Histoire et d'Archéologie, *Frontières de Savoie* (1986); P. Sahlins, 'Natural frontiers revisited: France's boundaries since the seventeenth century', *American Historical Review* 95 (1990), pp. 1438–41; D. Nordman and J. Revel, 'La formation de l'espace français', in J. Revel (ed.), *Histoire de la France I: L'Espace français* (Paris, 1989), pp. 29–169.

195. AE. CP. Prusse 210 fol. 25.

196. A.C. Carter, *The Dutch Republic in Europe in the Seven Years' War* (1971).

197. AE. CP. Esp. 537 fols 111, 128–9.

198. Scott, 'The importance of Bourbon naval reconstruction to the strategy of Choiseul after the Seven Years War', *International History Review*, 1 (1979), pp. 17–35;

R.J. Singh, *French Diplomacy in the Caribbean and the American Revolution* (Hicksville, New York, 1977), pp. 56–7.

199. J. Tramond, 'La Marine et les réformes de M. de Boynes', *La Revue maritime*, 61 (1925), pp. 153–80.

200. J. Michel, *La Guyane sous l'Ancien Régime* (Paris, 1989).

201. Joseph de Bauffremont, *Journal de campagne dans les pays barbaresques (1766)*, edited by M. Chirac (Paris, 1981).

202. S.P. Sen, *The French in India, 1763–1816* (Calcutta, 1958).

203. P. Prost, *Les forteresses de l'Empire. Fortifications, villes de guerre et arsenaux napoléoniens* (Paris, 1991), p. 40.

Chapter 5: Intervention in America and the policy of Vergennes, 1774–1787

1. AE. CP. Russie 121 fol. 293.

2. See, most recently, D.A. Baugh, 'Withdrawing from Europe: Anglo-French maritime geopolitics', *International History Review*, 20 (1998), pp. 1–32.

3. Boutaric, *Correspondance secrète*, II, 437.

4. J. Flammermont, *Les correspondances des agents diplomatiques étrangers en France avant la Révolution* (Paris, 1896), p. 115.

5. Flammermont, *Correspondances*, p. 102.

6. R.R. Crout, 'In search of a "Just and lasting peace": the treaty of 1783, Louis XVI, Vergennes, and the regeneration of the realm', *International History Review*, 5 (1983), pp. 364–98; J. Hardman, *Louis XVI* (New Haven, Conn., 1993); O.T. Murphy, 'Charles Gravier de Vergennes: profile of an Old Regime diplomat', *Political Science Quarterly*, 83 (1968), pp. 400–18, and 'Napoleon and French Old Regime international politics and diplomacy', *Consortium (1989)* (Tallahassee, Florida, 1990), p. 98.

7. G. Fagniez, 'La politique de Vergennes et la diplomatie de Breteuil, 1774–1787', *Revue Historique*, 140 (1922), pp. 1–25, 161–207.

8. AN. KK. 1393, 18 Jan. 1777, 7 Nov. 1778.

9. E. Buddruss, *Die Französische Deutschlandpolitik, 1756–1789* (Mainz, 1995).

10. AE. CP. Esp. 616 fols 193–4.

11. J. Dull, *A Diplomatic History of the American Revolution* (New Haven, Conn., 1985).

12. AE. CP. Ang. 528 fols 54–5.

13. R.D. Harris, 'French finances and the American war, 1777–1783', *Journal of Modern History*, 48 (1976), pp. 233–58.

14. M. Gómez del Campillo, *El Conde de Aranda en su Embajada a Francia, 1773–1787* (Madrid, 1945).

15. L. Kennett, *The French Forces in America, 1780–1783* (Westport, Conn., 1977).

16. S.P. Sen, *The French in India, 1763–1816* (Calcutta, 1958).

17. P. Fauchille, *La Diplomatie française et la ligue de neutres de 1780 (1776–1783)* (Paris, 1893).

18. Dull, *The French Navy and American Independence: A Study of Arms and Diplomacy, 1774–1787* (Princeton, New Jersey, 1975).

19. A.T. Patterson, *The Other Armada: The Franco-Spanish Attempt to Invade Britain in 1779* (Manchester, 1960).

20. A.P. Stockley, *Britain, France and the peace negotiations of 1782–83* (PhD, Cambridge, 1994).

21. PRO. FO. 27/2 fol. 60.

22. 'Un nouveau Vergennes?', Colloquium at Sorbonne, 1987, proceedings printed in *Revue d'historie diplomatique*, 101 (1987), nos. 3–4; J.F. Labourdette, *Vergennes: ministre principal de Louis XVI* (Paris, 1990).

23. A. Tratchevsky, 'La diplomatie de Vergennes ou la France et l'Allemagne sous Louis XVI', *Revue Historique*, 15 (1881), pp. 50–82. See also G. Grosjean, *La Politique Rhénane de Vergennes* (Paris, 1925).

24. O.T. Murphy, *Charles Gravier, Comte de Vergennes: French Diplomacy in the Age of Revolution, 1719–1787* (Albany, New York, 1982), pp. 473–6.

25. P. Pluchon, *Histoire de la colonisation française internationale. Le Premier empire colonial, des origines à la restauration* (Paris, 1991), pp. 686–8, 715, 737–50, 761.

26. AE. CP. Ang. 522 fols 50, 117–22, 134, 162–3, 401.

27. *Polit. Corr.* 46, 391.

28. AE. CP. Ang. 540 fol. 318; AE. CP. Ang. 547 fols 38–41.

29. *Polit. Corr.* 46, 351.

30. BN. NAF. 6498 fol. 298.

31. Vergennes to Bertin, controller-general, 11 July 1783, BN. NAF. 6498 fol. 298.

32. R. Salomon, *La Politique orientale de Vergennes, 1780–1784* (Paris, 1935).

33. AE. CP. Aut. 348 fol. 70, sup. 23 fol. 75.

34. AE. CP. Russie 116 fols 34–5, 38, 46, 123 fol. 13; AE. CP. Aut. 349 fols 353–4; AE. CP. Turquie 175 fol. 9.

35. AE. CP. Aut. 351 fol. 411.

36. M. Price, *Preserving the Monarchy: The Comte de Vergennes, 1774–1787* (Cambridge, 1995).

37. AE. CP. Aut. 348 fol. 225, suppl. 23 fols 28, 31–6; F. Magnette, *Joseph II et la liberté de l'Escaut* (Paris, 1897); M. Price, *The Comte de Vergennes and Baron de Breteuil: French Politics and Reform in the Reign of Louis XVI* (PhD, Cambridge, 1989), p. 233.

38. Flammermont, *Correspondances*, p. 115.

39. A. Beer (ed.), *Joseph II, Leopold II und Kaunitz* (Vienna, 1873), pp. 122–3.

40. AE. CP. Aut. sup. 23 fol. 35; Mercy, Austrian envoy in Paris, to Kaunitz, 27 Nov. 1784, in Alfred von Arneth and Flammermont (eds), *Correspondance secrète du Comte Mercy-Argenthau avec l'Empereur Joseph et le Prince de Kaunitz* (2 vols, Paris, 1889–91), I, 341. See also G. Grosjean, *La Politique Rhénane de Vergennes* (Paris, 1925).

41. Memoranda of 2 Jan. 1785, AE. CP. Aut. 349 fols 6, 11, 21, 24.

42. AE. CP. Aut. 349 fol. 10.

43. Hardman, *Louis XVI*, pp. 98–9.

44. AE. CP. Aut. 349 fols 33, 52–7.

45. AE. CP. Aut. 349 fol. 35.

46. AE. CP. Aut. sup. 23 fol. 86.

47. AE. CP. Aut. sup. 23 fol. 35.

48. AE. CP. Aut 349 fols 7, 18–19, 23, 283.

49. AE. CP. Aut. 351 fol. 411.

50. The best recent treatment is M.M. Donaghay, *The Anglo-French Negotiations of 1786–1787* (PhD. University of Virginia, 1970). Professor Donaghay has published

a number of articles including 'Calonne and the Anglo-French commercial treaty of 1786', *Journal of Modern History*, 50 (1978), sup. 1157–84, 'The Maréchal de Castries and the Anglo-French commercial negotiations of 1786–1787', *Historical Journal*, 22 (1979), pp. 295–312, 'The ghosts of ruined ships: the commercial treaty of 1786 and the lessons of the past', *Consortium (1981)*, pp. 111–18, 'À propos du traité commercial franco-anglais de 1786', *RHD*, 101 (1987), pp. 371–4, 'The vicious circle: the Anglo-French commercial treaty of 1786 and the Dutch crisis of 1787', *Consortium (1989)*, pp. 447–56.

51. J.C. Riley, 'Dutch investment in France, 1781–1787', *Journal of Economic History*, 33 (1973), pp. 732–60.

52. J.L. van Regemorter, 'Commerce et politique: préparation et négotiation du traité Franco-Russe de 1787', *Cahiers du Monde Russe et Soviétique*, 4 (1963), pp. 230–57; F. Fox, 'Negotiating with the Russians: Ambassador Ségur's mission to Saint Petersburg, 1784–1789', *French Historical Studies*, 7 (1971), pp. 47–71; J. Savant, 'Louis XVI et l'alliance Russe', *La Nouvelle Revue des deux mondes* (1975), pp. 306–24.

53. O.T. Murphy, 'Louis XVI and the pattern and costs of a policy dilemma: Russia and the Eastern Question, 1787–1788', *Consortium (1986)* (Athens, Georgia, 1987), pp. 266–7.

54. AE. CP. Russie 123 fol. 22.

55. AE. CP. Aut. 349 fols 120, 132; AE. CP. Esp. 616 fols 82, 275–6.

56. AE. CP. Ang. 558 fol. 191.

57. A. Cobban, *Ambassadors and Secret Agents: The Diplomacy of the First Earl of Malmesbury at The Hague* (London, 1954); P. Coquelle, *L'alliance franco-hollandaise contre l'Angleterre* (Paris, 1902).

58. Montmorin to ?, 20 Feb. 1787, 'Mélanges', *RHD*, 105 (1991), p. 178.

59. J. Egret, *The French Prevolution, 1787–1788* (Chicago, 1977), pp. 1–35; V.R. Gruder, 'Paths to political consciousness: the Assembly of Notables of 1787 and the "Pre-Revolution" in France', *French Historical Studies*, 13 (1984), pp. 323–55.

60. AE. CP. Prusse 207 fol. 31.

61. AE. CP. Hollande 573 fols 215, 411–13; AE. CP. Hollande 574 fols 17–18, 60–61.

62. Mirabeau to Calonne, July 1786, F. Salleo, 'Mirabeau en Prusse, 1786. Diplomatie parallèle ou agent secret?', *RHD* (1977), p. 347; AE. CP. Ang. 561 fol. 55; AE. CP. Prusse 207 fol. 103.

63. AE. CP. Hollande 574 fol. 541.

64. Comte de Ségur, *Le Maréchal de Ségur* (Paris, 1895), pp. 315–16; Hardman, *Louis XVI*, pp. 100, 128–9.

65. AE. CP. Hollande 574 fol. 411.

66. AE. CP. Prusse 207 fol. 103.

67. B. Stone, *The French Parlements and the Crisis of the Old Regime* (Chapel Hill, North Carolina, 1986), pp. 84–5; M. Price, 'Vergennes and the Baron de Breteuil', p. 166; Duc de Castries, *Le Maréchal de Castries, 1727–1800* (Paris, 1956), pp. 149–52; Ségur, *Ségur*, pp. 319–20; M. Price, 'The Dutch affair and the fall of the *Ancien Régime*, 1784–1787', *Historical Journal*, 38 (1995), pp. 875–905.

68. AE. CP. Prusse, sup. 9 fol. 71.

69. Batzel, *Treaties of Versailles*, pp. 450, 457.

70. AE. CP. Russie 122 fol. 216.

71. AE. CP. Turquie 175 fol. 93.

72. Pluchon, *Colonisation française*, pp. 737–42.

73. *Ibid.*, p. 710.

74. M. Leclère, 'Les reformes de Castries', *Revue des Questions Historiques*, 128 (1937), pp. 28–60; Glete, *Navies and Nations*, pp. 274–6.

75. AE. CP. Aut. 349 fol. 8; Castries, *Castries*, p. 131; Hardman, *Louis XVI*, pp. 73, 79.

76. AE. CP. Ang. 548 fol. 185.

77. M. Duffy, *Soldiers, Sugar and Seapower. The British Expeditions to the West Indies and the War against Revolutionary France* (Oxford, 1987), p. 7; P. Butel, 'Traditions and changes in French Atlantic trade between 1780 and 1830', *Renaissance and Modern Studies*, 30 (1986), p. 136, and 'France, the Antilles, and Europe in the seventeenth and eighteenth centuries: renewals of foreign trade', in J.D. Tracy (ed.), *The Rise of Merchant Empires* (Cambridge, 1990), pp. 164, 172; F. Crouzet, 'Angleterre et France au XVIIIe siècle: essai d'analyse comparée de deux croissances économiques', *Annales*, 21 (1966), pp. 261–3.

78. A. Smith, *An Inquiry into the Nature and Causes of the Wealth of Nations*, ed. R.H. Campbell and A.S. Skinner (Oxford, 1959), p. 586; J. Tarrade, *Le Commerce colonial de la France à la fin de l'Ancien Régime: L'Evolution du régime de "l'Exclusif" de 1763 à 1789* (2 vols, Paris, 1972), I, 33–4.

79. Tarrade, *Commerce colonial*, II, 759; J. Dupâquier (ed.), *Histoire de la population française. II: De la Renaissance à 1789* (Paris, 1988), p. 128.

80. R.W. Unger, 'The tonnage of Europe's merchant fleets, 1300–1800', *American Neptune*, 52 (1992), pp. 260–61.

81. P.P. Hill, *French Perceptions of the Early American Republic, 1783–1793* (Philadelphia, 1988); J. Meyer, 'Les Difficultés du commerce franco-americain vues de Nantes, 1776–1790', *French Historical Studies*, 11 (1979), pp. 159–83; Fohlen, 'The Commercial Failure of France in America', in N.L. Roelker and C.K. Warner (eds), *Two Hundred Years of Franco-American Relations* (Worcester, Mass., 1983), pp. 93–119.

82. Donaghay, 'Textiles and the Anglo-French commercial treaty of 1786', *Textile History*, 13 (1982), pp. 215–22, and 'The exchange of products of the soil and industrial goods in the Anglo-French commercial treaty of 1786', *Journal of European Economic History*, 19 (1990), pp. 377–401.

83. J.-P. Faivre, *L'Expansion française dans le Pacifique* (Paris, 1953); J.E. Martin-Allanic, *Bougainville Navigateur et les découvertes de son temps* (Paris, 1964); S. Chapin, 'Scientific profit from the profit motive: the case of the LaPerouse expedition', *Actes du XIIe Congrès International d'Histoire des Sciences* XI (Paris, 1971), pp. 45–9, and 'The men from across La Manche: French voyages, 1660–1790', in D. Howse (ed.), *Background to Discovery. Pacific Exploration from Dampier to Cook* (Berkeley, Cal., 1990), p. 113; C. Gaziello, *L'Expédition de Lapérouse 1785–1788* (Paris, 1984).

84. W.J. Koenig, *The Burmese Polity, 1752–1819* (Ann Arbor, Michigan, 1990), pp. 22–5; V. Lieberman, 'Political consolidation in Burma under the early Konbaung dynasty, 1750–1820', *Journal of Asian History*, 30 (1996), p. 162.

85. A. Faure, *Les Français en Cochinchine au XVIIIe siècle. Mgr. Pigneau de Béhaine* (Paris, 1891), pp. 123–7; G. Taboulet, *La Geste française en Indochine* (2 vols, Paris, 1955–6) I, 161–279; Pluchon, *Colonisation française*, pp. 760–64.

86. J. Charles-Roux, *L'Isthme et le Canal de Suez* (2 vols, Paris, 1901), I, 110–11, 421–2; F. Charles-Roux, 'La politique française en Egypte à la fin du XVIIIe siècle', *Revue Historique*, 92 (1906); Charles-Roux, *Les Origines de l'expédition d'Egypte* (Paris, 1910); Charles-Roux, *L'Angleterre, l'Isthme de Suez et l'Egypte au XVIIIe siècle* (Paris, 1922); Charles-Roux, *Le Projet française de conquête de l'Egypte sous le règne de Louis XVI* (Cairo, 1929).

87. Duparc (ed.), *Recueil . . . Turquie* (Paris, 1969), p. 473.

88. A. Auzoux, 'La France et Muscate', *RHD*, 22 (1909), pp. 529–36.

89. *Cambridge History of Iran*, VII (Cambridge, 1991), p. 368.

90. F.L. Nussbaum, 'The formation of the New East India Company of Calonne', *American Historical Review*, 38 (1933), pp. 475–97; J. Conan, *La Dernière Compagnie française des Indes, 1785–1875* (Paris, 1942); L. Dermigny, *Cargaisons indiennes: Solier et Cie, 1781–93* (Paris, 1959–60).

91. Charles-Roux, 'La Monarchie française d'Ancien Régime et la question de la Mer Noire', *Revue de la Méditerranée*, 27 (1948), pp. 533, 537; P.W. Bamford, *Forests and French Sea Power, 1660–1789* (Toronto, 1956), pp. 194–205; Duparc (ed.), *Recueil . . . Turquie*, pp. 472–3; F. Bilici, *La Politique française en mer Noire, 1747–1789, vicissitudes d'une implantation* (Istanbul, 1992).

92. AE. MD. Russie 16 fols 279–83; Charles-Roux, *L'Angleterre, L'Isthme*, p. 276.

93. O.T. Murphy, *The Diplomatic Retreat of France and Public Opinion on the Eve of the French Revolution, 1783–1789* (Washington, 1998), p. 175. For a structural interpretation of the period, B. Stone, *The Genesis of the French Revolution: a Global-Historical Interpretation* (Cambridge, 1994).

94. H. Legoherel, *Les Tresoriers généraux de la marine, 1517–1788* (Paris, 1963), pp. 351–5.

95. J. Merrick, 'Politics on pedestals: royal monuments in eighteenth-century France', *French History*, 5 (1991), p. 235.

96. R.R. Palmer, 'The national idea in France before the Revolution', *Journal of the History of Ideas*, 1 (1940), pp. 95–111.

97. AE. CP. Ang. 571 fol. 48.

98. B. Stone, '"Public opinion" and the international standing of the eighteenth-century French state', *Consortium (1992)*, pp. 164–5.

Chapter 6: The impact of Revolution, 1787–1799

1. AE. CP. Ang. 583 fols 171–2.

2. BL. Add. 58920 fol. 105.

3. AE. CP. Esp. 623 fols 196–7; AE. CP. Hollande 574 fol. 411.

4. A. Cobban, *Ambassadors and Secret Agents*, pp. 176–7, 196.

5. Eden to Marquis of Carmarthen, Foreign Secretary, 18 Oct. 1787, enclosing anon. French memorandum, PRO. FO. 27/26 fols 225–30.

6. Eden to Dorset, 22 Dec. 1787, Dorset to Pitt, 8 Nov. 1787, Maidstone, Kent Archive Office C183, 175; AN. AM. B7 454, report from Marianne, agent in Rotterdam, 31 Mar., draft instructions for Priest, envoy to The Hague, 14 May 1788.

7. V.G. Hatalkar, *Relations Between the French and the Marathas, 1668–1815* (Bombay, 1958), pp. 276–7; Faure, *Français en Cochinchine*, pp. 147–84.

8. S.P. Sen, *French in India* (2nd edn, New Delhi, 1971), p. 517.

9. J.B. Gentil, *Memoires sur l'Indoustan ou Empire Mogol* (Paris, 1822), pp. 316–38.

10. Memorandum read to *Conseil d'état* by Count César-Henri de la Luzerne, minister of the marine, 14 Dec. 1788, Hardman, *The French Revolution*, p. 79.

11. AE. CP. Aut. 353 fol. 131.

12. AE. CP. Russie 123 fol. 20.

13. AE. CP. Aut. 353 fols 174–6; AE. CP. Russie 122 fol. 211; AE. CP. Esp. 623 fols 293–4; H. Ragsdale, 'Montmorin and Catherine's Greek project: revolution in French foreign policy', *Cahiers du Monde Russe et Soviétique*, 27 (1986), pp. 27–44; Murphy, 'Louis XVI . . . policy dilemma', *Consortiom 1986*, pp. 264–74.

14. AE. CP. Russie 122, fols 218, 221, 263–5, 296, 308–9, Esp. 623 fol. 283.

15. AE. CP. Esp. 623 fols 198, 200.

16. A. Mousset, *Un témoigne ignoré de la Révolution: Le Comte de Fernan Nuñez, Ambassadeur d'Espagne à Paris, 1787–1791* (Paris, 1924), pp. 188–92; AE. CP. Esp. 626 fol. 9; AE. CP. Russie 122 fol. 320.

17. AE. CP. Aut. 353 fol. 210.

18. AE. CP. Ang. 566 fol. 309.

19. AE. CP. Aut. 357 fols 78–9.

20. AE. CP. Prusse 210 fols 58–9.

21. AE. CP. Prusse 210 fol. 67.

22. AE. CP. Prusse sup. 9 fols 82–3; AE. CP. Ang. 566 fol. 196.

23. *London Chronicle*, 12 Mar. 1757.

24. Earl of Bristol to Pitt, 13 Apr. 1757, PRO. SP. 92/65.

25. Sturgill, 'French army's budget', pp. 125, 127, 132; *Correspondance secrète du Comte Mercy-Argenthau*, II, 221.

26. AE. CP. Esp. 626 fols 241, 267.

27. AE. CP. Esp. 623 fol. 359.

28. *Polit. Corr.* 46, 460.

29. AE. CP. Esp. 626 fol. 27.

30. Price, 'The "Ministry of the hundred hours": a reappraisal', *French History*, 3 (1990), pp. 317–39.

31. AE. CP. Aut. 358 fol. 106; AE. CP. Russie 130 fols 203–4.

32. AE. CP. Aut. 357 fol. 283.

33. J.H. Rose, 'The Comte d'Artois and Pitt in December 1789', *English Historical Review*, 30 (1915), pp. 322–4.

34. Mousset, *Fernan Nuñez*, pp. 201–2.

35. AE. CP. Ang. 573 fols 50, 173.

36. AE. CP. Ang. 573 fols 115–16; *AP*, 15, 510–11.

37. *AP* 15, 518, 530, 559; B. Rothaus, 'The war and peace prerogative as a constitutional issue during the first two years of the Revolution, 1789–91', *PWSF 1974*, pp. 120–38. This is based on his *The Emergence of Legislative Control over Foreign Policy in the Constituent Assembly, 1789–91* (PhD, Wisconsin, 1968).

38. AE. CP. Esp. 629 fols 7–19.

39. AE. CP. Aut. 360 fol. 37.

40. AE. CP. Esp. 629 fols 231–7, 264.

41. PRO. 30/8/139 fols 123–8.

42. AE. CP. Esp. 629 fols 283, 296–7, 355, 376.

43. AE. CP. Ang. 576 fols 228, 235.

44. AE. CP. Ang. 577 fol. 112.

45. AE. CP. Ang. 578 fols 191, 235, 253–7; AE. CP. Ang. 579, fols 15–19, 37, 66.

46. AE. CP. Ang. 579 fols 71–2; A. Foucrier, 'Rivaltés européennes dans le Pacifique: l'affaire de Nootka Sound, 1789–1790', *Annales Historiques de la Révolution Française*, 307 (1997), pp. 24–5.

47. *AP* 15, 663.

48. AE. CP. Aut. 359 fol. 237.

49. AE. CP. Ang. 573 fols 249–5.

50. AE. CP. Aut. 360 fol. 110.

51. Hardman, *Louis XVI*, pp. 185–97.

52. A. Beer (ed.), *Joseph II, Leopold II und Kaunitz. Ihr Briefwechsel* (Vienna, 1873), pp. 405–6.

53. Aymes, 'Spain and the French Revolution', p. 65.

54. AE. CP. Ang. 579 fol. 111.

55. P. Muret, 'L'affaire des princes possessionnées d'Alsace et les origines du conflit entre la Révolution et l'Empire', *Revue d'Histoire Moderne et Contemporaine* I (1899–1900).

56. H.A. Goetz-Bernstein, *La Diplomatie de la Gironde. Jacques-Pierre Brissot* (Paris, 1912); E. Ellery, *Brissot de Warville: a study in the history of the French Revolution* (Boston, 1915).

57. M. Braubach, 'Frankreichs Rheinpolitik im Zeitalter der französischen Revolution', *Archiv für Politik und Geschichte*, 8 (1927), pp. 172–86; B.J. Kreuzberg, *Die politischen und wirtschaflichen Beziehungen des Kurstaates Trier zu Frankreich in der zwieten Hälfte des 18 Jahrhunderts bis zum Ausbruch der französischen Revolution* (Bonn, 1932); A. Sprunck, 'Die französischen Emigranten im kurfürstentum Trier', *Kurtrierisches Jahrbuch*, 6 (1966), pp. 133–42; J. Tulard, 'La Diplomatie française et l'Allemagne de 1789 à 1799', in J. Voss (ed.), *Deutschland und die französische Revolution* (Munich, 1983), pp. 43–8; E. Oberländer, ' "Ist die Kaiserin von Russland Garant des Westphälischen Friedens?" Der Kurfürst von Trier, die französische Revolution und Katharina II, 1789–1792', *Jahrbücher für Geschichte Osteuropas*, 35 (1987), pp. 219–22; E. Buddruss, 'Die Deutchlandpolitik der Französischen Revolution zwischen Traditionen und revolutionärem Bruch', in K.O. Aretin and K. Härter (eds.), *Revolution und Konservatives Beharren. Das Alte Reich und die französische Revolution* (Mainz, 1990), pp. 145–50.

58. *Recueil . . . Trèves*, pp. 310–14; *Recueil . . . Mayence*, pp. 270–6; *AP* 37, 410–11.

59. T.C.W. Blanning, *The Origins of the French Revolutionary Wars* (Harlow, Essex, 1986), pp. 96–123. See also J.H. Clapham, *The Causes of the War of 1792* (Cambridge, 1892); P. Howe, 'Belgian influence on French policy, 1789–1793', *Consortium 1986*, pp. 213–22.

60. *AP* 37, 89.

61. *AP* 37, pp. 491–3.

62. AE. CP. Ang. sup. 29 fols. 189–240; G. Pallain, *La Mission de Talleyrand à Londres en 1792. Correspondance inédite de Talleyrand avec le Département des Affaires Étrangères* (Paris, 1889).

63. *AP* 37, p. 470.

64. G. Wolf, 'Le Marquis Scipion de Chambonas, Ministre des Affaires Étrangères de

Louis XVI', *Annales historiques de la Révolution Française*, no. 259 (1985), pp. 25–45, 'Le Dernier Ministère Feuillant et la politique étrangère du Marquis Scipion de Chambonas', *Actes du 110e Congrès National des Sociétés Savantes, Montpellier 1985: Hist. Mod. et Cont.* (Paris, 1986), I, 265–71, 'Juin 1792: Faut-il négocier avec la Prusse ou avec l'Autriche?', *L'Information historique*, 49 (1987), pp. 191–3; 'Un oublié de la diplomatie sous la Révolution Française. Le Marquis Scipion de Chambonas', *Bulletin de la Société des Sciences Historiques et Naturelles de l'Yonne*, 123 (1991), pp. 76–9; AE. CP. Ang. 581 fols 218–19; *Recueil . . . Mayence*, pp. 283–4; G. Grosjean, 'Les Relations diplomatiques de la France avec Les Deux-Siciles de 1789 à 1793', *La Révolution française*, 15 (1888), pp. 28–31.

65.   F. Masson, *Le département des affaires étrangères pendant la Révolution* (Paris, 1877).

66.   H.A. Barton, 'The origins of the Brunswick Manifesto', *French Historical Studies*, 5 (1967), pp. 146–69.

67.   W.S. Cormack, *Revolutionary and Political Conflict in the French Navy, 1789–1794* (Cambridge, 1995) and 'Legitimate authority in revolution and war: the French navy in the West Indies, 1787–1793', *International History Review*, 18 (1996), pp. 1–27.

68.   AE. CP. Ang. 582 fol. 248; AE. CP. Ang. 583 fol. 134; S. Tassier, 'Aux origines de la première coalition: le ministre Le Brun Tondu', *Revue du Nord*, 36 (1954), pp. 263–72.

69.   Rothaus, 'Justice from the fall of the monarchy to the September massacres: the case of the Count of Montmorin', *PWSF*, 14 (1987), pp. 154–7.

70.   AE. CP. Ang. 583 fols 211–12, 302, 361–3; AE. CP. Ang. 586 fol. 79.

71.   AE. CP. Ang. 582 fols 51, 167.

72.   *AP* 53, 472–4.

73.   Grosjean, 'Relations', pp. 37–8.

74.   AE. CP. Ang. 584 fol 52.

75.   Grosjean, 'Relations', pp. 39–40.

76.   *AP* 56, 110–17; *AP* 57, 16–25; *AP* 58, 112–23.

77.   Black, *British Foreign Policy in an Age of Revolutions, 1783–1793* (Cambridge, 1994), pp. 406–71.

78.   *Recueil . . . Venise*, p. 312; *Recueil . . . Diète Germanique*, p. 380.

79.   BL. Add. 58920 fol. 108.

80.   J.P. McLoughlin, 'Ideology and conquest: the question of proselytism and expansion in the French Revolution, 1789–1793', *Canadian Historical Papers* (1976), pp. 49–66.

81.   AE. CP. Ang. 578 fol. 216; AE. CP. Ang. 581 fol. 49.

82.   AE. CP. Ang. 580 fol. 267.

83.   AE. CP. Ang. 581 fol. 233.

84.   AE. CP. Ang. 581 fol. 50.

85.   AE. CP. Ang. 581 fols 89, 280, 341; AE. CP. Hollande 583 fol. 298.

86.   BL. Add. 59021 fol. 16; Broomhall, Fife, Elgin Papers, 60/1/184.

87.   AE. CP. Ang. 582 fol. 113; L. and M. Frey, '"The reign of the charlatans is over". The French revolutionary attack on diplomatic practice', *Journal of Modern History*, 65 (1993), pp. 706–44.

88.   AE. CP. Ang. 583 fol. 172. For Talleyrand's criticism, Ang. 585 fol. 182.

89.   AE. CP. Ang. 582 fol. 256.

90.   M. Degos, 'Les Consulats de France sous la Révolution des États

Barbaresques . . . en Italie . . . en Espagne et au Portugal', *RHD*, 105 (1991), pp. 102–33, 107 (1993), pp. 243–77, 108 (1994), pp. 151–80.

91. F. Cadilhon, 'La Diplomatie pontificale en France à la fin de l'Ancien Régime, 1785–1791', *RHD*, 107 (1993), pp. 215–25.

92. F. Attar, *La Revolution française déclare la guerre à l'Europe* (Brussels, 1992).

93. K.A. Roider, *Baron Thugut and Austria's Response to the French Revolution* (Princeton, 1987).

94. G. Savage, 'Favier's heirs: the French Revolution and the *Secret du Roi*', *Historical Journal*, 41 (1998), pp. 225–58.

95. *Recueil . . . Diète Germanique*, pp. 376–7; S.S. Biro, *The German Policy of Revolutionary France. A Study in French Diplomacy during the War of the First Coalition, 1792–1797* (2 vols, Cambridge, Mass., 1957); P. Sahlins, *Boundaries. The Making of France and Spain in the Pyrenees* (Berkeley, 1989), p. 182.

96. AE. CP. Ang. 576 fol. 227.

97. A. Sorel, *L'Europe et la révolution française* (Paris, 1946); A. Sorel, *Europe and the French Revolution* (London, 1969).

98. D.E. Kaiser, *Politics and War. European Conflict from Philip II to Hitler* (Cambridge, Mass., 1990), pp. 203–10.

99. AE. CP. Ang. 581 fols 218–19, 277.

100. Blanning, *The French Revolutionary Wars, 1787–1802* (London, 1996).

101. A. Aulard, 'La Diplomatie du premier Comité de salut public', in *Études et leçons sur la révolution française*, 3rd series (Paris, 1902), pp. 51–240; A. Sorel, 'La Diplomatie française et le comité de salut public', *Revue Historique*, 17 and 18 (1881–2).

102. Blanning, *The French Revolution in Germany: Occupation and Resistance in the Rhineland, 1792–1802* (Oxford, 1983).

103. M. Bouloiseau, 'L'Organisation de l'Europe selon Brissot et les Girondins, à la fin de 1792', *Annales Historiques de la Révolution Française*, 57 (1985), pp. 290–94.

104. R. Guyot, *Le Directoire et la paix de l'Europe des traités de Bâle à la deuxième coalition, 1795–1799* (Paris, 1912); B. Narbonne, *La Diplomatie du directoire et Bonaparte, d'après les papiers inédits de Reubell* (Paris, 1951); G.D. Homan, *Jean-François Reubell: French Revolutionary, Patriot, and Director, 1747–1807* (The Hague, 1971).

105. P. Schroeder, *The Transformation of European Politics, 1763–1848* (Oxford, 1994), pp. 11–12.

106. M. Hutt, *Chouannerie and Counter-Revolution* (2 vols, Cambridge, 1983).

107. C. Parry (ed.), *The Consolidated Treaty Series*, vol. 64 (New York, 1969), pp. 55–8; M. Lyons, *France under the Directory* (Cambridge, 1975), p. 200.

108. M. Elliott, *Partners in Revolution: The United Irishmen and France* (New Haven, 1982); D. O'Carroll, 'France and the Irish revolutionary movement of the 1790s', in *L'influence de la Révolution française sur les armées en France, en Europe et dans le monde* (1991) II, 119–32.

109. A. Silvera, 'The origins of the French expedition to Egypt in 1798', *Islamic Quarterly*, 18 (1974), pp. 21–30.

110. J.C. Herold, *Bonaparte in Egypt* (London, 1962), pp. 3–4. See, more generally, H. Laurens, 'Bonaparte et l'Islam', *La Revolution française et l'Orient* (Paris, 1989), pp. 39–47, and *L'Expédition d'Egypte, 1798–1801. Bonaparte et l'Islam. Le choc des cultures* (Paris, 1989).

111. J.W. Marcum, 'Catherine II and the French Revolution: a reappraisal', *Canadian Slavonic Papers*, 16 (1974), pp. 187–202.

Chapter 7: The foreign policy of Napoleon, 1799–1815

1. Frey and Frey, '"Reign of charlatans"', p. 740.
2. W.B. Cohen, *The French Encounter with Africans: White Response to Blacks, 1530–1880* (Bloomington, Indiana, 1980), p. 119.
3. H. Ragsdale, *Détente in the Napoleonic Era* (Lawrence, Kansas, 1980).
4. R.B. Holtman, *Napoleonic Propaganda* (Baton Rouge, Louisiana, 1950), p. 24; C. Prendergast, *Napoleon and History Painting: Antoine-Jean Gros's 'La Bataille d'Eylau'* (New York, 1997).
5. E.A. Whitcomb, *Napoleon's Diplomatic Service* (Durham, North Carolina, 1979); M.S. Chrisawn, 'A military bull in a diplomatic China shop: General Jean Lanne's mission to Lisbon, 1802–1804', *Portuguese Studies Review*, 3 (1993–4), pp. 46–67.
6. F. Boyer, 'Les Résponsabilités de Napoléon dans le transfert à Paris des oeuvres d'art de l'étranger', *Revue d'histoire moderne et contemporaine* 11 (1964), pp. 241–62; M.L. Turner, 'French art confiscations in the Roman Republic, 1798', *Consortium* (1980), pp. 43–51.
7. S. Burrows, 'Culture and misperception: the law and the press in the outbreak of war in 1803', *International History Review*, 18 (1996), p. 815.
8. S. Woolf, *Napoleon's Integration of Europe* (London, 1991).
9. E. Driault, *Napoléon et l'Europe: la politique extérieure du premier consul, 1800–1803* (Paris, 1910).
10. P. Schroeder, 'Napoleon's foreign policy: a criminal enterprise', *Consortium (1989)* (Tallahassee, Florida, 1990), pp. 105–6, and *The Transformation of European Politics*, e.g. pp. 396–412. A much more positive recent account is offered by R.M. Epstein, 'Revisiting Napoleon: for and against', *Consortium 1998*.
11. J.-P. Bertaud, *Bonaparte et le duc d'Enghien* (Paris, 1972).
12. H.C. Deutsch, *The Genesis of Napoleonic Imperialism* (Cambridge, Mass., 1938).
13. O. Connelly, *Napoleon's Satellite Kingdoms* (New York, 1966); S. Woolf, *Napoleon's Integration of Europe* (London, 1991).
14. E. Driault, *La Politique Orientale de Napoléon, Sébastiani et Gardane, 1806–1808* (Paris, 1904), pp. 26–7.
15. A. Latreille, *Napoléon et la Saint-Siège, 1801–1808: L'Ambassade du Cardinal Fesch à Rome* (Paris, 1935).
16. G.C. Bond, 'Louis Bonaparte and the collapse of the Kingdom of Holland', *Consortium (1974)* (1975), pp. 141–53.
17. For an emphasis on a more hesitant approach to territorial expansion by Napoleon, M. Broers, *Europe under Napoleon, 1799–1815* (London, 1996), p. 145.
18. J. Mistler, 'Hambourg sous l'occupation française: observations au sujet du blocus continental', *Francia* 1 (1973), pp. 451–66.
19. H.T. Parker, 'Toward understanding Napoleon, or did Napoleon have a conscience?', *Consortium (1997)* (Tallahassee, Fla., 1998), p. 208.
20. J.R. Aymes, *La Guerre d'Indépendance Espagnole, 1808–1814* (Paris, 1973); D.W. Alexander, *Rod of Iron: French Counterinsurgency Policy in Aragon during the Peninsular War* (Wilmington, Delaware, 1985).
21. J. Gill, 'What do they intend? Austrian war aims in 1809', *Consortium (1996)* (Tallahassee, Fla., 1997), pp. 295–303.
22. P. Schroeder, 'The enduring rivalry between France and the Habsburg monarchy,

1715–1918', in W.R. Thompson (ed.), *The Evolution of Great Power Rivalries* (Columbia, South Carolina, 1999).

23. S. Askenasy, *Napoléon et la Pologne* (Brussels, 1925).

24. M. Jones, 'Sebastiani: soldier, diplomat', *Consortium (1996)* (Tallahassee, Fla., 1997), pp. 213–15.

25. S.S. Tatistcheff, *Alexandre Ier et Napoléon d'après leur correspondance inédite, 1801–1812* (Paris, 1891).

26. H.T. Parker, 'Why did Napoleon invade Russia? A study in motivation and the interrelations of personality and social structure', *Journal of Military History*, 54 (1990), pp. 131–46.

27. E. Weis, 'Bayern und Frankreich in der Zeit des Konsulats und des Ersten Empiere, 1799–1815', *Historische Zeitschrift*, 237 (1983), pp. 559–95.

28. J.W. Rooney, 'Continuity: French foreign policy of the First Restoration', *Consortium (1986)* (Athens, Georgia, 1987), pp. 275–88; V.J. Puryear, *Napoleon and the Dardanelles* (Berkeley, Cal., 1951), p. 403.

29. F. Crouzet, 'The second Hundred Years War: some reflections', *French History* 10 (1996), p. 447.

Chapter 8: France and the world

1. L. Bergeron, *Banquiers, négociants et manufacturiers parisiens du Directoire à l'Empire* (Paris, 1978), pp. 272–8.

2. M. Giraud, *A History of French Louisiana. I: The Reign of Louis XIV, 1698–1715* (French edn, Paris, 1953; trans. and repr. Baton Rouge, Louisiana, 1974), pp. 39–41, 45, 214, 218–21, 329, 353, and *II: Years of Transition, 1715–1717* (Baton Rouge, Louisiana, 1993), pp. 107–9, 155–6, 175; J. Higginbotham, *Old Mobile. Fort Louis de la Louisiane, 1702–1711* (Mobile, Alabama, 1977).

3. M. Giraud, *La Louisiane après le Système de Law, 1721–23* (Paris, 1974), and *A History of French Louisiana. V: The Company of the Indies, 1723–1731* (Baton Rouge, Louisiana, 1991), pp. 404, 419.

4. D. Van der Cruyse, *Louis XIV et le Siam* (Paris, 1991), p. 419.

5. S. Das, *Myths and Realities of French Imperialism in India, 1763–1783* (New York, 1992), p. 193.

6. A. Martineau, *Bussy et l'Inde française* (Paris, 1935).

7. A. Ray, 'France in Madagascar, 1642–1674', *Calcutta Historical Journal*, 6 (1982), pp. 33–63.

8. V.G. Hatalkar, *Relations between the French and the Marathas, 1668–1815* (Bombay, 1958), p. 273.

9. AE. CP. Ang. 451 fol. 481; AE. CP. Ang. 455 fol. 5.

10. AE. CP. Ang. 429 fol. 15.

11. J.F. Bosher, *Business and Religion in the Age of New France, 1600–1760* (Toronto, 1994).

12. P.A. Goddard, 'Christianization and civilization in seventeenth-century French colonial thought' (D.Phil., Oxford, 1990), pp. 278, 304; J.F. Bosher, 'The imperial environment of French trade with Canada, 1660–1685', *English Historical Review*, 108 (1993), pp. 77–8, and 'The Gaigneur clan in the seventeenth-century Canada

trade', in O.U. Janzen (ed.), *Merchant Organization and Maritime Trade in the North Atlantic, 1660–1815* (St John's, Newfoundland, 1998), pp. 31, 35.

13. C.A. Brasseaux, 'The image of Louisiana and the failure of voluntary French emigration, 1683–1731', and G.R. Conrad, 'Immigration forcé: a French attempt to populate Louisiana, 1717–1720', both *Proceedings of the Fourth Annual Meeting of the French Colonial Historical Society* (1979).

14. J.N. Biraben, 'Le Peuplement du Canada français', *Annales de démographie historique* (Paris, 1966), pp. 104–39; J. Dupâquier (ed.), *Histoire de la Population Française. II: De la Renaissance à 1789* (Paris, 1988), pp. 125–7.

15. P.N. Moogk, 'Reluctant exiles: the problems of colonisation in French North America', *William and Mary Quarterly*, 46 (1989), pp. 463–505.

16. J. Roach, 'Body of law. The Sun King and the Code Noir', in S.E. Melzer and K. Norberg (eds), *From the Royal to the Republican Body. Incorporating the Political in Seventeeth and Eighteenth-Century France* (Berkeley, Cal., 1998), pp. 113–30.

17. G.M. Hall, *Africans in Colonial Louisiana: The Development of Afro-Creole Culture in the Eighteenth Century* (Baton Rouge, Louisiana, 1992).

18. D. Miquelon, 'Jean-Baptiste Colbert's "compact colony policy" revisited: the tenacity of an idea', in P. Galloway (ed.), *Proceedings of the Seventeenth Meeting of the French Colonial History Society* (Lanham, Maryland, 1993), pp. 12–33.

19. Das, *Myths and Realities*, e.g. pp. 6–7, 275.

20. *Ibid.*, p. 276.

21. J.M. Lafont, 'L'Inde et la France en 1781–1783', *Rencontre avec l'Inde*, 16 (1987), pp. 58–72; 17 (1988), pp. 5–30; 18 (1989), pp. 51–96.

22. J.M. Lafont, 'Some aspects of the relations between Tipu Sultan and the French', in B.S. Ali (ed.), *Tipu Sultan. A Great Martyr* (Bangalore, 1993), p. 79.

23. O. Prakash, *European Commercial Enterprise in Pre-Colonial India* (Cambridge, 1998), p. 79. On India see, more generally, P. Haudrère, *La Compagnie française des Indes au XVIIIe siècle, 1719–1795* (Paris, 1989).

24. P.H. Boulle, 'French mercantilism, commercial companies and colonial profit-ability', in L. Blusse and F. Gaastra (eds), *Companies and Trade* (The Hague, 1981), pp. 97–117; O. Pétré-Grenouilleau, 'Dynamique sociale et croissance. À propos du prétendu retard du capitalisme maritime français', *Annales*, 52 (1997), pp. 1263–74.

25. T.J. Schaeper, *The French Council of Commerce* (Columbus, Ohio 1983); P. Haudrère, 'Un aspect des relations entre le pouvoir royal et le grand commerce maritime au XVIIIe siècle: les Commissaires du Roi auprès de la Compagnie française des Indes, 1720–1770', *L'Information Historique* (Dec. 1976), pp. 221–5.

26. M. Giraud, *Le Métis canadien: Son rôle dans l'histoire des provinces de l'Ouest* (Paris, 1945); H.A. Innis, *The Fur Trade in Canada* (2nd edn, Toronto, 1956); W.J. Eccles, *Canada under Louis XIV, 1663–1701* (Toronto, 1964); A.J. Ray, *Indians in the Fur Trade, 1660–1870* (Toronto, 1974); J. Brown (ed.), *The Fur Trade Revisited* (Lansing, Michigan, 1994).

27. J.G. Clark, *New Orleans, 1718–1812: An Economic History* (Baton Rouge, Louisiana, 1970); J.F. Bosher, 'Government and private interests in New France', *Canadian Public Administration*, 10 (1967), pp. 110, 124; D.R. Farrell, 'Private profit and public interest: individual gain, state policy and French colonial expansion', *PWSF*, 14 (1987), pp. 70–77.

28. AN. AM. B7 274, 21 Feb.

29. P. Masson, *Histoire du commerce français dans le Levant au XVIIIe siècle* (Paris, 1911), p. 94; Erdbrink, *On the Threshold of Felicity*, p. 208.

30. N. Svoronos, *Le Commerce de Salonique au XVIIIe siècle* (Paris, 1956), p. 168.

31. K. Banks, '"Lente et assez fâcheuse Traversée": Navigation and the Transatlantic French Empire, 1713–1763', *Proceedings of the Twentieth Meeting of the French Colonial Historical Society* (1997), pp. 92–4; W.E. Dunn, *Spanish and French Rivalry in the Gulf Region of the United States, 1678–1702* (Austin, Texas, 1917); H. Folmer, *Franco-Spanish Rivalry in North America, 1524–1763* (Glendale, California, 1953).

32. C. Manning, *Fortunés à faire. The French in Asian Trade, 1719–48* (Aldershot, Hants., 1996); A. Sinha, 'French trade in India in the XVIIIth Century', in *Indo-French Relations: History and Perspectives* (New Delhi, 1990), pp. 37–50.

33. AN. AM. B7 365, 13 May 1748.

34. J.F. Bosher, 'The French government's motives in the *Affaire du Canada*, 1761–1763', *English Historical Review*, 96 (1981), p. 72.

35. J. Meyer, 'Stratégies navales et terrestres: domaines complémentaires ou indépendantes? Le cas de l'Ancien Régime', *Le Soldat, la stratégie, la mort, Mélanges André Corvisier* (Paris, 1989), pp. 74–89; D. Gerhard, 'Kontinentalpolitik und Kolonialpolitik im Frankreich des ans gehenden ancien régime', *Historishe Zeitschrift*, 147 (1933), pp. 21–31.

36. J.M. Black, *Britain as a Military Power, 1688–1815* (London, 1999), pp. 109–13.

37. R. Chartrand, *The French Soldier in Colonial America* (Ottawa, 1984); W.J. Eccles, 'The social, economic, and political significance of the military establishment in New France', in Eccles, *Essays on New France* (Toronto, 1987), pp. 110–24; A. Greer, *The People of New France* (Toronto, 1997), pp. 111–14.

38. G. Debien, *Les Esclaves aux Antilles Française: XVII–XVIII Siècle* (Basse-Terre, Guadeloupe, 1974); R.L. Stein, *The French Slave Trade in the Eighteenth Century: An Old Regime Business* (Madison, Wisconsin, 1979); J. Tarrade, *Le Commerce colonial de la France à la fin de l'Ancien Régime* (Paris, 1972) II, 759. See, more generally, W.B. Cohen, *The French Encounter with Africans: White Response to Blacks, 1530–1880* (Bloomington, Indiana, 1980) and E. Saugéra, *Bordeaux port négrier. XVIIIe–XIXe siècles. Chronologie, économie, idéologie* (Paris, 1995); J. Dupâquier (ed.), *Histoire de la Population Française. II: De la Renaissance à 1789* (Paris, 1988), p. 127.

39. P. de Villette-Mursay, *Mes Campagnes de mer sous Louis XIV*, ed. by Michel Vergé-Franceschi (Paris, 1991), p. 170.

40. AE. CP. Esp. 533 fols 123–5.

41. AN. AM. B1 32 fols 372–3; M. Giraud, *A History of French Louisiana. II: Years of Transition, 1715–1717* (Baton Rouge, Louisiana, 1993), p. 181.

42. E.A.H. John, *Storms Brewed in Other Men's Worlds: The Confrontation of Indians, Spanish and French in the Southwest, 1540–1795* (College Station, Texas, 1975).

43. Murphy, *Vergennes*, p. 454.

44. R. Gaston, 'La France et la politique commerciale de l'Espagne au XVIIIe siècle', *Revue d'Histoire moderne et contemporaine*, 6 (1959), p. 287.

45. AE. CP. Esp. 537 fol. 258.

46. AE. CP. Esp. 506 fol. 62.

47. J.-F. Labourdette, *La nation française à Lisbonne de 1669 à 1790: entre colbertisme et libéralisme* (Paris, 1988).

48. AN. AM. B7 113.

49. AN. AM. B7 123 pp. 3–4.

50. L. Vignols, 'L'asiento française, 1701–1713, et anglais, 1713–1750, et le commerce franco-espagnol vers 1700 à 1730', *Revue d'histoire economique et sociale*, 17 (1929), pp. 403–36.

51. AN. AM. B7 123, pp. 53, 215, 286–7; G. Rambert, 'La France et la politique commerciale de l'Espagne au XVIIIe siècle', *Revue d'Histoire moderne et contemporaine* (1959), pp. 269–83.

52. *Sbornik*, 75, 372.

53. AE. CP. Ang. 288 fol. 12.

54. AE. CP. Esp. 419 fols 181–8.

55. AE. MD. Ang. 51 fol. 180; AE. CP. Esp. 522 fol. 31; AN. AM. B7 349, 10 Aug. 1744.

56. AE. CP. Ang. 582 fols 137, 167, 222.

57. AE. CP. Ang. 582 fol. 225; AE. CP. Ang. 583 fol. 49.

58. H.H. Kaplan, 'Russia's impact on the industrial revolution in Great Britain during the second half of the eighteenth century: the significance of international commerce', *Forschungen zur osteuropäischen Geschichte*, 29 (1981), p. 93. For limited trade earlier in the century, A. Kraatz, *La Compagnie française de Russie: Histoire du commerce franco-russe aux XVIIe et XVIIIe siècles* (Paris, 1993); AN. AM. B7 285, 3 Jan. 1724; BN NAF. 22009 fol. 10, *re* 1756.

59. V.T. Harlow, *The Founding of the Second British Empire, 1763–1793* (2 vols, London, 1952–64).

60. *AP* 37, 152.

61. S.P. Sen, *The French in India, 1763–1816* (Calcutta, 1958), pp. 530, 525–6.

62. C.L.R. James, *The Black Jacobins: Toussaint L'Ouverture and the San Domingo Revolution* (London, 1980); D.P. Geggus, 'The Haitian Revolution', in F.W. Knight and C.A. Palmer (eds), *The Modern Caribbean* (Chapel Hill, North Carolina, 1989), pp. 21–50.

63. J. Pachoński and R.K. Wilson, *Poland's Caribbean Tragedy. A Study of Polish Legions in the Haitian War of Independence, 1802–1803* (New York, 1986).

64. R.L. Tignor (ed.), *Napoleon in Egypt. Al-Jabarti's Chronicle of the French Occupation, 1798* (Princeton, New Jersey, 1993), pp. 154, 160–61; A. Palluel-Guillard, 'Napoléon et les Indes', in *L'Inde, la France, la Savoie. Le Général de Boigne* (Chambéry, France 1997), pp. 87–108.

65. Contre Amiral Sevaistre, 'Missions françaises en Perse en 1805', *RHD* (1996), pp. 191–200.

66. D.M. Lang, *The Last Years of the Georgian Monarchy, 1658–1832* (New York, 1957), pp. 208–9.

67. P. Galloway, 'Debriefing explorers: Amerindian information in the Delisles' mapping of the southeast', in G.M. Lewis (ed.), *Cartographic Encounters. Perspectives on Native American Mapmaking and Map Use* (Chicago, 1998), pp. 223–37.

68. M. Pelletier, 'La Martinique et La Guadeloupe au lendemain du Traité de Paris. L'oeuvre des ingénieurs géographes', *Chronique d'histoire maritime*, 9 (1984), pp. 22–30.

69. C. Fick, *The Making of Haiti: The Saint Domingue Revolution from Below* (Knoxville, 1991), p. 27.

70. M. Giraud, *A History of French Louisiana. V: The Company of the Indies, 1723–1731* (Baton Rouge, Louisiana, 1991), p. 317.

71. Goddard, 'Christianization and civilization', pp. 262, 364.

Chapter 9: Conclusions

1. For recent work casting valuable light on aspects of this process, J.L. Rosenthal, *The Fruits of Revolution. Property Rights, Litigation and French Agriculture, 1700–1860* (Cambridge, 1992); H.G. Brown, *War, Revolution and the Bureaucratic State. Politics and Army Administration in France, 1791–1799* (Oxford, 1995); W. Doyle, *Venality: The Sale of Offices in Eighteenth-Century France* (Oxford, 1996); Ken Alder, *Engineering the Revolution: Arms and Enlightenment in France, 1763–1815* (Princeton, 1997). The financial shift can best be approached through J.F. Bosher, *French Finances 1770–1795. From Business to Bureaucracy* (Cambridge, 1970).

2. Hanover, Niedersächsisches Hauptstaatsarchiv, Calenberg Brief Archiv, 24 Nr. 2009 fol. 25, *re* 1742.

3. P. Mathias and P.K. O'Brien, 'Taxes in Britain and France, 1715–1810: a comparison of the social and economic incidence of taxes collected for the central governments', *Journal of European Economic History*, 5 (1976), pp. 601–50.

4. M. Bertrand, *Suffren. De Saint-Tropez aux Indes* (Paris, 1991), pp. 311–12.

5. J.F. Bosher, 'The French government's motives in the *Affaire du Canada*, 1761–1763', *English Historical Review*, 96 (1981), p. 69.

6. D. Hudson, 'The Parlementary crisis of 1763 in France and its consequences', *Canadian Journal of History*, 7 (1970), pp. 97–117.

7. D.R. Weir, 'Tontines, public finance, and revolution in France and England, 1688–1789', and E.N. White, 'Was there a solution to the Ancien Régime's financial dilemma?', *Journal of Economic History*, 49 (1989), pp. 124, 545–68.

8. J.F. Bosher, 'French colonial society in Canada', *Transactions of the Royal Society of Canada*, 4th series, 19 (1981), p. 156.

9. R. Szostak, *The Role of Transportation in the Industrial Revolution. A Comparison of England and France* (Montreal, 1991).

10. I. Wallerstein, *The Modern World-System II: Mercantilism and the Consolidation of the European World-Economy, 1600–1750* (New York, 1980), pp. 75–125.

11. J. Pritchard, *Louis XV's Navy 1748–1762. A Study of Organisation and Administration* (Montreal, 1987).

12. J.C. Riley, *The Seven Years' War and the Old Regime in France: The Economic and Financial Toll* (Princeton, New Jersey, 1987), pp. 78–9.

13. *Ibid.*, p. 103.

14. A. Corvisier, *L'Armée française de la fin du XVIIe siècle au ministère de Choiseul* (2 vols., Paris, 1964) I, 220–21, 229.

15. A skilful recent example of such an approach is R.N. Lebow, 'Play it again, Pericles: agents, structures and the Peloponnesian War', *European Journal of International Relations*, 2 (1996), pp. 231–58.

16. I.L. Janis, *Victims of Groupthink: A Psychological Study of Foreign-Policy Decisions and Fiascoes* (Boston, 1972).

17. J. Swann, *Politics and the Parlement of Paris under Louis XV, 1754–1774* (Cambridge, 1995).

18. AE. CP. Bavière 129 fol. 188.

19. AE. CP. Esp. 532 fol. 68.

20. AN. KK. 1372, 4 Feb.

21. C.M. Desbarats, 'France in North America: the net burden of empire during the first half of the eighteenth century', *French History*, 11 (1997), pp. 1–28.

22. 'Memoire [de Louis XIV] pour servir d'instruction à Monsieur le comte de Frontenac sur l'entreprise de la Nouvelle-York', *Le Rapport de l'Archiviste de la Province de Québec* (Québec, 1927–8), pp. 12–16; M. Trudel, 'Louis XIV et son projet de deportation', *La Revue de l'histoire de l'Amerique française*, 4 (1950), pp. 157–71.

23. J.I. Israel, 'The emerging empire: the continental perspective, 1650–1713', in N. Canny (ed.), *The Oxford History of the British Empire. I: The Origins of Empire* (Oxford, 1998), pp. 440–43.

24. AE. CP. Ang. 348 fol. 56.

25. W. Beik, 'A social interpretation of the reign of Louis XIV', in N. Bulst, R. Descimon and A. Guerreau (eds), *L'État ou le Roi. Les fondations de la modernité monarchique en France, XIV–XVIIe siècles* (Paris, 1996), pp. 145–60, esp. pp. 145–6, 150–51; P. Benedict, 'More than market and manufactory: the cities of early modern France', *French Historical Studies*, 20 (1997), p. 538.

Select Bibliography

1. Manuscript sources

1.1 Within France

1.1.1 Paris: Ministère des Affaires Etrangères/Relations Extérieures

1.1.1.1 Correspondance Politique (CP)

Allemagne 322–3, 346, 373–5, 377, 379, 381, 597

Angleterre 89, 118–20, 127–9, 149, 154–6, 158–63, 165–7, 174–7, 180–81, 188, 191, 256–84, 288, 311–13, 322–4, 337–55, 359–71, 373–82, 384–97, 399, 404, 412–19, 421–33, 437–55, 460–61, 467, 472, 476, 483–4, 489–94, 498–500, 522, 528, 530–31, 538, 547–8, 555, 557–8, 561, 563, 565–8, 571, 575–86, 593, sup. 4, 7–9, 13, 24, 26, 29

Autriche 61, 63, 165, 247–8, 251–4, 256, 275, 295, 298, 301, 303, 348–51, 353, 357–8, 360, sup. 10–11, 23

Bavière 40–41, 70, 84, 94, 97–8, 100–04, 109–10, 113–15, 119–20, 129, 134, 172

Brunswick-Hanovre 25, 45–50, 52, sup. 2

Cologne 39, 70–72

Danemark 34, 136

Espagne 75, 225, 404, 413, 419, 441, 470–71, 475, 488, 491, 503, 506–7, 517, 522–3, 526–7, 532–7, 576–7, 616–17, 623, 626

États-Unis 35

Grisons 17

Hambourg 17

Hesse–Cassel 7

Hollande 155–7, 394–8, 442–6, 450, 460–62, 486–9, 506, 573–4, 580–81, 583, sup. 11

Lorraine 81, 90

Mayence 27

Palatinat 78

Pologne 144, 298, 314

Portugal 26, 70

Prusse 32, 34, 73, 83, 87–9, 91–5, 105, 171, 185–6, 207, 210, sup. 9
Rome 316, 321, 537–8
Russie 78, 116, 119, 121–3, 130
Sardaigne 229–31
Saxe 14, 70
Suède 67, 172, 272
Suisse 88
Turquie 175–6
Tuscany 145

1.1.1.2 Mémoires et Documents (MD)

Allemagne 42, 74–5
Angleterre 1–2, 6, 8, 24, 32, 40–41, 51, 55–6, 59
Autriche 7
Brunswick-Hanovre 9
France 36, 303, 445–6, 457, 503–5
Hollande 27, 60, 140
Russie 3, 16
Sardaigne 14

1.1.2 Paris: Archives Nationales

1.1.2.1 Archives de la Marine

This was the prime collection consulted. Within that the following were among those examined:

B1 10, 17–18, 32, 40, 48, 103, 754, 755–8, 760
B3 359, 364, 370, 384, 396, 401, 406–7
B7 111, 113, 121, 123, 138–9, 144–5, 265–90, 292–300, 304, 306–9, 311–17, 323–5, 327–9, 331–4, 341–54, 356, 358–65, 373–6, 379–84, 389, 396, 401, 406–7, 419–21, 423–5, 429, 434, 447–8, 450–51, 453, 455–7, 475

1.1.2.2 Other collections consulted include

K 1351, 1369, 1373
KK 1371–2, 1393–4, 1400–02
Archives Privée: entrée Fleury

1.1.3 Paris: Bibliothèque Nationale

1.1.3.1 Manuscrits Français (MF)

1328 naval events
6946 Dangervilliers–Noailles correspondence
7149 Cambis correspondence
7177–98 Villeneuve papers
10672 Torcy memoires
10681–2 Groffey correspondence

1.1.3.2 Nouvelles Acquisitions Françaises (NAF)

349 Blondel, Remarques
486–98 Correspondence of Charles Albert
6498 Vergennes–Bertin correspondence
6834 Villeneuve correspondence

9399–401 Mémoires sur la marine de Louis XV
9511, 9513–14 D'Aube, Réflexions sur le Gouvernement de France
10125 Hoym correspondence
10257 Berwick memoires
10716 memoire on France and Britain, 1760
14904–7, 14911–17 Montaigu papers
22009–10 Douglas correspondence
23291 Leurie–Estrées correspondence
23936 D'Antin memoires
23975 Douglas correspondence

1.1.4 Paris: Archives de la Guerre

A1 series. Volumes consulted included 1183, 2643, 2655, 2676–8, 2687, 2696–7, 2970, 2997, 3070–71, 3126

1.1.5 Paris: Bibliothèque de l'Arsenal

The prime collection consulted was the Archives de la Bastille. Within that, the following were among those examined: Gazetins secrets de la Police, vols. 10155–60, 10162–5

1.1.6 Paris: Bibliothèque Victor Cousin

Fonds Richelieu, vols. 30–32, 40, 58–9

1.1.7 Nancy Archives de Meurthe-et-Moselle

Fonds de Vienne, serie 3F, vols. 30, 32, 34, 86–8, 138–9, 202, 212–13

1.2 Outside France

1.2.1 Chewton Mendip: Chewton Hall

Papers of James, 1st Earl Waldegrave

1.2.2 Darmstadt: Staatsarchiv

M 14/1–3, 15/1–4, 16/1–5, 17/1–2
Boehmer's reports from Paris 1734–44, and agents' reports up to 1770

1.2.3 Dresden: Sachsisches Hauptstaatsarchiv

Geheimes Kabinett, Gesandtschaften
Reports from Le Coq and De Brais, 2733, 2735

1.2.4 Edinburgh: Scottish Record Office

Stair Papers

1.2.5 Genoa: Archivio di Stato

Lettere Ministri Francia 44–6

1.2.6 Hanover: Nieder Sachsisches Hauptstaatsarchiv

Calenberg Brief Archiv 24 Nr. 1988, French intercepts
Nr. 2009 Hardenberg Papers

1.2.7 Huntingdon: County Record Office

Manchester Papers

1.2.8 Ithaca, New York: Cornell University Library

Maurepas Papers

1.2.9 London: British Library

Department of Western Manuscripts, Additional Manuscripts, vol. 61573, D'Huxelles-
    Iberville intercepts
Auckland, Gualterio, Hardwicke, Newcastle, Townsend Papers

1.2.10 London: Public Record Office

State Papers France, United Provinces
State Papers Confidential (Intercepts)
Pitt Papers

1.2.11 Maidstone: Kent Archives Office

Dorset Papers

1.2.12 Marburg: Staatsarchiv

Series 4f France 1586, 1602, 1604, 1611–14

1.2.13 Munich: Bayerisches Hauptstaatsarchiv

1.2.13.1

Kasten Schwarz: 17070, 17072, 17074, 17076–7, 17079–80, 17083, 17085, 17087,
17090–91, 17100, 17104–6, 17111–2, 17122–3, 17132–3, 17142–3, 17189–91, 17194,
17221–4, 17313, 17726, 17728

1.2.13.2

Bayr. Gesandtschaft Paris: 13, 18, 25, 67, 72, 79–88, 216–27, 243–52

1.2.13.3

Kasten Blau 9/11, 9/20

1.2.14 Münster: Staatsarchiv

Deposit Nordkirchen, papers of the Plettenberg family
NB 33, 104

1.2.15 New Haven, Connecticut: Beinecke Library

Blathwayt, Manchester Papers

1.2.16 New York: Public Library

Hardwicke Papers: Schaub and Stair correspondence

1.2.17 Turin: Archivio di Stato

Lettere Ministri Francia 163–78, 180

1.2.18 Vienna: Haus-, Hof-, und Staatsarchiv

1.2.18.1

Staatenabteilung, Frankreich, Varia 10–13
Interiora Intercepte 1

1.2.18.2

Grosse Korrespondenz 85a, 102a, 150a

1.2.18.3

Nachlass Fonseca 3, 6, 11–13, 21

1.2.19 Vienna: Palais Kinsky

Papers of Counts Philip and Stephen Kinsky

1.2.20 Windsor, Berks: Royal Archives

Stuart, Cumberland Papers

1.2.21 Wolfenbüttel: Staatsarchiv

Seckendorf–Ferdinand Albrecht correspondence

2. Selected secondary works

There is no space to repeat the listing in the notes. The following recent works are of
value, not least because they also list earlier works.

G.J. Ames, *Colbert, Mercantilism and the French Quest for Asian Trade* (Dekalb, Illinois, 1996).

J. Baillou (ed.), *Les Affaires Étrangères et le Corps Diplomatique Français. I: De L'Ancien
Régime au Second Empire* (Paris, 1984).

J. Bély, *Les rélations internationales en Europe, XVIIe–XVIIIe siècles* (Paris, 1992).

J. Bérenger and J. Meyer, *La France dans le monde au xviiie siècle* (Paris, 1993).

T.C.W. Blanning, *The French Revolutionary Wars, 1787–1802* (London, 1996).

J. Cornette, *Le Roi de guerre: Essai sur la souveraineté dans la France du grand siècle* (Paris,
1993).

H. Duchhardt, *Balance of Power und Pentarchie, 1700–85* (Paderborn, 1997).

J. Dull, *The French Navy and American Independence: A Study of Arms and Diplomacy, 1774–
1787* (Princeton, 1975).

E. Dziembowski, *Un nouveau patriotisme français 1750–1770* (Oxford, 1998).

J. Hardman and M. Price (eds), *Louis XVI and the Comte de Vergennes: Correspondence,
1774–1787* (Oxford, 1998).

A. Lossky, *Louis XIV and the French Monarchy* (New Brunswick, 1994).

J.A. Lynn, *The Wars of Louis XIV, 1667–1714* (London, 1999).

J.R. McNeill, *Atlantic Empires of France and Spain: Havana and Louisbourg, 1700–1763*
(Chapel Hill, North Carolina, 1985).

K. Malettke, *Frankreich, Deutschland und Europa im 17. und 18. Jahrhundert* (Marburg,
1994).

O.T. Murphy, *Charles Gravier, Comte de Vergennes: French Diplomacy in the Age of Revolution, 1719–1787* (Albany, New York, 1982).

J.C. Riley, *The Seven Years' War and the Old Regime in France: The Economic and Financial Toll* (Princeton, 1986).

P.W. Schroeder, *The Transformation of European Politics, 1763–1848* (Oxford, 1994).

B. Stone, *The Genesis of the French Revolution: A Global-Historical Interpretation* (Cambridge, 1994).

Appendix 1: The later Bourbons

Louis XIV

Born 5 Sept. 1638.
Succeeded father 14 May 1643.
Assumed personal control with death of Mazarin 9 Mar. 1661.
Died 1 Sept. 1715.

Louis XV

Born 15 Feb. 1710.
Succeeded great-grandfather 1 Sept. 1715.
Declared of age 15 Feb. 1723.
Died 10 May 1774.

Louis XVI

Born 23 Aug. 1754.
Succeeded grandfather 10 May 1774.
Executed 21 Jan. 1793.

Appendix 2: Secretaries of State

Brienne	23 June 1643–3 Apr. 1663
Lionne	3 Apr. 1663–1 Sept. 1671
Pomponne	1 Sept. 1671–18 Nov. 1679
Croissy	12 Feb. 1680–26 July 1696
Torcy	28 July 1696–23 Sept. 1715
Huxelles	23 Sept. 1715–1 Sept. 1718
Dubois	1 Sept. 1718–10 Aug. 1723
Morville	16 Aug. 1723–19 Aug. 1727
Chauvelin	19 Aug. 1727–22 Feb. 1737
Amelot	22 Feb. 1737–26 Apr. 1744
Argenson	18 Nov. 1744–3 Jan. 1747
Puysieulx	18 Jan. 1747–11 Sept. 1751
Saint-Contest	11 Sept. 1751–24 July 1754
Rouillé	25 July 1754–25 June 1757
Bernis	29 June 1757–1 Nov. 1758
Choiseul	3 Dec. 1758–13 Oct. 1761, 8 Apr. 1766–24 Dec. 1770
Praslin	13 Oct. 1761–8 Apr. 1766
La Vrillière	24 Dec. 1770–6 June 1771
Aiguillon	6 June 1771–3 June 1774
Vergennes	21 July 1774–13 Feb. 1787
Montmorin	15 Feb. 1787–20 Nov. 1791
Lessart	20 Nov. 1791–10 Mar. 1792
Dumouriez	15 Mar. 1792–13 June 1792
Chambonas	14 June 1792–23 July 1792
Bigot de Sainte-Croix	1 Aug. 1792–10 Aug. 1792
Lebrun-Tondu	10 Aug. 1792–21 June 1793
Deforgues	21 June 1793–2 Apr. 1794

Committee of National Convention	2 Apr. 1794–4 Nov. 1795
Delacroix	4 Nov. 1795–18 July 1797
Talleyrand	18 July 1797–13 July 1799, 21 Nov. 1799–17 June 1807, 13 May 1814–10 Sept. 1814, 8 July 1815–23 Sept. 1815
Reinhard	20 July 1799–21 Nov. 1799
Champagny	8 Aug. 1807–16 Apr. 1811
Maret	17 Apr. 1811–19 Nov. 1813
Caulaincourt	20 Nov. 1813–2 Apr. 1814, 21 Mar. 1815–22 June 1815
Jaucourt	11 Sept. 1814–20 Mar. 1815
Bignon	23 June 1815–7 July 1815

Index